T0188694

The Official (ISC)²® CCSP® CBK® Reference

Fourth Edition

CCSP®: Certified Cloud Security Professional

An (ISC)²® Certification

The Official (ISC)²®
CCSP® CBK® Reference

Fourth Edition

Aaron Kraus

Acknowledgments

First and foremost, my deepest appreciation goes to my family, mentors, and colleagues. The support of my family during the long hours required to research, write, and review this book made it possible. Mentors and colleagues who have educated and guided me made it possible to produce this reference, and the excellent resources they have created are linked throughout the book for more information on a wide variety of topics.

I would also like to express appreciation to (ISC)² for providing the CCSP certification, certification preparation materials, and reference guides for many security topics. As the world continues the shift to cloud computing, it is essential for security practitioners to have validated real-world skills to properly secure these new computing resources.

The excellent team at John Wiley & Sons is a continuing source of support, including associate publisher Jim Minatel, project editor John Sleeva, and content refinement specialist Archana Pragash. Many thanks to them for entrusting me with the task of updating this reference guide and for their ongoing help to make it the best possible. Special thanks to my technical editor Gareth Marchant, whose knowledge and insight elevated every domain.

Above all, thank you to the readers. Whether you are preparing for your CCSP exam or brushing up on a crucial aspect of cloud security, it is your hard work securing cloud computing environments that makes the world a safer place.

About the Author

Aaron Kraus, CCSP, CISSP, is an information security executive with deep experience in security risk management, auditing, and teaching information security topics. He has worked in security and compliance roles across industries including U.S. federal government civilian agencies, financial services, and technology startups, and he is currently a security director for a property technology startup. His experience includes creating alignment between security teams and the organizations they support, by evaluating the unique threat landscape facing each organization and the unique objectives each organization is pursuing to deliver a balanced, risk-based security control program. As a consultant to a financial services firm, he designed, executed, and matured the third-party vendor audit programs to provide oversight of key compliance initiatives, and he led global audit teams to perform reviews covering physical security, logical security, and regulatory compliance. Aaron is a course author, instructor, and cybersecurity curriculum dean with more than 14 years of experience at Learning Tree International, and he most recently taught the Official (ISC)² CISSP CBK Review Seminar. He has served as a technical editor for numerous Wiley publications, including CISSP and CCSP study guides and practice tests, and is coauthor of *The Official (ISC)² CISSP CBK Reference* as well as coauthor of the previous edition of *The Official (ISC)² CCSP CBK Reference*.

About the Technical Editor

Gareth Marchant started his professional career as an electrical engineer and has worked in information technology for over 20 years. He has held systems engineering and senior leadership roles in both private and public sector organizations. The central theme throughout his career has been systems architecture and design, covering a broad range of technical services but always focused on resiliency. Gareth currently lives in Nashville, TN, but has recovered IT operations in Florida following tornado strikes and many hurricanes.

Gareth is an (ISC)² and EC-Council certified instructor and currently holds CISSP, CEH, ECIH, SSCP, GMON, CASP+, Security+, CySA+, Network+, Cybersec First Responder, Cyber Secure Coder, and other certifications, as well as a master's degree in computer information systems. In addition to cybersecurity certification prep, he also teaches information systems and cybersecurity courses as an adjunct instructor and is the author of the *Official CompTIA CASP+ Self-Paced Study Guide*.

Contents at a Glance

Contents

Chapter   4   Cloud Application Security   139

Foreword to the Fourth Edition

These are exciting times for the cybersecurity profession, and we are so glad that you are a part of it. Once recognized as a CCSP®, you will have a cloud security certification that will help you advance your career by demonstrating your expertise in securing critical assets in the cloud.

Cloud security is one of the most in-demand cybersecurity skillsets today. In fact, the opportunity has never been greater for dedicated professionals to carve out a meaningful career and make a difference in their organizations. Earning the CCSP® certification makes you a forerunner in the cybersecurity community, proving that you have the advanced skills and knowledge to design, manage, and secure data, applications, and infrastructure in the cloud.

Whether you are picking up this book in preparation to sit for the exam or you are an existing CCSP® using this as a reference, you'll find *Official (ISC)² CCSP CBK Reference* a valuable resource as you continue to learn about today's cloud security principles and practices.

We wish you all the best in your CCSP® journey. From the very beginning through the advancements and discoveries that you are sure to find along the way, (ISC)² will be by your side, always advocating for you, as we work together to create a safe and secure cyber world.

Sincerely,

Clar Rosso

Clar Rosso
CEO, (ISC)²

Introduction

The Certified Cloud Security Professional (CCSP) denotes a professional with demonstrated ability across important aspects of architecture, data security, and risk management in cloud computing. The exam covers knowledge and skills across six domains of practice related to cloud security, codified in the (ISC)[2] CCSP Common Body of Knowledge (CBK).

- Domain 1: Cloud Concepts, Architecture, and Design
- Domain 2: Cloud Data Security
- Domain 3: Cloud Platform and Infrastructure Security
- Domain 4: Cloud Application Security
- Domain 5: Cloud Security Operations
- Domain 6: Legal, Risk, and Compliance

Passing the exam is one condition of certification, and to qualify for the certification, a professional must have five years of experience in information technology, of which three years must be in a security-specific capacity and at least one year dedicated to one or more of the six CCSP domains.

Professionals take many paths into information security, and there are variations in acceptable practices across different industries and regions. The CCSP CBK represents a baseline standard of security knowledge relevant to cloud security and management, though the rapid pace of change in cloud computing means a professional must continuously maintain their knowledge to stay current. As you read this guide, consider not only the scenarios or circumstances presented to highlight the CBK topics, but also connect it to common practices and norms in your organization, region, and culture. Once you achieve CCSP certification, you will be asked to maintain your knowledge with continuing education, so keep topics of interest in mind for further study once you have passed the exam.

Domain 1: Cloud Concepts, Architecture, and Design

Understanding cloud computing begins with the building blocks of cloud services, which the Cloud Concepts, Architecture, and Design domain introduces. This includes two vital participants: cloud service providers and cloud consumers, as well as reference architectures used to deliver cloud services like infrastructure as a service (IaaS), platform as a service (PaaS), and software as a service (SaaS). There are business benefits inherent in these IT resource paradigms, like shifting spending from capital expenditure (CapEx) to operating expenditure (OpEx). This changes the way organizations budget and pay for the IT resources needed to run their business, so it is not uncommon to see financial leaders driving adoption of cloud services. New IT service models bring with them new forms of information security risks, however, which must be assessed and weighed so the organization achieves an optimal balance of cost (in the form of risk) with benefits (in the form of reduced IT spending). This will drive decisions on which cloud deployment model to adopt, like public or private cloud, as well as key internal governance initiatives when migrating to and managing cloud computing.

Domain 2: Cloud Data Security

Information security is fundamentally concerned with preserving the confidentiality, integrity, and availability of data. Although cloud computing upends many legacy IT models and practices, security risks to information systems remain. The Cloud Data Security domain introduces new concepts like the cloud data lifecycle, as well as cloud-specific considerations like data dispersion and loss of physical control over storage media that requires unique approaches to data disposal. Cloud security practitioners must understand how to implement controls for audit and accountability of data stored or processed in the cloud, as well as crucial oversight tasks like data discovery to create an inventory. This domain introduces proactive safeguards intended to manage sensitive data stored in the cloud, like masking, tokenization, data loss prevention (DLP), and classification of data. Cloud-specific considerations and adaptations of traditional controls are a primary concern, since cloud services remove security capabilities like physical destruction of disk drives. Cloud computing also introduces new capabilities like instantaneous global data replication, which can reduce availability risks.

Domain 3: Cloud Platform and Infrastructure Security

There are two perspectives treated in the Cloud Platform and Infrastructure Security domain. Cloud providers require skilled security practitioners to design, deploy, and maintain both physically and logically secure environments. This includes buildings, facilities, and utilities needed to provide the cloud service offering, as well as configuration and management of software systems like hypervisors, storage area networks (SANs), and software-defined networking (SDN) infrastructure. A key concern is the security of data stored by the cloud consumers, particularly the proper isolation of tenant data to avoid leakage between cloud tenants. From the perspective of the cloud consumer, traditional security controls will require adaptation for cloud environments, such as the use of virtualized hardware security modules (HSM) to generate and manage cryptographic keys, and additional layers of encryption required to reduce the risk associated with giving up physical control of storage media. Audit mechanisms like log collection are generally available in cloud environments, but abilities like packet capture and analysis may not be available due to multitenant data concerns. Disaster recovery and business continuity planning are also presented in this domain; while the inherent high availability of many cloud services is beneficial for organizations, proper configuration to take advantage of these features is required.

Domain 4: Cloud Application Security

Security practitioners working in cloud computing environments face the challenge of more rapid deployment, coupled with the relative ease with which more users can develop sophisticated cloud applications. Again, these are advantages to the business at the possible expense of security, so the Cloud Application Security domain presents key requirements for recognizing the benefits offered by cloud applications without introducing unacceptable risks. These begin with a focus on the importance of fostering awareness throughout the organization of common cloud security basics. Specific training for cloud app developers on vulnerabilities, pitfalls, and strategies to avoid them is also presented. Modifications to the software development life cycle (SDLC) are discussed, which help accommodate changes introduced by cloud-specific risks. These include system architecture concerns to avoid vendor lock-in and threat modeling specific to the broadly accessible nature of cloud platforms. Since many cloud computing services are delivered by third parties, this domain introduces assurance, validation, and testing methods tailored to address the lack of direct control over acquired IT services and applications. It also introduces common application security controls and specifics of their implementation for cloud environments, like web application firewalls (WAF), sandboxing, and Extensible Markup Language (XML) gateways. Many cloud services rely heavily on functionality offered via application programming interfaces (APIs), and key points regarding how data is exchanged, processed, and protected by APIs are presented in this domain.

Domain 5: Cloud Security Operations

The Cloud Security Operations domain is a companion to many of the concepts introduced in the Cloud Platform and Infrastructure Security domain. It deals with issues of implementing, building, operating, and managing the physical and logical infrastructure needed for a cloud environment. There is a heavy focus on the cloud service provider's perspective, so concepts in this domain may be unfamiliar to some security practitioners who have only worked to secure cloud services as a consumer. The concepts are largely similar to legacy or on-premises security, such as the secure configuration of BIOS and use of Trusted Platform Module (TPM) for hardware security, deployment of virtualization management tools, and configuring remote maintenance capabilities to allow remote administrative tasks. Considerations unique to cloud environments include the additional rigor required in the configuration of isolation features, which prevent data access across tenants, as well as the much larger demands of managing capacity, availability, and monitoring of vast, multicountry data centers. Traditional security operations (SecOps) are also of critical concern for security practitioners in a cloud environment, such as handling vulnerability and patch management programs, network access and security controls, and configuration and change management programs. Additional SecOps activities covered in this domain include supporting incident response and digital forensics when security incidents occur, as well as traditional security operations center (SOC) oversight and monitoring functions for network security, log capture and analysis, and service incident management. These tasks are also covered from the cloud consumer's perspective, as many cloud services and security tools provide log data that must be analyzed to support policy enforcement and incident detection.

Domain 6: Legal, Risk, and Compliance

Legal and regulatory requirements are a significant driver of the work many information security professionals perform, and cloud computing adds increased complexity due to its inherently global nature. The Legal, Risk, and Compliance domain details the conflicting international laws and regulations that organizations will encounter when using cloud services. These present financial risks, additional compliance obligations and risk, and technical challenges like verifying that cloud applications and services are configured in accordance with compliance requirements. Privacy legislation is a particularly important driver of many cloud security concerns; as many countries and localities introduce strict requirements to safeguard privacy data, organizations using the cloud must weigh financial benefits of a cloud migration against potential fines if they violate these laws. New challenges are also emerging around jurisdiction over multinational cloud services: how do you determine jurisdiction for a U.S.-based company operating a cloud data center in Kenya processing data belonging to a Swiss citizen? Three different laws potentially overlap in this scenario. Processes for audits, assurance, and reporting are also covered, as security practitioners must understand and be able to implement both internal oversight mechanisms like gap analysis and audit planning, while also selecting and supporting external auditors for standards like Service Organization Control (SOC) audit reports. Since cloud service providers are third parties not directly under the control of the organization, vendor risk management practices like contract design and service level agreements (SLAs) are often required tools for security risk management.

Chapter 1

Cloud Concepts, Architecture, and Design

Domain 1 establishes the foundation of knowledge required to adequately secure cloud environments, including an overview of key architectural concepts and security principles applied to cloud environments. This information is fundamental for all other topics in cloud computing. A set of common definitions, architectural standards, and design patterns will put everyone on the same level when discussing these ideas and using the cloud effectively and efficiently.

Understand Cloud Computing Concepts

The first task is to define common concepts. In the following sections, we will provide common definitions for cloud computing terms and will discuss the various participants in the cloud computing ecosystem. We will also discuss the characteristics of cloud computing, answering the question "What is cloud computing?" We will also examine the technologies that make cloud computing possible.

Cloud Computing Definitions

Cloud computing is a quickly evolving practice, with new concepts and paradigms of computing being introduced quickly. Cloud computing itself represented a major shift from traditional on-premises infrastructure, data centers, and colocation facilities, and to apply security to these new environments it is essential to have a firm understanding of core concepts.

Cloud Computing

The National Institute of Standards and Technology (NIST) Special Publication (SP) 800-145 provides a widely accepted definition of cloud computing: "a model for enabling ubiquitous, convenient, on-demand network access to a shared pool of configurable computing resources . . . that can be rapidly provisioned and released with minimal management effort or service provider interaction." The document formalizes definitions of cloud computing and services, including the five essential characteristics that define a cloud service, cloud service categories, and deployment models. These are discussed in more detail later in this chapter.

Cloud computing expands earlier concepts of distributed computing or parallel computing, even when done over a network, in a number of critical ways. It is a philosophy that creates access to computing resources in a simple, self-driven way. Although an organization or individual may negotiate a contract, rates, and service levels from a cloud provider, once access is granted a true cloud computing environment typically does not require involvement by the cloud service provider (CSP).

Cloud computing requires a network in order to provide broad access to infrastructure, development tools, and software solutions. It requires some form of self-service to allow users to reserve and access these resources at times and in ways that are convenient to the user.

The provisioning of resources needs to be automated so that human involvement is limited. Any user should be able to access their account and procure additional resources or reduce current resource levels by themselves, without the need for manual work by the CSP staff.

An example is Dropbox, a cloud-based file storage system. An individual creates an account, chooses the level of service they want or need, and provides payment information. Once this is done, the service and storage are immediately available. A company might negotiate contract rates more favorable than are available to the average consumer, but once the contract is in place, the company's employees can access this resource without the need for any additional provisioning by Dropbox staff.

A final important concept in cloud computing deals with the financial accounting for cloud services. While this is typically outside the role of the security practitioner, it is a key driver for many organizations adopting cloud computing and is helpful to understand. Purchasing servers and building data centers to house them are known as capital expenditures (CapEx), while services like cloud computing are known as operating expenditures (OpEx). In most places OpEx spending is preferable due to more favorable tax treatment; whatever an organization spends in OpEx reduces taxable income, thereby reducing the organization's tax bill.

Service and Deployment Models

There are three *service models* and four *deployment models* in which cloud services can be provisioned. These are discussed in detail later in this chapter, but a basic understanding is essential to begin exploring other cloud concepts.

The three service models are software as a service (SaaS), platform as a service (PaaS), and infrastructure as a service (IaaS). The key differences between these models include the level of control the consumer has over the cloud service as well as the level of effort required to use the service.

There are four deployment models for cloud services: public, private, community, and hybrid clouds. These define who owns and controls the underlying infrastructure of a cloud service and who can access a specific cloud service. Additionally, organizations may adopt a multi-cloud deployment strategy, combining two or more of these deployment models across their technology stack.

These concepts will be discussed further in the "Cloud Service Categories" and "Cloud Deployment Models" sections later in this chapter.

Cloud Computing Roles and Responsibilities

There are a number of roles in cloud computing, and understanding each role allows clearer understanding of each of the cloud service models, deployment models, security responsibilities, and other aspects of cloud computing.

Cloud Service Customer

The cloud service customer (CSC) is the company or person purchasing the cloud service, or in the case of an internal customer, the employee using the cloud service. For example, a SaaS CSC would be any individual or organization that subscribes to a cloud-based email service. A PaaS CSC would be an individual or organization subscribing to a PaaS resource. A PaaS resource could be a development platform. With an IaaS solution, the customer is a system administrator who needs infrastructure to support their enterprise. The CSC consumes the services provided by the cloud service provider.

Cloud Service Provider

The CSP is the company or other entity offering cloud services. CSPs may be public companies providing cloud services to any customer but can also be an internal IT department that provisions cloud platforms to other units of the organization. A CSP may offer SaaS, PaaS, or IaaS services in any combination. For example, major CSPs such as AWS, Microsoft Azure, and Google Cloud offer both PaaS and IaaS services. Major SaaS CSPs include companies like Salesforce and Dropbox, as well as Microsoft 365 and Google Workspace, which are SaaS offerings built on top of the same cloud components that make up Azure and Google Cloud.

As the cloud environment becomes more complicated, with hybrid clouds and community clouds that federate across multiple cloud environments, the responsibility for security becomes ever more complex. As the customer owns their data and processes, they have a responsibility to review the security policies and procedures of any and all CSPs in use at their organization, and the federated responsibilities that may exist between multiple CSPs and data centers.

Cloud Service Partner

A cloud service partner is a third-party offering a variety of cloud-based services (infrastructure, storage and application services, and platform services) using the associated CSP. An AWS cloud service partner uses AWS to provide their services. The cloud service partner can provide customized interfaces, load balancing, and a variety of services. It may be an easier entrance to cloud computing, as an existing vendor may already be a cloud service partner. The partner has experience with the underlying CSP and can introduce a customer to the cloud more easily.

The cloud partner network is also a way to extend the reach of a CSP. The cloud service partner will brand its association with the CSP. Some partners align with multiple CSPs, giving the customer a great deal of flexibility. Partners can extend the value of cloud services by selling additional services, support, management, and consulting to organizations that lack these skills or capabilities.

Cloud Service Broker

A cloud service broker is similar to a broker in any industry. Companies use a broker to find solutions to their cloud computing needs. The broker will package services in a manner that benefits the customer. This may involve the services of multiple CSPs. A broker is a value-add service and can be an easy way for a company to begin a move into the cloud. A broker adds value through aggregation of services from multiple parties, integration of services with a company's existing infrastructure, and customization of services that a CSP cannot or will not make. They may also be able to offer discounts due to volume purchasing of cloud services, which is beneficial to smaller organizations that lack the bargaining power of a high-volume purchaser.

Just as with any vendor, it is crucial to vet the capabilities and reputation of a CSB before engaging their services. Each serves a specific market, utilizing different cloud technologies. It is important that the CSBs selected are a good fit for the customer organization and its cloud strategy. While this is typically an operational concern rather than a security one, inadequate capabilities in the cloud solution can give rise to security problems if needed security controls cannot be implemented.

Regulator

Cloud computing itself is not heavily regulated, similar to most IT environments, which are merely tools. The use of those tools, specifically the processing of data, is regulated. Examples of regulatory frameworks that govern cloud data processing include the European Union General Data Protection Regulation (EU GDRP), the Graham-Leach-Bliley Act (GLBA), and the Personal Information Protection and Electronic Documents Act (PIPEDA), which are privacy laws in Europe, the United States, and Canada, respectively. While none explicitly identify cloud computing, they do require organizations that collect, process, or store data to properly safeguard it. Cloud customers must be aware of any regulations that affect their data or business processes and choose or configure CSP resources that meet those regulatory requirements.

Common regulatory issues that impact cloud usage include security of data at rest and in transit. When looking at data in a cloud environment, the broad network accessibility characteristic usually requires the use of the Internet to interact with systems, so these regulations demand adequate encryption to protect the data as it moves into and out of the cloud. Similarly, the shared multitenant nature of cloud services and involvement of third-party administrators working for the CSP demand proper controls for the data at rest; encryption is a common control that can mitigate the risk of unauthorized disclosure so long as keys are properly managed.

Regulatory bodies have published guidance for organizations utilizing cloud computing services to handle sensitive data, and CSPs share responsibility for providing service offerings that are compliant with their customers' regulatory requirements. For example, the major CSPs offer configurations of many services that are compliant with various regulations, though there may be additional costs associated with these specialized offerings. Ultimately it is the responsibility of the consumer to identify all requirements associated with their data and choose, architect, and maintain cloud solutions in line with those requirements.

Examples of regulator guidance on cloud computing include the following:

- UK Information Commissioner's Office, *Guidance on the use of cloud computing*: ico.org.uk/media/for-organisations/documents/1540/cloud_computing_ guidance_for_organisations.pdf

- Irish Data Protection Commission, *Guidance for Organisations Engaging Cloud Service Providers*: dataprotection.ie/sites/default/files/uploads/2019-10/ Guidance%20for%20Engaging%20Cloud%20Service%20Providers_Oct19.pdf
- U.S. Department of Health and Human Services Guidance on HIPAA & Cloud Computing: hhs.gov/hipaa/for-professionals/special-topics/health-information-technology/cloud-computing/index.html

Shared Responsibility Model

Depending on the service provided (SaaS, PaaS, or IaaS), the responsibilities of the CSP vary considerably. In all cases, security in the cloud is a shared responsibility between the CSP and the customer. This shared responsibility is a continuum, with the customer taking a larger security role in an IaaS service model and the CSP taking a larger role in the security of a SaaS service model. The responsibilities of a PaaS fall somewhere in between. But even when a CSP has most of the responsibility in a SaaS solution, the customer is ultimately responsible for the data and processes they put into the cloud.

The major CSPs publish their variations of a *shared responsibility model* detailing the assignment of various aspects of security to the CSP, the CSC, or both. In most cases, the CSP is solely responsible for operational concerns such as environmental controls within the data center, as well as security concerns such as physical access controls. Customers using the cloud service are responsible for implementing data security controls, such as encryption, that are appropriate to the type of data they are storing and processing in the cloud. Some areas require action by both the provider and customer, so it is crucial for a CCSP to understand which cloud service models are in use by the organization and which areas of security must be addressed by each party. The generic model in Table 1.1 identifies key areas of responsibility and ownership in various cloud service models.

TABLE 1.1   Cloud Shared Responsibility Model

Responsibility	IAAS	PAAS	SAAS
Data classification	C	C	C
Identity and access management	C	C/P	C/P
Application security	C	C/P	C/P
Network security	C/P	P	P
Host infrastructure	C/P	P	P
Physical security	P	P	P

C = Customer, P = Provider

A variety of CSP-specific documentation exists to define shared responsibility in each CSP's offerings, and a CCSP should be familiar with the particulars of the provider their organization is utilizing. The following is a brief description of the shared responsibility model for several major CSPs and links to further resources:

- **Amazon Web Services (AWS):** Amazon identifies key differences for responsibility "in" the cloud versus security "of" the cloud. Customers are responsible for data and configuration in their cloud apps and architecture, while Amazon is responsible for shared elements of the cloud infrastructure including hardware, virtualization software, environmental controls, and physical security.

  More information can be found here: `aws.amazon.com/compliance/shared-responsibility-model`.

- **Microsoft Azure:** Microsoft makes key distinctions by the service model and specific areas such as information and data and OS configuration. Customers always retain responsibility for managing their users, devices, and data security, while Microsoft is exclusively responsible for physical security. Some areas vary by service model, such as OS configuration, which is a customer responsibility in IaaS but a Microsoft responsibility in SaaS.

  More information can be found here: `docs.microsoft.com/en-us/azure/security/fundamentals/shared-responsibility`.

- **Google Cloud Platform (GCP):** Google takes a different approach with a variety of shared responsibility documentation specific to different compliance frameworks such as ISO 27001, SOC 2, and PCI DSS. The same general rules apply, however: customer data security is always the customer's responsibility, physical security is always Google's responsibility, and some items are shared depending on what service offerings are utilized.

  More information can be found here: `cloud.google.com/security`.

Key Cloud Computing Characteristics

The NIST SP 800-145 definition of cloud computing describes certain characteristics that must be present for an IT service to be considered a cloud service. Not every third-party solution is a cloud solution. Understanding the key characteristics of cloud computing will allow you to distinguish between cloud solutions and noncloud solutions. This is important as these characteristics result in certain security challenges that may not be shared by noncloud solutions.

On-Demand Self-Service

The NIST definition of cloud computing identifies an on-demand service as one "that can be rapidly provisioned and released with minimal management effort or service provider interaction." This means the user must be able to provision these services simply and easily when they are needed. If you need a Dropbox account, you simply set up an account and pay for the amount of storage you want, and you have that storage capacity immediately. If you already have an account, you can expand the space you need by simply paying for more space. The access to storage space is on demand; neither creating an account nor expanding the amount of storage available requires the involvement of people from the CSP. This capability is automated and provided via a dashboard or other simple interface.

On-demand self-service offers advantages of speed and flexibility compared to traditional IT services that required lengthy provisioning processes. However, this ease of use can facilitate the poor practice known as *shadow IT*. Any individual, team, or department can bypass company policies and procedures that handle the provisioning and control of IT services. A team that wants to collaborate can choose and provision OneDrive, Dropbox, SharePoint, or another service to facilitate collaboration. This can lead to sensitive data being stored in locations that do not adhere to required corporate controls and places the data in locations the larger business is unaware of and cannot adequately protect.

In the past, provisioning IT resources involved significant spending, but the pricing of cloud services may fall below spending thresholds that require reviews and approvals. Large projects typically require some reviews and approvals from departments such as finance, accounting, IT, security, or vendor management. Setting up a cloud service is typically much cheaper and can be done using a credit card, meaning the new IT service circumvents processes designed to evaluate and mitigate security risks.

If this behavior is allowed to proliferate, the organization can lose control of its sensitive data and processes. For example, the actuary department at an insurance company may decide to create a file-sharing account on one of several available services. As information security was not involved, company policies, procedures, risk management, and controls programs are not followed. As this is not monitored by the security operations center (SOC), a data breach may go unnoticed, and the data that gives the company a competitive advantage could be stolen, altered, or deleted. Counterintuitively, shadow IT can also lead to increased spending. If all departments set up and maintain their own cloud environments, the organization loses the ability to negotiate lower rates in exchange for volume purchasing, and different groups may even pay for the same services, potentially doubling costs.

Broad Network Access

Cloud services assume the presence of a network. For public and community clouds, this is the Internet. For a private cloud, it could be the corporate network—generally an IP-based network—and possibly the Internet and a secure remote access method such as a VPN. In either case, cloud services are not local solutions stored on your individual computer. They are solutions that require the use of a network to access services hosted in the cloud. Without broad and ubiquitous network access, the cloud becomes inaccessible and is no longer useful.

Not all protocols and services on IP-based networks are secure. Part of the strategy to implementing a secure cloud solution is to choose secure protocols and services. For example, Hypertext Transfer Protocol (HTTP) and File Transfer Protocol (FTP) should not be used to move data to and from cloud services as they send unencrypted data. HTTP Secure (HTTPS), Secure FTP (SFTP), and other encryption-based transmission should be used so that data in motion may be intercepted but not read.

If you are able to access the cloud service and obtain access to your data anywhere in the world, so can others. The requirement for identification and authentication becomes more important in this public-facing environment. The security of accessing your cloud services over the Internet can be improved in a number of ways including improved passwords, multifactor authentication (MFA), virtual private networks (VPNs), etc. The increased security needs of a system available over the network where security is shared between the CSP and customer makes these additional steps more important. For clouds that require remote access, traditional security models that assume a secure perimeter are no longer applicable. This drives new requirements for network security such as zero trust architecture, which is discussed later in this chapter.

Multitenancy

One way to get the improved efficiencies of cloud computing is through the sharing of infrastructure. CSPs provide a virtual set of resources including memory, computing power, and storage space, which customers share. This is known as a multitenant model, similar to an apartment building where tenants share resources and services but have their own dedicated space. Virtualization enables the appearance of single tenancy in a multitenancy situation. Ideally, each tenant's data remains private and secure in the same way that your belongings (data) in an apartment building remain secure and isolated from the belongings (data) of your neighbor. However, incorrect access settings and software flaws in virtualization software may be exploitable to grant unauthorized access.

In a multitenant model it is the responsibility of each tenant to exercise care to maintain the integrity and confidentiality of their own data. If your apartment door is left unsecured, any other tenant in the building could easily enter and steal your belongings. It is also necessary to consider the availability of the data, as the actions of the CSP or another tenant could make your data inaccessible for a time due to no fault of your own. A software upgrade that causes system outages could impact other users of shared infrastructure, just as a fire in one apartment could cause damage to surrounding apartments. A multitenant environment increases the importance of disaster recovery (DR) and business continuity (BC) planning; luckily, other aspects of cloud services make planning high-availability (HA) infrastructure easier and cheaper.

Rapid Elasticity and Scalability

In a traditional computing model, a company needs to plan and buy for anticipated infrastructure needs. If they estimate poorly, they will either have too little capacity, leading to loss of availability, or have excess capacity that represents wasted money. In a cloud solution, elastic infrastructure allows the service to grow or shrink as needed to support the customer's demand. If there is a peak in usage or resource needs, the service grows, or scales, to meet the demand. When usage falls back to normal levels, the resources are released. This supports a pay-as-you-go model, where a customer pays only for the resources they actually consumed rather than excess capacity for potential future needs.

For the CSP, this presents a challenge. The CSP must have the excess capacity to serve all their customers without having to incur the cost of the total possible resource usage. They must, in effect, estimate how much excess capacity they need to serve all of their customers. If they estimate poorly, the customer will suffer, and the CSP's customer base could decrease.

There is a cost to maintaining this excess capacity. The cost must be built into the cost model. In this way, all customers share in the cost of the CSP, maintaining some level of excess capacity. However, some cloud customers can achieve cost savings by sharing excess capacity only when they need it. For example, an online retail store is likely to need excess capacity during major holidays, while a tax preparer needs it at a different time. Both organizations can access the resources as demand peaks, without having to pay for the full set of resources during nonpeak seasons.

In the banking world, a bank must keep cash reserves of a certain percentage so that it can meet the withdrawal needs of its customers. But if every customer wanted all of their money at the same time, the bank would run out of cash on hand. In the same way, if every customer's potential peak usage occurred at the same time, the CSP would run out of resources, leading to a loss of availability and unhappy customers.

The customer must also take care in setting internal limits on resource use. Proper architectural decisions as well as process and procedure are required to ensure that resources that are no longer needed are deprovisioned. Otherwise, the customer continues to pay for resources that are not serving any purpose. Some cloud service offerings provide automated scale-up and scale-down capabilities, but it is possible to design cloud architecture that mimics traditional servers in a data center with no automated scaling.

Resource Pooling

In many ways, this is the core of cloud computing. Multiple customers share a set of resources including compute power, memory, storage, application services, etc. They do not each have to buy the infrastructure necessary to provide their IT needs. Instead, they share these resources with each other through the orchestration of the CSP. Everyone pays for what they need and use. Pooling these resources enables the other characteristics of cloud computing: self-service is possible because adding a new virtual server doesn't require a physical server to be installed and set up, and automating this based on demand is what enables elasticity.

This resource pooling presents some challenges for the cybersecurity professional, including issues of multitenancy as discussed earlier. A competitor or a rival can be sharing the same physical hardware. If the system, especially the hypervisor, is compromised, sensitive data could be exposed.

Resource pooling also implies that resources are allocated and deallocated as needed. The inability to ensure data erasure can mean that remnants of sensitive files could exist on storage allocated to another user. This increases the importance of data encryption and key management.

Measured Service

Metering service usage allows a CSP to charge for the resources used. In a private cloud, this can allow an organization to charge each department based on their usage of the cloud. For a public cloud, it allows each customer to pay for the resources used or consumed. With a measured service, everyone pays their share of the costs.

Measured service provides two key benefits. It is the foundation of shifting IT spending from CapEx to OpEx, and it provides additional visibility and transparency into actual IT needs. A CSP provides metrics on the services consumed, including network bandwidth, storage space, and computing power. This discrete measurement of services consumed is in contrast to estimating how much of a server's capacity is actually used and is beneficial for capacity planning.

Building Block Technologies

These technologies are the elements that make cloud computing possible. Without virtualization, there would be no resource pooling, while advances in networking allow for ubiquitous access. Improvements in storage and databases allow remote access to virtual storage in a shared resource pool, and orchestration puts all the pieces together and allows organizations to utilize the various cloud computing services. The combination of these technologies allows better resource utilization and improves the cost structure of technology.

Virtualization

Virtualization allows the resources of a physical server to be shared among multiple virtual servers. Virtualization is not unique to cloud computing and can be used to share corporate resources among multiple processes and services, typically offering more efficient utilization of resources. For example, a single physical server can be used to host virtual machines (VMs) running an email server and a web server, saving the organization the cost of buying and running two physical machines. This resource sharing also makes it easier to move VMs between physical hardware, providing availability benefits.

Cloud computing takes the idea of server virtualization and expands it to virtualizing all aspects of an information system, including the basic infrastructure such as networking, compute, memory, physical data storage, data storage systems like databases, and even applications that traditionally ran on a user workstation. The CSP shares resources among a large number of services and customers (also called *tenants*). Each tenant has full use of their environment without knowledge of the other tenants. This increases the efficient use of the resources significantly.

Most CSPs have multiple locations providing the cloud services, and high-speed connectivity allows services and data to move seamlessly between locations. This allows the CSP to evenly distribute workloads, provides failover capabilities, and allows regulated customers to access cloud services in locations that meet their regulatory requirements.

The use of all-virtualized infrastructure can create some security and compliance concerns, such as data leaving a geographic area where it may not be governed by the same set of laws and regulations. These issues may be handled during contract negotiation, though most CSPs offer solutions designed with common regulations in mind. For example, AWS, Azure, and GCP all offer GDPR-compliant services that retain data in EU data centers and also offer solutions to the U.S. federal government that retain data only in U.S.-based data centers.

Virtualization relies on technology known as a *hypervisor*, which is software that governs access by VMs to the hardware resources. If the hypervisor is compromised, it could allow an attacker to gain access to other VMs running on the same hardware. This type of attack is known as an *escape*, and properly securing and patching the hypervisor is the responsibility of the CSP.

Early virtualization focused on creating multiple virtual computers on a single piece of physical hardware, which increased efficiency in resource utilization and offered portability for virtual machines (VMs). Containers are a more recent evolution of these virtualization concepts. A *container*, or *containerized application*, is an application packaged along with its required software dependencies and configuration information. A container platform, such as Docker, can be installed on any physical hardware and run any compatible containers. The containerized application is inherently more portable, as it can run on any platform so long as the container software is also installed.

Storage

A variety of storage solutions allow cloud computing to work. Two of these are storage area networks (SANs) and network-attached storage (NAS). These and other advances in storage allow a CSP to offer flexible and scalable storage capabilities.

A SAN provides secure storage among multiple computers within a specific customer's domain. A SAN appears like a single disk to the customer, while the storage is spread across multiple locations. This is one type of shared storage that works across a network. SANs utilize block-level storage, where data being stored is broken down into blocks of uniform size. Blocks can be stored more efficiently than files due to their uniform size, and the SAN software is responsible for arranging all the needed blocks when a specific piece of data is requested.

Another type of networked storage is the NAS. This network storage solution uses TCP/IP and allows file-level access. A NAS appears to the customer as a single file system similar to the hard drive in a workstation. Many operating systems offer native support for NAS using a variety of formats.

The responsibility for choosing the storage technology lies with the CSP and will change over time as new technologies are introduced. These changes should be transparent to the customer—from the customer's perspective, the access speed, integrity of data, and allocated storage space are the important factors, not the underlying storage technology. The CSP is responsible for the security of the shared storage resource, while customers retain responsibility for security data they store in the cloud.

Shared storage can create security challenges if data remnants are present on a disk after it has been deallocated from one customer and allocated to another. A customer has no way to securely wipe the drives in use or physically destroy them; typically a CSP will offer some form of secure deletion. However, customers can utilize a practice known as *crypto-shredding* to make these fragments unusable if recovered, by encrypting data and securely destroying the key.

Networking

As all resources in a cloud environment are accessed through the network, a robust, available network is an essential element. The Internet is the network used by public and community clouds, as well as many private clouds. This network has proven to be widely available with broad capabilities. The Internet has become ubiquitous in society, allowing for the expansion of cloud-based services.

An IP-based network is only part of what is needed for cloud computing. Low latency, high bandwidth, and relatively error-free transmissions make cloud computing possible. The use of public networks also creates some security concerns. If access to cloud resources is via a public network, like the Internet, the traffic can be intercepted, and if data is transmitted in the clear, it can be read. The use of encryption and secure transport keeps the data in motion secure and cloud computing safer. Some CSPs even offer dedicated connectivity into the edge of their network for organizations with a high volume of sensitive data that prefer not to utilize the public Internet for connectivity.

Databases

Databases allow for the storage and organization of customer data. By using a database in a cloud environment, the administration of the underlying database becomes the responsibility of the CSP, including key tasks such as patching, tuning, and other database administrator services. The exception is IaaS, where the user is responsible for whatever database they install.

The other advantage of databases offered through a cloud service is the number of different database types and options that can be used together. While traditional relational databases are available, so are other types. By using traditional databases and other data storage tools as well as large amounts of data resources, data warehouses, data lakes, and other data storage strategies can be implemented. The cost savings offered by the scale of cloud computing make big data applications such as these more affordable than they would otherwise be.

Orchestration

Cloud orchestration is the use of technology to manage cloud infrastructure. In a modern organization, there is a great deal of complexity, including a mix of on-premises infrastructure and multiple cloud services. Even small organizations are likely to have multiple cloud offerings, such as infrastructure hosted in a traditional CSP like AWS, GCP, or Azure, as well as SaaS applications used by the business like Google Workspace, GitHub, or Salesforce.

This complexity can lead to data being out of sync, processes being broken, and a fragmentation that leaves the IT department unable to keep track of all the cloud services, business processes, and data locations. Like the conductor of an orchestra, cloud orchestration partners keep all of these pieces working together including data, processes, and application services. Orchestration is the glue that ties all of the pieces together through programming and automation. Orchestration is valuable whether an organization runs a single cloud environment or a multi-cloud environment.

This is more than simply automating a few tasks. Automation is heavily used by cloud orchestration services to create one seemingly seamless organizational cloud environment. In addition to hiding much of the complexity of an organization's cloud environment, cloud orchestration can reduce costs, improve efficiency, and support the overall workforce.

The major CSPs provide orchestration tools. These include IBM Cloud Orchestrator, Microsoft Operations Management Suite (OMS), and AWS Cloud Formation. These offerings are typically best suited to manage their respective CSP's services. Organizations utilizing multiple CSPs can utilize multi-cloud orchestration tools to deploy infrastructure across various CSPs, such as Kubernetes.

Describe Cloud Reference Architecture

The purpose of a reference architecture (RA) is to allow a wide variety of cloud vendors and services to be interoperable and to provide consumers with guidance on optimal deployment of resources in the cloud. An RA creates a framework or mapping of cloud computing activities and cloud capabilities to allow the services of different vendors to be mapped and potentially work together more seamlessly. An example of this approach is the seven-layer Open Systems Interconnection (OSI) model of networking, which allows interoperability of networking protocols between different operating systems. As companies engage a wide variety of cloud solutions from multiple vendors, interoperability is becoming more important, and the reference architecture makes the process easier.

NIST provides a cloud computing reference architecture in SP 500-292, which was based on a Cloud Security Alliance (CSA) working group project for cloud enterprise architecture. CSA has continued to update material related to this RA, including mapping control frameworks to the RA providing guidance to security practitioners for securely deploying cloud services.

Some RA models like NIST are role-based and describe the activities needed to provision, use, and maintain cloud services. The NIST RA is intended to be vendor neutral and defines five roles: cloud consumer, cloud provider, cloud auditor, cloud broker, and cloud carrier. Other RAs, such as the IBM Cloud Computing Reference Architecture (CCRA), are layer-based, although they also identify key activities performed by cloud provider and consumer.

Cloud Computing Activities

Some organizations will be a mix of cloud consumer and cloud provider. Internal IT departments may migrate legacy computing environments to a private cloud model for consumption by the organization's users, while other services will be consumed strictly from external cloud providers; as an example, an organization might retain its on-premises Exchange environment while also consuming Microsoft 365 SaaS for collaboration. Cloud-native organizations are those with no traditional, on-premises IT environments. New organizations, such as startups, often pursue this model due to the ease of use, while some older organizations have migrated completely to the cloud for cost savings. Regardless of the organization's status, there are several key activities related to each role, which are detailed here:

- **Cloud consumer:** The consumer procures and uses, or consumes, the cloud services. This involves reviewing available providers and services to determine which one best fits the organization's needs and then entering into a relationship, usually defined by a contract, with the CSP. Once the service is active, the consumer is responsible for setting up accounts, configuring the service, and then actually using it. These activities will be different across different CSPs and cloud service models, but there are some common activities. For a SaaS consumer, the typical end-user management is required, including provisioning accounts and configuring settings such as multifactor authentication (MFA). End users consuming the service will perform whatever activity the SaaS platform enables, such as collaboration and communication. In a PaaS environment the customer activities center on software development efforts, business intelligence, and application deployment. IaaS customers focus on activities such as business continuity and disaster recovery and building higher-level services on top of the basic infrastructure such as storage and compute.

- **Cloud service provider:** The provider makes the service available. These activities include service deployment, orchestration, and management as well as security and privacy. The CSP is also responsible for constructing physical infrastructure such as data centers and computer rooms, deploying physical security controls including fences and security guards, and monitoring and maintaining environmental controls such as air handling and fire suppression.

- **Cloud auditor:** An auditor is an entity capable of independent examination and evaluation of cloud service controls and is usually charged with issuing a report on the effectiveness of those controls. These activities are especially important for consumers with contractual or regulatory compliance obligations, as the auditor's independent review of controls provides assurance that the cloud service is properly secured. Audits are usually focused on compliance, security, or privacy.

- **Cloud broker:** This entity is involved in three primary activities: aggregation of services from one or several CSPs, integration with consumers' existing on-premises infrastructure, and customization of services.

- **Cloud carrier:** The carrier provides the network and telecommunication connectivity that permits the delivery and use of cloud services. This role is often performed by an Internet service provider (ISP) along with other standard Internet access, though dedicated cloud carrier functions may be useful for organizations that require high-security communications or dedicated connectivity.

Cloud Service Capabilities

Capability types are another way to look at cloud service models. In this view, we look at the capabilities provided by each model. The three service models are SaaS, PaaS, and IaaS, and each provides a different level and type of service to the customer. The shared security responsibilities differ for each type as well.

Application Capability Types

Application capabilities include the ability to access an application over the network from multiple devices and from multiple locations. Application access may be made through a web interface, through a thin client, or in some other manner. As the application and data are stored in the cloud, the same data is available to a user regardless of the device they connect from. Depending on the end user's authorization and device, the look of the interface may be different. Administrators will typically see the full set of features, while users on mobile devices may see a subset of functionality tailored to a smaller screen.

Users do not have the capability to control or modify the underlying cloud infrastructure, although they may be able to customize their interface of the cloud solution. This often takes the form of customizing or whitelabeling the application so it looks like a part of the organization's branded tools, though more advanced customization is also possible. This can include defining available data fields, access to different modules within an application, and integration with other tools or platforms. The organization typically does not have to be concerned with the different types of endpoints in use in their organization, so long as the devices are capable of running a modern web browser. Supporting different device types is the responsibility of the application service provider, and support for the organization's installed technology is often a key decision point for acquiring the cloud service.

Platform Capability Types

A platform has the capability of developing and deploying solutions through the cloud. These solutions may be developed with available tools, may be acquired solutions that are delivered through the cloud, or may be solutions that are acquired and customized prior to delivery. The user of a platform service may modify the solutions they deploy, particularly the ones they develop and customize. However, the user has no capability to modify the underlying infrastructure. A standard build of Windows Server deployed on a cloud machine is an example of a PaaS solution. The consumer might modify which software components are installed, such as a web or file server, but they do not have the ability to specify the underlying infrastructure.

What the user gets in a platform service are tools that are specifically tailored to the cloud environment. In addition, the user can experiment with a variety of platform tools, methods, and approaches to determine what is best for a particular organization or development environment without the expense of acquiring all those tools and the underlying infrastructure costs. It provides a development sandbox at a lower cost than doing it all in house. Some platform services focus on vital business functions like big data analytics and business intelligence. In these cases the consumer gets access to a shared environment needed to perform the tasks without the up-front cost of building the massive storage and processing infrastructure needed.

Infrastructure Capability Types

An infrastructure customer cannot control the underlying hardware but has full control over the operating system as well as tools, applications, and solutions installed on top of their infrastructure. The consumer can also provision infrastructure tailored to their needs, including the amount of computing power, storage space, and network bandwidth. This is similar to building out legacy IT, except the infrastructure is virtualized instead of physical.

This capability provides the customer with the ability to quickly spin up an environment and also quickly deprovision when it is no longer needed. This combines the characteristics of elasticity and self-service to provide lower-cost access to the computing capabilities.

Cloud Service Categories

There are three primary cloud service categories: SaaS, PaaS, and IaaS. In addition, other service categories are sometimes suggested, such as storage as a service (STaaS), database as a service (DBaaS), and even everything as a service (XaaS). Marketing combined services is also popular using the -aaS name, such as penetration testing as a service (PTaaS). However, the three fundamental service models for delivering cloud computing are used across providers and are defined in NIST SP 800-145.

Security of systems and data is a shared responsibility between the customer and service provider. The point at which the provider's responsibility ends and the consumer's responsibility begins varies by service category, and the major CSPs publish their shared responsibility model mapping different services they offer to the service categories.

If you are an end user, you are likely using a SaaS solution. If you are a developer, you may be offering a SaaS solution you developed in-house or delivered to your customers using a PaaS development environment. If you are building and managing entire infrastructure in the cloud similar to an on-premises IT deployment, you are using IaaS.

Software as a Service

SaaS is the most common cloud service that most people have experience with. This is where we find the end user performing common tasks like collaborating in Google Docs, sharing files via Dropbox, or documenting project work status by updating a Jira ticket. SaaS is usually subscription-based and billed by the number of users or licenses acquired, and SaaS is typically very easy to set up and use. Some SaaS providers offer site licenses for large volumes of users.

Consumer-configurable security in a SaaS environment is typically limited to application settings and user access controls. Security of the underlying infrastructure from the virtual servers to operating systems is maintained by the provider, though some limited options may be available to the consumer. For example, the deployment of a major upgrade to a SaaS application might be configurable so that the downtime required for the upgrade does not impact system availability. The amount of control over security will vary by the CSP, the service offering, and often the size of the contract.

Platform as a Service

PaaS is the domain of developers. With a PaaS solution, the service provider is responsible for infrastructure, networking, virtualization, compute, storage, and operating systems. Everything built on top of that is the responsibility of the developer and their organization.

Many PaaS service providers offer tools that may be used by developers to create their own applications, leaving choices about how tools are used and configured to the developers and their organizations. PaaS offers cost savings over building and maintaining traditional infrastructure and speeds development activities by providing ready-built platforms for developers to deploy applications.

With a PaaS solution, a developer can work from any location with an Internet connection. The CSP is responsible for maintaining the security of the platform, such as patching and updating the services provided rather than requiring internal IT staff to manage these tasks. Major CSPs offer PaaS solutions for common operating systems and databases and support multiple programming languages for custom development.

Infrastructure as a Service

IaaS is where we find the system administrators (sysadmins). In a typical IaaS offering, the service provider is responsible for provisioning hardware, networking, and storage infrastructure, and for exposing this hardware through virtualization. Consumers use tools provided by the CSP such as a web console or command line to create and maintain infrastructure, and the CSP's systems allocate resources from the virtualized pool as needed. The sysadmin is responsible for everything built on top of the virtualized infrastructure, including the operating system, developer tools, middleware applications, and end-user applications as needed.

IaaS provides the most flexibility to build and deploy computing resources but also requires the most administrative effort from the consumer. It mirrors processes needed for traditional infrastructure but provides additional flexibility and cost savings due to the shared nature of cloud computing.

Cloud Deployment Models

There are four cloud deployment models defined in NIST SP 800-145, and a fifth model is emerging as organizations utilize multiple cloud environments at either an application or organization level. Each deployment model has advantages and disadvantages for both cost and security considerations. The defining element of each model is who owns the cloud and who can access the cloud—or at least, who controls access to the cloud.

Public Cloud

In a public cloud, anyone with access to the Internet may access the resources provided, usually through a subscription-based service. The resources and application services are provided by third-party service providers, and the systems and data reside on third-party servers. For example, Dropbox provides a file storage product to end users. The details of how Dropbox provides this service are not exposed directly to the end users, and for the customer it is simply a publicly available cloud data storage service that can be consumed using a PC or mobile device, or even integrated into an application.

There are concerns with privacy and security in a public cloud. While this was a major concern in the past that could prevent organizations from utilizing public cloud services, advances in regulation and service offerings have made public cloud a viable option for virtually all organizations. The responsibility for data privacy and security remains with the data owner, who is typically the customer, which includes the decision about which cloud service model to utilize. Concerns about reliability can sometimes be handled contractually through the use of a service-level agreement (SLA); however, most CSPs offer standard uptime SLAs that are robust enough for a majority of organizations. This is also a key part of the shared responsibility model, as different services provide different SLAs, and it is the responsibility of the consumer to architect their application and use of cloud services to meet their availability requirements.

Concerns also exist for vendor lock-in and access to data if the service provider goes out of business or is breached. While unlikely, the major CSPs have suffered temporary disruptions, and each offers customized service offerings that can make it difficult or impossible to move an application hosted by one CSP to another. A more frequent risk is the retirement or removal of certain services, which is a business decision made by the CSP. If you are a customer of the CSP and rely on that service, you likely have no control over when and how the service is retired, potentially creating availability issues and unexpected effort to upgrade or migrate.

Private Cloud

A private cloud is built in the same manner as a public cloud, but the difference is in ownership. A private cloud belongs to a single company and contains data and services for use by that company, meaning there is no subscription or access for the general public. In this case, the infrastructure may be built internally or hosted on third-party servers. Private clouds continue the trend toward virtualization and delivery of IT shared services across an organization and are often driven by cost measures designed to maximize efficiency.

A private cloud is usually more customizable, since the provider and consumer are the same entity. This offers benefits for access control, security, and privacy. A private cloud is also generally more expensive, as it requires building out the infrastructure required. There are no other customers to share the infrastructure costs, so the cost of providing excess capacity is not shared. However, in a very large organization a private cloud might be able to more evenly share costs across different units.

A private cloud may not save on infrastructure costs, but it provides cloud services to the company's employees in a more controlled and secure fashion. The major cloud vendors provide both a public cloud and the ability for an organization to build virtual private cloud environments, and some have dedicated private cloud environments for specific customers such as government.

The primary advantage to a private cloud is security and control, while the primary disadvantage is cost. With more control over the environment and only one customer, it is easier to avoid security issues of multitenancy, and issues such as scheduling patches or maintenance downtime are easier. When the cloud is internal to the organization, secure data destruction is also a possibility because the organization retains physical control of its infrastructure.

Community Cloud

A community cloud falls somewhere between public and private clouds. The cloud is built for the needs of multiple organizations that are typically in the same industry. These common industries might be banks, regional governments, or a cloud hosted by a game manufacturer and provided to a specific community of gamers with specific hardware. Universities often set up consortiums for research, and this can be facilitated through a community cloud. Structured like public and private clouds, the infrastructure may be hosted by one of the community partners or by a third party. Access is restricted to members of the community and may be subscription based.

While a community cloud can facilitate data sharing among similar entities, each remains independent and is responsible for what it shares with others. As in any other model, the owner of the data remains responsible for its privacy and security, sharing only what is appropriate, when it is appropriate. Because of the smaller scale compared to a public cloud, a community cloud may be more expensive. This may be offset by the shared interests or requirements of the community that can be implemented in the cloud, such as enhanced privacy.

Hybrid Cloud

A hybrid cloud is a combination of one or more cloud deployment models and is often a combination of private and public cloud. This offers additional flexibility and scalability for different types of computing needs. For example, high-sensitivity data requires additional security controls that a public cloud cannot offer, while lower-sensitivity data can be handled in a public cloud at much lower cost. In this arrangement, sensitive data like intellectual property would utilize only the private cloud, while the organization's external-facing systems like email and website hosting can take advantage of public cloud cost savings.

When an organization has highly sensitive information, the additional cost of a private cloud is warranted, since the potential risk impact is greater. A private cloud still offers benefits of broad network access and resource pooling but provides more control to the organization over security controls such as physical access, data destruction, and system access.

Most organization will also have less sensitive information, such as marketing materials, emails, and public information, on a company website. A public cloud's cost benefits likely outweigh the minor risk increase inherent with giving up physical control of infrastructure, so the business decision will likely require the organization to take advantage of these cost savings.

In a hybrid model, the disadvantages and benefits of each type of cloud deployment are the same for the different elements that make up the organization's hybrid cloud environment. Additionally, the added complexity of managing multiple clouds is itself a risk, so a clear justification needs to exist. Cloud orchestration can be useful to make the job of managing a hybrid cloud environment easier, particularly ensuring that configurations are uniformly applied across different cloud services.

Multi-cloud

Multi-cloud is not one of the cloud deployment models identified in NIST SP 800-145, but it is not an entirely new concept. An organization with a multi-cloud model consumes cloud computing services from multiple CSPs. Multi-cloud is different from hybrid cloud because the entire system is spread across multiple CSPs, rather than specific subsystems being in different cloud environments. An organization that utilizes public cloud for its website and a private cloud for company confidential data is utilizing a hybrid cloud deployment model.

By contrast, a system with both databases and application servers that are located across both AWS and Azure is a multi-cloud deployment. By utilizing open-source or standardized cloud orchestration tools that work across different CSPs, such as Kubernetes and YAML definition files, the organization can deploy the same infrastructure regardless of the underlying CSP. Modern applications increasingly rely on application programming interfaces (APIs) for communicating and sharing data, and these APIs allow for dynamic location of hosts via DNS records. Application servers in AWS can easily communicate with a database in AWS or Azure, as long as the DNS records are maintained for the current location of the database.

Multi-cloud deployments can provide enhanced reliability and availability in the event that a CSP suffers an outage, and issues of vendor lock-in may be reduced with the more portable infrastructure created by a multi-cloud architecture. Potential cost savings can also be recognized if one CSP offers a cheaper service than their competitors. Additionally, if different CSPs offer unique services, a multi-cloud deployment allows the organization to take advantage by locating relevant system elements in that CSP.

The added complexity of multiple CSPs with potentially different service offerings, security capabilities, and technical requirements can make multi-cloud deployment risky. Each CSP offers its own interface and methods of interacting with the cloud service offerings from setup to deployment to administration, so performing routine tasks can require additional time and effort. Operational issues can include increased latency of communications and potential difficulty in assigning costs to specific systems that are spread across multiple CSP invoices.

Cloud Shared Considerations

All cloud customers and CSPs share a set of concerns or considerations. It is no longer the case that all companies use a single CSP or SaaS vendor. In fact, larger companies may use multiple vendors and two or more CSPs in their delivery of services. The business choice is to use the best service for a particular use (best being defined by the customer based on features, cost, or availability). The sections that follow discuss some major considerations that cloud customers must consider when deciding if cloud computing is appropriate for specific tasks and if it should be part of the organization's cloud computing strategy.

Interoperability

With the concern over vendor lock-in, *interoperability* is a primary consideration. Interoperability creates the ability to communicate with and share data across multiple platforms and between traditional IT and cloud services provided by different vendors. Avoiding vendor lock-in allows the customer to make decisions based on the cost, feature set, or availability of a particular service regardless of the vendor providing the service. Interoperability leads to a richer set of alternatives and more choices in pricing.

Portability

Portability may refer to data portability or architecture portability. Data portability is focused on the ability to move data between traditional and cloud services or between different cloud services without having to port the data using potentially lossy methods, and architecture portability allows for migration of applications or systems without significant changes to or loss of service.

Data portability matters to an organization that uses a multi-cloud approach, as data will move between CSPs. Moving data between the CSPs should not be a burdensome task leading to loss of system availability or loss of data. It is also important in a cloud bursting scenario, where peak usage expands from on-premises hosting to include services in a cloud environment to meet demand, as the system must remain fully available both during the cloud burst and when demand returns to normal and the on-premises system resumes handling all requests. This must be seamless to make the strategy useful. Data backups are increasingly stored in the cloud, and restoration to in-house servers must be handled easily.

Architecture portability is concerned with the ability to access and run a cloud service from a wide variety of devices, running different operating systems. This allows users on a Windows laptop, iPadOS tablet, or Android smartphone to use the same application services, share the same data, and collaborate easily.

Reversibility

Reversibility can be a challenging concept to separate from portability, but it is concerned with a very specific question: once an organization moves an application or workload into a CSP, can it be moved back out again without causing significant impact? This move-out might entail switching to another CSP, deploying a multi-cloud strategy, or even migrating back to traditional on-premises infrastructure.

Elements of reversibility include the ability to avoid vendor lock-in. These might take the form of tools that can be used for both importing data and exporting it easily, or cloud architectures that allow for portability such as standardized PaaS, which can be replicated by another CSP. Another element of reversibility is the potential impact on the system operations. If migration takes days or weeks, during which the system cannot be used, this is a barrier to reversibility and creates a potential vendor lock-in to a specific CSP.

Availability

Availability is obviously important as it is one leg of the CIA triad. Within the constraints of agreed-upon SLAs, the purchased cloud services must be made available to the customer by the CSP. If the SLA is not met, there should be penalties or recourses available to the consumer. As an example, if a customer has paid for Dropbox and the service is not available when the customer attempts to access their data, the service availability has failed. If this failure is not within the requirements of the SLA, the customer has a claim against the service provider and may be entitled to compensation such as a reduced price for the service.

An important aspect of availability is concerned with the elasticity and scalability of the cloud service. If the CSP has not properly planned for capacity expansion, customers with growing needs will not find the service adequate to their requirements. Consider a SaaS tool like Salesforce. If customers are successful, their list of potential customers will grow, and they would expect a tool like Salesforce to scale up to this new demand. If Salesforce does not provision adequate storage and computing power to grow with customer demand, then successful businesses will be forced to migrate to another solution as their businesses expand.

Security

Cloud security is a challenging endeavor. It is true that the larger CSPs spend resources and focus on creating a secure environment, and the shared nature of the cloud means these resources are available to organizations that would otherwise not have access to them. It is equally true that large CSPs are very attractive targets for attackers, and there are aspects of cloud computing like multitenancy that create new security challenges.

The fundamental architecture of cloud services, which make data and service portability extremely simple, also introduce a new security complexity. Laws and regulations that restrict cross-border data flow, such as GDPR, can make choosing a CSP and architecting infrastructure in a cloud environment more challenging. With cloud computing the actual hardware could be anywhere, so it is vital to know where your data resides. When there are law enforcement issues, location of the data may also be a jurisdictional challenge as law enforcement may lack the means to gain access to data stored outside their jurisdiction.

The owner of data retains ultimate responsibility for the security of the data, regardless of what cloud or noncloud services are used. Cloud security involves more than protection of the data and includes the applications and infrastructure used as well. Security practitioners must ensure that their organizations are aware of any potential security risks introduced by cloud computing and that such risks do not outweigh potential cost savings from a cloud migration.

Privacy

The involvement of third-party providers, in an off-premises situation, creates challenges to data protection and privacy. In most privacy laws and regulations there are concepts of data owners and data processors. Owners are typically the organizations that collect the data, and processors act on behalf of the owner to perform some data tasks. Data subjects are the individuals whose data is being handled, and their rights are enforced through privacy laws like GDPR. This creates a requirement for the data owner to ensure that they choose appropriate cloud service options and architectures.

Privacy concerns include access to data both during a contract and at the end of a contract, as well as the erasure or destruction of data when requested or as required within the contract. Regulatory and contractual requirements such as HIPAA and PCI are also key concerns. Monitoring and logging of data access and modification, and the location of data storage, are additional privacy concerns that must be considered when evaluating a cloud solution.

Resiliency

Resiliency is the ability to continue operating under adverse or unexpected conditions. This involves both business continuity and disaster recovery planning and implementation.

Business continuity might dictate that a customer store their data in multiple regions so that a service interruption in one region does not prevent continued operations, and many cloud services offer this type of resiliency by design.

The cloud also provides resiliency when a customer suffers a severe incident such as weather, facilities damage, terrorism, civil unrest, or similar events. A cloud strategy allows the company to continue to operate during and after these incidents. The plan may require movement of personnel or contracting personnel at a new location. The cloud strategy handles the data and processes as these remain available anywhere network connectivity exists.

Major CSPs use multiple regions and zones to provide redundancy and support recovery or continuity abilities. An organization may choose to build an entire continuity strategy around a single CSP, with multiple regions or zones used to continue providing system availability in the event of a disaster. Multi-cloud can be another strategy to support continuity, as the system can run even if a specific provider is not available.

Performance

Performance is measured through the requirements agreed upon in an SLA and is generally quite high as major CSPs build excess capacity and redundancy into their systems. The major performance concerns are network availability and bandwidth, which may be outside the control of the CSP. A network is a hard requirement of a cloud service, and if the network is down, the service is unavailable. Areas of limited bandwidth or network providers may be at higher risk for poor performance, or loss of system availability, and may drive design requirements such as seeking out or even building alternate network options.

Governance

Cloud governance uses the same mechanisms as governance of your on-premises IT solutions, including policies, procedures, controls, and oversight. Controls include encryption, access control lists (ACLs), and identity and access management. As many organizations have cloud services from multiple vendors, a cloud governance framework and application can make the maintenance and automation of cloud governance manageable. This may be another cloud solution, and many cloud security SaaS offerings exist in the market.

A variety of governance solutions, some cloud based, exist to support this need. Without governance, cloud solutions quickly grow beyond what can be easily managed. For example, a company may want to govern aspects of the cloud services used such as the number of CSP accounts, number of server instances, amount of storage utilized, and size of databases or other storage tools. Each of these adds to the cost of cloud computing, and without adequate governance the organization's cloud bill will continue to grow. A tool that tracks usage and associated costs will help an organization use the cloud efficiently and keep its use under budget.

Maintenance and Versioning

Maintenance and versioning in a cloud environment have some advantages and disadvantages. Each party is responsible for the maintenance and versioning of their portion of the cloud stack. In a SaaS solution, the maintenance and versioning of all parts is the responsibility of the CSP, from the hardware to the SaaS solution. In a PaaS solution, the customer is responsible for the maintenance and versioning of the applications they acquire and develop. The platform and tools provided by the platforms, as well as the underlying infrastructure, are the responsibility of the CSP. In an IaaS solution, the CSP is responsible for maintenance and versioning of hardware, network and storage, and the virtualization software. The remainder of the maintenance and versioning is the responsibility of the customer.

What this means in practical terms is that updates and patches in a SaaS or PaaS environment may occur without the knowledge of the customer. If properly tested before being deployed, it will also be unnoticed by the customer. There remains the potential for something to break when an update or patch occurs, as it is impossible to test every possible variation that may exist in the cloud environment of the customers. This is true in a traditional on-premises environment as well. In an IaaS environment, the customer has much more control over patch and update testing and deployment.

Virtualization made maintenance and versioning much easier, and the cloud's foundation on virtualization extends this advantage to cloud services. In most cases it is easy to create a snapshot of a virtualized resource, which supports rollback if a patch causes operational issues. The distributed nature of the cloud also means that many services exist in multiple places; updates are typically deployed in stages, so if an issue is encountered, other regions or zones can handle processing without causing downtime. Additionally, SaaS solutions solve issues of potentially unlicensed or unpatched software by centralizing the control with the CSP.

In a PaaS or IaaS, the customer is responsible for some of the maintenance and versioning and is required to define their own policies, procedures, and oversight to ensure that they are followed. However, each customer that connects to the PaaS and IaaS environment will be accessing the most current version provided by the CSP, ensuring that at least some issues addressed by patching are handled in a timely manner.

Service Levels and Service Level Agreements

Contractually, an SLA specifies the required performance parameters of a solution. This negotiation will impact the price, as more stringent requirements can be more expensive. For example, if you need 24-hour support, this will be less expensive than 4-hour support.

Some CSPs will provide a predefined set of SLAs, and customers choose the level of service they need. The customer can be an individual or an organization. For the customer contracting with a CSP, this is a straightforward approach. The CSP publishes their performance options and the price of each, and the customer selects the one that best suits their needs and resources.

In other cases, a customer specifies their requirements, and the CSP will provide the price. If the CSP cannot deliver services at the level specified or if the price is more than the customer is willing to pay, the negotiation may continue, or the organization may need to find an alternative provider. Once agreed upon, the SLA becomes part of the contract, and the SLA is executed along with other documents like a contract or master services agreement (MSA). The cost of negotiating and customizing an SLA and the associated environment is not generally cost effective for smaller organizations and individuals, though most CSPs offer a large variety of services at predefined service levels. This allows smaller entities to choose the services they need without the cost of negotiation.

Auditability

A cloud solution needs to be auditable for the customers to gain assurance that their data is adequately protected. Audits require an independent examination of the cloud services controls, and the auditors express an opinion on the effectiveness of the controls examined. The audit activities seek to answer questions such as "Are the controls properly implemented?" and "Are the controls functioning adequately and achieving their intended risk reduction goals?"

A CSP will rarely allow a customer to perform on audit on their controls. Instead, independent third parties will perform assessments that are provided to the customer. Some assessments require a nondisclosure agreement (NDA), while others are publicly available. These audit reports include SOC reports, FedRAMP packages, vulnerability scans, and penetration tests. More details of audit processes, methodologies, and the types of audits a CSP might furnish to customers are covered in Chapter 6.

Regulatory

Proper oversight and auditing of a CSP makes regulatory compliance more manageable. A regulatory environment is one where a principle or rule controls or manages the activities of an organization. For example, the Payment Card Industry Data Security Standard (PCI DSS) dictates how organizations processing payment card transactions must handle the data. Governance of the regulatory environment involves implementing policies, procedures, and controls that assist an organization in meeting regulatory requirements.

One form of regulations are those governmental requirements that have the force of law. The Health Insurance Portability and Accountability Act (HIPAA), the Gramm-Leach-Bliley Act (GLBA), the Sarbanes-Oxley Act (SOX) in the United States, and the GDPR in the European Union are examples of laws that are implemented through regulations and have the force of law. If any of these apply to an organization, governance will put a framework in place to ensure compliance with these regulations.

Another form of regulations are those put in place through contractual requirements. SLAs are one example of a contractual obligation that regulates business activities, and PCI DSS is another example of contractual obligations that credit and debit card processors are required to implement in order to continue processing payments. Enforcement of contractual rules can be through the civil courts governing contracts. Governance must again put in place the framework to ensure compliance.

A third form of regulations is found through standards bodies like the International Organization for Standardization (ISO) and NIST, as well as nongovernmental groups such as the Cloud Security Alliance and the Center for Internet Security. These organizations make recommendations and provide best practices in the governance of security and risk. While this form of regulation does not usually have the force of law, an organization or industry may voluntarily adopt a specific set of guidelines as a framework for implementing security and risk management. In other cases these may be required based on legal or contractual requirements. For example, contractors to the U.S. federal government are often required to implement the NIST control set in order to secure data shared with them, and private organizations may have customer-enforced requirements for an ISO 27001 certification over their security program.

Outsourcing

As previously discussed, use of the cloud involves giving up some control, which has both benefits and possible disadvantages. Shared resources tend to lower costs, which is a major benefit of outsourcing and a huge driver for organizations to both outsource business processes and migrate to cloud computing. The loss of visibility into service provisioning is also a potential drawback of outsourcing; in SaaS the CSP is supposed to provide patching, but there may be little to no visibility other than application interface changes to indicate whether all relevant patches have actually been applied.

The loss of control inherent in outsourcing can be a source of additional security risks. Outsourcing firms are often located in different countries, and sharing data across borders can be a violation of privacy or security laws and regulations like the EU GDPR. Outsourcing services like system administration or even data entry can lead to issues under the U.S. International Traffic in Arms Regulations (ITAR), which requires that certain activities be performed only by U.S. citizens.

Both cloud consumers and CSPs need to consider the advantages and risks of outsourcing when developing business strategies. The cost savings can be significant, but so too can the added risks. Major CSPs offer specialized cloud services designed to meet major regulations like ITAR, PCI DSS, HIPAA, and GDPR. It might even be possible to simplify meeting regulatory obligations by using such a prebuilt service, as it removes many potential pitfalls from the process of standing up your own infrastructure in a heavily regulated environment.

Impact of Related Technologies

The technologies in this section may be termed *transformative technologies*. Without them, cloud computing still works and retains its benefits, but these technologies are providing increased capabilities and improvements, and many leverage the quickly evolving set of technologies that cloud computing is built on. In the following sections, the specific use cases for the technology will be described.

Data Science

The field of *data science* has expanded rapidly in recent years and combines elements of the scientific method with data management and usage to derive new approaches to understanding, manipulating, and extracting valuable information from large volumes of data. Its applications to security are obvious to any practitioner who has observed log data from even a small computer network—computer systems can easily generate hundreds of log entries per minute, leading to an overwhelming amount of data for human analysis.

Advances in data storage and processing, enabled by the massive scale of cloud computing resources, have made data science a critical tool for information security. Defining a baseline of expected system behavior and then spotting anomalies or suspicious patterns in real time is virtually impossible for human analysts to do. A machine learning (ML) model can be trained on the unique circumstances of a particular system, then continuously monitored for anomalies like unexpected connections, user behavior that does not conform to expectations, or entirely novel attacker methods that deviate from expected system activity.

Training is a key element of data science. This is not the same as security training for end users; data scientists develop models that ML platforms can use to analyze data. These models must be trained using datasets, often using the ML to make a guess and then verifying it with human analysis. CAPTCHA authentication mechanisms are an example. First, systems designed to recognize objects in photos guess what types of objects each photo contains; then when a user is presented a CAPTCHA challenge, they can confirm or refute the ML model's guess. Such systems need a large quantity of data, and if the input data for training is not high quality, the results may be unreliable or entirely unusable.

Data science tools include big data storage locations like data warehouses and data lakes. Because these locations aggregate large amounts of data, they can present a number of security challenges. Personnel working on the data will have broad access, so robust authentication mechanisms are required. These locations are also likely to be highly attractive targets since a compromise grants access to a large volume of likely sensitive data.

Machine Learning

ML is a key component of *artificial intelligence* (AI) and is becoming more widely used in the cloud. Machine learning creates the ability for a solution to learn and improve without the use of additional programming. Many of the CSPs provide ML tools designed for organizations to build their own ML models, as well as services that include ML like speech or image recognition. There is some concern and regulatory movement when ML makes decisions about individuals without the involvement of a person in the process.

The availability of large amounts of inexpensive data storage coupled with vast amounts of computing power increases the effectiveness of ML. A data warehouse, or even a data lake, can hold amounts of data that could not be easily used before, likely because of the extremely high cost of storage and processing power. ML tools can mine this data for answers to questions that could not be asked before and can be used to train systems to automatically spot patterns or trends.

The security concern inherent with ML has to do with both the data and the processing. If all your data is available in one large data lake, access to the data must be tightly controlled, and that data lake is a high-value target for attackers. If the data store is breached, all your data is at risk, so controls to protect the data at rest, control access, and audit access are crucial to make this capability safe for use.

The other concern is with how the data is used. More specifically, how will it impact the privacy of the individuals whose data is in the data store? Will questions be asked where the answers can be used to discriminate against groups of people based on some characteristics? Might insurance companies refuse to cover individuals when the health history of their entire family tree suggests they are an even greater risk than would be traditionally believed?

Governmental bodies and nongovernmental organizations (NGOs) are addressing these concerns to some degree. For example, Article 22 of the EU GDPR has a prohibition on automated decision making, which often involves ML, when that decision is made without human intervention if the decision has a significant impact on the individual. For example, a decision on a mortgage loan could involve ML, but the final loan decision cannot be made by exclusively the ML solution. A human must review the information and make the final decision.

Artificial Intelligence

The goal of AI is to create a machine that has the capabilities of a human and cannot be distinguished from a human, especially when it comes to situations that the machine was not preprogrammed to deal with. It is possible that AI could create intelligent agents online that are indistinguishable from human agents. This has the potential to impact the workforce, particularly in jobs that do not require a great deal of situational analysis or critical thinking. There is also concern about how agents could be manipulated to affect consumer behavior and choices. An unethical individual could use these tools to impact humanity, leading to a need for safeguards in the technology and legal protections that will need to be in place to protect the customers. The rapid evolution of this field has so far outpaced the rate of regulation and legislation.

With the vast amount of data in the cloud, the use of AI is a security and privacy concern beyond the data mining and decision making of ML, though many AI endeavors rely on training systems using ML models, so there are shared concerns. This greater ability to aggregate and manipulate data through the tools created through AI research creates growing concerns over security and privacy of that data, as well as the potential applications that will be devised for any AI systems.

Many security solutions offer ML or AI as features that can supplement human analysts in processing large quantities of security data. One example is intrusion detection, where hundreds of thousands or even millions of data points may be generated by an organization's network in a day. Human analysis of that much data is virtually impossible, but a computer system could easily handle the load. Since most organizations have some uniqueness in their IT setup, an ML model can be trained to spot activity that is anomalous for the given network. However, a true AI that can analyze all relevant data and make a decision on whether the activity is truly suspicious or simply unexpected is still many years away.

Blockchain

A blockchain is an open distributed ledger of transactions, often financial, between parties. This transaction is recorded in a permanent and verifiable manner, where the records, or *blocks*, are linked cryptographically and are distributed across a set of computers, owned by a variety of entities. All parties participating in the blockchain can write new transactions and verify previous transactions but cannot modify those previous transactions.

Blockchain provides a secure way to perform anonymous transactions that also maintain nonrepudiation. The ability to securely store a set of records across multiple servers, perhaps in different CSPs or on-premises across different organizations, can be a method for achieving data integrity. Any data transaction committed to the chain is verifiable and secure and relies on advances in cryptography and distributed computing.

In cloud computing, blockchains are often implemented as part of financial systems to record transactions. Most CSPs and many other IT service providers offer blockchains that can be used as high-integrity data storage methods for any application. Any organization that requires this level of integrity can build a solution on top of a specific blockchain. This can, in turn, lead to similar issues with utilizing a given CSP, particularly the problem of vendor lock-in.

One example of a security application for blockchain is the collection of audit evidence. Once an audit artifact is created, such as an access review, it is recorded to the blockchain to definitively prove that the security control activity has occurred. When the organization's compliance team or auditors review that evidence, they have a high level of assurance that the control was executed and is functioning as intended.

Internet of Things

With the growth of the Internet of Things (IoT), a great deal of data is being generated and stored by a large volume of distributed devices. The cloud is a natural way to store this data, as data from IoT devices such as thermostats, cameras, or irrigation controllers is generated by devices with limited storage capabilities but persistent network connectivity. The ability to store, aggregate, and mine this data in the cloud from any location with a network connection is beneficial.

The manufacturers of many IoT devices do not even consider the cybersecurity aspects of these devices, and many of the manufacturers lack robust software development and security practices. To an HVAC company, a smart thermostat may simply be a thermostat with hardware that allows it to connect to a Wi-Fi network and communicate via APIs. These devices can be in service for many years, may never receive software or firmware updates, and lack processing power to run security tools like anti-malware or firewalls.

For many IoT devices, the data may not be the primary target, but instead the device itself may become part of a botnet for use in a DDoS attack. This was the case for the Mirai botnet, which infected vulnerable IoT devices like cameras and used them to send floods of network traffic. Devices with cameras, microphones, or location tracking abilities are frequently a target, as those features may be used to surveil individuals. Processes controlled by IoT devices can be interrupted in ways that damage equipment (e.g., Stuxnet) or reputations.

Few organizations are sufficiently mature to really protect IoT devices. This makes these devices more dangerous because they are rarely monitored. The cloud provides the ability to monitor and control a large population of devices from a central location. For some devices, such as a thermostat, this may be a small and acceptable risk. However, audio and visual feeds raise privacy, security, and safety concerns that must be addressed.

Containers

Virtualization is a core technology in cloud computing. It allows resource pooling, multitenancy, and other important characteristics. Containers are one approach to virtualization. In a traditional virtualization environment, the hypervisor sits atop the host OS, while the VM sits atop the hypervisor. The VM contains the guest OS and all files and applications needed for the functioning of that VM. A physical server can have multiple VMs, each running a different machine.

In containerization, there is no hypervisor and no guest OS. A container runtime sits above the host OS, and then each container uses the runtime to access needed system resources. The container contains the files and data necessary to run, but no guest OS. The virtualization occurs higher in the stack and is generally smaller and can start up more quickly. It also uses fewer resources by not needing an additional OS in the virtual space.

The smaller size of the container image and the low overhead are the primary advantages of containers over traditional virtualization, as well as increased portability as it allows for increased abstraction from underlying hardware resources.

Containers make a predictable environment for developers and can be deployed anywhere the container runtime is available, specifically across different CSPs, which enables multi-cloud deployment. Similar to the Java Virtual Machine, a runtime is available for common operating systems and environments. Containers can be widely deployed. Versioning and maintenance of the underlying infrastructure do not impact the containers as long as the container runtime is kept current.

The container itself is treated like a privileged user, which creates security concerns that must be addressed. Techniques and servers exist to address each of these security concerns such as a cloud access security broker (CASB). Security concerns exist and must be carefully managed. All major CSPs support some form of containerization.

Quantum Computing

Quantum computers use quantum physics to build extremely powerful computers. When these are linked to the cloud, it becomes quantum cloud computing. IBM, AWS, and Azure all provide a quantum computing service to select customers, though many of these are still in a research and development stage and require highly specialized knowledge to use. The increased power of quantum computers and the use of the cloud may make AI and ML more powerful and will allow modeling of complex systems available on a scale never seen before. Quantum cloud computing has the ability to transform medical research, AI, and communication technologies.

A concern for quantum computing is that traditional methods for encryption/decryption could become obsolete as the vast power of the cloud coupled with quantum computing makes cryptographic attacks much simpler. This would effectively break current cryptographic methods, which necessitates new quantum methods of quantum encryption. Quantum cryptographic attacks are still theoretical, but as with all cryptography it is only a matter of time before current methods are rendered obsolete.

Edge Computing

Edge computing refers to processing or acting on data at the source where it is collected. It assumes distributed devices that can collect, analyze, and act on data, and is a frequently used model for IoT devices. For example, smart thermostats throughout a campus can gather local temperature data and set the temperature in individual floors, buildings, or even zones without the need for centralized management.

Edge computing can enhance availability by reducing single points of failure (SPOFs), since the edge devices can act independently and synchronize when a centralized system is available. They can provide enhanced customization as well—zones on the side of a building that get afternoon sun might need a lower temperature than zones on the side that is not heated, leading to significant energy cost savings. Processing data on device also reduces bandwidth consumption, which can be useful for extending services to areas with poor connectivity.

Security at the edge can be a challenge for many of the same reasons IoT devices are a security issue. IoT, industrial control systems (ICSs), and embedded systems at the edge may be low-power, stripped-down devices incapable of running traditional security controls like antimalware or host-based firewalls.

Edge devices may be deployed in areas where the organization has limited control as well. Physical devices like IoT may be located in areas with limited physical access controls, while virtual edge devices such as servers may be located across a wide range of hosting services. The issue of data integrity can also be problematic. Similar to distributed computing systems where data must be reconciled into a single data store, processing by edge devices and the communication needed to move data from the edge to a centralized store creates opportunities for data to be intercepted or modified in transit.

Confidential Computing

Confidential computing employs cryptography to protect data in use when it is being processed in a cloud environment. Data that is to be processed typically must be stored in memory and sent to a processor in an unencrypted state, which leaves it potentially vulnerable to unauthorized access by other processes such as malware or compromised applications.

In confidential computing, a trusted execution environment (TEE) is utilized to perform data decryption only when an authorized program attempts to access data. The TEE acts as a secure enclave, with access controls enforced to verify that only authorized applications can make calls for the data being protected. If a malware application attempts to access data processed in the TEE, it is denied access, because it is not authorized to view the keys needed to decrypt the data.

Organizations that want to recognize benefits of cloud computing, such as elasticity and cost savings from metered services, often must balance security risk against the potential benefits. Confidential computing can be deployed to ensure that data processed in the cloud is readable only by authorized applications and not by other cloud tenants or even cloud administrators.

Confidential computing also supports distributed workloads such as edge computing and can be deployed on edge devices as a countermeasure to a failure of physical access controls where the edge devices are deployed. A Confidential Computing Consortium was developed in 2019 to develop models, reference architectures, and best practices for the use of confidential computing. More information can be found at `confidentialcomputing.io`.

DevSecOps

Although not a technology itself, *DevSecOps* represents an evolution of DevOps, which creates a pipeline from system development to operational execution, to include important concepts of security at various stages of the pipeline. DevOps identifies ways to remove inefficiencies and misunderstandings between development teams and operational teams like IT by blending the practices. As the name implies, DevSecOps inserts security concerns into this cross-functional discipline.

A fundamental tenet of DevSecOps is the principle of "shifting left," or taking security activities and embedding them where appropriate throughout the development and deployment lifecycle. Rather than perform security activities after a system is built and deployed, when it may be costly or impossible to fix issues, DevSecOps embeds security activities at earlier phases of the system lifecycle. This generally leads to lower-cost fixes that are easier to implement. For example, code reviews performed after a developer checks in a module can uncover bugs that can be fixed with a few simple code changes rather than weeks of hunting to determine the source of a flaw.

In addition to distributing security activities, DevSecOps also seeks to create a more holistic view of security and provision resources most appropriate to various types of tasks. A security analyst is unlikely to be skilled at performing code reviews. A DevSecOps team can hire and manage resources directly and remove the bottleneck of a separate security team's involvement. DevOps and Agile development are widely deployed and popular with cloud computing organizations. By embedding key security activities throughout the development and operations lifecycle, organizations can ensure that security objectives are met without adversely impacting project timelines or deliverable schedules.

Understand Security Concepts Relevant to Cloud Computing

Security concepts for cloud computing mirror many concepts in on-premises security, though some unique considerations exist. Most of these differences are related to the customer not having access to the physical hardware and storage media, as well as the assumption of broad network accessibility. These concepts and concerns will be discussed in the following sections.

Cryptography and Key Management

Cryptography is essential in the cloud to support security and privacy. Cloud computing presents three key challenges for encryption. First, data must move between the consumer and CSP, so data in transit must be protected. Second, multitenancy and the inability to securely wipe the physical drives used in a CSP's data center make data at rest and disposal more challenging. The primary solution is cryptography.

Data at rest and data in motion must be securely encrypted. A customer will need to be able to determine whether a VM or container has been unaltered after deployment, requiring cryptographic tools. Secure and reliable communications are essential when moving data and processes between the consumer and the CSP, so encryption and integrity checks by hashing are essential.

One of the challenges with cryptography has always been key management. With many organizations using a multi-cloud strategy, key management becomes even more challenging. The questions to answer are

- Where are the keys stored?
- Who generates and manages the keys (customer or CSP)?
- Should a key management service be used?

In a multi-cloud environment, there are additional concerns:

- How is key management automated?
- How is key management audited and monitored?
- How is key management policy enforced?

The power of a key management service (KMS) is that many of these questions are answered. Most CSPs offer a KMS and supporting services like virtual hardware security modules (HSMs) that can be attached to VMs to provide secure cryptographic functions.

One benefit of a KMS is that it stores keys separately from the data, so a breach of encrypted data is less severe because the attackers are less likely to be able to read it. Many data breach and privacy laws provide an exemption if a breach occurs and there are no signs attackers were able to decrypt the data. This benefit disappears if the encryption/decryption keys are stored with the data or if evidence points to attackers accessing the KMS. If the keys are to be stored in the cloud, they must be stored separately from the data and have robust logging capabilities. Outsourcing this has the benefit of bringing that expertise to the organization. However, like any outsourcing arrangement, you cannot turn it over to the KMS and forget about it—someone still needs to oversee the KMS.

Using a KMS does not mean that you turn over the keys to another organization any more than using a cloud file repository gives away your data to the service storing your files. You choose the level of service provided by the KMS to fit your organization and needs. The level of integrity and confidentiality required will determine which services make sense for an organization to engage from an external KMS.

The last three questions—automation, monitoring and auditing, and policy enforcement—are the questions to keep in mind when reviewing the different KMSs available. Like any other service, the features and prices vary, and each organization will have to choose the best service for their situation. More details of managing encryption and cryptographic keys in cloud environments, including topics such as key escrow, are covered in Chapter 2.

Identity and Access Control

There are multiple types of access control, and in the shared responsibility model of cloud computing the CSP and customer have different, but important, responsibilities. Some examples include physical access control, technical access control, and administrative access control.

Physical Access

Physical access control refers to actual physical access to the servers and data centers where the data and processes of the cloud customer are stored. Physical access is entirely the responsibility of the CSP, since the CSP owns the physical infrastructure and the facilities that house the infrastructure. Only they can provide physical security.

Physical access control to cloud customer facilities remains the purview of the customer. Some cloud services offer physical transportation options for data migration to the cloud, whether for initial migration or for making data backups available. In these cases, the customer must choose an appropriate courier or other secure transportation service.

User Access

Administrative access control refers to the policies and procedures a company uses to regulate and monitor access. These policies include who can authorize access to a system, how system access is logged and monitored, and how frequently access is reviewed. The customer is responsible for determining policies and enforcing those policies as related to procedures for provisioning/deprovisioning user access and reviewing access approvals.

Technical access control is the primary area of shared responsibility. While the CSP is responsible for protecting the physical environment and the customer is responsible for the creation and enforcement of policies, both the customer and the CSP share responsibilities for technical access controls.

For example, a CSP may be willing to federate with an organization's identity and access management (IAM) system. The CSP is then responsible for the integration of the IAM system, while the customer is responsible for the maintenance of the system. If a cloud IAM system is used (provided by the CSP or a third party), the customer is responsible for the provisioning and deprovisioning of users in the system and determining access levels and system authorizations while the CSP or third party maintains the IAM system.

Logging system access and reviewing the logs for unusual activity can also be a shared responsibility, with the CSP or third-party IAM provider logging access and the customer reviewing the logs or with the CSP providing both services. Either choice requires coordination between the customer and the CSP. Access attempts can come from a variety of devices and locations throughout the world, making IAM an essential function.

Privilege Access

Privilege access control refers to the privileged access granted to cloud infrastructure as well as systems, applications, and data hosted in a CSP. A related field is known as *privileged access management* (PAM) and is focused on reducing the risk of compromise or abuse related to such accounts. A system administrator is an example of a privileged account. An attacker who gained access to that user's account could perform a number of functions, including adding new users, accessing confidential information, and misusing resources.

Managing privileged access in the cloud may rely on an existing IAM solution or a separate PAM solution that is integrated with the IAM. Additional controls for privilege accounts are often justified by the capabilities granted to these accounts. Those controls might include stronger password or multifactor authentication (MFA) requirements, separate accounts for administrative and nonadministrative tasks, and more frequent access reviews.

Service Access

Service access refers to controlling access by the CSP to customer data. CSP administrators require access to infrastructure elements of the cloud service in order to perform necessary services such as patching, troubleshooting, and other maintenance. This access can be a problem for highly sensitive workloads such as regulated data and could be a deciding factor for an organization to avoid using cloud computing.

Major CSPs publish details of their service access control policies and may implement additional controls to give customer assurance over the safety of their data in the cloud environment. Data-at-rest encryption for many cloud services can be configured to utilize customer-controlled keys, meaning the cloud administrators can see encrypted data but nothing else. Implementing confidential computing via a TEE is another safeguard against snooping of data by cloud service personnel, since their administrative tools can be blocked from access to the keys needed to decrypt data in use.

Some CSPs offer transparency reports that show when, why, and how CSP personnel accessed customer data. For organizations looking to mitigate risks associated with service access, such a report can provide needed oversight to understand whether the CSP's access is a risk to the organization. In other cases, the requirement for cloud administrators to have access may be too great a risk, so a different deployment model like a community or private cloud is required.

Data and Media Sanitization

It is possible to sanitize storage media when you have physical access to the media, as is the case with on-premises architecture. You determine the manner of sanitization, such as software-based overwriting or even physical destruction of the storage media. You also determine the schedule for data deletion and media sanitization.

In the cloud this becomes more challenging. The data storage is shared and distributed, and CSPs do not allow access to the physical media. The CSP will not allow customer organizations access to the physical disks and will certainly not allow their destruction. In addition, data in the cloud is regularly moved and backed up, making it impossible to determine which disks might contain a copy of any one organization's data. This is a security and privacy concern. The customer will never have the level of control for data and media sanitization that they had when they had physical access and ownership of the storage hardware.

While some CSPs provide access to wipeable volumes, there is no guarantee that the wipe will be done to the level possible with physical access. Encrypted storage of data and cryptoshredding are discussed in the following sections. While not the same as physical access and secure wipe, they provide a reasonable level of security. If, after review, this level of security is not adequate for an organization's most sensitive data, this data should be retained on-premises in customer data centers or on storage media under the direct physical control of the customer.

Overwriting

Overwriting of deleted data occurs in cloud storage over time. Deleted data areas are marked for reuse, and eventually this area will be allocated to and used by the same or another customer, overwriting the data that was previously stored. There is no specific timetable for overwriting, and the data or fragments may continue to exist for some time. Encryption is key in keeping your data secure and the information private. Encrypting all data stored in the cloud works only if the cryptographic keys are inaccessible or securely deleted.

Cryptographic Erase

Cryptographic erase, also known as cryptographic erasure, is an additional way to prevent the disclosure of data. In this process, the cryptographic keys are destroyed (*cryptoshredding*), eliminating the key necessary for decryption of the data. Although data remains on drives or other storage media owned by the CSP, it is unreadable without the decryption key. Like data and media sanitization and overwriting, encryption is an essential step in keeping your data private and secure. Secure deletion of cryptographic keys makes data retrieval nearly impossible.

Network Security

Broad network access is a key component of cloud computing. However, if you have access to cloud resources over an uncontrolled network, bad actors can also gain access, which threatens the security of the cloud service you are using. These bad actors might be able to intercept data in transit or gain access to cloud services by observing the traffic you send, threatening the privacy and security of your data.

There are a number of ways to provide network security. This list is not exhaustive, not all concepts apply to all organizations, and the concepts are not mutually exclusive. Network security starts with controlling access to cloud resources through IAM, discussed previously. Controlling access to the cloud resources limits their exposure and provides accountability for authorized users.

Network security tools like VPNs, cloud gateways, and proxies can be used to reduce exposure to the public Internet and therefore reduce the attack surface bad actors might exploit. The use of VPNs for secure remote access across the Internet is common, though organizations may find cost savings by transitioning from legacy architecture that requires a VPN to a SaaS offering that allows users to dynamically create secure connections without the need for additional hardware or software. Evolving methods of network security, such as zero trust architecture (ZTA), are leveraging new capabilities to provide security with less overhead than a traditional VPN.

Network Security Groups

Security remains an important concern in cloud computing. A network security group (NSG) is one way of protecting a group of cloud resources. The NSG provides a set of security rules that control access, like a virtual firewall, to those resources. The NSG can apply to an individual VM, a network interface card (NIC) for that VM, or even a subnet. The NSG is essentially an access control mechanism protecting the asset and fills the same role as a traditional firewall in a layered defense strategy.

Configuration of the NSG is typically the responsibility of the cloud customer, as they are familiar with the architecture of their applications and systems. Concepts that applied to traditional firewall configuration also apply to NSGs, including default deny all and routine review of allowed access. Although configuration is the responsibility of the customer, most CSPs offer some security tools that can identify common issues with NSGs, such as missing deny all configuration, redundant or broken rules that can hinder access, and public access to resources that typically require stricter access control such as database services.

Zero Trust Network

Zero trust is a relatively new term in security. It is often applied as a marketing label to a wide variety of products, which can make it difficult to discern what the actual concept means. Zero trust is a fundamental approach to security that focuses on protecting assets by never implicitly assuming that other resources are trusted.

Older approaches to security often assumed a well-defined perimeter, like the edge of an organization's network, and implicitly trusted assets inside that perimeter. In this model a database server might have robust firewall rules and access controls for any remote access from outside the organization's firewall but would not enforce the same controls for a user inside the network. Obviously if a bad actor were to gain access to the network, they would be able to access a great deal of information with few barriers.

A zero trust network is modeled on the idea of making access control enforcement as granular as possible. Put another way, every request for access should be verified before access is granted. In a zero trust network, users must authenticate to join the network, they must authenticate to any and all systems or resources they try to access, and, where possible, the system should enforce access approval for each transaction or action performed.

A formal definition of zero trust architecture was published by NIST in SP 800-207. The document formally defines zero trust, identifies applications for network security, and provides guidance on implementing these principles. The document can be found at nist.gov/publications/zero-trust-architecture.

Ingress and Egress Monitoring

Traditional secure perimeter architecture placed security monitoring devices at major entry and exit points to the network, known as *ingress* and *egress monitoring*. Ingress controls can block unwanted external access attempts, while egress controls can prevent internal resources from communicating with unknown or unwanted resources outside the perimeter. However, an organization with even a simple mix of SaaS applications and infrastructure in a PaaS environment will find such monitoring difficult because of the lack of a traditional network perimeter.

Many CSPs offer monitoring solutions native to their environment, which can take the place of traditional perimeter monitoring. In a complex environment with multiple CSPs or cloud applications, it can be helpful to aggregate these monitoring logs into a single platform, such as a security information and event management (SIEM) tool. The SIEM provides centralized monitoring but must be able to ingest information from the organization's entire cloud environment to prevent blind spots in the monitoring.

Virtualization Security

Virtualization is an important technology in cloud computing. It allows for resource sharing and multitenancy, but like all technology there are benefits and security concerns. Security of the virtualization method is crucial. Several components make up virtualization, such as a hypervisor and VMs, and the ability to create virtual computing resources has led to the development of other technologies such as serverless computing.

Hypervisor Security

A *hypervisor*, such as Hyper-V or vSphere, packages resources into a VM. Creating and managing the VM are both done through the hypervisor, and the hypervisor is responsible for scheduling and mediating a VM's access to the underlying physical hardware. For this reason, it is important that the hypervisor be secure. Hypervisors such as Hyper-V, VMware ESXi, and Citrix XenServer are type I hypervisors or native hypervisors that run on the host's hardware.

A type I hypervisor is generally faster and more secure but requires special skills to set up and maintain compared to a type II hypervisor such as VMware or VirtualBox. Type II hypervisors run on top of a host operating system like Windows or macOS. These are easier to set up, typically requiring only the skills needed to install the virtualization application, but they are generally less secure.

A hypervisor is a natural target of malicious users, because a compromise of the hypervisor grants a malicious user control of all the resources used by each VM. If a hacker compromises another tenant on the server you are on and can then escalate the attack to compromise the hypervisor, they may be able to attack other customers through the hypervisor. This type of attack is known as a VM escape, and hypervisor vendors are continually working to make their products more secure.

For the customer, security is enhanced by controlling admin access to the virtualization solution, designing security into your virtualization solution, and securing the hypervisor. All access to the hypervisor should be logged and audited. Access to the network should be limited for the hypervisor to only the necessary access. This traffic should be logged and audited. Finally, the hypervisor must remain current, with all security patches and updates applied as soon as is reasonable. More detailed security recommendations are published in NIST SP 800-125A Rev 1 and by hypervisor vendors.

Container Security

Containerization, such as through Docker or LXC, has many benefits and some vulnerabilities. These include resource efficiency, portability, easier scaling, and agile development. Containers are portable environments that package up an application and its dependencies. This is often a key enabler for a multi-cloud strategy, as containers can be run in any cloud environment compatible with the container technology used. Containerization improves security by isolating the cloud solution and the host system, but inadequate identity and access management and misconfigured containers can be a security risk. Software bugs in the container software can also be an issue. The isolation of the container from the host system does not mean that security of the host system can be ignored.

The security issues of containerization must first be addressed through education and training. Traditional DevOps practices and methodologies do not always translate to secure containerization. The use of specialized container operating systems is also beneficial as it restricts the capabilities of the underlying OS to only those functions a container may need. Much like disabling network ports that are unused, limiting OS functionality decreases the attack surface. Finally, all management and security tools used must be designed for containers. A number of cloud-based security services are available.

There are many containerization solutions provided by major CSPs, and the choice of which solution to use will depend on a variety of factors. The choice of a container platform should be made based on the features and ability to support the organization's existing or defined future-state architecture. Ideally security should be a primary deciding factor, but at a minimum the ability to provide adequate security must be a consideration.

Ephemeral Computing

Ephemeral means "lasting for a very short time." *Ephemeral computing* refers to resources that are created when needed and immediately deprovisioned when no longer needed. They are a crucial part of the metered service characteristic of cloud computing—if an organization needs a server for only a few minutes each day, then paying for 24 hours of computing power is wasteful.

Ephemeral computing can offer a major security advantage. A system that does not exist is impossible to attack, and a system that is briefly created and then deprovisioned reduces the amount of time a malicious user has to exploit it. However, the transient nature of these devices also means that traditional monitoring and security controls are not available. Running an antimalware agent on a server that is only briefly in existence is nearly impossible.

The key to securing ephemeral computing lies in properly specifying configuration of the ephemeral asset. When the asset is needed, a definition file is used to create the needed resources. This definition file must specify appropriate configurations like access controls and security settings like encryption to ensure that the resulting asset is properly secured during use. When the asset is no longer needed, care must be taken to ensure that any data in the ephemeral asset is also securely disposed. The use of cryptographic erasure is common, which ensures that the data cannot be easily recovered.

Serverless Technology

The name *serverless* is something of a misnomer, as there are still servers involved in serverless computing. The CSP is solely responsible for maintaining servers and exposes their computing capacity to customer applications on demand. Code written for serverless computing is deployed into an environment that supports a standard set of programming languages and functions.

When serverless code is run, the CSP's serverless environment allocates resources needed for the requested functions and performs the requested data processing. Results are stored in persistent memory rather than volatile memory like RAM, and the requesting function reads the data from its persistent data store.

Serverless applications offer the ability to scale very efficiently due to fewer constraints from system resources, and developers do not need to worry about setting up or tuning any infrastructure. The customer pays only for the actual amount of computing time that they utilize. Serverless applications may be more secure since they do not inherit security vulnerabilities of a traditional operating system.

However, similar to ephemeral computing, there can be security risks such as a lack of traditional security controls designed to run on a full operating system like intrusion detection systems (IDSs). Many serverless applications rely on APIs for communication and executing functions, so authentication of API calls becomes more important than in a traditional application where requests for data or processing are coming from a known location.

Common Threats

Previous sections dealt with threats that are related to the specific technologies that are key parts of cloud computing, such as virtualization, media sanitization, and network security. However, all other threats that may attack traditional services are also of concern. Controls that are used to protect access to software solutions, data transfer and storage, and identity and access control in a traditional environment must be considered in a cloud environment as well.

Cloud computing is evolving quickly. Each new service or capability offers advantages but also poses potential security risks. The Cloud Security Alliance (CSA) publishes a list of common cloud threats known as the Egregious Eleven. This list highlights threats that target unique elements of cloud computing, such as a lack of cloud security architecture or strategy in immature organizations or those with a significant shadow IT problem. Other threats on the list are common across all computing systems, such as inadequate access controls and insider threats.

Security Hygiene

Hygiene refers to basic practices designed to maintain health and is typically associated with practices like handwashing and cleaning surfaces. Cyber hygiene is basically the same—practices that maintain the health and security posture of systems. These practices include, but are not limited to, the following:

- Vulnerability scanning to detect known vulnerabilities and allow the organization to remediate them

- Penetration testing to identify weaknesses or misconfigurations that could be exploited

- Maintaining asset inventories to ensure that the organization is aware of what assets might be at risk and what controls are deployed to protect them

- Data backups that allow recovery or reconstitution of data if it suffers a loss of integrity or availability

Patching

The single most important element of a security hygiene program is applying software patches. All software contains flaws and vulnerabilities, and patches remove them before bad actors can exploit them. Traditional patching advice has often established windows for patch deployment, such as patches that address critical security issues must be installed within 30 days of release. However, the rapid pace of exploitation means that such windows often leave an organization exposed to risk, so faster patching cycles are recommended. Many systems and application support automatic installation of patches, and it is quickly becoming a security best practice to enable this setting.

Patching in a cloud environment is a crucial shared responsibility. Patches for SaaS applications are the responsibility of the CSP, as are patches for underlying platform software in PaaS such as operating systems and database management systems. Custom software or applications deployed on top of the PaaS are the responsibility of the customer. In IaaS, the CSP is responsible only for patching underlying systems that provide virtualized resources to the customer, such as a hypervisor. Patching of all systems and applications deployed on top of IaaS are the responsibility of the customer.

Baselining

A *baseline* refers to a known set of configuration attributes for a system. Security hygiene related to baselines is twofold. First, it is important to ensure that any new systems or applications added follow the defined baseline, which should be configured to enforce all relevant aspects of security. In cloud computing environments, this can be achieved relatively easily by using infrastructure as code (IAC).

Specifications for cloud infrastructure are documented in a text file that the CSP reads when provisioning new infrastructure. Unlike traditional IT, this removes the potential for errors if a deployment technician missed a step or misread the deployment guide. The concept of *immutable architecture* is also important to baselines, as it prohibits changes to environments once they are built. Patching immutable infrastructure is done by tearing down the old and building a new environment with all the latest patches and updates. Although this sounds like a great deal of work, the cloud characteristic of rapid elasticity makes it trivial to build a new environment from IAC definitions, and tools exist to check all elements contained in a definition and update to the latest version when the environment is built.

The second requirement for baselines is an audit or review of the current environment configuration against the baseline. CSPs offer tools that can alert when a system deviates from the expected baseline. In immutable architecture the baseline is always re-established when the environment is rebuilt, as any drift in the configuration is removed when the new environment is built.

Understand Design Principles of Secure Cloud Computing

As processes and data move to the cloud, it is only right to consider the security implications of that business decision. Cloud computing is as secure as it is configured to be. With careful review of CSPs and cloud services, as well as fulfilling the customer's shared responsibilities for cloud security, the benefits of the cloud can be obtained securely. The following sections discuss methods and requirements that help the customer work securely in the cloud environment.

Cloud Secure Data Lifecycle

As with all security efforts, the best outcomes are achieved when security is designed into a system from the very beginning; this is the principle of *secure by design*. Since many cloud service offerings do not move through traditional system development phases, it can be helpful to instead identify the phases that data flows through. Each phase has accompanying risks and potential security controls. The cloud secure data lifecycle comprises six steps or phases.

- **Create:** This is the creation of new content or the modification of existing content. Controls that typically operate at the creation phase can include labeling data according to its sensitivity and applying encryption.

- **Store:** This generally happens at creation time and involves storing the new content in some data repository such as a database or file system. Choosing an appropriate storage location based on the data's sensitivity level is a critical security task during this phase.

- **Use:** This includes all the typical data activities such as viewing, processing, and modifying data, collectively known as *handling*. Data spends most of its life in this phase, and the majority of an organization's security controls apply here. These include encryption of the data at rest and underlying storage media, encryption of data in transit when it is accessed, access controls, and auditing data use.

- **Share:** This is the exchange of data between two entities or systems. Ensuring adequate confidentiality and integrity of data when it is shared is a vital security control and is typically achieved by encryption and hashing. Access controls are also crucial as the sharing parties must be properly authorized and authenticated to avoid unauthorized access.

- **Archive:** Data is no longer used but is being stored. Data controls such as a retention schedule are important during this phase, and additional encryption concerns may apply due to the long life of data in archives. The proper key is required to decrypt data, so if keys are rotated, a backup is required to ensure that data in archives remains accessible.

- **Destroy:** Data has reached the end of its life, as defined in a data retention policy or similar guidance. It is permanently destroyed, and the method of destruction or sanitization must meet the organization's requirements to avoid data recovery by an unauthorized party.

At each of these steps in the data's lifecycle, there is the possibility of a data breach or data leakage. As discussed, encryption plays a vital role in data security in multiple ways. Other security tools are also important, such as data loss prevention (DLP), which can help identify, inventory, and classify information stored in both on-premises and cloud systems.

Cloud-Based Business Continuity and Disaster Recovery Plan

A *business continuity plan* (BCP) is focused on keeping a business running following a disaster such as weather, civil unrest, terrorism, fire, etc. The BCP may focus on critical business processes necessary to keep the business going while disaster recovery takes place. A *disaster recovery plan* (DRP) is focused on returning to normal business operations, which can be a lengthy process. The two plans work together, since most business processes documented in the BCP rely on the technology and services the DRP is concerned with.

In a BCP, business operations must continue, but they often continue from an alternate location. So, the needs of BCP include space, personnel, technology, process, and data. The cloud can support the organization with many of those needs. A cloud solution provides the technology infrastructure, processes, and data to keep the business going.

Availability zones in a region are independent data centers that protect the customer from data center failures. Larger CSPs like AWS, Azure, and Google define regions. Within a region, latency is low. However, a major disaster could impact all the data centers in a region and eliminate all availability zones in that region. A customer can set up their plan to include redundancy across a single region using multiple availability zones or redundancy across multiple regions to provide the greatest possible availability. This is a concept known as *resiliency*, which describes system architecture that accounts for and anticipates failure by design, without affecting availability. Some cloud concepts, like serverless computing and containerization, are inherently portable and make a resilient architecture relatively inexpensive.

One drawback of multiregion plans is that the cost grows quickly. For this reason, many organizations put only their most critical data—the core systems that they cannot operate the business without—across two or more regions, but less critical processes and data may be stored in a single region. To minimize costs, an organization might back up only critical data and infrastructure definitions in another region but not maintain fully duplicate architecture. The cost of simply storing the data is relatively low, and in the event of an interruption, the environment can be rebuilt, though there will be a temporary loss of availability.

Functions and data that are on-premises may also utilize cloud backups, which help reduce backup costs compared to fully redundant architecture. However, these will also not be back up and running as quickly as a multiregion cloud architecture.

DRP defines processes the organization will use to resume normal operations, such as rebuilding the original computing environment and supporting business infrastructure like office buildings. Depending on the cloud backup strategy used, this might involve restoring data and processing to rebuilt on-premises infrastructure or to the original cloud region.

One failure of many DRPs is the lack of an offsite or offline backup, or the ability to quickly access necessary data backups. In the cloud, a data backup exists in the locations (regions or availability zones) you specify and is available from anywhere network access is available. A cloud-based backup works only if you have network access and sufficient bandwidth to access that data. That network infrastructure must be part of the DRP, and if that is deemed impossible in certain circumstances, a physical, local backup can also be beneficial.

Business Impact Analysis

Performing a business impact analysis (BIA) allows an organization to identify critical assets and capabilities that allow the organization to deliver its products or serve its missions. The BIA identifies the impact to the business if an asset or process is lost and enables prioritization of limited resources for business continuity and disaster recovery planning.

Collaboration tools like email and instant messaging are critical assets for many organizations. Company A has employees who do not communicate with the outside world, so the loss of email would have a minimal impact as long as instant messaging is still available. Company B is reliant on outside communications, so a loss of email would be highly disruptive.

Once all assets and processes are identified, the most critical should be prioritized for planning. The criticality of a process or asset determines the level of resources committed to its continuity. In the previous example, Company A might choose to take no proactive steps to plan for a loss of email, instead relying on an ad hoc strategy if a disruption occurs. Company B, by contrast, should have a plan and resources prepared to ensure continuity of their operations.

Cost-Benefit Analysis

Cloud computing is not always the correct solution. Choosing correct solutions is a business decision guided by a cost-benefit analysis. Cloud computing benefits include more resilient architecture and potential business cost savings as cloud services can be written off as operating expenses. CSPs typically offer incredibly robust solutions that provide uptime that exceeds levels most organizations can achieve due to the costs involved.

These benefits come with certain risks, or costs. These include the loss of control over physical infrastructure, as well as potential for unauthorized data access by CSP staff or other tenants using the cloud services. While most CSPs offer extremely reliable services, in the event of an outage the customer has no control over the recovery process and must wait for a CSP to restore the service. In addition, a migration to the cloud can disrupt traditional perimeter-based security controls since the computing services are no longer located inside an organization-controlled network.

The *cost-benefit analysis* must take all of these factors into account, and business decision makers should weigh them when deciding on a CSP, a deployment model, and what security infrastructure to implement.

Return on Investment

Measuring how much value an organization receives from investing in something is known as *return on investment* (ROI) and is often part of a security practitioner's work in justifying spending on security tools and resources. For example, the salary and benefits paid to a salesperson are an investment by the organization. A positive ROI in this example would be new business that brings in more revenue than the salesperson's compensation, allowing the organization to show a profit.

In security terms, ROI is often measured by risk reduction and is typically measured in financial terms. If an organization faces a risk of losing €1,000,000 due to a data breach, then a security control that costs €5,000 per year provides a positive ROI if it can produce significant risk reduction. Another common measure of ROI is efficiency or productivity of resources. A security tool has a positive ROI if it can speed up detection and remediation of security incidents or can automate tasks and free up resources to focus on more important issues.

Functional Security Requirements

Defining functional security requirements and ensuring that the chosen CSP can meet them is essential when developing a secure cloud solution. Some areas that require particular attention include portability of systems and data, interoperability with other CSPs and on-premises architecture, and the issue of vendor lock-in.

These challenges can be lessened through the use of a vendor management process to ensure standard capabilities, clearly identifying the responsibilities of each party and the development of SLAs as appropriate. For complex or expensive systems, the RFP process can be utilized to clearly state customer security requirements. A vendor that cannot meet the customer's security needs can be eliminated early on, and working with a cloud service partner or cloud service broker can be useful when selecting cloud services.

Portability

One time movement is when a customer moves to a cloud platform with no intention of moving again. Moving between CSPs may not occur frequently, but there are potential risks associated with being completely dependent on a single vendor like a CSP. The migration process can be challenging, as each CSP uses different tools and templates. A move from one CSP to another requires mapping service capabilities between the CSPs and possibly performing data cleanup if needed. Moving from your own infrastructure to a CSP has the same challenge.

Frequent movement between CSPs and between a CSP and your own infrastructure can be very difficult, and data can be lost or modified in the process, leading to a loss of availability or integrity. Portability means that the movement between environments is possible with minimal impact. Portable movement will move services and data seamlessly and may be automated, and recent changes like containerization have made this problem significantly easier.

The movement of data between software products is not a new issue. Legacy on-premises systems often had their own data models and formats, and migrating between them required conversion and cleanup. Similar challenges in the cloud may be additionally constrained by the cost of maintaining both old and new cloud infrastructure, which was less of an issue for on-premises systems where ongoing costs to operate systems were limited to utilities.

Interoperability

With customers using a variety of cloud services, often from different vendors, interoperability is an important consideration. The ability to share data between different cloud environments and between cloud and on-premises systems is important. Interoperability challenges include differences in the security tools and control sets between CSPs. A gap in security may result, and differing controls can lead to gaps in monitoring and oversight. Careful planning is essential, and the services of a cloud broker may also be warranted.

One way to improve the situation is through APIs. If properly designed, the API can reduce interoperability challenges by providing a standardized and consistent way to access systems and data across different cloud environments and on-premises architecture. For example, if a SaaS tool is used to build a data inventory and supports the corporate data/system classification scheme, an API could be built to securely share that information with the governance, risk management, and compliance (GRC) or system inventory tool. This allows the GRC tool to act as a single source for data, sharing it with relevant systems, and removes the potential of multiple inventories and processes for tracking assets.

Vendor Lock-in

Solving interoperability and portability challenges reduces vendor lock-in, which occurs when an organization does not have alternatives to a specific vendor. This can occur if a customer utilizes features that are specific to one CSP. Moving would incur significant financial costs, technical challenges, or possibly legal issues like early contract termination fees.

Vendor lock-in remains a significant concern with cloud computing and can be caused by taking advantage of newly created services in one CSP that other CSPs have not yet offered. Continued advances in virtualization, improvements in portability and interoperability, and a careful design within a reference architecture can decrease this issue.

An additional concern is the use of CSP-specific services. If a system is reliant on these proprietary or unique features, then moving to a different CSP could lead to a loss of system availability. This mirrors challenges with legacy environments when moving from one major application to another, such as a move from IBM Lotus Notes to Microsoft Exchange for email service. Both systems provide similar functionality, but resources are needed to migrate data and business processes built on top of these email functions.

One example is the use of AWS Lambda for serverless computing. Applications written to run on Lambda cannot be directly migrated over to the equivalent Azure Functions without being rewritten. Both CSPs offer some unique functions like security monitoring of serverless computing processes. A migration from one platform to the other requires engineering effort to update applications and at least some reconfiguration of security monitoring, if not entirely new tools.

Emerging cloud-agnostic technologies like containers and careful architecting of cloud systems can reduce vendor lock-in. Cost-benefit analyses can be useful to guide the business when making decisions about unique CSP features. An increasing number of security tools are designed to support multiple CSPs' offerings and interact via standardized means like APIs.

Security Considerations for Different Cloud Categories

In a cloud environment, security responsibilities are shared between the service provider and the customer. In the SaaS model, the customer has the least responsibility, and in the IaaS model, the customer has the most responsibility. In a PaaS, the responsibility is shared more equally.

The Shared Responsibility Model for cloud services is widely used to identify which security tasks are owned by the CSP, which are owned by the customer, and which require participation by both parties. The basics of the shared responsibility model are presented earlier in this chapter, and each CSP publishes their own version of a shared responsibility model tailored to their unique offerings.

Cloud security is designed to address risks that exist in a typical cloud infrastructure stack, which usually has most of the following components:

- Data
- APIs
- Applications/solutions
- Middleware
- Operating systems
- Virtualization (VMs, virtual local area networks)
- Hypervisors
- Compute and memory
- Data storage
- Networks
- Physical facilities/data centers

It is generally understood that the CSP is responsible for the last five items on the list in all delivery models. Customers always have ultimate responsibility for data they place in the cloud, and the responsibility for the items in between varies depending on the service model. Those responsibilities are detailed in the following sections.

Software as a Service

From a security standpoint SaaS offers the most limited security options. Most of the security responsibility falls to the SaaS provider, such as securing the infrastructure, operating system, application, networking, and storage of the information on their service.

The customer may have limited application-specific security options, such as configuring the type of encryption or supplying their own keys to be used for encrypting data. Access control to the SaaS application is also the responsibility of the customer, including user access and access to any APIs. All other layers are the responsibility of the CSP.

The user of a SaaS solution has responsibilities as well. When a service is subscribed to by an organization or an individual, it is important to understand the security policies and procedures of the SaaS provider to the extent possible. In addition, the user determines how information is transferred to the SaaS provider and can do so securely through end-to-end encryption. The SaaS user is responsible for determining how the data is shared. Finally, the user can provide access security through proper use of login credentials, secure passwords, and multifactor authentication when available.

Platform as a Service

In a PaaS solution, security of the underlying infrastructure, including the servers, operating systems, virtualization, storage, and networking, remains the responsibility of the PaaS service provider. The developer is responsible for the security of any solutions built on the PaaS offering. This includes patching any applications other than the PaaS offering, as well as adequate security for the data used by the application. Just as with SaaS, the customer is responsible for controlling user access to the solutions developed.

In the Shared Responsibility Model, this means the customer is responsible for the data, APIs, and applications, with potentially some middleware responsibility.

Infrastructure as a Service

IaaS places most security responsibility on the customer. The CSP secures the virtualization computing, storage, and networking resources, which may exist on servers or hardware devices. The IaaS customer is responsible for the security of everything built on top of this virtualized computing environment, including the operating system and anything built on top of it.

In the Shared Responsibility Model, the customer is responsible for everything above the hypervisor. As in the other delivery models, the exact responsibility along this line can vary between the CSP and customer and must be clearly understood in each case. For example, the CSP may provide secure access to their network, which can then be used to access the customer's IaaS resources. Maintaining the secure access service falls to the CSP, while the customer is responsible for all other aspects of security.

Cloud Design Patterns

Similar to a reference architecture, cloud design patterns provide a set of guidelines and practices designed to create secure cloud computing services. Many of these are frameworks or models created by cloud organizations like CSPs and the Cloud Security Alliance. Utilizing these frameworks can guide organizational decisions such as choosing cloud service and deployment models, deploying cloud security technologies, and managing cloud environments once deployed.

SANS Security Principles

SANS (sans.org) is an organization that provides a variety of services to security practitioners, including training, templates, and the CIS control framework. This control framework is lightweight and is prioritized to address the most-prevalent security threats seen on the Internet. They provide a solid foundation for organizations looking to secure cloud infrastructure, due to the broad network accessibility of cloud solutions.

SANS security principles follow a risk-management approach that begins with inventorying assets. These include on-premises and cloud assets, as well as critical service providers like CSPs. Once inventoried, the risks facing these assets are documented, and risk mitigation strategies are implemented. SANS is vendor agnostic, and the security principles are designed to be applied to cloud infrastructure in any CSP.

Well-Architected Framework

The Well-Architected Framework comprises pillars, which are a collection of best practices that can be used to evaluate and manage cloud infrastructure. Each CSP publishes a Well-Architected Framework unique to their offerings, but there are similarities among those. These include the following:

- **Security:** Protecting system and data assets is an obvious concern for security practitioners and appears in all CSPs' versions of the framework. Tasks that fall under this pillar typically include identity and access management, encryption, and monitoring.

- **Reliability:** Maintaining access to systems and data is the focus of this pillar, which aligns with the availability objective.

- **Performance:** In many CSP frameworks, this pillar is also focused on availability, though it focuses on the perspective of a well-architected system to scale up and down based on demand.

The selection and use of a Well-Architected Framework will be driven by the organization's choice of CSP. Although the elements are common, some frameworks include more pillars, and each CSP's documentation has implementation guidance specific to their service offerings. Several CSP frameworks are presented here:

- **AWS:** docs.aws.amazon.com/wellarchitected/latest/framework/welcome.html

- **Azure:** docs.microsoft.com/en-us/azure/architecture/framework

- **IBM Cloud:** ibm.com/cloud/architecture/articles/well-architected-framework/introduction

Cloud Security Alliance Enterprise Architecture

The CSA Enterprise Architecture (CSA EA) is a framework for modeling IT resource architecture in a way that aligns it to business needs within the organization. It is maintained by a working group and has been published as a freely available standard in NIST SP 500-299 and SP 500-292.

The CSA EA comprises four domains where IT services are required and associated security concerns within each domain. The domains include Business Operation Support Services (BOSS), IT Operations & Support (ITOSS), Technology Solution Services (TSS), and Security and Risk Management. The last domain contains the practices that security often owns, such as identity and access management, vulnerability management, and data protection. Infrastructure protection services are a specific area of focus within this domain, and guidance is provided for identifying tools, processes, and practices needed to address the items in this domain.

Full details of the CSA EA and related supporting documents are available at the EA Working Group site: `cloudsecurityalliance.org/research/working-groups/enterprise-architecture`.

DevOps Security

DevOps represents an integration of development and operations teams, with the goal of speeding delivery of quality software. When this concept evolved, security either was usually an afterthought or was an entirely siloed function within the organization. The reality, however, is that security is vital in both development and operations tasks; otherwise, it is significantly less effective. For example, catching a bug in code as soon as it is written requires fewer resources to find and fix and poses less risk to application availability than designing a workaround or patch.

Integrating security into DevOps follows a fundamental practice of shifting left, that is to say, taking security activities traditionally performed at the end of a system development lifecycle and shifting them to the left on a timeline. Instead of all testing being done after a system is code complete, testing can begin while code is being written.

There are different approaches to solving this problem. DevSecOps and SecDevOps have both emerged as models for integrating security into DevOps processes. Both approaches share the goal of shifting left but have different philosophies regarding how to effect this change. The choice of a model will be driven largely by the DevOps mindset in a given organization, as the practices and philosophy of each model align with development and management practices like Agile and Six Sigma.

A NIST working group for integrating security into DevOps is a popular resource for DevOps security and can be found here: `csrc.nist.gov/projects/devsecops`.

Evaluate Cloud Service Providers

Evaluation of CSPs should be done through objective criteria, and using standardized criteria makes it easier to compare offerings from different CSPs. Standards may be voluntary, and a CSP would choose them as a way to demonstrate security capabilities to customers. Other standards are required for CSPs offering services with specific functions or to specific markets.

For example, SOC 2 is a voluntary standard that a CSP can implement, and a SOC 2 Type II audit report demonstrates to potential customers that the CSP's security program is in place and operating as intended. In contrast, PCI DSS is a required standard for any organization that is accepting and processing payment card transactions.

Some standards are required for certain organizations and may be adopted by others voluntarily. For example, the U.S. federal government requires that technologies conform to the Federal Information Processing Standards (FIPS) in order to be used by federal agencies. These standards are not required for nongovernmental organizations, but many have chosen to use these standards because they are robust, well understood, and widely deployed by technology providers.

Verification Against Criteria

Different organizations have published compliance criteria for technology products and systems. For cloud computing, there are a mix of regulatory and voluntary standards, depending on the market that the CSP is serving. The International Organization for Standardization/International Electrotechnical Commission (ISO/IEC) standard is voluntary, but it may be a customer requirement in some parts of the world. By contrast, the PCI Council contractually requires compliance with PCI DSS in order to process payment card transactions, and CSPs looking to work with the U.S. federal government must undergo an audit against the standards defined in the Federal Risk and Authorization Management Program (FedRAMP).

International Organization for Standardization/International Electrotechnical Commission

ISO 27017 and 27018 standards extend guidance from ISO 27001, which establishes an organization's information security management system (ISMS), and ISO 27002, which provides related security controls. 27017 guides the implementation of these controls in cloud computing environments, while 27018 extends the controls to implement protection of personally identifiable information (PII) processed in the cloud. 27017 added 35 supplemental controls and extended 7 existing controls to the original ISO documents.

ISO 27018 serves as a supplement to ISO 27002 and is specifically geared toward PII processors, so it is often implemented where privacy controls are required. Like ISO 27017, these principles are recommendations and not requirements, though the requirements of privacy regulations are usually mandatory. ISO 27018 added 14 supplementary controls and extended 25 other controls. As an international standard, adherence to this standard can help an organization address a wide and ever-changing data protection and privacy environment, as laws like GDPR in the EU and PIPEDA in Canada continue to evolve.

While these are recommendations and not requirements, many international corporations strive to be ISO-compliant. In that case, the criteria provided by ISO/IEC become governing principles for the organization, including the reference framework, cloud service models (of which there are seven instead of just SaaS, PaaS, and IaaS), and the implementation of controls from the approved control set. Auditing the controls and conducting a risk assessment should help identify which controls best address identified risk.

The ISO standard is important for companies in the international marketplace due to their wide acceptance throughout the world. These standards are also well suited to the international nature of cloud services, which rely on broad network accessibility. Cloud security practitioners must understand the context of their business, legal, and regulatory requirements that arise from it and select control frameworks or standards as appropriate to address them.

Payment Card Industry Data Security Standard

The PCI Council regularly updates its Data Security Standard to include updated guidance for emerging technologies and evolving threats. Although the PCI DSS is legally required for organizations, the payment card companies that comprise the council make it a contractual requirement that payment processors maintain compliance. The 12 requirements in the standard are designed to reduce the risk of payment fraud and unauthorized access to sensitive payment information and maintain the integrity of transaction data.

Although originally written before cloud computing became widespread, the PCI DSS contains high-level guidance for information system security. This means it is adaptable to any organization's computing environment, whether it is cloud-based, on-premises, or some mix of the two. Some of the key requirements that deal with cloud computing can be summarized as follows:

- Ensure that a customer's processes can only access their data environment.
- Restrict customer access and privileges to their data environment using the concept of least privilege.
- Enable logging and audit trails that are unique to each environment.
- Provide processes to support forensic investigations.
- Provide an isolated, access-controlled environment for processing cardholder data, known as the cardholder data environment (CDE).

Because of the commoditized nature of payment processing, many organizations utilize an external payment processor rather than implementing these functions internally. This has the benefit of shifting some risk and elements of PCI DSS compliance away from the organization. However, the outsourcing arrangement brings its own shared responsibility model, meaning the consuming organization must still implement some controls to ensure the security of the payment data.

Government Cloud Standards

Governments around the world have recognized the benefits and cost savings that cloud computing offers. While they lack the motivation to maximize profitability, fiscal responsibility with taxpayer dollars makes cloud computing an attractive option. Because of the sensitive nature of data processed by government agencies, a number of standards have been created. These offer the governments, which are cloud customers, assurance that the CSPs they engage implement adequate protection of sensitive data like PII, financial data, or possibly even national security information.

As a CSP it is important to implement standards required by any government customers your organization serves. Some private organizations may also choose to use these higher-security services due to additional controls offered. Some standards used by governments around the world include the following:

- FedRAMP is required by the U.S. federal government and provides a set of risk-based security controls that CSPs must implement. In addition, there is an audit process known as assessment and authorization (A&A) designed to validate the proper implementation and function of those controls.

- The UK G-Cloud is a marketplace of cloud services that have implemented controls in line with the G-Cloud framework, which can be consumed by UK governmental agencies. They are divided into categories of service, including cloud hosting, cloud software, and cloud support.

CSA Security, Trust, Assurance, and Risk

CSPs can enroll in the CSA Security, Trust, Assurance, and Risk (STAR) registry as a way to demonstrate the security and privacy controls they offer. This allows customers with specific security needs to select a CSP or specific services that meet their needs.

CSA STAR is a voluntary scheme and offers two levels of assurance. CSPs can provide evidence of their security controls, privacy controls, or both, and the registry has two levels of assurance. Level 1 is a self-assessment and allows the CSP to detail their controls in a standardized format so customers can easily compare across CSPs. The CSP completes either a CSA Cloud Controls Matrix (CCM) or Consensus Assessments Initiative Questionnaire (CAIQ) and submits it to the STAR registry.

Level 2 of CSA STAR provides an additional layer of assurance for customers by requiring the CSP to undergo a third-party audit. This audit assesses the security control implementations at the CSP and their effectiveness, so customers have additional evidence that the services of the CSP provide adequate security. The audit may be done as a stand-alone activity or may be incorporated into an existing SOC 2 or ISO 27001 audit.

System/Subsystem Product Certifications

The following are system/subsystem product certifications. Unlike certifications that attest to overall capabilities in a cloud environment, like FedRAMP or ISO 27001, these certifications apply to smaller parts of a system, such as a cryptographic module. For organizations with very specific security needs, they provide a way to choose products that can meet those requirements.

Common Criteria

Common Criteria (CC) is an international set of guidelines and specifications to evaluate information security products. These evaluations are typically done on systems configured according to specific standards and provide customers with assurance that the system can meet requirements when configured appropriately. There are two parts to CC.

- **Protection profile:** This defines a standard set of security requirements for a specific product type, such as a network firewall. This creates a consistent set of standards for comparing like products.

- **Evaluation assurance level:** Known as EAL, these are scores from 1 to 7, with 7 being the highest. This measures the level of rigor and amount of testing conducted on a product. It should be noted that a level 7 product is not automatically more secure than a level 5 product. It has simply undergone more testing. The customer must still decide what level of testing is sufficient. The manufacturer chooses the level of testing they want to pursue; the costs can be significant, so not all products are assessed to EAL 7 unless a viable definite market for such a solution exists.

The testing is performed by an independent lab from an approved list. Successful completion of this certification allows sale of the product to government agencies and may improve competitiveness outside the government market as CC becomes better known. Customers must define what component or system capabilities they require and pick systems matching that protection profile. Furthermore, the customer must determine the level of assurance they need and choose the correct EAL required. Using those criteria, the customer can then select a system that meets their needs. The goal of the CC is validation and ability to reliably compare systems and to provide a framework for product vendors to improve their products through testing.

FIPS 140-2

To secure data processed by government agencies, the United States publishes FIPS for various information processing use cases. The use of cryptography to protect data is one such use case, and FIPS 140-2 provides a scheme for validating the strength of cryptographic modules.

Organizations that want to do business with the U.S. government must meet the FIPS criteria. Because the U.S. federal government is such a large technology purchaser, FIPS 140-2 is widely implemented in hardware and software products and can be used by any organization. Specifications for data security like the Advanced Encryption Standard (AES) arose from FIPS requirements for data protection and have become widespread. In many cryptography implementations, using FIPS-validated encryption is simply a configuration option that can be enabled, giving organizations access to strong data security controls.

FIPS-validated cryptographic modules undergo testing to check the implementation of the cryptographic functions. These modules are considered adequate for government use if they are configured in the same manner as the validated test environment. This usually requires enabling only FIPS-validated encryption algorithms like AES, and disabling algorithms like 3DES that do not provide adequate security.

There are many cryptographic modules and algorithms that are not FIPS validated. The lack of validation does not mean these are automatically insecure, but an organization must determine what level of assurance is required before selecting cryptographic functions. The public nature of FIPS and its wide acceptance simply make it an easy standard to adopt for any organization.

FIPS 140-2 is scheduled to be retired by 2026, and the process of transition to FIPS 140-3 began in 2019. The basic functions of FIPS validation will remain the same, but the new standard addresses emerging technologies and security challenges that encryption faces.

Summary

Cloud security practitioners must be familiar with the basic terminology surrounding this technology. This understanding includes characteristics of cloud computing, as well as the service models and deployment models of cloud computing. It also includes the role of the CSP in cloud computing, the shared security model that exists between the CSP and the customer, and the implications this has for ensuring that cloud services and data are adequately protected. Finally, the technologies that make cloud computing possible were discussed in this chapter alongside the emerging technologies that will support and transform cloud computing in the future. Understanding this chapter will make it easier to access the discussion in each of the following domains and allows a security practitioner to evaluate cloud computing technologies based on their organization's security requirements.

Chapter

2

Cloud Data Security

Responsibility for many elements of cloud security are shared between the cloud service provider (CSP) and the cloud consumer, while each party retains exclusive control over some elements. For example, the CSP is always responsible for the physical security of the infrastructure, while the consumer retains control over the identity and access management concerns of their applications and services. When it comes to securing data stored in the cloud, the most important thing to remember is that the consumer is always accountable. Securing the data and ensuring that the CSP implements adequate security practices are essential activities the cloud consumer must perform.

Describe Cloud Data Concepts

Data is a crucial element to most modern organizations, so processes to provision and secure the systems that store, process, and transmit that data are essential. The cloud strategy for most organizations will include a variety of personnel in different roles, from the top C-level executives or other executive management all the way to operational personnel responsible for day-to-day functions such as data input and processing. To provide adequate security, it is vital to have a model for understanding how data is created, stored, and used in the cloud environment such as the cloud data lifecycle.

Cloud Data Lifecycle Phases

Unlike valuable physical assets such as precious metals or other objects, information can be hard to definitively identify and secure. Data is constantly being generated, used, stored, transmitted, and, once it is no longer valuable, destroyed. In such a dynamic environment, it can be useful to model the phases that information passes through. This model provides a generic way of identifying broad categories of risk facing the data and allows an organization to design security controls that address data risks specific to each phase.

The secure cloud data lifecycle is roughly linear, though some data may not go through all phases, and data may exist in multiple phases simultaneously. Regardless, data should be protected in each phase by controls commensurate with its value. Figure 2.1 illustrates the lifecycle.

The cloud data lifecycle is not generally iterative; that is, it does not repeat in the same way as other lifecycles like the systems development lifecycle (SDLC). Data may also exist in one or more of the phases simultaneously; for example, data being created may be shared and stored at the same time if the user saves a file to a shared drive that other users can access. However, data in each phase of the lifecycle faces specific risks, and the cloud security practitioner should thoroughly understand these risks and appropriate mitigations specific to each phase.

FIGURE 2.1   The secure data lifecycle

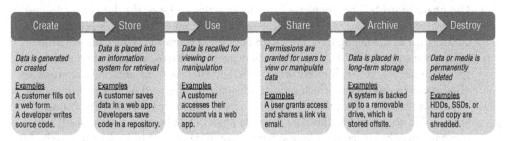

- **Create:** Data is created when it is first entered into a system or whenever it is modified. Examples include a user writing a document and saving it, a process collecting data through an API and placing the data into a database, or a user opening a shared document and updating its contents. If data is being modified, the data lifecycle iterates, but it is also normal for data to be created once and never updated.

  - **Create phase controls:** Data classification is a foundational security control, as it allows the organization to identify data's value and implement appropriate controls. During creation, data should be classified by the creator or owner. In some systems, this might be a manual process such as placing the classification in a document header/footer. In other cases, the classification of data may be done by a system owner. In this case, the users do not make classification decisions, but all data stored in the system will be classified the same and protected by system-level controls.

- **Store:** Storage is the act of saving data in a retrievable location, such as a solid-state drive (SSD), application database, or hard-copy records. In many cases, storage occurs simultaneously with creation, for example, when a user uploads a new document to a fileshare.

  - **Store phase controls:** Data being stored may need protection in transit, especially for cloud services where the data must cross public networks to reach the organization's cloud apps. These protections include the use of Transport Layer Security (TLS), a virtual private network (VPN), Secure Shell (SSH), or other secure data-in-transit controls. The actual act of storing data should be governed by policies and procedures, such as restrictions on where data of differing classification levels may be stored, access control and granting procedures, and technical controls like encryption by default for highly sensitive data. Once stored, data should be protected using appropriate access controls and encryption management to preserve confidentiality, as well as adequate backups to preserve both integrity and availability.

- **Use:** The use phase comprises accessing, viewing, and processing data, which is collectively referred to as *handling*. Data can be handled in a variety of ways, such as accessing a web application, reading and manipulating files, or fetching data via an API.

    - **Use phase controls:** The use phase is the most active phase of the data lifecycle, and it is where data typically faces the most risks. The number of controls is commensurate, such as managing data flow with data loss prevention (DLP), information rights management (IRM), technical system access controls, authorization and access review processes, network monitoring tools, and the like. Accountability controls are also crucial in this phase, which require adequate logging and monitoring of access. Note that the data states, which are data in use, data in transit, and data at rest, are not directly related to this data lifecycle phase. Data being actively "used" by a company may be stored on a laptop hard drive (data at rest) or be sent to a web app for processing (data in transit). The use phase is simply when data is actively being handled.

- **Share:** The share phase is relatively self-explanatory: access to data is granted to other users or entities that require access. Not all data will be shared, and not all sharing decisions will be made explicitly. Highly classified data may be severely restricted to access by just a few critical personnel, while less sensitive data may be shared by virtue of being stored in a shared system like a collaboration app.

    - **Share phase controls:** Access controls form the majority of security safeguards during the share phase and should be designed to be both proactive and reactive. Proactive access controls include role-based access authorizations and access-granting procedures. Reactive controls such as DLP, IRM, and access reviews can detect when unauthorized sharing occurs and, in some cases, prevent the shared data from leaving organizational control.

- **Archive:** Data that has reached the end of its useful life often needs to be retained for a variety of reasons, such as ongoing legal action or a compliance mandate. Archiving data is the act of placing it into long-term retrievable storage. Several industries and types of data, such as financial and healthcare, have mandated retention requirements. Archiving is also an operational cost benefit, as it moves data that is not actively being used to cheaper, though possibly slower, storage.

    - **Archive phase controls:** Data controls in the archive phase are similar to the store phase, since archiving is just a special type of storage. Because of long timeframes for storage in archives, there may be additional concerns related to encryption. Specifically, encryption keys may be rotated on a regular basis. When keys are rotated, data encrypted with them is no longer readable unless you can access that older key; this leads to solutions such as key escrow or the cumbersome process of decrypting archived data and re-encrypting it with a new key. Additionally, storage formats may become obsolete, meaning archived data is not readable, or archival media may degrade over time, leading to losses of integrity or availability.

- **Destroy:** Data that is no longer useful and no longer subject to retention requirements should be securely destroyed. Methods of destruction range from low security, like deleting files using standard filesystem commands, to more secure options such as overwriting disks, physical destruction of storage media, or the use of cryptographic erasure or *cryptoshredding*. Cryptoshredding does not destroy the sensitive data itself but instead securely deletes the keying material needed to decrypt it. Data destruction can be a particular challenge for cloud security practitioners as the CSP has physical control over media, preventing the use of options like physical destruction. Additionally, cloud services such as platform as a service (PaaS) and software as a service (SaaS) typically do not provide access to underlying storage for tasks such as overwriting.

    - **Destroy phase controls:** Choosing the proper destruction method should balance two main concerns: the value of the data being destroyed and the options available in a cloud service environment. Low-sensitivity data such as public information does not warrant extraordinary destruction methods, while high-value information such as personally identifiable information (PII) does. Various resources provide guidance for selecting a destruction method, such as the NIST SP 800-88, *Guidelines for Media Sanitization*, available here: csrc.nist.gov/publications/detail/sp/800-88/rev-1/final.

Data Dispersion

Data dispersion refers to a technique used in cloud computing environments of breaking data into smaller chunks and storing them across different physical storage devices. It is similar to the concept of striping in redundant arrays of independent disks (RAIDs), where data is broken into smaller segments and written across multiple disks, but cloud-based data dispersion also implements *erasure coding* to allow for reconstruction of data if some segments are lost.

Erasure coding is similar to the idea of a parity bit calculation in RAID storage. In simple terms, data being written is broken into multiple segments, a mathematical calculation is conducted on the segments, and the result is stored separately from the data. In the event that some segments are lost, the parity bit and the remaining segments can be used to reconstruct the lost data, similar to solving for a variable in an algebra equation.

Data dispersion in cloud environments can have both positive and negative impacts on an organization's security. The benefit of availability is obvious—even if a physical storage device fails, the data on it can be reconstructed, and if a physical device is compromised, it does not contain a complete, usable copy of data. However, dispersing the segments can cause issues. If data is dispersed to countries with different legal or regulatory frameworks, the organization may find itself subject to unexpected laws or other requirements. Most CSPs have implemented geographic restriction capabilities in their services to allow consumers the benefit of dispersion without undue legal/regulatory complexity.

Properly configuring the cloud service is a crucial task for a cloud security practitioner to meet the organization's compliance objectives. If the organization is subject to European Union (EU) General Data Protection Regulation (GDPR) requirements, it may be preferable to maintain data in the European Union rather than dispersing it to all countries the CSP operates in. This may be a simple configuration for a particular service or may require complex information system architecture planning.

One potential downside of data dispersion is latency, because of the additional processing overhead required to perform the erasure coding and reconstruct data. This is similar to the performance considerations in RAID setups that implemented a parity bit. The additional time and processing capacity may introduce system latency, which can have negative consequences on system availability. This is especially true for high-volume, transaction-based systems or for systems with data that is highly dynamic like fileshares.

Data Flows

Cloud systems and modular application architecture offer significant benefits, such as decreased development time and faster deployment of new system features. However, this new paradigm mirrors the migration from on-premises data centers to the cloud. Organizations now have reduced visibility into where data and systems reside, how data moves between different system elements, and even what ports or services must be open for all the communication needed in such a distributed system.

Documenting a data flow diagram (DFD) is useful to gain visibility and ensure that adequate controls are implemented. These diagrams resemble traditional system architecture and network diagrams. They show how system components are connected and add another layer of information: how data flows between system components.

For example, a simple web application diagram would show a web server, an application programming interface (API), and a backend database. System interconnections allow for data to be exchanged via the API, while users access the application using a web frontend that also makes calls to the API for data. Figure 2.2 diagrams the system architecture and data flow.

FIGURE 2.2 Cloud web app data flow diagram

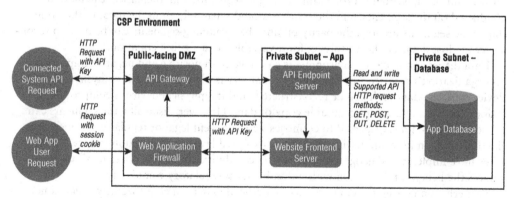

More complex DFDs can also capture the use of and data flows between different cloud regions, availability zones, or even CSPs in a multi-cloud setup. This can be essential for legal and compliance purposes, as the organization's responsibility to protect data rests on knowing where that data actually is and how it moves about. For example, identifying any data flow across borders is crucial to demonstrating compliance with privacy regulations like GDPR. Security practitioners can leverage a DFD to identify risks, such as data leaving geographic boundaries or data exchanges with systems that do not implement adequate security controls. Some compliance frameworks require DFDs to capture specific information, such as the geographic location of data flows or ownership of systems where data is flowing, so creating the DFD can be both a risk assessment activity and a crucial compliance activity.

Design and Implement Cloud Data Storage Architectures

Pooling resources is one of the key elements of cloud services. Virtualized storage pools are more flexible than installing and maintaining individual disks or storage networks, but it can be difficult to identify exactly where and how data is being stored in these broad pools. Understanding the storage options available in different cloud service models is essential. Security practitioners should be aware of general storage types, threats, and countermeasures associated with each, as well as the specific offerings of their chosen CSP. Traditional decisions such as directly choosing SSDs for high-speed storage needs may be replaced instead by a set of configurable parameters including the quantity and speed of data access.

Storage Types

Each of the three cloud service models offers unique storage types designed to support the needs and use cases of the particular service model. These options are detailed in the following pages, and it is important to note that CSPs may offer storage of a particular type but with unique branding or naming conventions. There are also novel storage solutions used for specific industries or purposes, and an organization should thoroughly review such solutions to ensure that they meet both operational and security needs before they are used for data storage.

IaaS

Infrastructure as a service (IaaS) typically offers consumers the most flexibility but also requires the most configuration. Types of storage available in IaaS include the following:

- **Ephemeral:** Unlike the other storage types discussed in the following sections, ephemeral storage is not designed to provide extended storage of data. Similar to random access memory (RAM) and other volatile memory architectures, ephemeral storage lasts as long as a particular IaaS instance is running, and the data stored in it is lost when the virtual machine (VM) is powered down. Ephemeral storage is often packaged as part of compute capability rather than storage, as modern operating systems (OSs) require temporary storage locations for system files and memory swap files.

- **Raw:** Raw device mapping (RDM) is a form of virtualization that allows a particular cloud VM to access a storage logical unit number (LUN). The LUN is a dedicated portion of the overall storage capacity for use by a single VM, and RDM provides the method for a VM to access its assigned LUN.

- **Long-term:** As the name implies, long-term storage is durable, persistent storage media that is often designed to meet an organization's records retention or data archiving needs. The storage may offer features such as search and data discovery as well as unalterable or immutable storage for preserving data integrity.

- **Volume:** Volume storage behaves like a traditional drive attached to a computer, but in cloud data storage, both the computer and drive are virtualized. Volume storage may store data in blocks of a predetermined size, which can be used for implementing data dispersion. Because the disk is virtualized, the data may be broken down into blocks and stored across multiple physical disks, along with erasure coding needed to reconstruct the data if some blocks are missing.

- **Object:** Object storage is similar to accessing a Unix sharepoint or Windows file server on a network. Data is stored and retrieved as objects, often in the form of files, and users are able to interact with the data objects using file browsers. Metadata may be stored along with objects or within applications that utilize the object storage, which provides flexibility for applications as they can be decoupled from the underlying storage medium.

PaaS

Some PaaS offerings provide the ability to connect to IaaS storage types, such as connecting a volume to a PaaS VM to provide a virtual disk for storing and accessing data. There are storage types unique to PaaS, however, including the following:

- **Disk:** This is a virtual disk that can be attached to a PaaS instance and may take the form of a volume or object store, depending on the CSP offering and consumer needs. Many PaaS offerings allow the customer to specify parameters for storage connected to the PaaS instance, such as speed and volume of I/O operations or data durability. The CSP provisions appropriate storage space based on the configurations specified by the consumer.

- **Databases:** This is both a storage type and a PaaS offering. Platforms that can be delivered as a service include popular database software such as Microsoft SQL Server and Oracle databases, as well as CSP-specific offerings such as AWS Relational Database (RDS) or Microsoft Azure Databases. In most cases, these databases will be offered in a multitenant model with logical separation between clients, and data is accessed via API calls to the database.

- **Binary Large Object (blob):** Blobs are unstructured data; that is to say, data that does not adhere to a particular data model like the columns in a database. These are often text files, images, or other binary files generated by applications that allow users to generate free-form content. It is possible to apply some loose organization to blobs, but in a less structured way than strict models like a database. This is similar to manually organizing files into folders, such as word processing files by date of writing or photos by vacation destination. Blob storage services such as AWS Simple Storage Service (S3) and Azure Blob Storage provide such storage, and access to data by applications or users is provided via a URL.

Some types of storage platforms or storage types may be specific to a particular CSP's offerings. Examples include blob storage for unstructured data in Microsoft Azure, and a variety of queue services available in AWS that support the short-term storage, queueing, and delivery of messages to users or services.

SaaS

SaaS offerings are the most abstracted service model, with CSPs retaining virtually all control including data storage architecture. In some cases, the data storage type is designed to support a web-based application that permits users to store and retrieve data, while other storage types are actual SaaS offerings themselves, such as the following:

- **Information storage and management:** This storage type allows users to enter data and manipulate it via a web GUI. The data is stored in a database managed by the CSP and often exists in a multitenant environment, with all details abstracted from the users.

- **Content and file storage:** Data is stored in the SaaS app in the form of files that users can create and manipulate. Examples include filesharing and collaboration apps, as well as custom apps that allow users to upload or attach documents such as ticketing systems.

- **Content delivery network (CDN):** CDNs provide geographically dispersed object storage, which allows an organization to store content as close as possible to users. This offers advantages of reduced bandwidth usage and lower latency for end users as they can pull from a server physically closer to their location.

One feature of most cloud data storage types is their accessibility via application program interfaces (APIs). The virtualization technologies in use for cloud services create virtual connections to the pooled storage resources, replacing physical cable connections. These APIs mean the storage types may be accessible from more than one service model; for example, object storage may be accessed from a PaaS or SaaS environment if an appropriate API call is made. Many CSPs have specifically architected their storage APIs for broad use in this manner, like Amazon's Simple Storage Service (S3), which is an object storage type accessible via a REST API. This enables IaaS, PaaS, SaaS, on-premises systems, and even users with a web browser to access it.

Threats to Storage Types

There are universal threats to data at rest (in storage) regardless of the location, including on-premises or legacy environments, local workstation storage, and cloud services. These affect all three elements of the confidentiality, integrity, and availability (CIA) triad. Unauthorized access, improper modification, and loss of connectivity are threats to confidentiality, integrity, and availability, respectively. Security tools that are appropriate for on-premises environments may not work in a distributed cloud environment, so it is essential to be aware of how these threats impact cloud storage and corresponding countermeasures.

- **Unauthorized access:** Any user accessing data storage without proper authorization presents obvious security concerns. Appropriate access controls are required by the consumer to ensure that only properly identified and authorized internal users are able to access data stored in cloud services. Because of the multitenant nature of cloud storage, the CSP must provide adequate logical separation to ensure that cloud consumers are not able to access or tamper with data that does not belong to them.

- **Unauthorized provisioning:** This is primarily a cost and operational concern. The ease of provisioning cloud services is one of the selling points versus traditional, on-premises infrastructure. This ease of use can lead to unofficial or shadow IT, leading to unrestricted growth in the cloud services and associated costs. Unauthorized storage can also act as a blind spot when it comes to security; if the security team is not aware of where the organization is storing data, the team cannot take appropriate steps to secure that data.

- **Regulatory noncompliance:** Certain cloud service offerings may not meet all the organization's compliance requirements, which leads to two security concerns. First are the consequences of noncompliance like fines or suspension of business operations. Second is the reason for the compliance requirements—to protect data. Requirements like the use of a specific encryption algorithm are driven by a need to protect data, and using cloud services that do not meet the compliance objectives represents a failure to adequately protect that data.

- **Jurisdictional issues:** The major CSPs are global entities and offer highly available services, many of which rely on global redundancy and failover capabilities. Unfortunately, the ability to transfer data between countries can run afoul of legal requirements, particularly privacy legislation that bars the transfer of data to countries without adequate privacy protections. Many cloud storage services support global replication by default, so security practitioners must understand both their organization's legal requirements and the configuration options available in the CSP environment.

- **Denial of service:** Cloud services are broadly network accessible, which means they require active network connectivity to be reachable. In the event a network connection is severed anywhere between the user and the CSP, the data in storage is rendered unavailable. Targeted attacks like a distributed denial of service (DDoS) can also pose an issue, though the top CSPs have robust mitigations in place and are usually able to maintain some level of service even during an attack.

- **Data corruption or destruction:** This is not a concern unique to cloud data storage. Issues such as human error in data entry, malicious insiders tampering with data, hardware and software failures, or natural disasters can render data or storage media unusable.

- **Theft or media loss:** This threat applies more to devices that can be easily accessed and stolen, such as laptops and USB drives; however, the risk of theft for cloud data storage assets like hard drives does exist. CSPs retain responsibility for preventing the loss of physical media through appropriate physical security controls. Consumers can mitigate this risk by ensuring that adequate encryption is used for all data stored in the cloud, which renders the stolen data useless unless the attacker also has the key.

- **Malware and ransomware:** Any location with data storage and processing abilities is at risk from malware, particularly ransomware. Attackers have become more sophisticated when writing ransomware, so it not only encrypts data stored on locally attached drives but also seeks common cloud storage locations like well-known collaboration SaaS apps. Proper access controls and antimalware tools can prevent or detect malware activities, while data backups and versioning can be useful countermeasures to data that has been impacted by malware.

- **Improper disposal:** Like physical drive loss, the CSP has the majority of responsibility when it comes to disposal of hardware. Ensuring that hardware that has reached the end of its life is properly disposed of in such a way that data cannot be recovered must be part of the CSP's services. Consumers can protect data by ensuring that it is encrypted before being stored in the cloud service and that the encryption keys are securely stored away from the data.

Design and Apply Data Security Technologies and Strategies

Data security in the cloud comprises a variety of tools and techniques. According to the shared responsibility model published by the major CSPs, consumers are responsible for securing their own data. Under most privacy legislation, the data owner, who is usually the cloud consumer, is ultimately accountable and legally liable for data breaches. However, adequately securing data requires actions by both the cloud consumer and the CSP to properly secure elements such as the hardware infrastructure and physical facilities.

Encryption and Key Management

Encryption is the process of applying mathematical transformations to data to render it unreadable. It typically requires the use of a key or cryptovariable, which is a string of data used by the cryptographic system to transform the data. The steps taken to achieve the transformation are known as an *algorithm*, and the encryption operation can be reversed if the encrypted data, cryptovariable, and algorithm are known.

Modern cryptographic algorithms like Rijndael, which is part of the Advanced Encryption Standard (AES), offer data protection that could take thousands or millions of years to break. Trying every possible combination of keys and permutation steps in the algorithm would take more time and resources than most attackers have available, but the process of encrypting and decrypting is comparatively quick if you know the key. Encryption is a foundational element of modern data security, particularly in cloud environments where data is stored outside the organization's direct control.

Due to the criticality of encryption, organizations should focus attention on properly implementing and managing cryptographic systems. One area of focus is managing encryption keys. Auguste Kerckhoffs, a Dutch cryptographer, defined a simple doctrine that underpins key management: a cryptosystem should be secure even if everything about the system, except the key, is public knowledge. Known as *Kerckhoffs' principle*, this simple maxim guides security in cryptographic systems by placing the emphasis on protecting keys.

Keys should be classified at the highest data classification level available in the organization and protected as other high-value assets would be. It is appropriate to implement controls across all categories including policies for creating and managing keys, operational procedures for securing and using keys, and tools and systems for handling keys. As a data asset, the keys should be protected at each stage of their lifecycle, including the following:

- Creating strong, random keys using cryptographically sound inputs like random numbers

- Storing keys in a secure manner, whether encrypted inside a key vault or stored on a physical device, and handling the process of storing copies for retrieval if a key is ever lost (known as key escrow)

- Using keys securely, primarily focused on access controls and accountability

- Sharing keys is not as common due to their highly sensitive nature, but facilities should exist for sharing public keys, securely transferring symmetric keys to a communications partner, and distributing keys to the key escrow agent

- Archiving keys that are no longer needed for routine use but might be needed for previously encrypted data

- Secure destruction of keys that are no longer needed or that have been compromised

Federal Information Processing Standards (FIPS) 140-3 provides a scheme for U.S. government agencies to rely on validated cryptographic modules and systems, though it has become a globally recognized framework as many tools offer FIPS-validated modes for encryption. FIPS 140-3 establishes a framework and testing scheme for validating the strength of protection provided by a cryptographic module and defines levels of protection for such modules, including physical tamper-evident hardware security modules (HSMs). FIPS 140-3 is the successor to FIPS 140-2; cryptographic module validations done under FIPS 140-2 may still be in use but are gradually being phased out for validations performed under the newer standard. Details on the standard can be found here: `csrc.nist.gov/publications/detail/fips/140/3/final`.

Cloud security practitioners will need to understand where encryption can be deployed to protect their organization's data and systems. Many CSPs offer virtualized HSMs that are validated against the FIPS standard and can be used to securely generate, store, and control access to cryptographic keys. These virtual HSMs are designed to be accessible only by the consumer and never by the CSP and are usually easy to integrate into other cloud offerings from the same CSP.

Organizations that use multiple cloud providers or need to retain physical control over key management will need apps architected to allow for a bring-your-own-key strategy. This is more technically challenging, as hosting any such on-premises systems requires more skills and resources, but it offers more control over the configuration and use of encryption as well as physical control over the HSMs.

Encryption in cloud services may be implemented at a variety of layers, from the user-facing application all the way down to the physical storage devices. The goals of safeguarding data, such as counteracting threats of physical theft or access to data by other tenants of the cloud service, will drive decisions about which types of encryption are appropriate to an organization. Some examples include the following:

- **Storage-level encryption** provides encryption of data as it is written to storage, utilizing keys that are controlled by the CSP. It is useful in cases of physical theft as the data should be unreadable to an attacker, but CSP personnel may still be able to view data as they control the keys.

- **Volume-level encryption** provides encryption of data written to volumes connected to specific VM instances, utilizing keys controlled by the consumer. It can provide protection in the case of theft and prevents CSP personnel or other tenants from reading data, but it is still vulnerable if an attacker gains access to the instance.

- **Object-level encryption** can be done on all objects as they are written into storage, in which case the CSP likely controls the key and could potentially access the data. For high-value data, it is recommended that all objects be encrypted by the consumer with keys they control before being stored.

- **File-level encryption** is often implemented in client applications such as word processing or collaboration apps like Microsoft Word and Adobe Acrobat. These apps allow for encryption and decryption of files when they are accessed using keys controlled by the user, which prevents the data from being read by CSP personnel or other cloud tenants. The keys required may be manually managed, such as a password the user must enter, or automated through IRM, which can verify a user's authorization to access a particular file and decrypt it based on the user's provided credentials.

- **Application-level encryption** is implemented in an application typically using object storage. Data that is entered or created by a user is encrypted by the app prior to being stored. Many SaaS platforms offer a bring-your-own-key ability, which allows the organization to prevent CSP personnel or other cloud tenants from being able to access data stored in the cloud.

- **Database-level encryption** may be performed at a file level by encrypting database files or may utilize transparent encryption, which is a feature provided by the database management system (DBMS) to encrypt specific columns, whole tables, or the entire database. The keys utilized are usually under the control of the consumer even in a PaaS environment, preventing CSP personnel or other tenants from accessing data, and the encrypted data is also secure against physical theft unless the attacker also gains access to the database instance to retrieve the keys. The underlying storage media may also be encrypted using storage-level encryption, which can be effective when developing a layered security strategy.

Hashing

Hashing, sometimes known as *one-way encryption*, is a tool primarily associated with the integrity principle of the CIA triad. Integrity deals with preventing, detecting, and correcting unintended or unauthorized changes to data, either malicious or accidental. Cryptographic algorithms called *hash functions* take data of any input length and perform mathematical operations to create a unique hash value of the data similar to a unique fingerprint. This process can be performed again in the future and the two hash values compared; if the input data has changed, the mismatched hash values are proof that the data has been altered.

Hashes can provide multiple security services in cloud environments. They can verify that copies of data like backups are accurate and can be used to verify the integrity of messages like email. They are also widely implemented in many security tools to detect changes that indicate system compromise.

File integrity monitoring is used by some antimalware and intrusion detection systems to identify changes to key system files, and highly secure systems may create hashes of data about system hardware such as manufacturer, devices connected, or model numbers. In both cases, there is an expectation that these items should not change; comparing a current hash with a previously calculated hash identifies unwanted changes. Due to the network accessibility of cloud services, data in transit can be altered by a malicious user in the middle or by network issues. Sending a hash value for data sent over a network allows the recipient to determine whether any changes occurred during transit.

Hashes form an integral part of digital signatures, which provide users the ability to verify both the integrity and the source of a message, file, or other data such as an app. The signing party calculates a hash and encrypts the hash value with their private key. A receiving party, who may be a user receiving a message, downloading an app, or pulling software from a repository, calculates a hash of the received data and then decrypts the sender's digital signature using the sender's public key. If the two hashes match, it can be assumed the data is original as no other user would be able to change the data, calculate a hash, and use the original sender's private key to create the digital signature. A CCSP should be aware of digital signatures as a method for verifying messages and apps used in cloud environments, especially when third-party software is being integrated.

When implementing hash functions, it is important to choose a strong function that is collision resistant. A *collision* occurs when two different inputs produce the same hash value as an output. When that occurs, it is impossible to rely on the hash function to prove integrity. As with many aspects of information security, there is a U.S. federal government standard related to hashes. FIPS 180-4, *Secure Hash Standard (SHS)*, provides guidance on the Secure Hash Algorithm (SHA-3). As with FIPS 140-2 and 140-3 encryption, many popular tools and platforms provide FIPS-compliant modes for hash algorithms. More details on SHS can be found here: `csrc.nist.gov/publications/detail/fips/180/4/final`.

Data Obfuscation

Obfuscation is often implemented when sensitive data needs to be used in a different situation from the primary use case. For example, obfuscation can remove or replace sensitive data elements when data from a live production system is copied for testing purposes. Testers are likely not authorized to view the data and can perform their jobs using synthetic data, which is similar to live data. Regulations often require obfuscation or de-identification of data prior to its use for purposes outside normal operations, especially privacy regulations that specify that data use must be limited to specific purposes, such as providing services to customers.

There are a number of ways to obfuscate data, outlined next. These methods can be implemented as part of database export functions or in data management programs such as spreadsheets, and they may also be implemented in business applications when users need to access or use a data set without requiring access to all sensitive data elements.

- Substitution works by swapping out some information for other data. This may be done randomly, or it may follow integrity rules if the data requires it. As an example of integrity rules, there are certain phone numbers that are never used for individuals, such as emergency phone numbers like 911, 999, and 111. Synthetic phone numbers should not start with these digits, as many programs will flag these numbers and prevent normal program functions unless the user provides a valid number.

- Shuffling involves moving data around. This can be done on an individual column; for example, a name like Chris would become Hrsci, though this is fairly easy to reverse engineer. More robust shuffling can be performed by shuffling individual data points between rows; for example, swapping Mary Jones's and Bob Smith's purchase history information. Shuffled data still looks highly realistic, which is advantageous for testing but removes identifiability.

- Value variance applies mathematical changes to primarily numerical data like dates, accounting or finance information, and other measurements. An algorithm applies a variance to each value, such as +/− $1,000. This can be useful for creating highly realistic test data from a live dataset.

- Deletion or nullification simply replaces the original data with null values. A similar practice is redaction, where a document's sensitive contents are simply blacked out. The resulting document may not be useful if too much of the data has been redacted, and nullified data may be problematic for testing as zero values are often unrealistic or generate errors where nonzero data is required.

- Encryption may be used as a tool for obfuscation, but it is problematic. Encrypted data is not useful for research or testing purposes, since it cannot be read. This challenge has given rise to the field of *homomorphic encryption*, which is the ability to process encrypted data without first decrypting it. Once returned to the original data set, the processed data can be decrypted and reintegrated; however, homomorphic encryption is challenging to implement and not widely used.

Obfuscating data often incorporates rules to ensure that the output data remains realistic. For example, credit card numbers conform to known patterns—usually 16 digits broken into groups of 4—so the replacement data must use only numerals. Information may also need to be verifiable against external sources, such as postal codes and telephone area codes that indicate geographic locations. Modifying a data set with address, post code, and telephone numbers may need to conform to the rules of these numbering systems or the relationships that data implies, such as taxes calculated on shipping to a specific region. If an organization does not serve customers outside a specific area, then constraints must be placed on the obfuscation process to ensure that only valid postal codes or addresses within the service area are substituted for the real data.

Masking

Masking is similar to obfuscation and can be used to prevent disclosure of sensitive data without removing the data itself. Masking involves hiding specific elements of data for certain use cases, primarily when there is a need for data to be retrievable for some but not all users or processes. As an example, a corporate human resources (HR) system may need to store a user's bank account number for salary payment and expense reimbursement. Daily users accessing the HR system do not have a need to see the full account number, so the system instead displays "XXXXX1234." The last four digits should be sufficient to confirm the bank account details if needed without exposing the data every time a user is logged into the HR system.

Data masking can be useful in preventing unintended disclosures by limiting the amount of data displayed. It is a very granular implementation of minimum necessary access. Although a user may be authorized to view full information about employees, they likely do not require that information on a daily basis. Masking the data prevents access by unauthorized individuals who may be looking over the user's shoulder and provide a secondary data security control if the authorized user leaves their workstation unlocked and unattended. Masked data is often displayed by default, and to display the full unmasked data the user must reauthenticate.

Unstructured data can present problems for masking, as well as tokenization, obfuscation, and de-identification. When data is structured in a database, it is easy to identify and apply these techniques. Unstructured data can be stored in files, in free-form text or comment fields in databases, or in applications that store data objects without structure. As an example, it would be quite simple to identify and apply masking to a database column labeled Social Security Number (SSN), but if users have entered SSNs elsewhere like a notes or comments field, those records will not be properly masked. Data handling and system use policies should dictate the proper use of information, including where to store sensitive data elements. If the organization utilizes unstructured storage or formats, data security tools must also be chosen to deal with unstructured data types.

Data De-identification and Anonymization

De-identifying data is primarily used when the data contains PII, known as *direct identifiers*, or contains information that could be combined with other data to uniquely identify an individual, known as *indirect identifiers*. Direct identifiers consist of information such as name and financial account numbers, while indirect identifiers are often demographic information like age or personal behavior details like shopping history. Removing these identifiers makes data anonymous rather than identifiable, so this process is often known as *anonymization*. This differs from pseudonymization, where the goal is to allow the re-identification of data, unlike anonymization, which is designed to be permanent.

Most privacy regulations require data anonymization or de-identification for any use of PII outside live production environments. For example, U.S. healthcare entities regulated by the Health Insurance Portability and Accountability Act (HIPAA) are required to de-identify medical records information when it is to be used for anything other than patient treatment, such as research studies. Details that could be used to specifically identify a patient must be removed or substituted, including full name, geographic location information, payment information, dates more specific than the year, email address, health plan information, etc.

Removing indirect identifiers can be more of a challenge, and the challenge starts with identifying what information could be uniquely identifiable. Trend information such as frequently browsed product categories at an online shopping site can be cross-referenced to a user's social media posts to identify them with relative certainty. If an online retailer removed all direct identifiers and published their sales trend data, it might still be possible to uniquely identify individual users by combining this data with users' social media posts. Combining multiple obfuscation and anonymization techniques can be useful to combat this threat, such as deleting names, substituting postal codes, and shuffling rows so that purchase history and location are no longer linked.

A process known as *pseudo-anonymization* or *pseudonymization* (often *pseudonymisation* due to its presence in the EU GDPR and use of British English spellings in EU documents) is a process of obfuscating data with the specific goal of reversing the obfuscation later. This is often done to minimize risk of a data breach and is performed by the data owner or controller prior to sending data to a processor. For example, if an organization wants to store large volumes of customer purchase orders in a cloud service, where storage is cheaper and more durable, they could remove PII and replace it with an index value prior to upload. When the data is retrieved, the index value can be looked up against an internal database, and the proper PII inserted into the records. The cost of storing that PII index would be small due to the lower volume of data, and the impact of a cloud data breach is also minimized by avoiding storage of PII in the cloud.

Tokenization

Tokenization is a process whereby a nonsensitive representation of sensitive data, otherwise known as a *token*, is created and used in place of the sensitive data. The token can be used as a substitute to more sensitive data like a credit card number, often called a *primary account number* (PAN). Rather than storing and using PANs, which is risky due to the value of a

PAN, tokens are used since theft of the token does not automatically give an attacker access to an individual's payment details.

Tokens can be traced back to the original information by making a proper request to the tokenization service, which usually implements access controls to verify user identities and authorization to view sensitive data. Tokens are implemented for many online payment systems where credit card numbers are stored. The payment card data is not stored in the app but is instead tokenized. When the user makes a purchase, the app supplies the token along with user identity information to the tokenization server; if the tokenization server accepts the information provided, it accesses the relevant credit card data and supplies it to complete the transaction.

Using tokens instead of the actual data reduces risk by adding an additional layer of access control to sensitive data needed by an application. A database of live credit card PANs and customer data would be incredibly valuable to a thief, who could use those cards to make purchases. The same database with tokens and customer data is worth considerably less. Tokenization systems are obviously high-value targets, but due to their specialized function, it is possible to more robustly secure them versus a general-purpose application.

Although tokenization is widely used in credit card processing transactions and is a recommended control for Payment Card Industry Data Security Standard (PCI DSS) compliance, any sensitive data can be tokenized to reduce risk. Implementations vary, but the process of tokenizing data generally follows the same basic steps:

1. An application collects sensitive information from the user.

2. The app secures, often using encryption, and sends the sensitive data to a tokenization service.

3. Sensitive data is stored in the token database, and a token representing the data is generated and stored in the token database along with the sensitive data.

4. The token is returned to the original application, which stores it instead of the original sensitive data.

5. Any time the sensitive data is required, the token and appropriate credentials can be used to access it. Otherwise, the sensitive data is never revealed, as the tokenization service should be tightly access controlled.

Data Loss Prevention

DLP, sometimes also known as *data leakage prevention*, refers to a technology system designed to identify, inventory, and control the use of data that an organization deems sensitive. It spans several categories of controls including detective, preventative, and corrective. DLP systems can identify where sensitive data is stored and being used, prevent data loss by enforcing policy requirements on the storage and sharing of sensitive data, and correct potential data breaches by displaying an alert to the user informing them of the policy violation and preventing inappropriate action like sending sensitive data via email.

Due to the multiuse nature of DLP, many organizations will implement only some of the functions at one time. An organization is unlikely to be successful attempting to simultaneously perform an organization-wide data inventory, deploy new technology in the form of DLP agents and network devices, and manage process changes due to the new DLP functionality. In cloud security environments, particularly when the enterprise architecture combines on-premises and cloud services, DLP can be useful for enforcing policies on the correct use of various systems, such as storing regulated data only in approved on-premises repositories rather than cloud storage.

A typical DLP installation will comprise three major components:

- **Discovery:** This is a function of DLP that allows the organization to identify, categorize, and inventory data assets. In large organizations, this may be the first step of a phased rollout, while in smaller organizations with fewer assets, it may not be required. DLP scanners identify data storage locations belonging to the organization, typically by performing network scans to identify targets such as fileshares, storage area networks (SANs), databases, common collaboration platforms like SharePoint, and cloud services like Google Drive or Dropbox. The scan requires input details regarding the organization, such as IP ranges or domains, over which it will perform the scans.

   Once the tool has a created a blueprint of the organization's network and identified storage sources, it will scan the identified targets to identify data based on common formats such as xxx-xx-xxxx, which represents a U.S. Social Security number. Organization-defined sensitive data can also be identified, such as documents that contain strings like "Confidential—for internal use only" in document footers or utilizing regular expressions to identify sensitive data unique to the organization. Many DLPs allow scanning using privileged credentials to provide more accurate results, so managing access controls for the DLP scanner is a major focus. Most scanners offer the ability to categorize information based on standard categories including PII, protected health information (PHI), payment information, etc., and some support organization-defined classification levels. The result of the scan is an inventory of organization data sets.

- **Monitoring:** This is the most important function of a DLP system, as it enables the security team to identify how data is being used and prevent inappropriate use. The choice of DLP tool should be made in light of its capability to monitor the platforms in use at an organization; for example, some legacy tools do not provide monitoring for emerging instant-message tools like Slack. Another critical concern for monitoring is the placement of the DLP's monitoring capabilities. A network-based DLP monitoring traffic on an organization LAN is unable to monitor the actions of remote workers who are not always connected to the network and may not provide sufficient coverage to mitigate risk.

  - **In-motion** data monitoring is typically performed by a network-based DLP solution and is often deployed on a gateway device such as a proxy, firewall, or email server. Some DLP agents deployed on user workstations can perform in-motion monitoring as data leaves the workstation by scanning the contents and attachment emails or files being uploaded before the transfer is completed. This type of DLP must be placed in appropriate locations to be able to monitor unencrypted data; otherwise, users could create an encrypted tunnel, and the DLP will not be able to scan the data being sent. Workstation agent- or proxy-based tools can prevent this issue by scanning data before it is sent over an encrypted connection.

- **At-rest** monitoring is performed on data in storage and is usually performed by an agent deployed on the storage device, though some network-based DLP can perform scans of storage locations with proper credentials. These can spot policy violations such as sensitive information stored outside prescribed locations; for example, users entering credit card details or PII in unencrypted notes/comments fields rather than fields where encryption, tokenization, or other controls have been applied. Compatibility is a particular concern for agent-based DLP solutions, as the organization's storage solutions must be supported for the DLP to be effective.

- **In-use** monitoring is often referred to as *endpoint* or *agent-based DLP,* and it relies on software agents deployed on specific network endpoints. These are particularly useful for monitoring users interacting with data on their workstations or other devices and enforcing policy requirements on the use of those endpoints. Compatibility is a major concern for these agents as the DLP must support the devices and OSs in use. Most DLP solutions offer support for popular business operating systems, but support for some platforms such as the macOS and mobile operating systems like iOS and Android may be limited.

- **Enforcement:** DLP applies rules based on the results of monitoring to enforce security policies. For example, a DLP agent running on a user workstation can either generate an alert or block the user from saving sensitive information to a removable USB drive. A network-based DLP can look for information by analyzing traffic entering or leaving a network (like a virtual private cloud) or monitor information sent to and from a specific host. Alerts typically call attention to a policy violation and may allow a user to proceed after dismissing the alert. Blocking the action prevents a data breach but may unintentionally create a denial-of-service condition if the DLP generated a false positive. Alerts and enforcement actions taken by the DLP should be monitored and investigated as appropriate and are a valuable source of security incident detection.

Deploying DLP in a cloud environment can be a particular challenge, especially in SaaS or PaaS service models where the organization lacks the ability to install software, or in cloud services that do not permit scanning such as DLP discovery. There are many cloud-native DLP tools, and security practitioners must ensure that the organization's system requirements are well defined, particularly which operating systems and cloud environments must be supported. DLP can create operational overhead due to the time and resources needed to scan network traffic or resources consumed on endpoints when monitoring. This impact should be considered as part of the cost-benefit analysis associated with the DLP solution deployment.

Keys, Secrets, and Certificates Management

Information systems rely on a variety of supporting technologies to provide security controls. Encryption systems rely on keys, access control systems may implement shared secrets to authenticate users or connection requests, and digital certificates are implemented for a variety of purposes like mutual authentication and access control. The practice of secrets management comprises handling these types of credentials.

Many organizations face a challenge of secrets sprawl, similar to the predicament users face with unique passwords required across a multitude of systems. Secrets are typically associated with nonhuman accounts or access needs like API keys and device-based certificates designed to authenticate remote systems making requests.

Secrets management comprises both tools and processes for managing this highly sensitive data. From a process standpoint, developers and system engineers should never hard-code or store secrets in easily accessible locations such as code repositories or script files. Management tools, similar to password managers for human accounts, can provide secure storage and APIs that allow other programs to access secrets in a secure manner only when needed. To identify the secrets in use by the organization, a discovery and inventory process must be conducted.

Specific best practices for managing the various types of secrets are detailed here:

- **Keys** are most often used for encryption operations and can be used to uniquely identify a user or system. Security of the key is crucial as encrypted data is often exchanged over untrusted networks and encryption algorithms are widely known. Keys should be stored in a tool that implements encryption and requires a strong passphrase or multifactor authentication (MFA) to access.

- **Secrets** are often a secondary authentication mechanism used to verify that a communication has not been hijacked or intercepted. Secure storage is essential, and access must be tightly controlled. Secrets used to verify the integrity of communications must be stored in such a way that a malicious user intercepting communications traffic is not also able to capture the secret.

- **Certificates** are used to verify the identity of a communication party and can also be used for asymmetric encryption by providing a trusted public key. This is often used to encrypt data like a session key or secret and provide it securely to a remote host over an untrusted connection. Since certificates are publicly distributed, there are few concerns about confidentiality, but the ability to verify the validity of a certificate is crucial. Well-architected public key infrastructure (PKI) is needed to ensure that certificates are issued only to trusted individuals or organizations. Certificates that are used as access tokens may need additional layers of access control similar to keys and secrets to ensure that they are not easily accessed by or transferred to a malicious user.

Regardless of the type of secret being used, all secrets management tools should be configured to log access requests and use of secrets. These logs should be closely monitored for anomalous behavior or inappropriate access, and access to the secrets manager should be reviewed at the same frequency as other highly sensitive systems. In addition, systems generating secrets, keys, and certificates require robust capabilities such as well-tested pseudorandom number generation and secure storage for newly generated keys, secret material, and certificates.

Implement Data Discovery

Data discovery has two primary meanings in the context of information security. Discovery of data stored in your environment is the purview of DLP solutions, which helps build an inventory of critical data assets your organization needs to protect. This is not the same as eDiscovery, which deals with collecting evidence in legal situations, but utilizes many of the same principles.

Discovering trends and valuable intelligence within data is the second meaning, and one that is less a dedicated concern of the security department. Analyzing data to uncover trends or make predictions, such as what products are likely to be in demand or what a given customer might be interested in shopping for, can drive meaningful business improvements like ensuring adequate inventory of goods. In these cases, security is not a primary concern of data discovery, but the business intelligence (BI) is itself a valuable intellectual property (IP) data asset, which requires security commensurate with its value. Supporting tools such as algorithms or proprietary data models used for analysis may also be valuable IP and should be included in the organization's asset inventory, assessed for risks, and protected with appropriate controls.

Many security tools, especially those monitoring large-scale deployments of user workstations, servers, and cloud applications, make use of data discovery. Analysis tools can be used to drive security operations by identifying suspicious events that require investigation, such as system vulnerabilities, misconfigurations, intrusion attempts, or suspicious network behavior. This data, comprising details of an organization's vulnerabilities, is obviously an asset worth protecting as it would be useful to an attacker. It is important for a security practitioner to understand both the value of these tools in supporting security operations and how to adequately protect them.

There are a number of important terms associated with data discovery and BI, including the following:

- **Data lake and data warehouse:** These terms are similar but not the same. Both are designed to consolidate large amounts of data, often from disparate sources inside or outside a company, with the goal of supporting BI and analysis efforts. A lake is an unstructured data storage mechanism with data in the form of files or blobs, while a warehouse is structured storage in which data has been normalized to fit a defined data model.

  - *Normalization* is the process of taking data with different formats—for example, one system that stores MM-DD-YYYY and another that uses YYYY-MM-DD—and converting it to a common format. This is often known as *extract, transform, load* (ETL), as the data is extracted from sources like databases or apps, transformed to meet the warehouse's data model, and loaded into warehouse storage. Normalizing data improves searchability.

- **Data mart:** A data mart contains data that has been warehoused, analyzed, and made available for a specific use like sales forecasting. Data marts typically support a specific business function by proactively gathering data needed and performing analysis and then presenting the data needed for reporting and decision making.

- **Data mining:** Mining data involves discovering, analyzing, and extracting patterns in data. These patterns are valuable in some way, much like minerals mined from the ground; they may support business decision making or enhance human abilities to identify important trends, patterns, and knowledge from large sets of data. Even small organizations with only a few users and systems generate enormous volumes of security log data, and data mining tools can be useful for isolating suspicious events from normal traffic.

- **Online analytic processing (OLAP):** As the name implies, OLAP provides users with analytic processing capabilities for a data source. OLAP consists of consolidation, drill-down, and slice-and-dice functions. Consolidation gathers multidimensional data sets into cubes, such as sales by region, time, and salesperson. Drill-down and slice-and-dice allow users to analyze subsets of the data cube, such as all sales by quarter across all regions or sales of a particular product across all salespeople. Security incidents that require forensic analysis often make use of OLAP to extract relevant information from log files.

- **ML/AI training data:** Machine learning (ML) and artificial intelligence (AI) are emerging areas of data science. ML is concerned with improving computer algorithms by experience, such as asking a computer to identify photos of dogs and then having a human verify which photos actually contain dogs and which contain other animals instead. The computer algorithm learns and refines future searches; these algorithms can be used across a wide variety of applications such as filtering out unwanted emails by observing which messages users mark as spam, and they are widely implemented in security tools designed to learn and adapt to an organization's unique environment. AI is a field of computer science with the goal of designing computer systems capable of displaying intelligent thought or problem solving, though the term is often used to describe systems that simply mimic human tasks such as playing strategy-based board games or operating autonomous vehicles. Both AI and ML require large sets of data to learn, and there are myriad security as well as privacy concerns, especially when the data sets include personal information like photos used for training ML facial recognition.

Security practitioners working with cloud services should be aware that their organization retains accountability for protecting data, including data discovery processes to identify and inventory sensitive data. CSPs may be subject to contractual obligations for implementing specific data protections, but they are not the data owners and are therefore not legally liable under most privacy and security laws for data breaches. An adequate inventory of sensitive data is a vital input to security risk assessment and mitigation.

Structured Data

Structured data refers to data that has been formatted in a consistent way. This often takes the form of a database where all records conform to a known structure: data is separated into columns, and each row contains the same type of information in the same place. Stand-alone data may also be structured using a markup language such as XML or JSON, which utilizes tags to provide context around data like `<Account>123456</Account>`.

Data discovery is simplified with structured data, as the process only needs to understand the data's context and attributes to identify where sensitive data exists, such as PII, health-care data, transaction information, etc. Columns and data attributes are typically named in a self-explanatory way, simplifying the identification of sensitive or useful data. Many security information and event management (SIEM) tools also provide functionality to ingest data from multiple sources and apply structure to the data, which facilitates analysis across disparate sources. As an example, the SIEM tool might normalize log data from multiple operating systems to include human-readable usernames in log files, rather than a numeric global user ID (GUID) value.

Structured data is often accompanied by a description of its format known as a *data model* or *schema*, which is an abstract view of the data's format in a system. Data structured as elements, rows, or tuples (particularly in relational databases) is given context by the model or schema. For example, defining a particular string as a user ID can be achieved using tags defined in a schema. Understanding the relationship of a user belonging to a particular business unit can be achieved with data in a particular column; for example, the user's business unit designation appears in the "Bus. Unit" column. These relationships and context can be used to conduct complex analysis, such as querying to see all failed login attempts for users from a specific business unit.

Metadata, or data that describes data, is a critical part of discovery in structured data. *Semantics*, or the meaning of data, is described in the schema or data model and can be useful when analyzing the relationships expressed in data. A particular user record, for example, may contain a tag `<BusUnit>EMEA</BusUnit>`, which identifies that the user belongs to the EMEA business unit and might be considered sensitive information as it provides some location information for that user. Similarly, column names can also be used to identify specific types of regulated data, such as credit card numbers, which require specific protections.

Unstructured Data

Structured data simplifies the process of analysis by providing context and semantics, which speed up discovery and analysis. Unfortunately, not all data is structured—human beings tend to create data in a variety of formats like documents or photos containing infinite types and configurations of data. Unstructured data refers to information stored without following a common format. For example, credit card data may be stored in tables or as strings inside a word processing document or in a spreadsheet with user-defined columns like CC, Card Number, PAN, etc. The variety of unstructured data makes it harder to identify and analyze, but it is nonetheless valuable and therefore requires protection.

Applying *data labels* is one approach to dealing with unstructured data. Labels can identify the classification level of a particular file and, by extension, the protections required. Files or other objects stored in a particular system may have a label applied by virtue of being stored in that system; for example, all documents stored in a "Restricted" fileshare are also given a "Restricted" classification. Labels may also be applied individually via metadata in a file management system or inside documents as a header, footer, or watermark. Security tools such as DLP should be able to detect these unstructured files based on the labels and take appropriate actions, such as blocking files with "Restricted" in the footer from being sent as email attachments. Note that this is an imperfect approach, as users can simply delete the label data or might use incorrect templates and thereby mislabel the data.

Another approach to unstructured data discovery is content analysis, which requires a great deal of resources to parse all data in a storage location and identify sensitive information. Analysis can be performed using one of several methods, such as the following:

- **Pattern matching,** which compares data to known formats like credit card numbers that are 16 numeric digits, or unique organization-defined patterns such as user account information like "j.smith." Patterns are typically defined using a regular expression or *regex*, which allows for more powerful search capabilities by defining not just exact match conditions, but flexible conditions as well. For example, searching for j.smith@ company.com would return only exact matches of that email address. If the user has both j.smith and john.smith aliases, a regex can be created to search for j*.smith@ companyname.com, which returns both email aliases.

- **Lexical analysis** attempts to understand meaning and context of data to discover sensitive information that may not conform to a specific pattern. This is useful to flag highly unstructured content like email or instant message communications where users may utilize alternate phrasing like "payment details" instead of "card number." However, it is prone to false positives as linguistic meaning and context are quite complex.

- **Hashing** attempts to identify known data such as system files or important organization documents by calculating a hash of files and comparing it to a known set of sensitive file hashes. This can be useful for documents that do not change frequently.

Semi-structured Data

Data that has some structure but is not strictly structured is known as *semi-structured*. Object-oriented databases often implement this concept, where files or other unstructured data can be stored as objects. Metadata about the objects is stored to provide a schema, but the entirety of the data is not formatted as it would be in a relational database. Tags are often used to provide this structure; common examples of tagged semi-structured data include HTML, XML, and JSON.

Semi-structured data can be advantageous from both operational and security perspectives. Strict data models require very precise planning; otherwise, the data model may not be able to capture necessary data. Semi-structured data is more flexible and can more readily adapt to business changes. The inclusion of some structure makes security tasks like discovery and indexing easier.

One particular challenge for data discovery is the inclusion of unstructured data inside structured data sets. This often occurs as an unstructured text field in an otherwise structured database, like a free-form notes or comments field into which users can enter any information. Systems that support both types of data are also problematic, like ticketing systems with form fields and file attachments. In both scenarios, users are required to enter information into defined fields, but they may enter or upload anything in free-form text or file attachments. The result is a system with a wide variety of data at differing classification levels, including more sensitive data than originally planned. The organization's data discovery tool must be flexible enough to identify both types of data within the same system, which increases cost and complexity.

Data Location

The location of data will impact both its discoverability and the choice of tools used to perform discovery. Cloud systems offer inherent flexibility with respect to the actual storage location of data. Unlike legacy systems where data could be easily traced to a single data center, a distributed cloud system might have data stored all over the world. This, and other features of cloud computing, can lead to problems with respect to data discovery.

Discovery tools must be able to access data to perform the scanning and analysis needed in the discovery process. On-premises systems can be scanned relatively easily by placing a DLP agent on servers comprising the system or a network-based DLP that can monitor traffic inside the network. However, cloud-based systems may not provide the ability to install local agents, especially in PaaS and SaaS situations. Network-based DLP may not be able to analyze traffic between user workstations and cloud services, as the connection is encrypted, which renders the data unreadable by the DLP.

It is essential to identify the services and locations in use by the organization before choosing and implementing a data discovery scheme. Architectural changes and major system changes like moving from on-premises to the cloud must be carefully analyzed for impact to data discoverability. Additional or new tools may be required, and existing tools might need to be relocated or configured differently to ensure that they have the required visibility into data regardless of its location.

Implement Data Classification

Class has many meanings, but as it relates to data, it is a way to identify common attributes that drive protection requirements. These may include regulated categories such as PII, which is covered by a variety of regulatory and legal schemes like privacy legislation. Classification can also follow an internally defined scheme such as Business Confidential information, which offers your organization some competitive advantage and therefore should be highly protected.

Data Classification Policies

Data classification is the act of forming classes, or groups, by identifying these common attributes. The term *categorization* is often used, especially when discussing systems or large data sets, and describes the process of determining which class a system or data set belongs to by eliciting requirements for protecting the system's confidentiality, integrity, and availability. Each classification level should have an associated set of control expectations, such as data classified as "Public" does not require encryption in transit, while data classified as "Internal Use Only" must be encrypted both at rest and in transit. These requirements are mitigations for the risk presented to the organization by the data or system, as described by the operational impact of a loss of confidentiality, integrity, and/or availability.

Data classification is a way for organizations to provide a uniform set of controls and expectations, as well as a method for speeding up security decision making. Creating a classification scheme, such as Low, Moderate, and High, allows the organization to bundle security control expectations and simplify the process of determining required actions. When a new system is brought online, security practitioners do not need to perform exhaustive research to determine the security requirements they need to meet. The classification scheme provides a clear set of risk-based security controls and expectations based on the sensitivity of the data handled by the system.

Data classification levels and schemes are driven by multiple aspects of data. They may be prescribed by an outside entity such as a regulator or government agency or may be driven by purely internal risk management requirements. Here are some examples:

- **Data type:** Different types of data are regulated by different rules, such as healthcare, sensitive PII, financial, educational, or legal. Data classification schemes based on data type often point to a set of external requirements that must be met if a system or data set includes the given data type.

- **Legal constraints:** If data on EU citizens is collected by a company based in another country, that company may have to either implement privacy protection similar to the EU's GDPR or be based in a country with privacy laws recognized by the EU as equivalent to GDPR. Understanding the legal constraints attribute allows the organization to make decisions such as geolocation of cloud computing architecture.

- **Ownership:** Many organizations utilize data that is shared with business partners and customers, and these external entities may impose requirements such as not sharing the data with third parties or securely destroying data after a specified retention period.

- **Value/criticality:** Some data's value is context-specific. A database of contact details for restaurant suppliers is of little value to an IT services company, but that same database would be mission-critical to a company operating a chain of restaurants. The data classification scheme must take into account how valuable and critical data is to the organization, often by measuring the impact that a loss of the data would have on operations.

The drivers for classification levels, types of data the organization handles, and references to required protections should all be documented in the organization's data classification policy. This may be a stand-alone policy document or may be part of a larger data management plan that specifies classification and security responsibilities. The procedures required to adequately secure data may be specified in a variety of supporting documents, such as system configuration guides that specify configuration of needed encryption or approved cloud solutions that can be used to store data of varying classification levels.

Because of the information provided in a data classification policy, it is often a foundational document for an organization's security program. Rather than specifying a long list of system-specific security requirements for each system individually, such as approved encryption or data retention schedules, a classification label provides a common vocabulary for communicating security needs in a consistent manner. Every system with the same classification level is expected to have the same controls. Other information security policies will likely refer to the data classifications to specify appropriate controls for data or systems, such as approved cryptographic modules, access control procedures, and data retention periods and destruction requirements.

Common Sensitive Data Types

The organization's data classification policy should cover a number of requirements for handling data, many of which will be driven by external laws and regulations. These external obligations will typically provide guidance for handling sensitive classes of information such as the following:

- **Personally identifiable information (PII):** Governed globally by privacy laws and often by laws or regulations specific to certain industries covering the collection, use, and handling of PII. Examples include the EU GDPR and Canadian Personal Information Protection and Electronic Documents Act (PIPEDA) laws, which broadly cover PII, and the U.S. Graham-Leach-Bliley Act (GLBA), which covers banking uses of PII.

- **Protected health information (PHI):** Defined and governed primarily by the U.S. HIPAA, though personal health records are considered PII by most global privacy laws such as GDPR.

- **Cardholder data (often referred to as a cardholder data environment, or CDE):** Defined and regulated by PCI DSS, it provides guidance on the handling, processing, and limited allowable storage of information related to credit and debit cards and transactions.

Handling Sensitive Data

Data protection should be specified for all sensitive data discovered and may be a mix of requirements defined in the various laws mentioned earlier as well as an organization's own risk-management goals. Some elements appropriate to specify in a data classification policy include the following:

- **Compliance requirements inherent at various classification levels:** While this may be too complex for an average user, it ensures that vital security requirements are not overlooked. As a best practice, points of contact who are skilled at managing sensitive data should be identified in the policy so users can seek assistance as needed.

- **Data retention and disposal requirements:** Many data protection laws specify retention periods, such as customer records must be held indefinitely while the customer is still active and then for five years thereafter. Classification and retention policies and procedures should be tightly aligned and provide guidance on approved disposal or destruction methods for data that has reached the end of its retention period.

- **What is considered sensitive or regulated data:** Some regulations include exceptions for a variety of circumstances, and an untrained individual may not fully understand the subtle nuances of when healthcare data is considered PHI or not, for example. The classification policy should provide clear guidance on what data is considered sensitive or regulated and explicitly state any exceptions that may apply.

- **Appropriate or approved uses of data:** Many regulations provide explicit guidance on approved use and processing of data, frequently related to the intended purpose or consent given by the data subject. Classification policies must provide guidance on how to identify these approved uses, such as with explicit system instructions or a point of contact who can provide definitive guidance. Explicit instructions should also be provided on approved or unapproved environments where data may be used, and any requirements for modifying the data if it is to be used elsewhere. For example, a system that handles healthcare information requires valid diagnostic codes and patient records for testing purposes, so using data from a live production system would be very easy. However, those testing activities could lead to unwanted or unapproved healthcare activities since they can alter patient data. In such a case, data sanitization procedures, such are removing actual patient names and other identifiers, might be required before the production data may be used in a nonproduction environment.

- **Access control and authorization:** Controlling logical and physical access to assets is, along with encryption, one of the most powerful tools available to security practitioners. Classification can be used to determine access rights; for example, only users in the payments team are allowed to see plaintext payment card data to process customer transactions. This clearly identifies the need for obfuscation, tokenization, or other methods of blocking users on other teams from accessing the data.

- **Encryption needs:** Encryption is a multipurpose tool for security and privacy, so the application and configuration of encryption must be clearly documented for users to ensure that it is properly applied.

Mapping

Data mapping comprises a number of activities in the overall practice of data science—the application of scientific methods and algorithms to identify knowledge or useful information from data sets. One particular practice related to data mapping is relevant to the role of a security practitioner: identifying the locations of data.

Identifying and mapping the location of data within the organization is a critical inventory task, which is in turn a critical input to risk assessments. Identifying what needs protecting—system and data assets belonging to the organization—and where they exist are crucial to ensure that a security program is designed appropriately. Many DLP tools provide this functionality by scanning a network, domain, or other set of organization-controlled resources to identify data storage locations.

Mapping may be further extended by identifying metadata such as asset ownership like a person, role, or organizational unit, which provides the organization with key information on responsibility and accountability for security processes. Ensuring that all information is located and assigned an owner responsible for protecting it forms the foundation of sound data security practices.

Labeling

Once a data set or system has been classified, the classification level must be communicated in some way so that users, administrators, and other stakeholders know how to protect it. The use of labels simplifies this communication. Rather than forcing users to memorize which systems they can print data from and which systems ban printing, users are instead instructed that systems labeled "Internal" allow printing, while systems labeled "Top Secret" do not allow printing.

Labeling data can be tricky, as we typically think of labels in physical terms but obviously are not able to stick a label on a collection of digital 0s and 1s. There are a variety of labeling methods for different types of assets, such as the following:

- **Hard-copy materials,** primarily printed information on paper, which can be labeled with a printed watermark, stamps, or a physical container such as a folder or box. Hard-copy materials are the easiest to affix labels to because they are physical objects and do not change often.

- **Physical assets,** including servers, workstations, disc drives, optical disks, and removable media, which can be physically labeled with a sticker or badge. These are somewhat tricky to label as the information on these devices can change quite easily. It can also be more challenging to identify and label found physical assets, as the user needs to have appropriate equipment to read the data on the asset; there may also be security issues around plugging in found media due to the possibility of introducing malware.

- **Digital files,** which may come from common collaboration tools, databases, or other programs, and can often be labeled with metadata. This includes content inside the document like a digital watermark or signature or text like a document footer containing the classification level. File metadata such as the filename or document attributes stored in a database can also be used to apply a classification label.

- **Some complex or shared systems and data sets** will have subcomponents that can be labeled, but the overall system cannot. In these cases, labeling of components along with supporting procedures, such as training and reference materials for users or a master organization-wide list of systems, can be useful to ensure that users are aware of the protection requirements they must meet. Classification level is frequently captured in asset inventories for such complex systems.

When it comes to labeling data sets, there are a number of best practices that facilitate the use of the classification level to ensure that adequate protection is applied. The first is to ensure that labels are appropriate to all types of media in use within a system; for example, if both digital files and hard-copy documents are to be used, a digital watermark that also appears when the document is printed helps ensure that the data label is visible across all media states. Labels should be informative without disclosing too much—stamping a folder "Top Secret" makes it easy to recognize for both legitimate users and bad actors! Labels may include only an owner or asset number that can be used to determine the sensitivity of the data in the event it is lost. Finally, when media is found, it should be classified at the highest level supported by the organization until an examination proves otherwise, ensuring that sensitive data is not disclosed.

The organization's DLP tool may be a crucial consumer of data labels, as many DLP tools allow organization-defined labels to be used when performing data identification and classification. If DLP is being used, labels should be applied in a consistent and accessible manner, such as text in the file identifying the classification or common filename conventions to facilitate the discovery process.

Design and Implement Information Rights Management

Since electronic data is highly portable and there is great value in collaborating and sharing access, it is often necessary to ensure that an organization's security controls can be extended to offer protection for the data wherever it might be. Data that is shared outside the organization will likely end up on information systems and transit networks not controlled by the data owner, so a portable method of enforcing access and use restrictions is needed: information rights management, sometimes also called *digital rights management* (DRM). There are two main categories of IRM.

- Consumer-grade IRM is more frequently known as DRM and usually focuses on controlling the use, copying, and distribution of materials that are subject to copyright. Examples include music, videogame, and application files that may be locked for use by a specific (usually paying) user, and the DRM tool provides copy protections to prevent the user from distributing the material to other, nonpaying users.

- Enterprise-grade IRM is associated with digital files and content such as images and documents. IRM systems enforce copy protection as well as usage restrictions, such as PDFs that can be read but prevent data from being copied or printed, and images that can be accessed for only a certain duration based on the license paid for. IRM can also be a form of access control, whereby users are granted access to a particular document based on their credentials and can be applied both internally and externally.

IRM is often implemented to control access to data that is designed to be shared but not freely distributed. This can include sensitive business information shared with trusted partners but not the world at large, copyrighted material to which a user has bought access but is not authorized to share, and any information that has been shared under a license that stipulates limitations on the use or dissemination of that information.

Objectives

Most IRM solutions are designed to function using an access control list (ACL) for digital files, which specifies users and authorized actions such as reading, modifying, printing, or even onward sharing. Many popular file-sharing SaaS platforms implement these concepts as sharing options, which allow the document owner to specify which users can view, edit, download, share, etc.

IRM systems should ideally possess a number of attributes, including the following:

- **Persistence:** The ACL and ability to enforce restrictions must follow the data. Some tools allow users to set a password required to open a document, but the tools also allow other users to disable this password-based access control once they have opened the document, which defeats the purpose.

- **Dynamic policy control:** The IRM solution must provide a way to update the restrictions even after a document has been shared. If a user no longer requires access, the IRM solution must provide a way for the document owner to revoke the permission and enforce it the next time the document is opened regardless of its location. This leads to a key usability challenge, as IRM tools often require users to have an active network connection so the policy can be validated before access is granted.

- **Expiration:** IRM tools can enforce time-limited access to data as a form of access control, which reduces the amount of time a bad actor has to exploit a document to which they have gained unauthorized access. While this can be an element of dynamic policy control, which requires the ability to query an IRM server, it may also be done by calculating and monitoring a local time associated with the file. One example is the timer that begins when a user first starts playback of a rented digital movie: the user's ability to play the movie is restricted to 24 hours after that initial start time.

- **Continuous audit trail:** Accountability is a key attribute of access control systems, so the IRM solution must ensure that protected documents generate an audit trail when users interact with protected documents.

- **Interoperability:** Different organizations and users will have a variety of tools, such as email clients and servers, databases, and operating systems. IRM solutions must offer support for users across these different system types. Document-based IRM tools often utilize a local agent to enforce restrictions, so support for specific operating systems or applications is a critical consideration. System-based IRM tools, such as those integrated into document repositories or email systems, are capable of broad support despite the user's OS, but may offer limited support for user applications like browsers or email clients. Lastly, sharing documents across systems can be challenging, especially with outside organizations that may utilize different services like Google Workspace Apps instead of Microsoft Office for collaboration tools.

IRM restrictions are typically provisioned by a data owner, whose responsibilities will vary depending on the access control model being used. In a discretionary access control (DAC) model, the owner is responsible for defining the restrictions on a per-document or data set basis. This may involve manual configuration of sharing for documents, specifying user authorizations for a database, or defining users and their specific rights for a data set. In non-discretionary access control models such as mandatory access control (MAC), the owner is responsible for specifying metadata like a classification rating or a user role. The IRM system then utilizes this metadata to enforce access control decisions, such as allowing access to users with the same clearance level or denying users who are not assigned specific job roles.

Appropriate Tools

IRM tools comprise a variety of components necessary to provide policy enforcement and other attributes of the enforcement capability. This includes creation, issuance, storage, and revocation of certificates or tokens, which are used to identify authorized users and actions. This requires a centralized service for identity proofing and certificate issuance, as well as a store of revoked certificates that can be used to identify information access that is no longer authorized. This model is used for software distribution via app stores, where developers digitally sign code and user devices validate the signature each time the app is launched. This can ensure that the device is still authorized and the user is still the authentic license holder but also offers the ability for the entity controlling the app store to prevent apps from running if their certificates have been revoked. Such a solution obviously requires network connectivity between devices and the centralized management system.

Both centralized and decentralized IRM solutions will require local storage for encryption keys, tokens, or digital certificates used to validate users and access authorizations. This local storage requires protection primarily for the integrity of data to prevent tampering with the material used to enforce IRM and is an example of a secret that must be properly managed in order for the IRM security control to function properly. Modifying these access credentials could lead to loss of access control over the IRM-protected data; for example, a user might modify the permissions granted to extend their access beyond what the data owner originally specified. If the secret is improperly protected, an unauthorized user might be able to gain access to IRM-protected information. Since the access is made with a valid user credential, the unauthorized user action is essentially undetectable, which violates the access control principle of accountability.

Plan and Implement Data Retention, Deletion, and Archiving Policies

Data follows a lifecycle starting with its creation and ending when it is no longer needed by the organization. There are many actions that may be performed in this end-of-life phase including disposal, retention, archiving, and deletion. The specific action taken when data has reached the end of its useful life may be dictated by legal or compliance requirements, and data classification levels may be used to determine the appropriate action for a given record or data set based on these requirements.

Data disposal is most often associated with the destruction or deletion of data. The term can also be used to mean disposition, which implies a change of location for data such as moving it from active production to a backup or archival environment. When data is still required for use by the organization or must be held for a set period of time to meet a regulatory or compliance objective, the practice of data retention will be used. Once data is no longer needed by the organization and is not subject to any compliance requirements for retention, it should be deleted using tools and processes commensurate with its value.

Data archiving is a subset of retention typically focused on long-term storage of data not required for active processing, or data that has historical value and will therefore have high integrity requirements. Data retention, archive, and destruction policies are highly interconnected, and the required practices may be documented in a single policy or set of procedures governing the use, long-term storage, and secure destruction of data.

Data Retention Policies

Data retention is driven by two primary objectives. Operational needs, like data that must be available to support the organization's operations, as well as compliance requirements, will drive retention policies and practices. Compliance is particularly applicable when sensitive, regulated data such as PII, healthcare, or financial information is used. Many regulatory documents refer to data as records; hence, the term *records retention* is often used interchangeably. Data retention policies should define several key practices for the organization and need to balance organizational needs for availability, compliance obligations, and operational objectives such as cost.

Cloud services can be used in several ways for backups, which are often a key subset of data retention practices related to availability. Cloud backup can replace legacy solutions such as backing up to tape drives and sending them to offsite storage. A network-accessible cloud backup can be used to perform more frequent backups with lower costs, since sending data over a network is typically cheaper than having a courier pick up physical drives. This advantage must be weighed against the potential downside of making the organization's network connection a single point of failure.

Cloud backup can be architected as a mere data storage location, or a full set of cloud services can act as a hot site to take over processing in the event the on-premises environment fails. This scenario may be cost effective for organizations that are unable to use the cloud as a primary processing site but do not want to incur the costs of a full hot site. Temporary use of the cloud as a contingency helps to balance cost and security.

Cloud services, particularly SaaS and PaaS deployments, may offer intrinsic data retention features. Most cloud storage services provide high availability or high durability for data written into the environment, which allows the organization to retain vital data to meet operational needs. Some services also offer compliance-focused retention features designed to identify data or records stored and ensure that compliance obligations are met. In all cases, security practitioners need to be aware of the features available in their organization's chosen cloud environment and ensure that their organization properly architects or configures the services to meet internal and compliance obligations.

Storage Costs and Access Requirements

Data retention has associated storage costs, which must be balanced against the requirements of speed to access it. In many cases, older data is accessed less frequently, such as old emails or archived documents. This data may not be accessed at all for routine business matters but is needed occasionally for reasons like archival research or a legal action where it is acceptable to wait a few hours for a file to be retrieved. Organizations may also have compliance or regulatory obligations to retain data even after it is no longer useful for daily operations.

The costs associated with this storage can be significant, so CSPs offer a variety of storage services that balance cost and retrieval speeds. These solutions typically offer a combination of either low price and slow retrieval speed or higher price and quick retrieval. As an example, Amazon Simple Storage Service (S3) offers higher-priced S3 Standard, where retrieval is in real time, or lower-priced S3 Glacier, where retrieval time ranges from 1 minute to 12 hours. Similarly, Microsoft's Azure Blob Storage offers Hot, Cool, and Archive tiers, in order of higher cost/retrieval speed to lower cost/speed.

To model this cost-benefit analysis, consider Alice's Blob Cloud (ABC), which offers the following storage service levels (currency is USD per gigabyte):

- **Rabbit Storage:** $0.5, real-time access (>50 milliseconds)
  - Storing 5TB of data (5000GB) would cost $2,500/month or $30,000/year.
- **Turtle Storage:** $0.005, access times from 1 to 12 hours
  - Storing 5TB of data (5000GB) would cost $25/month or $300/year.

The cost savings of using Turtle are significant: $29,700 per year in this limited example. Most organizations will generate significantly more than 5TB of data. If the data is used infrequently, such as once a quarter, the data retention policy should specify appropriate storage options to balance costs with the access speed requirements. Data like customer records that is used frequently is more likely to use the more expensive, but faster, storage. Active customers calling a support representative for help with their recent transactions are unlikely to be satisfied with a wait time of 12 hours, which could lead to lost business. Inactive customers who have questions about prior transactions are more likely to accept a delay in accessing their information from archives.

The storage location and conditions for various records to move to different locations should be specified in a records retention schedule. For example, all data that is older than 12 months is moved to Turtle to reduce storage costs. These conditions may also be defined in a data classification policy or data handling procedures; for example, live production data is classified as Business Confidential. All data at this level must be encrypted at rest with key rotation, and the data must be stored in Rabbit. Once it is moved to the Archived classification level, the data is encrypted with archival keys that are not rotated but utilize stronger access controls, and the data is stored in Turtle.

Specified Legal and Regulatory Retention Periods

All organizations should retain data for as long as it is functionally useful; otherwise, the organization faces a loss of availability or ever-increasing data storage costs. The useful life of data may be marked by obvious milestones such as the end of a customer relationship or project, after which the data is no longer valuable to the organization and can be deleted. Any organization dealing with regulated data like PII is likely to have external obligations for data retention that are legally enforceable. Some examples of external regulations include the following:

- **HIPAA:** Affects all U.S. residents and specifies a six-year retention period for documents, such as policies and procedures, relevant to the HIPAA compliance program. Retention of patient medical data is not directly mentioned in HIPAA but is specified by many state-level laws that require that medical records be retained for as long as a patient is active and then for a set period of time thereafter.

- **EU GDPR:** Affects data of EU citizens and does not set a specific retention period but rather provides for indefinite retention so long as a data subject has given consent and the organization has a legitimate need for the data. If consent is revoked or the organization no longer has a legitimate need, the organization must act by deleting, destroying, or anonymizing the data.

Data Retention Practices

The organization's data retention policy should specify what data is to be retained and why. Procedures should also be documented to specify how those retention goals will be met, including details regarding the following:

- **Schedules:** Data and records retention often refers to a schedule of retention, which is the period of time the data must be held for. These are often included in data labels to enable the discovery of data that is no longer required and can be destroyed.

- **Integrity checking:** Whenever data is copied, there is a chance something could go wrong, and data stored may fall victim to environmental issues like heat or humidity, which damage the storage media. Integrity checking procedures should be established to verify data when it is written and periodically thereafter to ensure that it is readable and complete.

- **Retrieval procedures:** Data may have different access requirements across different environments. Typically, there will be more users authorized to access data in a live production environment as it is needed to support operations. Data in an archive may be needed only by a limited set of users, like the legal department when responding to a lawsuit or auditors reviewing regulatory compliance. Retrieval procedures should include proper authorization steps like approved access requests and enforced accountability for archived data usage.

- **Data formats:** The format of data, including programs, apps, and hardware needed to read and write it, requires consideration. Over time, file formats and hardware change, so procedures such as virtualizing legacy environments, purchasing reserves of obsolete equipment, or converting data to new formats may be appropriate. Encryption keys used for data that is archived must also be stored to ensure that data can be decrypted, and the keys must be protected as a highly valuable data asset.

Data Security and Discovery

Retained data will face unique security challenges, particularly driven by the fact that it is long lived and may be difficult to access or manipulate as threat conditions change over time. For example, data encryption standards evolve quite frequently; today's state-of-the-art cryptography may be trivially easy to crack in a few years. It may not be technically or financially feasible to decrypt data retained in archives and re-encrypt using more robust cryptography.

Security practitioners should consider defense-in-depth strategies such as highly secure key storage and tightly limited access control over archival data as a compensating control for weaker legacy encryption standards. Similarly, keys that are rotated out of use in live production environments may need to be securely stored to grant access to archival data.

Data retention supports after-the-fact investigations such as legal action and review by regulators. Methods for retaining data must support the ability to discover and extract data as needed to meet these compliance obligations. For legal actions the requirements of eDiscovery must be considered. eDiscovery is covered in detail in Domain 6: Legal, Risk, and Compliance, but in short, it is the ability for data to be queried for evidence related to a specific legal action, such as all records during a certain time period when fraudulent activity is suspected.

Data Deletion Procedures and Mechanisms

When data is no longer required for operational needs and has been retained for the mandated compliance period, it can be disposed of. It may, however, still be sensitive, such as medical records of a patient who is no longer being treated at a particular facility but is still living and is legally entitled to privacy protections for their medical data. In this case, simply disposing of the data by selling old hard drives or dumping paper files into the trash would open the organization and the patient to risk, so proper controls must be enforced to ensure that the confidentiality of information remains intact during destruction.

NIST SP 800-88, *Guidelines for Media Sanitization*, is a widely available standard for how to securely remove data from information systems when no longer required. It defines three categories of deletion actions for various types of media to achieve *defensible destruction*—the steps required to prove that adequate care was given to prevent a breach of data confidentiality. These categories, in hierarchical order based on protection they provide, are as follows:

- Clear: The use of tools to remove or sanitize data from user-addressable storage. Clearing may include standard operating system functions like deleting data from a trash can/recycle bin, which renders the data invisible but recoverable using commonly available tools. These options are typically the fastest and lowest cost but are inappropriate for very sensitive data.

- **Purge:** The use of specialized tools like overwriting drives with dummy data, physical state changes such as magnetic degaussing, or built-in, hardware-based data sanitization functions designed to provide secure destruction of data. Purged media can typically be reused, which may be a cost factor to consider, but the time required to perform purge actions can make it infeasible for use. For example, writing 35 passes of dummy data over a modern high-capacity hard drive can take hundreds of hours, and purging actions like overwriting shorten the lifespan of media to such an extent that its remaining useful life is negligible. Data may be recovered from purged media using highly specialized tools and laboratory techniques, which makes purging appropriate for moderate-risk data where no determined attacker with adequate means exists.

  - *Cryptographic erasure*, or *cryptoshredding*, is a form of purging that utilizes encryption and the secure destruction of the cryptographic key to render data unreadable. This is effectively a positive denial-of-service attack and is often the only option available for cloud-based environments due to loss of physical control over storage media and the dispersion of data in cloud environments. Solid-state drives (SSD) cannot be reliably overwritten, which leaves cryptoshredding as the only viable means of protecting data if the SSD cannot be physically destroyed. Organizations utilizing the cloud can encrypt all data using organization-controlled keys that can be securely destroyed, rendering data stored in the cloud economically infeasible to recover. Modern smartphone, tablet, and workstation operating systems also implement this feature using technologies such as Apple FileVault or Microsoft BitLocker, which can be used to eliminate costs associated with purging and extend the useful life of storage media.

- **Destroy:** The most drastic option that renders storage media physically unusable and data recovery infeasible using any known methods. Destruction techniques include physical acts like disintegrating, pulverizing, melting, incinerating, and shredding. It is unlikely a CSP will provide the capability for cloud consumers to physically destroy media, but this may be an appropriate control for the CSP to implement for information system components that contain sensitive customer data but that are no longer needed.

The choice of data deletion procedures should be driven by a cost-benefit analysis. Cost including replacement of the media, fines, or legal settlements if a data breach occurs, and the actual implementation of destruction methods should be accounted for. As an example, hard drives containing high-sensitivity information may simply be cleared if they are to be reused in the same environment where the risk of a data breach is low, but the drives may be physically destroyed if they are leaving the organization's control. The full NIST SP 800-88 document covering data destruction and associated risk factors can be found here: csrc.nist.gov/publications/detail/sp/800-88/rev-1/final.

Data Archiving Procedures and Mechanisms

Data archiving refers to placing data in long-term storage for a variety of purposes: optimizing storage resources in live production environments and meeting the organization's retention requirements are both examples. The procedures and mechanisms in place need to ensure that adequate security controls are in place for data as it moves from live systems to the archive, which may implement significantly different access controls and cryptography.

Access controls for production environments are typically more complex than for archive environments, but that does not mean the archive deserves less rigor. Archivists or retention specialists may be the only users authorized to routinely access data in the archive, and procedures should be in place to request, approve, and monitor their access to the data. Procedures governing the handoff between production and the archive should be documented as well, to ensure that the change of responsibility is well understood by the personnel assigned, and data is adequately protected as it moves between environments.

Cryptography serves multiple important roles for archival data just as it does in other environments. Data in transit to an archive will need to be protected for both confidentiality and integrity. For cloud-based systems or backup tools, this means encrypting data in transit to preserve confidentiality as the data moves between on-premises and cloud environments and verifying the integrity of data copied to the cloud environment.

Hashing may be appropriate for data with high integrity requirements. Data can be hashed at a later date when accessed from the archive, and the values compared to an initial hash calculated when the data was first stored. This will identify if changes have occurred. In some cases, integrity can also be verified by loading backup data into a production-like environment to verify that it is readable and conforms to expectation. This would be particularly appropriate for a cloud hot site where failover needs to happen quickly.

In addition to mandated retention periods, security practitioners must understand requirements for data formats mandated by their legal and regulatory obligations. For high-sensitivity data, particularly in the financial services industry, there may be a requirement for data to be stored immutably, that is, in a format where it cannot be changed. The integrity of the data is required to support investigations of regulated activity like financial transactions, and this requirement will influence decisions on where and how to store the data. Once data is written, it will require adequate physical and environmental protections as well, to prevent theft, tampering, or degradation.

Write once, read many (WORM) media is one example of high-integrity storage: data written to the media is physically unalterable, preventing a user from covering up evidence of fraudulent activity. Some cloud storage services implement similar write protections for integrity along with highly durable storage media, so the security practitioner must ensure that proper storage solutions are chosen to meet the organization's need. Blockchain technology is also being used for verifiable integrity, as blockchains rely on hashing to defensibly prove that data is legitimate. An organization's storage solution might be integrated with a blockchain ledger to prove that data has not been modified since it was written to prove the integrity of the data.

Legal Hold

Legal hold is a simple concept but has important implications for data retention. When data is placed under legal hold, its retention schedule is indefinitely suspended. If it is normally retained for seven years but is placed under legal hold, it must be retained until the legal hold is lifted even if the seven-year retention period passes. Determining legal hold is usually not within the purview of the security department, but they should be prepared to respond to such requests when the organization is involved in legal action such as a lawsuit.

The primary challenges surrounding legal hold include identifying applicable records to be held and implementing a way to exclude records from standard deletion procedures while under hold. Legal requests can be vague or specifically broad, as they may be handed down as a way to obtain evidence of suspected wrongdoing. This leads to problems for data archivists and security practitioners when determining which records to place under hold. Legal counsel should always be consulted for guidance, and in general it is better to retain more rather than less.

The second challenge of excluding records under legal hold from deletion is a data management problem. Hard-copy records under hold can be easily separated from other records by moving them to a secure facility and ignoring them when performing deletion, but electronic information systems are more complex. Copying records to a separate storage solution may be feasible but introduces challenges of preserving integrity during the process, as well as the need to set up an access-controlled legal hold archive location. One approach is the use of metadata to electronically flag records to exclude them from deletion. Many databases and filesystems support this functionality, but the archivist or security practitioner must also ensure that supporting systems such as cryptographic key management are aware of records under legal hold. Otherwise, encrypted records may be retained because they are flagged, but the key needed to decrypt is deleted when its retention period expires.

Records placed under legal hold are often included in the process of discovery, which is done as part of investigating and gathering evidence of suspected wrongdoing or noncompliance. This is different from data discovery discussed as part of DLP and is often known as eDiscovery. Legal requirements and the role of security practitioners in supporting eDiscovery are covered in Chapter 6.

Design and Implement Auditability, Traceability, and Accountability of Data Events

All the topics discussed thus far fall into broad categories of data governance and data management. Just like other valuable assets, an organization must identify strategic goals and requirements for managing, using, and protecting data. Despite best efforts to safeguard these assets, there will be times when it is necessary to collect evidence and investigate activity that could support assertions of wrongdoing. Gathering this digital evidence requires the existence of relevant data in logs or other sources, as well as capabilities to identify, collect, preserve, and analyze the data. An organization with no preparation for these activities will find this task difficult or impossible, and security practitioners should ensure that their organizations are not put in situations where they are unable to investigate and hold bad actors accountable.

Definition of Event Sources and Requirement of Event Attribution

There are formal definitions of events used in IT service management as well as security incident response. In general, an event is any observable action that occurs, such as a user logging in to a system or a new virtual server being deployed. Most IT systems support some ability to capture these events as running logs of past activity, though cloud-based systems can present a number of challenges that can complicate this logging effort.

The primary concern regarding information event sources in cloud services is the accessibility of the data. This will vary by the cloud service model in use. IaaS will obviously offer the most data events as the consumer has more control over the system elements and can capture detailed logs from network, OS, and application data sources, while in SaaS, the consumer may be limited to only data events related to their application frontend with no access to infrastructure, OS, or network logs. This loss of control is one cost factor organizations should weigh against benefits of migrating to the cloud and may be partially offset with contract requirements for expanded data access or investigation support from the CSP in exceptional circumstances like a data breach.

The Open Web Application Security Project® (OWASP) publishes a series of guides called *cheat sheets*, including one on logging. The guide covers a variety of scenarios and best practices and also highlights security challenges associated with cloud services, particularly the inability to control, monitor, or extract data from resources outside the organization's direct control. Some of these scenarios include the following:

- **Synchronize time across all servers and devices:** The timestamp of events in a log is crucial to establish a chain of activity performed by a particular user. If a cloud service is hosted and generates logs in a time zone different from the user's workstation, it will time conversions to trace events. Without this conversion, crucial log data may be overlooked because search parameters will exclude it from the investigator's review.

- **Differing classification schemes:** Different apps and platforms will categorize events with different metadata. For example, one OS may identify user logins as "Informational" events, while apps running on that OS log the same activity as "User Events." Constructing queries on such varied data can be difficult.

- **Identity attribution:** Ultimately logs should be able to answer the basic question "Who did what and when?" Sufficient user ID attribution needs to be easily accessible; otherwise, it may prove impossible to definitely state that a particular user took a given action. The organization's identity and access management system may offer the ability to utilize a single identity across multiple services, but many cloud services enforce their own user management, complicating the attribution of events to a specific user. Additional elements of identity attribution include the following:

- **User identity:** This is most often associated with a username, though other forms can include a user ID (UID), globally unique identifier (GUID), process name or ID number, etc. These can be used to identify both human and nonhuman user access, such as service, system, and process accounts that are interacting with data and systems. The logs should capture as much detail as needed to tie events back to a single entity that made the request or performed an action.

- **IP address:** The IP address associated with a system event can be used to a limited extent when identifying a user or system. When the organization has complete control over network configuration, such as static IP address assignments or properly logged dynamic host configuration protocol (DHCP) logs that can trace an IP address to a specific workstation, the IP address can be used to uniquely identify a workstation. When communicating over the Internet, IP addresses are much less deterministic of location, as many organizations and ISPs utilize techniques that cause their public-facing IP addresses to change. IP address can be useful as a beginning point of an investigation, such as determining a rough geographic location for suspicious activity, so it is an important data element to capture in logs.

- **Geolocation:** Similar to IP addresses, geolocation information is an important data element to capture in logs. Organizational users based in the same country are likely to access organization resources from within the country, so activity that originates from foreign locations is an anomaly. It could be a nonmalicious user traveling and logging in to do work or a bad actor who has stolen credentials and is attempting to exfiltrate data. IP address can be used as a rough geolocation identifier, and many modern devices like smartphones, tablets, and laptops can actually provide very specific location information through the use of network locations or GPS signals. Geolocation is also frequently used as a proactive safeguard, as dynamic access control systems may require additional authentication factors if a user account is observed logging in from a foreign country not usually associated with a particular user.

- **Application-specific logs:** Apps may offer the ability to generate logs, but unlike widely standardized tools like operating systems or web server software, they may log information in a unique format. SaaS platforms may offer even fewer configuration options over internal functionality like event logging, since configuration is not exposed to the end users. Making sense of this data in relation to other sources, such as one app that uses a numeric ID value for users while others use an email address, can be challenging. Data normalization is one way of overcoming this challenge, and a log aggregation platform will need to be properly configured to ensure that the data it collects is useable.

- **Integrity of log files:** App and OS log files typically reside on the same hosts as the software generating the logs and are susceptible to tampering by anyone with privileged access to the host. If a user has administrative permissions, they may be able to not only perform unauthorized actions but then cover up evidence by modifying or deleting log files. A centralized log management tool with tightly controlled access can overcome this challenge by denying privileged users the ability to cover up fraudulent actions.

The full Logging Cheat Sheet is available here: cheatsheetseries.owasp.org/ cheatsheets/Logging_Cheat_Sheet.html.

Logging, Storage, and Analysis of Data Events

Logs are made valuable only by review; in other words, they are valuable only if the organization makes use of them to identify activity that is unauthorized or compromising. Because of the sheer volume of log data generated, it is unlikely that a human being would be capable of performing log reviews for any computing environment more complex than a single application.

SIEM tools, which are covered in detail in Domain 5: Cloud Security Operations, can help to solve some of these problems by offering these key features:

- **Log centralization and aggregation:** Rather than leaving log data scattered around the environment on various hosts, the SIEM platform can gather logs from operating systems, applications, network appliances, user workstations, etc., providing a single location to support investigations. This is often referred to as *forwarding* logs when looked at from the perspective of individual hosts sending log files to the SIEM.

- **Data integrity:** The SIEM platform should be on a separate host with access permissions unique from the rest of the environment, preventing any single user from tampering with data. System administrators may be able to tamper with logs on the systems they are authorized to access but should be denied write access to log data stored on the SIEM platform.

- **Normalization:** The same piece of data can often be formatted in a variety of ways, such as dates written YYYY/MM/DD, DD/MM/YYYY, or even the Unix format, which is a count of the number of seconds measured from a start time of January 1, 1970. SIEMs can normalize incoming data to ensure that the data is presented consistently; for example, all timestamps are converted to utilize UTC rather than the time zone of the originating system.

- **Automated or continuous monitoring:** Sometimes referred to as *correlation*, SIEMs use algorithms to evaluate data and identify potential attacks or compromises. These can often be integrated with other security tools such as intrusion detection systems (IDSs) and firewalls to correlate information; for example, a large number of failed logins by a user after that user also visited a particular website could indicate the presence of malware attempting to brute-force access. This is indicative that users may have fallen for a phish, and the attackers are now trying to use those credentials. Crucially, this monitoring can be automated and is performed continuously, cutting down the time to detect a compromise.

- **Alerting:** SIEMs can automatically generate alerts such as emails or tickets when action is required based on analysis of incoming log data. Some also offer more advanced capabilities like intrusion prevention systems (IPSs), which can take automated actions such as suspending user accounts or blocking traffic to/from specific hosts if an attack is detected. Of course, this automated functionality will suffer from false positives, but it performs at much greater speed compared to a human being when an incident occurs.

- **Investigative monitoring:** When manual investigation is required, the SIEM should provide support capabilities such as querying log files, generating reports of historical

activity, or even providing concise evidence of particular events that support an assertion of attack or wrongdoing. For example, a particular user's activity can be definitively
tracked from logging in to their workstation to accessing sensitive data in a web application and performing unauthorized actions like copying the data to send it outside the
organization.

Chain of Custody and Nonrepudiation

Data that is collected in support of an investigation has unique requirements for integrity,
particularly an investigation in which civil or criminal prosecution is called for. It is vital
to establish a *chain of custody*, or a defensible record of how evidence was handled and by
whom, from its collection to its presentation as evidence. If data has been altered after it was
collected, the defendant can make a case that the evidence has been altered to make them
look guilty.

Chain of custody and evidence integrity do not imply that data has not changed since
collection, but instead they provide convincing proof that it was not tampered with in a
way that damages its reliability. For example, data on a user's workstation will physically
change location when the workstation is collected from the user, and the data may be copied
for forensic analysis. These actions, when performed by properly trained professionals, do
not change the underlying facts being presented or the believability of evidence. However,
if the workstation is left unattended on a desk after it is taken from the user, then the user
can claim the data was altered in a way that incriminates them, and thus the evidence is no
longer reliable.

Nonrepudiation can be a challenging term because it is proving a negative. Repudi-
ating an action means denying responsibility for the given action, so nonrepudiation is a
characteristic whereby you can definitely hold a particular user accountable for a particular
action. In nontechnical terms, it can be difficult to hold anyone accountable for drinking the
last of the office coffee from a shared coffee maker; everyone can repudiate the assertion that
they finished the coffee without brewing more. If users are required to enter a PIN to unlock
the coffee maker, then it is possible to defensibly prove, when the coffeepot is found to be
empty, that the last person whose code was used is the culprit.

Information systems enforce nonrepudiation through the inclusion of sufficient evidence
in log files, including unique user identification and timestamps. System architecture and
limitations that can pose challenges include shared user accounts that are tied to a group
of users, as well as processes that act on behalf of users. In both cases, it may be possible to
narrow down a group of users who might be responsible, but the actual identity of the bad
actor is obscured because other users could also have performed the action. Nonrepudiation
is a concern not just for data event logging but also access control and system architecture.
Security practitioners must ensure that their access control, logging, and monitoring
functions support nonrepudiation, including compensating controls when a single system or
control does not provide sufficient evidence to support nonrepudiation.

One final note on chain of custody and nonrepudiation: the process of investigating
digital crimes can be quite complex and is best left to trained professionals with appropriate

tools, skills, and experience. Simple acts like plugging in a drive can cause irreversible data loss or corruption, and destroying evidence may limit the organization's ability to seek legal redress if a crime has occurred. While security practitioners should be familiar with these practices, it is also advisable to know when expert professionals are required. The field of digital forensics and incident response (DFIR) includes security professionals with specialized skills, and many firms offer services on retainer to speed access to these skills in a time of crisis.

Summary

Cloud services offer many benefits for accessing, managing, and handling data that is crucial to modern business operations, but they are not free from risk. The cloud data lifecycle provides a convenient framework for identifying the types of activities, risks, and appropriate security controls required to ensure that data remains secure. This, coupled with an understanding of the storage architectures available in different cloud service models, guides security practitioners when designing and applying appropriate safeguards such as data discovery, encryption, and tokenization, as well as countermeasures like DLP and incident response. Proper cloud data security requires organizations to know what kind of data they handle and where it is stored, and deploy adequate policies, procedures, and technical controls to ensure that the business benefits of cloud environments are not offset by increased information-security risks.

Chapter 3

Cloud Platform and Infrastructure Security

The cloud security professional must understand the architecture and infrastructure that supports each of the cloud delivery models. The infrastructure includes the physical components of the cloud, the services they provide, and the communication infrastructure that allows us to connect with the cloud. Each part of the infrastructure has specific security needs and shared security responsibilities.

In the shared security model of cloud computing, it is easy, but incorrect, to assume that security is the sole responsibility of the cloud service provider (CSP). Security practitioners need to understand the unique security requirements of cloud computing and the technologies, such as virtualization, that make the cloud possible. There are important differences between cloud security and security for on-premises systems, including responsibility that is divided between the CSP and the customer. A security professional must be clear on what the CSP provides with respect to security and which items are the customer's responsibility to protect. In general, the data put into a cloud environment will always be the responsibility of the customer, but other aspects of securing the system will vary based on the cloud delivery model used.

Finally, the cloud security professional must understand how the cloud can support the organization's objectives. This may include crucial functions such as business continuity and disaster recovery, scalable architecture to keep up with demand, and cost savings that make entirely new business models financially viable for some organizations.

Comprehend Cloud Infrastructure and Platform Components

There are infrastructure components that are common to all cloud service delivery models. These components are all physically located with the CSP, but many are accessible via the network. In the shared responsibility security model, both the customer and the CSP share security responsibilities for the elements of the cloud environment. Those responsibilities are discussed with each component.

Physical Environment

The physical environment is composed of the server rooms, data centers, and other physical locations of the CSP. The identity of the CSP may vary by the different cloud security models, as follows:

- A private cloud is often built by a company on its own premises, such as an IT group that runs cloud services supporting multiple business units or departments. If this occurs, the organization is the CSP, and the units or departments are customers; though they are all part of the same organization, costs associated with cloud services are usually tracked in the same manner as using a public cloud. This allows the organization to be very granular in identifying resource usage. Private clouds can also be virtual, and major CSPs including AWS, Azure, and Google Cloud offer the ability to use their infrastructure in an isolated virtual private cloud (VPC).

- In a community cloud, a member of the community hosts the space and equipment needed and is responsible for physical security. The community member hosting the cloud is the CSP. Similar to VPCs, a community cloud may be built using a private section of a commercial CSP, and the CSP is responsible for physical security.

- In public clouds, the CSP is the company providing the service, such as AWS, Microsoft, Google, IBM, and so on. This commercial vendor is the CSP and is responsible for the physical security of their cloud infrastructure.

The physical environment is under the sole control of the CSP, and it is their responsibility to provide all physical security. This includes responsibility for monitoring, auditing, and maintaining a secure environment. Security risks that affect cloud infrastructure are the same as those affecting any data center, regardless of whether they are on-premises or provided by a third party. These include physical security of the equipment, access control to the facility, environmental controls like heating and air conditioning, and utilities at the site like water and electricity.

CSPs utilize common controls to address these risks. For physical security these include standard measures such as locks, security personnel, lights, fences, visitor check-in procedures, and the like. Identity and access management (IAM) for CSP technical personnel will require tools including a single sign-on (SSO) provider, logging of user actions, and multi-factor authentication (MFA) to provide robust access controls and logging.

CSPs will address controls for data confidentiality and integrity in a similar manner to cloud customers, but with much broader controls. For example, ensuring that communication lines are not physically compromised might involve locating telecommunications equipment inside a controlled area of the CSP's building or campus. This makes it easier to guard against and detect any physical tampering, such as wiretapping or cutting communication lines.

Network and Communications

Physical networking gear is housed in facilities controlled by the CSP, and it is the CSP's responsibility to physically secure the device as well as logical security controls like proper configuration. Any components housed at the customer's facility (on-premises) are the responsibility of the customer. The largest area of concern is the public Internet that exists between these two. Since the Internet is a shared resource, the responsibility for securing data transiting the Internet falls to the individuals using it, so both the CSP and cloud customer must identify and implement ways of securing data in transit. This will most often involve the use of cryptography.

For this reason, the CSP must support secure protocols like HTTPS, and the customer must use the secure protocols. Encrypting data prior to transmission is also an effective method for preserving confidentiality and may involve the customer encrypting the data before it leaves the customer's network or using a VPN to securely transmit data over untrusted networks like the Internet. At each end of the transmission pipeline, both the customer and the CSP are responsible for the firewalls and other systems needed to maintain secure communications. Some organizations may find the use of dedicated communication lines a more effective way of protecting their data in transit, avoiding the use of untrusted networks.

In the shared security model, the CSP provides tools for secure computing, logging, encryption, and so on. However, customers do retain responsibility for activating and configuring these features to meet their needs. In all service delivery models, it is the responsibility of the customer to connect to and transmit data to the cloud service securely.

Consider, for example, that you are a company shipping a product. You have many ways in which you can accomplish this.

- You could create your own fleet, leasing aircraft from a supplier but providing your own pilots and cargo personnel. In this case, it is similar to an infrastructure as a service (IaaS) environment. The supplier is responsible for the aircraft provided, but not how you use the aircraft or the safety and security of your product.

- In a different approach, the supplier may provide the aircraft and pilots, and you handle the storage and security of the cargo. You remain responsible for the safety and security of your product, and the supplier provides a safe aircraft operated by qualified personnel, equivalent to a platform as a service (PaaS) environment.

- In the simplest method, you drop off the package with the supplier. Once it's in their possession, the supplier is responsible for the security and delivery of the package. They are not responsible for the manner in which the product is packaged or the condition of the product when it is dropped off with the service. Although they make a best effort to deliver the package in good condition, it is possible for the package to be damaged, so compensating controls like insurance are recommended. This is similar to using a software as a service (SaaS) environment.

This package delivery example is a useful metaphor for the security of data in transit with the IaaS, PaaS, and SaaS delivery models. Each model has potential benefits in terms of the amount of flexibility offered, which is offset by associated costs.

- In an IaaS service model, the customer is responsible for configuring the environment as well as enforcing company policies in the use of systems, as if the systems were on-premises as well as the connection to the CSP. The CSP is responsible for the technology provided but not how it is used, and the cost of that responsibility remains with the customer.

- In a PaaS module, the CSP is responsible for the physical components, the internal network, and the tools provided. The customer is responsible for the proper use of those tools and the connection to the CSP. Services provided by the CSP are likely to be cheaper than what the customer could do in house, due to the shared resources, but the customer also gives up some control.

- In a SaaS model, the customer remains responsible for access to the cloud service in a secure manner—using appropriate technologies to connect with and transmit data to and from the service securely. Once the data is in the CSP, the customer has less control over it, but the shared nature of the cloud means these services are available at significantly lower cost.

Compute

The compute resources are the infrastructure components that deliver virtual machines (VMs), disk, processor, memory, and network resources. These resources are owned by and under the direct control of the CSP. The security issues are the same for these resources in a cloud environment as they are on-premise with the additional challenge of multitenancy.

The CSP in every delivery and service model remains responsible for the maintenance and security of the physical components. These are owned and supported by the CSP. The customer in every delivery and service model remains responsible for their data and their users. Between the physical components, there is a vast array of software and other components. Who is responsible for each of these remaining parts varies by service and delivery model and sometimes by the CSP. The contract between the customer and the CSP should spell out the responsibilities for each part of the cloud environment. Typical responsibilities will be described for each service model (IaaS, PaaS, and SaaS).

In an IaaS environment, the CSP provides the hardware components and may provide networking, virtualization, and virtualization operating systems. The CSP is responsible for the security of any software components it provides, such as virtualization and operating system (OS) software, and the CSP is also responsible for the versioning and security of those components.

When the CSP provides the virtualization and OS software, some of the software configuration may be left to the customer, such as controlling access to the VMs the customer creates in the cloud. When this is the case, the customer is responsible for the security implications of the configuration they choose, and in IaaS the customer has the most responsibility for security. Other than the hardware components and system software provided, the customer remains responsible for all other security for the tools they install, software they develop, and, of course, all identity and access management, customer records, and other data. These responsibilities include patching and versioning of the software installed or developed by the customer and the security of data at rest and in motion.

In a PaaS environment, the CSP takes on more responsibility for providing services, and the corresponding security requirements. In addition to the responsibilities of IaaS, the CSP takes on security responsibility for services including operating systems, database management systems (DBMSs), or whatever other platforms are being offered in the cloud environment. While the customer has some ability to configure these services, all services provided by the CSP will usually be maintained by the CSP, including patching and versioning. The customer is responsible for the configuration and use of all systems and services provided as well as the patching and versioning of any software they install or develop on the platform. The customer is always responsible for the security of their data and users. The contract with the CSP should address these issues.

In a SaaS environment, the customer is usually responsible for only the customization of the SaaS service, as well as the security of their users and the data used or produced by the service. The CSP is responsible for the security of all other compute resources.

Virtualization

There are two types of hypervisors that provide virtualization. These are Type 1 hypervisors, also known as *bare-metal hypervisors*, and Type 2 hypervisors, also known as *hosted hypervisors*. Among the major CSPs the Type 1 hypervisor is more common, such as the Xen hypervisor provided by AWS and the Hyper-V hypervisor provided in Azure.

Type 1 hypervisors run directly on a physical server and its associated hardware components, rather than running on top of a traditional OS. In this scenario, the hypervisor provides the OS functionality, with VMs running atop the hypervisor. The hypervisor and virtualization environment are managed with a management console separate from the hypervisor. VMs running on a Type 1 hypervisor can move between physical machines, and when done properly, it is invisible to the end user. In addition to Hyper-V and the XenServer hypervisors, other common Type 1 hypervisors include VMware vSphere with ESX/ESXi and Oracle VM.

Type 2 hypervisors are more complex, as they run on top of a traditional OS. At the bottom is the hardware, and running on top of that is a host OS, such as Windows, macOS, or Linux. The hypervisor runs as a program on top of the OS; examples include Oracle VM VirtualBox, VMware Workstation Pro/VMware Fusion, Parallels Desktop, and Windows Virtual PC. These are not usually used for enterprise solutions because they are less efficient than Type 1 hypervisor environments, but Type 2 hypervisors are frequently used for individual needs or environments like testing where absolute efficiency is not as important. Management of the VMs is built into the Type 2 hypervisor, and usually includes options like specifying individual VM compute, storage, and memory parameters.

The security of the hypervisor is always the responsibility of the CSP. The virtual network and virtual machine may be the responsibility of either the CSP or the customer, depending on the cloud service model as described in the earlier "Compute" section.

Hypervisor security is critical. If unauthorized access to the hypervisor is achieved, the attacker can access every VM on the system and potentially obtain the data stored on each VM. A *VM escape* is a type of attack in which a malicious user can break the isolation between VMs running on a hypervisor by gaining access outside their assigned VM. In both Type 1 and Type 2 hypervisors, the security of the hypervisor is critical to avoid hypervisor takeover or VM escape. In a Type 2 hypervisor, host OS security is also important, as a breach of the host OS can potentially allow takeover of the hypervisor and all associated VMs as well. Proper IAM and other controls limiting access to those with both proper credentials (authentication) and a business need (authorization) can protect your systems and data. In a cloud computing multitenant model, there is another challenge: once an attacker gains access to be on a server hosting multiple VMs, they can compromise systems or data belonging to however many customers are running workloads on that server. Security of the hypervisor is the responsibility of the CSP, and a robust set of controls should be in place to provide customers with assurance that their virtualized systems are safe.

CSP hypervisor security includes preventing physical access to the servers and limiting both local and remote access to the hypervisor. The access that is permitted must be logged, and hypervisor maintenance or administrative access should be thoroughly monitored. The CSP must also keep the hypervisor software current and updated with patch management procedures.

The virtual network between the hypervisor and the VM is also a potential attack surface. The responsibility for security in this layer is often shared between the CSP and the customer. In a virtual network, you have virtual switches, virtual firewalls, virtual IP addresses, etc. The key to security is to isolate each virtual network so that only permitted traffic is able to move between virtual networks. This isolation will reduce the possibility of attacks being launched from the physical network or from the virtual network of other tenants, preventing attacks such as VLAN hopping, while preserving desired system communications such as access by a web server to application servers in a different VLAN. The security of the network virtualization hardware and software is the responsibility of the CSP, while proper VLAN configuration for a specific application is the responsibility of the customer.

A control layer between the real and virtual devices such as switches and firewalls and the VMs can be created through the use of software-defined networking (SDN). In AWS, when you create a virtual private cloud (VPC), the software-defined networking creates the public and private networking options (subnets, routes, etc.). To provide security to the software-defined network, you will need to manage both certificates and communication between the VM management plane and the data plane. This includes authentication, authorization, and encryption.

The security methods for a virtual network are not that much different from physical networks. However, certain tools may be better suited to certain tasks in a virtual environment, and some legacy tools may not function at all. For example, some network monitoring tools require a device plugged into the mirror or span port of a switch so they can analyze traffic.

However, a virtualized network does not provide such a capability, so these types of tools will not provide any security benefit. Using security tools designed specifically for virtual environments or even tools designed explicitly for cloud security are recommended.

The final attack surface in the virtualization space is the VM itself. Responsibility for VM security may be shared, but it is usually the responsibility of the customer in an IaaS model. In the PaaS model the security of the VM is the responsibility of the CSP if the platform is also the responsibility of the CSP, as in a hosted database platform. The CSP is responsible for securing the VM used to provide the hosted database in this model, while the customer would be responsible for secure configuration of the database. If the customer is creating VMs on top of a virtualization platform, then security of any VMs created remains the responsibility of the customer. In a SaaS model, the VM is created and used by the CSP to provide a service, and the responsibility of VM security rests on the CSP.

Storage

Various types of cloud storage technologies are discussed in Domain 1, "Cloud Concepts, Architecture, and Design." Cloud storage has a number of potential security issues, and the importance of the shared responsibility model with respect to cloud storage cannot be overstated. Data spends most of its life at rest, so understanding who is responsible for securing cloud storage is a key undertaking. At a basic level, the CSP is responsible for physical protection of data centers and the storage infrastructure they contain, while the customer is responsible for the logical security and privacy of data they store in the CSP's environment. The CSP is responsible for the security patches and maintenance of data storage technologies and other data services they provide, while the customer is responsible for properly configuring and using the storage tools.

CSPs provide a set of controls and configuration options for secure use of their storage platforms. The customer is responsible for assessing the adequacy of these controls and properly configuring and using the controls available. These controls can include how the data is accessed, such as over the public Internet, via a VPN, or only internally from other cloud VLANs. The customer is also responsible for ensuring adequate protection for the data at rest and in motion based on the capabilities offered by the CSP. For example, the CSP may provide the ability to encrypt data when it is written to the storage device. If the encryption is done using a customer-provided key, then keys must be securely generated and stored to safeguard the data. Similarly, many cloud storage tools can be configured for either public or private access. Failure to properly configure secure storage using available controls is the fault of the customer.

In a cloud environment, you lose control of the physical medium where your data is stored, but you retain responsibility for the security and privacy of that data. These challenges include the inability to securely wipe physical storage and the possibility of a tenant being allocated storage space that was previously allocated to you. This creates the possibility of fragments of your data files existing on another tenant's allocated storage space. You retain responsibility for this data and cannot rely on the CSP to securely wipe the physical storage areas.

Compensating controls for the lack of physical control of the storage medium include only storing data in an encrypted format and retaining control of the keys needed to decrypt the data. This permits crypto shredding when data is no longer needed, rendering any recoverable fragments useless.

Management Plane

The management plane provides the tools (web interface and APIs) necessary to configure, monitor, and control your cloud environment. It is separate from and works with the control plane and the data plane. If you have control of the management plane, you have control of the cloud environment; similar to system administration tools, it is a high-value target of attackers and should be tightly controlled.

Control of the management plane is essential and starts with limiting and controlling access. An attacker who can gain access to the management plane will have free rein over your cloud environment. Since virtualized infrastructure is all accessible through management plane tools like a cloud console, the impact of a compromised account or malicious access is significant.

The most important account to protect is root, or any named account that has administrative/superuser functionality. The start of this protection is the enforcement of a strong password policy. The definition of a strong password is an evolving question that has recently been addressed by updated guidance in NIST in SP 800-63, *Digital Identity Guidelines*. The most important factor in a secure password is length—longer is better, so passphrases are preferred over passwords—and secure use practices like not sharing passwords or reusing them across sites or services. Human factors include making passphrases easy to remember but difficult to guess, which discourages bad habits like reuse.

A strong password policy needs to be coupled with other measures for the critical root and administrative accounts due to the broad access they grant. MFA should be implemented for these accounts and may take the form of a hardware token that is stored securely or other methods like an authenticator app on a trusted device like the user's smartphone. In general, software solutions add some protection, but not as much as the hardware solutions. Widespread MFA is also relatively new, and novel attacks against it are still developing, so any solution should be routinely reviewed as part of risk assessments to ensure that it is still providing adequate security. SMS was considered an acceptable method for MFA, but attackers found simple ways to capture the codes being sent, which rendered the protection meaningless.

 Real World Scenario

$16 USD: The Price of Cracking SMS MFA

In 2021 a reporter for Vice worked with an ethical hacker to demonstrate how SMS MFA codes could easily be intercepted. Coupled with a phishing attack that compromised the reporter's username and password, this relatively simple and cheap attack allowed for a complete takeover of the reporter's email account. From there, the attacker was able to gain access to several other services, since many online services use email as a username and support password resets under the assumption that the legitimate user has control over their email.

The ethical hacker utilized a tool that intercepts text messages sent over the SMS protocol. While the tool has legitimate uses for marketing, it can also be used to capture the MFA codes sent via SMS. The ubiquity and simplicity of SMS made it an easy way to provision MFA codes, but since it was never designed as a high-security delivery method, its useful-ness was short lived.

More details of the compromise can be found at `vice.com/amp/en/article/y3g8wb/hacker-got-my-texts-16-dollars-sakari-netnumber`.

Role-based access control (RBAC) or access groups are another method to limit access to these sensitive accounts. Using RBAC or access groups makes management of these groups and permissions important. If rights are not deleted when an employee changes posi-tions or employment, access can become too broad very quickly. Another step is to limit access to users connecting from a known on-premises network or through a VPN, if remote work is required. This approach, however, is rapidly being replaced by zero trust network architecture (ZTNA), which does away with trusted networks in favor of verifying every user request. This minimizes risks associated with trusted insiders or malicious users who have gained unauthorized access to secure networks.

Another method for limiting access is to use attribute-based access control (ABAC), also called policy-based access control. Using this method, a variety of attributes can be used with complex Boolean expressions to determine access. Typical attributes such as username are one part of the policy, which can also include attributes like the usual time a user logs in, location they log in from, or even details of the device they are connecting from. ABAC can be used to ensure that only authorized users connecting from a corporate-managed endpoint are allowed access. If the user is accessing a system from a new geographic location, ABAC can be configured to require additional proof of the user's identity, such as an MFA prompt. Many social networks implement such a feature to prevent stolen devices from gaining access to social media accounts—even if the authorized user has traveled and taken a device with them, they must prove their identity by answering security questions since the device is not logging in from the normal, expected location.

Each of these methods can make accessing critical root or administrative accounts more difficult for both legitimate users and malicious users alike. How tightly you lock down these accounts is in direct proportion to the value of the information and processes in your cloud. As with all security measures, it requires a balance to create as much security as possible while maintaining reasonable business access.

Root and administrative accounts are typically the only accounts with access to the management plane. The end user may have some limited access to the service offering tools for provisioning, configuring, and managing resources, but should not be allowed access to manage the entire cloud environment. The degree of control will be determined by each business, but end users will normally be restricted from accessing the management plane. The separation of management and other workforce users makes the creation of separate accounts for development, testing, and production an important method of control.

In instances where the management functions are shared between the customer and the CSP, careful separation of those functions is necessary to provide proper authorization and control. In a Cisco cloud environment, the management plane protection (MPP) tool is available. AWS provides the AWS Management Console.

These are some of the methods that can be used to protect the cloud management plane. A layered defense is important, and the amount of work used to protect the management plane is, in the end, a business decision. The cloud security professional must be aware of the methods available for protection in order to be a trusted advisor to the business in this matter. Major CSPs including AWS and Azure publish security reference architectures, which detail best practices for utilizing each cloud's particular services and offerings. This includes security configurations, identity and access controls, and best practices like creating separate management plane accounts for production, testing, and staging environments.

Design a Secure Data Center

Designing a secure data center can be challenging with the physical siting; environmental, logical, and physical controls; and communication needs. In a cloud environment, many of these traditional concerns are the responsibility of the CSP or cloud vendor as they have physical control and ownership of the data center and the physical infrastructure. The customer may be able to review the physical, environmental, and logical controls of the underlying infrastructure of the vendor in limited cases but usually has no direct control over them.

The distributed nature of cloud computing environments makes security oversight even more challenging. Major CSPs like AWS, Google, Microsoft, and IBM run data centers all over the world. Even if the CSP allowed auditing of their physical infrastructure, customers would need to travel the world and audit hundreds of data centers! Most CSPs do not allow individual customers to perform audits, but they do provide third-party audit reports like SOC 2 Type II and the Cloud Security Alliance STAR Level 2 report. Customers can review these reports to gain assurance regarding the security controls implemented by the CSP.

Cloud customers have the ability to create a logical data center within the cloud environment. A logical data center is a construct, much like a container, where the customer designs the services, data storage, and connectivity within their instance of the cloud service, and it is effectively a virtual private cloud inside the public cloud infrastructure. The physical mapping of this design to the underlying architecture is not controlled by the customer as it would be in an on-premises data center; however, some CSP offerings do provide additional controls like geographic selection to prevent data from leaving specific countries.

Logical Design

The logical design of a data center is an abstraction. In designing a logical data center, the customer utilizes software and services provided by the CSP, and a chief concern in provisioning such a data center is implementing security controls appropriate to the data that will be handled in the cloud. The needs of a data center include access management, monitoring for compliance and regulatory requirements, patch management, log capture and analysis, and secure configuration of all services used.

In a logical data center design, a perimeter needs to be established with IAM and monitoring of all attempts to access the data. Access control can be accomplished through various IAM methods, including authentication and authorization, security groups, and VPCs, as well as the management consoles. Each major CSP offers services equivalent to software firewalls, traffic monitoring, and security monitoring like intrusion detection systems (IDS), which can be implemented to monitor data center activities and alert on potentially malicious behavior.

All services used should have a standard configuration that is reviewed and approved for use by the organization. This configuration is determined by the business and specifies how each approved cloud service is to be configured and can be used, and it is similar to hardening guides or configuration baselines in on-premises environments. Using a standard pattern/configuration makes administering and maintaining cloud services simpler and provides a consistent level of security. Deviations from approved configurations should be approved through an exception process that includes analysis of the risk presented by the deviation and any additional mitigations required. Secure baseline configurations can provide a more secure environment for the data center, and it is essential to monitor these configurations to detect drift. If unexpected changes occur, they should generate an alert and be investigated.

Connections to and from the logical data center must be secured to provide data in transit security. This may be achieved by VPNs, Transport Layer Security (TLS), or other secure transmission methods. With an increasingly remote and mobile workforce, remote access is increasingly important, and a careful logical design can help to provide a secure data center environment while also enabling a remote workforce to accomplish tasks regardless of location.

Tenant Partitioning

Multitenant models make cloud computing more affordable but create some security and privacy concerns. If the walls between tenants are breached, then your data is at risk. Multitenancy is not a new concept, as many business centers physically housed multiple tenants, and colocation data centers supported multiple customers. Both of these examples offered access controls designed to isolate individual tenants, but the risk remains that another tenant could breach the security controls and gain access to physical offices or computer systems belonging to other tenants. Both the provider and the tenant share responsibility for implementing, enforcing, and monitoring controls that address these unique risks in a multitenant environment.

In a cloud computing environment, the separation between tenants can be purely logical, unlike a colocation facility where physically separate server racks are provisioned for different customers. The vendor provides some basic security services, as well as maintenance and other services. Tenant partitioning is typically achieved through the use of access controls in the virtualized environment. Each tenant is able to access their own virtualized resources, but not the resources of other tenants.

Data that is placed into the shared environment is still the responsibility of the cloud customer. Compensating controls like encryption can be used to mitigate the risk of another tenant gaining access to your organization's virtual resources. Additional access monitoring and robust IAM tools provide additional mitigation of this multitenant risk.

In a physical business center, if you lock up your servers and all of your data but leave the keys in a desk drawer or with the business center owner, security is lessened. In the same way, the security provided by encryption is improved if the customer securely maintains their own encryption keys external to the cloud vendor. A well-architected encryption implementation can render attacks against physical hardware or hypervisors less effective, as the attacker gains access to encrypted data but not the keys needed to read it.

Access Control

When creating a logical data center, controlling access is a primary concern. A single point of access makes access control simpler and facilitates monitoring, but any single point can become a failure point as well. If you have a physical data center with multiple doors and windows, securing the data center is more difficult, and this is no different in a logical data center. However, having only a single door with no emergency exits is a recipe for disaster in the event the primary door is inaccessible.

One method of access control is to federate a customer's existing IAM system with the customer's cloud resources. Depending on the sophistication of the customer's IAM and their chosen CSP, this can be a simple and secure way to extend existing IAM policies and tools to new cloud services. This choice allows the customer to control access more directly, and it simplifies oversight into what users have access to and how they are using that access. Many cloud services also offer other options for existing IAM solutions, such as SAML integration that allows per-system integration with an IAM tool rather than full federation.

Another method to prevent cross-connection between cloud and on-premises resources is to use identity as a service (IDaaS) to provide access to a company's cloud services. Gartner refers to this as SaaS-provided IAM or simply SaaS IAM. An IDaaS solution has the benefit of providing a service that is tailored to cloud resources and services, and many IDaaS solutions are adding features that allow integration into legacy environments for organizations that have on-premises infrastructure that is still in use. A SaaS IAM may be included with another CSP service, such as Login With Google as part of Google Workspace SaaS tools, or it may be a stand-alone SaaS tool itself.

Regardless of whether a customer's current IAM system can be used, a well-educated workforce is a critical part of any access control system. Users who understand the fundamentals of access security, such as long passphrases and never reusing passphrases, are a critical element in preventing unauthorized access. This vital line of defense is best built by offering security training and reinforcing best practices through awareness materials.

Physical Design

Physical design is the responsibility of the owner of the cloud data center. This is generally the cloud vendor or CSP. Physical design considerations are the same as for on-premises data centers, but the CSP's task is generally more complex due to the size and requirement for multitenant access.

Location

Physical siting of a data center can limit some risks related to disasters or disruptions. Areas commonly impacted by natural disasters, civil unrest, utility interruptions, or similar problems should be avoided if possible. This is not always a possibility, as many large population centers are also located in areas prone to earthquakes, tornadoes, wildfires, etc. Despite these risks, organizations and people still expect access to services, so cloud data center designers must find ways to mitigate these risks while also locating data centers in areas close to their customers.

Multiple locations for data centers are a recommendation when designing an on-premises data center but can be so costly that organizations do not utilize them. Because of the size and scale of operations a CSP is likely to run, multiple data centers are a cost-effective way to mitigate risks related to disasters. No location is immune to all disasters, so locations that have different disaster risk profiles will increase the availability of cloud resources. The location should also have stable power/utilities and access to multiple communication paths when possible.

Buy or Build

Many business decisions come down to a fundamental question: is it better to build something custom to the organization or buy something premade by another organization? Build to suit is generally more expensive but allows the organization to build exactly what is needed, whether it is a data center, headquarters building, or even software. By contrast, buying a ready-made facility or commercial software is usually cheaper but may not meet all the organization's needs.

Most cloud customers have made the decision to buy their cloud services instead of building their own on-premises data centers and IT service components. If the cost savings generated by cloud services are greater than the costs associated with data security and regulatory compliance, then cloud computing is a sound business decision. If public cloud options are inadequate for the data sensitivity, then a private or community cloud might be a middle-ground option.

CSPs building public clouds generally opt to build data center facilities due to the scale of their operations. When considering a single data center, build versus buy is a legitimate concern, but finding existing facilities to build a global network of cloud computing data centers is unlikely. Community or private clouds may be hosted out of an existing data center or colocation facility due to cost savings of sharing some infrastructure with other tenants. Ultimately, the build-versus-buy decision requires well-documented requirements and a decision process designed to identify whether any existing facilities exist and can be purchased. If existing facilities do not exist or do not meet the organization's needs, then buying is the best course of action.

Environmental Design

The environmental design, like the physical location of a data center, is the responsibility of the CSP or cloud vendor, with the exception of the private cloud deployment model. Environmental design primarily impacts the availability of cloud resources, such as adequate cooling necessary to keep electrical equipment running. For the cloud customer, reviewing the basic design of a vendor or CSP's environmental controls can be part of the risk analysis of the vendor. Similar to physical security controls, this review may not be performed in person, instead relying on a third-party audit of the CSP's environmental design.

Environmental design is in many cases concerned with utility services needed to keep computing equipment running, as well as providing for habitation by support staff. This includes electricity needed to power the hardware comprising the cloud, as well as lighting needed by support personnel working in the facility. Some data centers will make use of water for cooling, while others will use air handling to provide cooling for electronics. These are also required by human occupants of the building, and guarding against leaks is a primary concern where water is needed for human occupancy but could cause damage to electrical equipment.

Heating, Ventilation, and Air Conditioning

Appropriate heating, ventilation, and air conditioning (HVAC) support is a requirement for data centers that provide cloud computing services. HVAC concerns will be dependent on the physical location and construction of the facility. A facility in Canada, which has very cold temperatures, will need to consider heating and ventilation more carefully than air conditioning (AC). Similarly, a data center near the equator will have greater concerns for cooling and will likely require more robust AC. Environmental concerns may even be a key consideration for the physical location of a facility—several major CSPs have placed data centers in locations with naturally cold climates, where cold outside air can be used without the need for additional cooling or refrigeration.

HVAC needs should be well understood and used as a requirement when choosing the site for CSPs building a data center or for customers reviewing potential cloud vendors. An HVAC failure can reduce the availability of computing resources much the same as an electrical or communication disruption. Because of the importance of HVAC in a CSP data center, customer reviews of the CSP should include the adequacy and redundancy of HVAC systems. In the event of an environmental failure, moving systems between data centers is possible if an application has been properly architected. This can provide a compensating control if a CSP's HVAC capacity is insufficient or suffers an outage.

A number of documents can help assess HVAC concerns. If a CSP has a SOC-2 Type II report with a review of the availability criteria, the report should contain details about the configuration and redundancy of HVAC systems. Because of the confidential nature of information contained in a SOC 2 Type II, most CSPs will require a nondisclosure agreement

(NDA) prior to sharing. A routine review of the most current SOC 2 report is a critical part of a cloud customer's due diligence for their cloud service vendor. Other documents that may assist in determining a CSP's environmental design sufficiency would be business continuity and disaster recovery plans.

Multivendor Pathway Connectivity

Connectivity is critical in a cloud computing environment. The ability for a customer to remain connected to cloud resources requires planning, and the network-accessible nature of cloud services makes communication pathways a potential single point of failure (SPOF). While it is not a perfect network, the Internet rarely suffers complete failures, so in most cases a network issue is likely caused by the CSP or cloud customer's network service provider. Network connectivity provided by multiple vendors is a proactive way to mitigate the risk of losing network connectivity.

The cloud customer should consider multiple paths for communicating with their cloud vendor. In an era of an increasingly dispersed workforce, often working from locations separate from the business network, strategies to keep the workforce connected to the Internet and the cloud vendors must be developed and tested.

In a legacy on-premises network, this often required the organization to acquire network connectivity from multiple Internet service providers (ISPs), but the network-accessible characteristic of cloud computing has made this task easier. A system that users access from their workstations over the Internet can just as easily be accessed by users working from home. If a facility loses connectivity, users may be able to simply work from home. This can even be used for higher-security environments, such as those that require a VPN; as long as users can access the Internet, they can still access the cloud services.

Cloud providers must also deploy strategies that support multiple connectivity options. If the CSP cannot access the Internet, then all customers will be blocked from accessing their cloud services, leading to a denial of service. Best practice for CSPs or data centers is dual-entry, dual-provider for high availability. Physically separated cabling, providing connectivity to two or more ISPs, should enter the facility in two physically separated locations. This way if one vendor loses connectivity, the data center is still reachable, and if an accident affects one side of the building, the facility still has network connectivity from another location.

Design Resilient

Resilient designs are engineered to respond positively to changes or disturbances, such as natural disasters or man-made disturbances. A data center that loses connectivity each time a rainstorm happens is not resilient, while a data center designed with local weather conditions in mind will be able to withstand storms and continue providing service even when severe weather occurs. A-frame chalets are an example of resilient design: in areas of heavy snowfall a flat roof accumulates snow and will eventually collapse under the weight. A pitched roof allows gravity to pull the snow down without causing the roof to collapse, ensuring that the structure can withstand the anticipated weather conditions.

Data center and office facility designs can be made without considering local conditions. While functional, these structures will require additional maintenance and may be rendered unusable in the event of severe weather or man-made disasters. Resilient-design buildings adopt construction principles that make them less likely to be severely damaged or unusable. This includes locating critical systems like HVAC and electrical in areas where they will not be damaged by anticipated disasters such as flooding.

In 2012 Hurricane Sandy caused significant damage to the East Coast of the United States, and many buildings in New York City lost both primary power and backup power due to flooding. Backup generators used to provide emergency power were located in the basements of buildings, and floodwaters caused by the hurricane naturally gathered in these basements because they were below ground level—generators with combustion engines require oxygen and generally do not work underwater. A resilient design should take into account the likelihood of flooding and either locate backup generators away from likely flood areas or provide a method of preventing floodwater from submerging the generators.

Resilient design takes into account multiple physical and environment aspects, including electrical power, HVAC, human occupation, and design practices like natural heating and cooling alternatives that minimize reliance on electric-powered HVAC. These principles can be applied at a single building, at a community scale, or even at a regional scale. The Resilient Design Institute publishes strategies and principles for resilient design; more information can be found at resilientdesign.org.

Analyze Risks Associated with Cloud Infrastructure and Platforms

All data centers have risk, whether they are organization-controlled, provided by a colocation facility, or hosted by a CSP. Organizations moving from on-premises to cloud hosting must properly consider risks associated with such a move, and organizations that are cloud-native must ensure that they implement risk assessment and management strategies that account for the unique circumstances of cloud infrastructure. Utilizing cloud-based resources is no less risky than hosting your own infrastructure, but with proper controls in place and a thorough cost-benefit analysis, organizations can find both cost savings and increased security in the cloud. For many organizations, a hybrid environment is likely the best solution, as it provides greater control over high-value assets while also providing cost savings.

Risk Assessment

The process of risk management is fundamental to information security, since the entire practice involves mitigating and managing risks to data and information systems. Cloud-based systems can pose a challenge to risk management for a variety of reasons. Many organizations assume that the CSP is in charge of all security concerns and that customers have no responsibility.

This is untrue, as demonstrated by the explicit shared responsibility guidance published by most CSPs—they are responsible for some things like physical and environmental, but the customer ultimately owns the risk to their data and must manage it accordingly. Doing so can pose another challenge, as cloud providers are third-party vendors to most organizations. Assessing and mitigating risks posed by third parties requires modified risk management practices, and the customer must also be proactive in addressing their assignments under the shared responsibility model.

Identification

Identifying risks is the first step in managing them. Many risk management frameworks follow an asset-based approach, which begins with the organization identifying its critical assets. The definition of an asset can vary by organization, but in general an asset is anything essential to or deemed valuable by the organization, such as computer hardware, data, people, business processes, critical suppliers and vendors, and the like. These assets should be documented in an inventory.

Once assets are identified, security practitioners and risk managers can then begin to identify potential causes of disruption to the assets. This can be done as a brainstorming activity, with participants asking "What could go wrong?" Any event that could disrupt the confidentiality, integrity, or availability of data and systems is a potential risk, and risks can be categorized by their source, such as deliberate man-made, natural disasters, and errors or omissions.

Several risk frameworks exist that provide processes and procedures for designing and implementing a risk management framework. This includes the process of inventorying assets and identifying risks. Example risk frameworks include the ISO/EC 31000:2018, *Risk Management*; NIST SP 800-37, *Guide for Applying the Risk Management Framework to Federal Information Systems;* and IT governance frameworks like COBIT. These frameworks provide a structured methodology for risk management, as well as libraries of common risks and threats to help first-time assessors.

Risks specific to cloud environments should be identified when making the decision to use a cloud service. As previously discussed, some common risks include giving up physical control over the infrastructure used to process your data, and the possibility of less customization available when using SaaS. These risks should be monitored over the lifetime of the cloud service; if the risks change significantly, it might be necessary to move to an alternative CSP or bring the system back to on-premises hosting.

Analysis

Analyzing identified risks continues the conversation started by "What could go wrong?" and seeks to answer two questions: "What will the impact be if that goes wrong, and how likely is it to happen?" Risks are typically measured by these two criteria: likelihood of occurrence and impact to the organization.

For example, a transient network outage is highly likely, as most networks experience minor issues that can disrupt traffic. The impact will be determined by the importance of what that outage disrupts: users checking routine emails will be able to continue work until the network is restored. The impact to an emergency call center that relies on network connectivity for calls is higher, as people will be blocked from accessing critical resources. Risk management decisions will be based on these measurements—the email users do not require an expensive, high-availability network, but that mitigation would be justified for the call center.

Analysis of a CSP or cloud solution and the associated risks involves many departments. These include business units, vendor management, privacy, and information security. The new risks with a cloud solution are mostly associated with privacy and information security, though operational concerns should also be addressed. There are some key issues when conducting a risk assessment for a CSP or cloud solution.

One risk to address is authentication. Will the cloud solution provide authentication services, or is the customer responsible for providing that solution? Using the CSP's authentication solution may be simpler for operations, but the organization is giving up control over a key piece of its access management capability, including configuration choices and monitoring capabilities.

If the customer provides their own IAM system, it may be accomplished through a SaaS IAM solution or through federation with the customer's on-premises IAM manager. Each solution has pros and cons. For example, a SaaS IAM system is most likely designed specifically for the cloud, since it is a cloud-based platform itself. This can mean easier integration with disparate cloud service providers but again involves giving up control of a key system to a service provider. Federating an on-premises IAM with the cloud provides more control for the customer but can introduce compatibility issues for legacy IAM systems that are not cloud-native. Operationally, the cost of running the IAM must also be considered, and a SaaS IAM may get support from the finance team since it has cost advantages compared to on-premises infrastructure.

Data security is always a concern when utilizing a third-party service provider. How a vendor encrypts data at rest is important, including the strength of the cryptography used and access controls that prevent unauthorized access by cloud service personnel or other tenants. Security of the data in transit between the organization and the CSP is also critical. In addition, the vendor's third parties can introduce additional risk, so adequate supply chain risk management (SCRM) is required. Data remains the responsibility of the customer even when stored on a vendor's system.

Assessing risks posed by a vendor's policies and processes is a crucial part of SCRM. This include the vendor's privacy policy, incident response process, cookie policies, information security policy, etc. You are no longer assessing only your organizational policies but also the policies of the organizations with whom you are doing business, since they have access to your data and systems. For some key systems, it is important to assess the support provided for incident response. This includes an assessment of logging support, vulnerability scans of the vendor, application vulnerability scans, and external assessments of the vendor being considered or currently used.

Most CSPs do not allow direct auditing of their operations, due to the number of customers they support. Instead, they provide standardized reports and assurance material regarding their security practices, such as a SOC 2 report, ISO 27001 certification, and more specialized reports showing control in place for specific types of regulated data. These may include HIPAA for U.S. healthcare data; ISO 27017 and 27018, which deal specifically with cloud services and processing of PII in cloud computing; and FedRAMP for U.S. federal government cloud services. Reviewing these materials allows the organization to analyze the risk and effectiveness of any vendor-supplied controls.

Common Cloud Risks

One risk that has been discussed is the organization losing ownership and full control over system hardware assets. While this change can be difficult, with careful selection of CSPs and the development of SLAs and other contractual agreements, these concerns can be addressed. In addition, the service model used affects the amount of control that is retained, so the organization may be able to balance cost savings with risk by building a system on top of IaaS or PaaS, rather than utilizing a SaaS solution.

Regardless of which deployment or service model is used, there are some risks that are common to all cloud computing environments. These risks, and common mitigation strategies, can include the following:

- **Geographic dispersion of the CSP data centers:** The disaster risk profile may be unknown to the customer and may be very different from their own. For example, the CSP data center may be in an area subject to hurricanes, while the customer is not. If the cloud service is properly architected, a disruption at one data center should not cause a complete outage, and it is incumbent on the customer to verify the resilience and continuity controls in place at the CSP.

- **Downtime:** CSPs must be network accessible in order for customers to utilize the service. Resilience for network disruptions can be built in multiple ways, such as multivendor connectivity to individual data centers, and the availability of multiple regions or zones should a data center suffer an outage.

- **Compliance:** Some data types are regulated, and the use of cloud services can be problematic. For example, privacy data in some jurisdictions cannot be transferred to other countries, so a cloud solution with globally distributed data centers is not appropriate for that type of data. Major CSPs have compliance-focused service offerings, and some cloud services can be architected to avoid issues like transfer of data outside specific geographies.

- **General technology risk:** Cloud systems are not immune to standard security issues like system abuse or cyberattacks. CSPs can be large and attractive targets to attackers due to the ability to cause significant damage to a wide number of organizations that utilize the cloud. The CSP's cyber defenses should be documented and tested, and customers should require details of these activities in the form of audits and reports from activities like penetration testing or red team exercises.

Cloud Vulnerabilities, Threats, and Attacks

The primary vulnerability in the cloud is that it is an Internet-based model. Anyone with access to the Internet has the potential to attack your CSP, your cloud provider, or you. Even organizations that deploy their own connectivity to a cloud provider could be at risk if the

CSP's public-facing infrastructure comes under attack. A private cloud is unlikely to face such an attack, but this protection comes at higher cost than public cloud services.

Any attack on your CSP or cloud vendor may be unrelated to you as an organization, so typical threats considered when assessing risks may not be adequate to address the threat model of a cloud environment. Threat actors may be targeting the CSP or another tenant of the CSP, or the CSP might be vulnerable to location-based threats due to weather or geological conditions in another part of the world. Customers of the CSP may simply be collateral damage; a denial-of-service attack against the CSP becomes an attack against all the cloud customers as well.

Risks can come from the other tenants as well. If protections keeping customer data separate fail, your data may be exposed to another tenant, who could be a competitor or bad actor. Even if the data exposed is not used maliciously, it is still a breach and may trigger legal or regulatory issues. Encryption is the best protection, with customer-managed keys that make any exposed data worthless to outsiders. The customer may also consider not storing their most sensitive data in the cloud, and a hybrid cloud approach with data stored in public cloud platforms can be an effective mitigation.

There can be an additional risk from the cloud vendor. Employees of cloud vendors have been known to exfiltrate customer data for their own purposes. Contractual language may provide the only remedy should this occur, though CSPs do design their services to minimize these risks—otherwise no customers would trust them with sensitive data or systems. Prevention becomes the best defense. As with other tenants, encryption with the customer managing their own keys (separate from the cloud) prevents data exposure.

The Cloud Security Alliance publishes the "Egregious 11: Top Threats to Cloud Computing." This is a list of common threats and risks to cloud computing, as well as recommended mitigation strategies that cloud customers can implement.
The full list is available here: `cloudsecurityalliance.org/artifacts/`
`top-threats-to-cloud-computing-egregious-eleven.`

Risk Mitigation Strategies

There are several approaches to risk mitigation in cloud environments. The start of security is with the selection of a CSP, and a set of documented requirements and comparison of CSP offerings against those requirements is a key due diligence activity. Choosing a CSP that is incapable of meeting the organization's security and operational needs is inherently risky, so selecting a qualified CSP is an essential first step.

Once the CSP is selected, the next step is designing and architecting systems and services. Security should be considered at every step and designed in from the beginning. CSPs offer a wide range of services, so well-documented requirements can once again be useful. If encryption of data at rest is important, then the customer must choose a cloud storage offering with adequate encryption capabilities to start with and then properly configure the service to meet the organization's needs.

The next risk mitigation tool is encryption, which is an essential countermeasure for data security when, as is the case in cloud computing, data is outside the organization's control. Encryption should be enabled for all data at rest and data in motion. Most CSP offerings include encryption service; depending on the type of service, there may be some configuration action required by the customer. Data in transit must be protected using TLS, IP security

(IPSec), VPNs, or another encrypted transmission method, while data at rest can often be encrypted by the CSP's storage platforms using customer-controlled keys. In addition, limiting the ingress/egress points in each cloud service can provide monitoring capabilities to ensure that data security measures are adequately applied.

Each major CSP provides the ability to manage your secure configuration, monitor changes to cloud services, and track usage. For example, AWS provides Inspector, Cloud-Watch, CloudTrail, and other tools to assist your management of your cloud environment. However, just like other tools, it is incumbent on the customer to properly use them for implementation and monitoring of security. If you log all system activity but never review it, then suspicious activity will go unnoticed.

Plan and Implementation of Security Controls

The risks associated with cloud computing can be mitigated with the proper selection of controls. This is the same approach used in traditional risk management tailored to the risks associated with cloud computing. Some controls will be designed to compensate for the loss of direct control when using cloud computing, while others will be similar to the measures used for managing risk throughout a supply chain. In both cases, the organization is giving up some direct involvement in return for cost savings and other operational efficiency, so the security program must ensure that these business benefits are not outweighed by security risks.

Physical and Environmental Protection

The location housing the physical servers in a cloud environment must ensure adequate protection against physical threats, like natural disasters, as well as provide necessary environmental controls to ensure that systems remain operational, such as power and HVAC. These controls are usually the purview of the CSP, meaning that a third party is responsible for them, though in a community or private cloud delivery model the organization consuming cloud services may have responsibility.

The primary consideration is the site location, as it will have an impact on both physical and environmental protections. A data center along the waterfront in an area subject to regular hurricanes or flooding is likely to be routinely damaged by these threats. If possible, a less susceptible location should be chosen; otherwise, additional locations and redundant system architecture may be required. For large CSPs, this risk is easily compensated for; the globally dispersed network of data centers utilized by a modern CSP results in data centers that are unlikely to be affected by the same threats.

Once facilities are constructed, there are additional physical and environmental requirements that must be addressed. Cloud data centers share requirements with traditional colocation providers or individual data centers. These include the ability to restrict physical access at multiple points, ensuring a clean and stable power supply, adequate utilities like water and sewer, and the availability of an adequate workforce.

A cloud data center also has significant network capability requirements. All data centers require network capabilities, but a CSP typically serves more customers than other data centers. More than one ISP and redundant cabling into the facility may improve the reliability of connectivity.

The customer has no control over the physical location of a cloud data center, except for a private or community cloud where the customer is also a service provider. Customers of public clouds do have some control over where their data is stored and processed, as most CSPs offer services that can be restricted by geography. To the extent possible, the customer should review the location of cloud data centers and be aware of the cloud vendor's business continuity and disaster recovery plans, as a CSP outage will lead to a loss of system availability. The ability of the cloud vendor or CSP to respond to disasters directly affects the ability of the cloud customer to serve their customers. Ensuring that cloud applications are properly architected to be resilient against loss of a single cloud data center is also an effective control against physical and environmental risks.

System, Storage, and Communication Protection

Properly securing information systems can be a difficult task due to the sheer number of elements that make up a system. Breaking systems down into components and applying security controls at this level can make the overall task more manageable. Information systems commonly comprise processes and operational technology like servers and applications, storage media where data resides, and communication pathways used to place information into the system and retrieve it when needed.

One source for controls is NIST Special Publication 800-53, "Security and Privacy Controls or Information Systems and Organizations," which contains a family of controls specific to systems and communications. Section 3.18, "System and Communications Protection (SC)," is a comprehensive set of guidelines for addressing system- and communications-specific risks, and similar controls can be found in ISO and other control frameworks. The NIST SC control family includes 51 specific controls, including the following:

- **Policy and Procedures:** This is a primary control, as policies and procedures serve as a foundation and guide to other security activities. They establish requirements for system protection, and define the purpose, scope, roles, and responsibilities needed to achieve it.

- **Separation of System and User Functionality:** This is a core control. Separation of duties is a fundamental security principle, and separating system administration functions from regular end user functions can prevent users from altering and misconfiguring systems and communication processes.

- **Security Function Isolation:** Separating security-specific functions from other roles is another example of separation of duties. Security functions can include configuring data security controls like encryption and logging configuration, as well as separate hardware-based security modules for high-security systems.

- **Denial-of-Service Protection:** A DOS attack is a threat to all information systems and specifically those that rely on network connectivity as cloud services do. Preventing a DOS attack involves dealing with bandwidth and capacity issues and detecting attacks. Most CSPs offer DOS mitigation as a service, and there are also dedicated providers like Akamai and Cloudflare.

- **Boundary Protection:** This control deals with both ingress and egress protections. This includes preventing malicious traffic from entering the network, as well as preventing malicious traffic from leaving your network, protecting against data loss (exfiltration), and applying protection mechanisms like routers, gateways, or firewalls to isolate sensitive system components.

- **Cryptographic Key Establishment and Management:** Cryptography provides a number of security functions including confidentiality, integrity, and nonrepudiation. Ensuring that keys are securely generated, stored, distributed, and destroyed is crucial, especially in cloud environments where physical control is lost over storage media and information system components.

Cloud computing has a shared security model, and which controls are the responsibility of the CSP and which are the responsibility of the customer should be carefully reviewed and understood. For example, the CSP should have a strategy to maintain service availability in the event of a DOS attack, but organizations can also choose services or architect applications to utilize an alternate cloud region or CSP if one is not available.

The cloud customer can also implement controls for system and communication protection, like redundant connectivity in the event of a network outage. This can be achieved via multiple ISPs serving an office building, or users might be assigned cellular hot spots that can be used when wired communications are unavailable. In addition to availability considerations, data confidentiality and integrity in transit must be addressed. Encryption tools like TLS or a VPN can be used to provide confidentiality. Hashing can be implemented to detect unintentional data modifications, and additional security measures like digital signatures or hash-based message authentication code (HMAC) can be used to detect intentional tampering.

Protection of business data remains a critical issue, and since data spends a significant amount of time on storage media, this is a crucial area of focus. Encryption is, once again, a primary method of providing security for data at rest and is also a key area of shared responsibility. The CSP is responsible for maintaining adequate hardware security as well as configuring storage media to utilize encryption.

Cloud customers must choose and configure storage solutions to meet their needs, such as disabling public access to cloud storage. For added protection, client-controlled encryption may be used, and this requires the customer to securely provision, store, and manage encryption keys. Public cloud storage may be inappropriate for very high-security systems or highly sensitive data, so architecting a hybrid cloud with private data storage can be a viable option.

Identification, Authentication, and Authorization in Cloud Environments

Organizations with existing IAM solutions may choose to extend those solutions to newly acquired cloud systems. Organizations may also choose to acquire a SaaS IAM, sometimes known as identity as a service (IDaaS), and this is appropriate for organizations making a clean start with cloud computing services rather than migrating. This is a business decision that must account for existing technology, future growth, and the availability of adequate solutions that meet the organization's needs.

Some CSPs offer their own IAM solution that integrates with other services offered by the CSP. This includes AWS IAM for AWS cloud environments, and Azure AD in the Microsoft Azure cloud. Use of these solutions is simple if all cloud services are running in the respective CSP's environment, but they may be less optimized for other services. The decision to use such an IAM should balance the benefits of efficiency with potential risks like vendor lock-in, single point of failure if all critical services are in the same CSP, and the security capabilities of the CSP's IAM solution.

IAM practices can be generally described by the acronym IAAA, which stands for Identification, Authentication, Authorization, and Accountability. IAM systems should provide capabilities in each of these areas, and some cloud-specific considerations for each are as follows:

- **Identification:** Users assert an identity by providing something unique, such as a username or employee ID number. An organization with different IAM solutions for cloud and on-premises environments may face difficulty with visibility into user activity but may also encounter compatibility issues between legacy on-premises IAM and cloud environments. Modern IDaaS tools were built with broad compatibility in mind, and they may provide the best solution to bridge on-premises and cloud.

- **Authentication:** Users must prove the identity they assert, typically by providing authentication material like a password, PIN, or biometric scan. Common authentication material like passwords can be managed with an IAM solution, and additional security options like multifactor authentication (MFA) should be considered where additional security is required. IDaaS providers offer MFA solutions like smartphone apps that generate MFA codes from Microsoft, Okta, and Google.

- **Authorization:** Users who are successfully identified and authenticated are granted access to the resources for which they are authorized. Managing authorization across cloud systems can be challenging as different clouds will implement different permission models and require unique administration. For example, an organization that utilizes Google Workspace for collaboration, Dropbox for file sharing, and Salesforce for customer management will need to administer user authorization in three separate tools. Solutions like a cloud access security broker (CASB) can be implemented to centralize this control and provide a meta later for administering user access that is automatically configured on various target services by the CASB.

- **Accountability:** Users who take action on a system are held accountable for following policies and procedures. Accountability is typically enforced with adequate logging and monitoring of system activity, which is covered in a later section on audit mechanisms.

In any IAM deployment, user education is important. End users often take actions that can weaken IAM controls, such as reusing or sharing passwords. An employee may use the same username and password on all work-based systems. If a vendor or CSP system is compromised, then other corporate systems will be similarly compromised since attackers have valid access credentials. The cloud vendor may not notify you of a compromise of the IAM for an extended period of time, if they are even aware of a compromise. This puts your business systems at further risk.

Cloud applications and platforms are, by definition, accessible from anywhere. While this supports a globally distributed workforce, it can also make identifying suspicious user behavior more challenging. In a legacy environment all users access an application hosted in a data center from their workstations in an organization-controlled facility, but a cloud-based SaaS application can have users logging in from various countries as they travel. This makes it more difficult to identify potentially malicious behavior, since a user logging in from a different country is no longer inherently suspicious activity.

More flexible authentication capabilities provide one answer to these challenges. For example, users who log in every day from the same IP address and browser are likely authentic, correctly authorized users. By contrast, a user who logs in from Argentina one day, China the next day, and Canada the day after could be a traveling salesperson, or it could indicate a user whose credentials have been stolen, and attackers are attempting to use the stolen credentials from various countries. Conditional authentication policies, such as requiring MFA when a user logs in from a different country or workstation, are a common feature of cloud computing platforms. They strike a balance between usability and security; requiring MFA at every login is an inconvenience to users, but it is warranted for users whose activity is highly irregular.

Audit Mechanisms

It can be more difficult to audit systems and the processes of a CSP, just as with any vendor that is outside the organization's direct control. A customer will not have broad access to the physical security of cloud data centers, vendor networks, or activity logs maintained by the CSP. This is due to both logistics and the presence of other tenants. Most CSPs have a number of data centers that are geographically dispersed and hundreds or thousands of customers. The logistics of customers performing physical security control audits make the practice virtually impossible, and similar challenges exist when performing system or network audits.

Broad access to the vendor network is also a security risk. If you have access to the network, you may intercept privileged information belonging to another customer, violating the boundaries needed in a multitenant environment. If the CSP provides one organization with access to data that violates these boundaries, other organizations will trust the CSP less with their sensitive data.

Some cloud services provide access to log data, some do not provide access, and many provide limited access to organization-specific data that does not violate the confidentiality of other tenants. These limited logs can be useful but may not provide all the needed details if a security incident occurs. Different service models will provide different levels of logging ability; for example, IaaS allows the customer to build virtually all the logging infrastructure they need, while SaaS logs may only provide information about user actions and customer-specific application details like patch deployments.

Log Collection

One common problem with logs is the volume of data collected in logs. Setting thresholds is important to ensure that only relevant events are captured, which can cut down on the over-whelming amount of data. Cloud services will offer different controls over what information is logged, but at a minimum security-relevant events such as the use of or changes to privileged accounts should be logged.

Unusual system activity should also be logged, but this will be very organization-specific since normal activity varies across organizations. Determining events to be logged can be difficult, but there are resources that provide useful guidance. NIST SP 800-53 contains a family of controls related to audit logs, and specific controls like AU-3 provide guidance on specific information to capture in audit records. OWASP also has a cheat sheet for logging that is generally applicable to any system, though it is focused on application-level logging. It can be useful as a guide when configuring SaaS logging capabilities and is found here: cheatsheetseries.owasp.org/cheatsheets/Logging_Cheat_Sheet.html.

A log aggregator can ingest the logs from all the on-premises and cloud resources for review in the SOC. These logs must be monitored daily with privileged account alerts getting immediate attention. If not reviewed, logs become much less valuable. Log collection will remain valuable for incident response and audit purposes. But without regular and consistent log review, the value of log collection is not fully realized.

Correlation

Log data is generated to provide an account of past activity. Log data generated across multiple systems, such as an IAM platform, user workstation, and various cloud applications, can make it difficult to find relationships due to the volume of data. *Correlation* refers to the ability to discover relationships between two or more events. Data points in logs can be correlated to gain important insight into system activity, such as establishing a baseline of normal activity and detecting anomalous events.

A user logging into their workstation at a normal time of day—during regular business hours—and accessing a cloud-based webmail client is a normal event. That same user logging in from a mobile device in a different country might be normal, if the user frequently travels, or it might indicate that the user's credentials were compromised. Correlating the information in logs, such as baseline normal activity and other user activity, can allow for the detection of potential security incidents.

Log centralizations, correlation, and other activities like detection and alerting are often performed by a security information and event management (SIEM) platform. These tools and capabilities are discussed in more detail in Domain 5, "Cloud Security Operations."

Packet Capture

Packet capture, sometimes shortened to *pcap*, refers to the capture of network communication packets. These can be used to monitor activity on a network, detect malicious network activity like data exfiltration, and can be useful in detecting certain types of network attacks like worms propagating between systems. Packet capture can be performed by running applications like Wireshark on a computer attached to a network or by copying data that is sent through a network device like a router or switch.

Since cloud environments are broadly network accessible and are maintained by third parties, packet capture can be difficult or impossible. If users are not connected to a centrally managed network, then packets sent between their workstations and the cloud are difficult to capture without specialized software running on the device they are using. Similarly, the cloud environment may not provide any facility for capturing packets. This is often the case with SaaS applications that run in a web browser; the user's network traffic is encrypted from their workstation to the CSP's network; even if the packets are captured, the data is encrypted and essentially worthless for monitoring purposes.

If packet capture is necessary in a system, some CSPs provide tools that allow packet capture functionality to a limited degree. If a customer is utilizing a hybrid cloud or mix of on-premises and cloud systems, packet capture is possible in customer-controlled networks. To achieve the same functionality in a CSP's public cloud, tools such as the following might be used:

- Amazon provides AWS VPC Traffic Monitoring. This tool allows a customer to mirror the traffic of any AWS network interface in a VPC they have created and to capture that traffic for analysis by the customer's security team. This can be done directly in AWS using CloudShark to perform network analysis on the packet capture. This tool creates what is essentially a virtual network tap, and it is able to capture all network traffic in the customer's virtual private cloud. Non-VPC traffic cannot be monitored, as this could lead to a breach of other tenants' data.

- Microsoft provides a similar capability with Azure Network Watcher. This tool allows packet capture of traffic to and from a customer's VMs. Packet capture can be started in a number of ways. This toolset also allows for packet capture to be automatically triggered by certain conditions, reducing the amount of noise that investigators must navigate.

The specific tools available and the use of these tools will change over time. For security purposes, the ability to capture packets in the cloud services used by the customer can be important. This is a requirement that the security team should thoroughly document prior to a cloud migration, and the organization should evaluate cloud services to ensure that they meet these needs.

Plan Disaster Recovery and Business Continuity

The cloud has transformed both disaster recovery (DR) and business continuity (BC) by providing the ability to easily and cost-effectively operate in geographically distant locations and by providing greater hardware and data redundancy. All of this leads to lower recovery time objectives (RTOs) and recovery point objectives (RPOs) at price points organizations could not achieve previously. While DR and BC are still important, this change has also enabled organizations to plan for cyber resilience in new ways—rather than making plans for what happens if a data center is destroyed, cloud applications can be architected to remain online even if multiple data centers, system components, or network segments fail.

Business Continuity/Disaster Recovery Strategy

Business continuity planning is concerned with ensuring that the organization is able to continue functioning after an adverse event has occurred. The result of the planning process is a business continuity plan (BCP), sometimes called a continuity of operations plan (COOP). This is a proactive risk mitigation strategy, as the BCP contains likely scenarios that could affect the organization and provides guidance on how the organization should respond.

Not all the processes an organization executes will be covered in a BCP or COOP. Some processes are essential to the organization's continued functioning, such as the ability to handle payments or communicate critical information to employees, while others can be considered "nice to have," such as internal communications about company social events. The business impact assessment (BIA) is used to determine which processes are critical and which are not. The impact of specific systems and processes is measured by the BIA, and any that are deemed critical to the organization's functioning must be prioritized in an emergency situation.

For example, many financial services firms are required to plan for pandemic readiness assuming that some percentage of staff are not available due to illness and that even healthy staff may be restricted from working in the office to contain the pandemic spread. In a scenario like this, the organization must have adequate remote work capabilities, such as a VPN, and necessary supplies for workers to utilize when working remotely. This ensures that critical functions of the firm, such as handling financial transactions, can continue even with reduced staffing levels. Cloud services can be easily integrated into this plan, as the broad network accessibility they provide means that workers can easily log in and work from any location.

Other common BCP scenarios include risks like natural disasters, loss of utilities, and civil unrest or war. If needed, the BCP is activated by formal declaration of a disaster, and the organization switches into contingency operation mode following the guidelines established in the BCP. The goal of the BCP is to maintain critical business processes and operations, which may involve alternate work locations, alternative business processes, or even the use of cloud environments in place of on-premises data centers if those facilities are unusable.

While a BCP keeps business operations going after a disaster, the DRP works on returning business operations to normal. Not all incidents will require the activation of both plans. A major ISP failure might activate the BCP and send workers to an alternate building while the ISP restores the connectivity. In contrast, a natural disaster like a tornado that destroys an office or data center will require activation of both the BCP and DRP.

If a tornado renders a primary data center unusable, procedures in the BCP are used to handle shifting to an alternate processing facility, such as temporary use of cloud computing. The DRP is activated to handle the process of cleaning up and restoring or replacing the destroyed facility. DRP operations are concluded when the infrastructure and facilities are returned to their normal, operational state; the BCP operations are concluded when the organization's processes return to the pre-incident state using the restored or rebuilt infrastructure.

A cloud data center that is affected by a natural disaster will likely activate multiple BCPs and DRPs. The cloud provider will obviously activate both plans to deal with the interruption to their service; one key element of the BCP is communicating incident status to relevant parties. In this case, the CSP must communicate to all customers impacted by the incident. In turn, the customers may activate their BCPs or DRPs as needed to handle the interruption to their services, such as migrating applications to another cloud region or possibly even another CSP for the duration of the outage.

The cloud supports the BCP/DRP strategy. The high availability of cloud services provides strong business continuity and can serve as a core part of an organization's BCP strategy. In effect, the cloud allows the business to continue regardless of disasters affecting the customer's business facilities. The high availability of cloud services also impacts DRP strategy, as the cloud can provide resilient services at cost-effective price points. Customers may focus more on resilient services that survive a disaster rather than processes to recover from disasters. As always when discussing security, BC and DR strategies should always prioritize the life, health, and safety of humans over systems and data.

The customer is responsible for determining how to recover in the case of a disaster and may choose to implement backups, or utilize multiple availability zones, load balancers, or other techniques to provide disaster recovery and resilience. A CSP can help support recovery objectives by not allowing a data center to have two availability zones. Otherwise, if you are using two zones and they are in the same data center, a single disaster can affect both availability zones. CSPs can also provide monitoring that can be used as an early warning system, such as a spike in traffic or utility issue that could lead to an incident. This gives any customers the ability to take preventative actions like shifting to other availability zones or activating alternate processes.

Business Requirements

Business-critical systems require more recoverability than is often possible with local resources and corporate data centers. Designing high availability or resilient systems in such an environment requires significant resources and is cost-prohibitive for many organizations.

Cloud computing provides options to support high availability, scalable computing, and reliable data retention and data storage at significantly reduced cost.

Although it is cheaper to build highly resilient systems in the cloud, there are still costs associated with such an architecture. To justify system and architecture resiliency decisions, there are three important metrics that the organization should consider. These metrics are outlined in the following sections, and include RTO, or how long are you down; RPO, or how much data may you lose; and recovery service level (RSL), which measures how much computing power (0 to 100 percent) is needed for production systems during a disaster. This does not usually include compute needs for development, test, or other environments, as these are usually nonessential environments during a disaster.

Recovery Time Objective

The amount of time the organization is willing to do without a system can be used to establish the recovery time objective (RTO). The organization may only be able to function for a matter of minutes without a mission-critical system, so adequate resources and designs must be implemented to ensure that disruptions are resolved swiftly. Such a system would have a very short RTO. Less critical systems, like email or collaboration tools, can go offline for hours or days before the organization suffers permanent harm, so these systems will have a longer RTO.

All systems should be categorized based on their criticality to the business, and this is usually achieved by performing a business impact analysis (BIA). Once prioritized, all systems should have a maximum tolerable downtime (MTD) established, which represents the absolute limit of time the organization can live without the system. The RTO should be less than the MTD; otherwise, a system disruption will have significant negative consequences.

At the end of the day, RTO is a business decision and not an IT decision. The role of IT is to support the business with options and costs. When conducting a BIA, many system owners will rank their systems as critical or essential but then reevaluate that ranking once the BC and DR costs of a short RTO are presented. Business leaders need this information to make decisions about system design, architecture, and recovery strategies, and once a decision is made, IT is responsible for implementing the resources needed to recover within the defined RTO.

Recovery Point Objective

The RPO is a measure of the amount of data that the business is willing to lose if a disaster or other system disruption occurs. RPO is most often used to guide the design and operation of a backup strategy, and RPO can be expressed as a number of transactions or amount of time. If the organization can afford to lose the last 24 hours of data but no more, then backups must occur at least daily. A weekly backup would fail the 24 hour RPO, because up to seven days of data could be lost if a disaster occurs.

Backup frequency and cost are generally correlated; more frequent backups require more resources for data storage and compute power. As with RTO many business leaders might want the most robust backup strategy possible, but the costs associated must be considered against the value of the data. Manual weekly or monthly backups of nonessential systems may be appropriate given their value. Regulated data like PII or financial information needed for public disclosure might carry regulatory fines if reasonable data backups are not performed, so the cost of noncompliance is greater than backup costs.

RPO can also be measured by the number of transactions the organization can afford to lose. These do not necessarily have to be financial transactions, but instead refer to data transactions. A user enters information into a web application and hits Save; the steps needed to process and store that data constitute a transaction. A low RPO might state that only the current in-process transaction can be lost, which means that all previous transactions either are backed up or can be re-created.

Cloud storage solutions can make such a low RPO cost-effective, because they are designed for high data durability. Even if there is a system failure, the data has been duplicated and is stored in multiple locations for recovery. Alternatively, application-level controls might be implemented to allow transactions to be recovered if an error occurs. One such approach is journaling transactions, which creates a separate journal of activity performed. If a database or storage media is destroyed or corrupted, the actions in the journal can be replayed to reconstitute the data and meet the RPO.

Recovery Service Level

RSL measures the compute resources needed to keep production environments running during a disaster. This measure, from 0 to 100 percent, gives an indication of the amount of computing used by production environments when compared to other environments like development, test, and QA. These nonproduction environments can be shut down during a disaster, with the goal of reducing unnecessary resource utilization.

During a disaster, the focus is on keeping key production systems and business processes running until the disaster is largely resolved and other activities can restart to pre-disaster levels. The customer organization should identify these service levels and ensure that any BC or DR actions do not implement processes or services that do not meet the RSL. For example, shifting an on-premises workload that requires 100 web servers to a cloud environment provisioned with only 10 web server VMs may not provide adequate system availability. If the workload requires 90 servers for development and testing activities, then the BCP and DRP should specify that only the 10 production servers are to be migrated in the event of a disaster. Testing and development activities can follow ad hoc procedures to recover, or those activities may be suspended until the normal environment is recovered or rebuilt.

Creation, Implementation, and Testing of Plan

There are three parts to any successful BCP/DRP, and each is vital to the success of the organization. These include the creation, implementation, and ongoing maintenance and testing of the plans.

Because of their inherent differences, BCPs require different roles and responsibilities within the business. Although frequently combined and considered a single practice area, the two plans do require different sets of resources and focus on different activities. If the business does not continue to function, which is the goal of the BCP, there is no reason to have a DRP as there will be nothing to return to normal.

The plans should each be developed with knowledge of the other, including key integration points, joint responsibilities between the BC and DR teams in the event of a disaster, and definitions of both common and unique resources. These plans will include many of the same members of the workforce and serve the same ultimate goal of helping the organization continue to function during and after a disaster, but they are separate plans.

Plan Creation

Performing a BIA is the first step in any comprehensive BCP. The BIA identifies the impact of process/system disruption and helps determine time-sensitive activities and process dependencies. It also identifies critical business processes and their supporting systems, data, and infrastructure. The BIA is essential to determining requirements and resources for achieving the RTO and RPO necessary for business continuity.

Systems can be grouped in a number of ways, such as by identifying critical processes, important processes, and support processes, along with the systems and data that support these processes. Critical business processes are those that impact the continued existence of the organization. Email, for example, is rarely a critical business process. For a company like Amazon, inventory, purchasing, and payment may be critical processes, and the systems that support them are also critical to the continued functioning of the company.

Along with the selection of critical processes is a prioritization of systems. If you can bring up only one system at a time, which is first? Some systems will not work until other systems are back online, such as a single sign-on (SSO) required for users to access other systems. In that case, the support system recovery must be prioritized before the processes that depend on it can be recovered. All critical processes and systems must be prioritized over other processes.

Important processes should be prioritized after critical processes are recovered. These are processes that are a value-add and can have an impact on the organization's profitability or smooth operation but are not absolutely essential for survival. Once again, these must have a prioritization or ordering.

After the important processes are online, other useful and beneficial processes are brought back online. It is possible that a business decision may be made to not restore some processes until restoration of normal operations is achieved. In the event of a disaster, an employee social calendar app is unlikely to be useful, so restoring this system before the disaster is concluded is not helpful.

Processes based on legacy systems can be difficult to return to pre-disaster configurations. The technical debt of continuing to run legacy systems unless essential to the business may make them expendable. If there are systems that may be in this category, it may be worthwhile to consider replacing and retiring them prior to an emergency. Legacy systems often have legacy hardware and software requirements that are not easily restored after a disaster.

The challenges associated with legacy system recovery are an operational consideration and may be compounded by security risks like lack of support for SSO or MFA. These risks should be accounted for as part of risk assessment activities, and the proper mitigation may be a migration to a newer platform. One advantage to a cloud-based BCP/DRP is the expectation of a modern and up-to-date infrastructure. While a legacy system could potentially be hosted in the cloud, the move to a cloud position may provide the opportunity to modernize.

The creation of the DRP often follows the BCP. Knowing the critical business processes and the supporting infrastructure needed provides a roadmap to returning the system to pre-disaster operations.

Both the BCP and DRP should be created considering a range of potential disasters. History is a good starting point for environmental disasters, and government agencies such as FEMA and private/public partnerships like InfraGard can provide guidance on the likely disasters that need to be considered in any geographic location. The CSP is also a source for BCP/DRP planning. Recommendations and solutions for surviving specific business disruptions and returning to normal operations are from major CSPs, and security reference architectures published by the CSPs highlight BC and DR best practices and recommendations.

The creation and implementation of a DRP or BCP is a lengthy process. It is simplified by having the system criticality and prioritization determined prior to beginning plan development. The identification, criticality, and prioritization of business processes, systems, and data are a necessary first step to creating a complete and functional plan. If this prerequisite step is omitted, the creation of the plan can be disruptive. Often, every business unit and all process owners view their processes, systems, and data as important, if not essential. It is important for senior leadership to make these decisions in advance so that each group knows their place within the plan for bringing the organization back online.

BCP/DRP Implementation

Identifying key personnel is a crucial step in creating and implementing a BCP or DRP. The executive sponsor provides key resources for creating the plan. Implementation of the BCP/DRP can include identifying alternate facilities, contracts for services, and training of key personnel, and this process requires the resources the executive sponsor brings.

Implementing BCP or DRP processes may necessitate utilizing cloud computing for critical services, which takes advantage of the cloud's high availability features like multiple availability zones, automatic failover, and even direct connection to a CSP. These choices come with costs that must be considered. The cost of high availability in the cloud is generally less than a company trying to achieve high availability on their own, and if possible, the cost of building resiliency may be far less than the cost of business interruption. By identifying the critical business processes, a business can also avoid the cost of implementing high availability for noncritical systems. In many conversations on availability with business process owners, it has become clear that everyone wants high availability, but justifying the associated costs is a good way to identify those systems that do not actually need it.

Critical business processes can be supported through component/data center redundancy and may run as an active-active configuration. This allows near instantaneous continuation of critical processes. Important but noncritical business processes may use the less expensive active-passive configuration. This allows a more rapid restoration of services when a specific region or zone becomes unavailable. Less important business processes may be run in a single region or zone and may take more time to return to service, and this configuration usually operates at a much lower cost.

Methods to provide high availability and resiliency continue to evolve. The ability to automate monitoring and deployment through orchestration and other methods supports high availability in the cloud and automated failure recovery that is faster than manual recover options. New tools and methods will continue to be developed that should lead to increasingly resilient cloud environments at attractive prices.

BCP/DRP Testing

A BCP and DRP should be tested at least annually. This test should involve the key personnel needed for all disasters. In addition, many tests will include a roleplaying scenario that involves members of the workforce who have responsibilities under the BCP or DRP. This training is useful in the event of a disaster, as employees will be familiar with processes and able to execute them more quickly and effectively in stressful situations.

There are some basic scenarios that apply to most if not all organizations. It is not necessary to test all of them each year, but a robust plan should test all likely scenarios over time. A well-tested plan will function even for an unexpected disaster. Common disaster scenarios include the following:

- Data breach
- Data loss
- Power outage or loss of other utilities
- Network failure
- Environmental or natural disasters (e.g., fire, flooding, tornado, hurricane, or earthquake)
- Civil unrest or terrorism
- Pandemics

The plan should test the most likely scenarios first and can be tested in a number of ways. The maturity of the plan and the people implementing the plan will determine the type of testing that takes place. There are a variety of standard test methods.

Tests should be both scheduled and unscheduled. Particularly for new plans and organization immature in the BCP/DCP space, a scheduled test ensures that key personnel are available and will begin the maturation process. Tests that have the potential of being very disruptive should also be scheduled to minimize disruption.

Eventually, some tests should be conducted without prior warning. Surprise tests do not mean unscheduled. Instead, only high-level approvers and a few key individuals are aware of an upcoming test, which gives a more realistic result since members of the recovery team respond as if an actual disruption took place. The high-level approval is essential in case some amount of unexpected business disruption occurs. Executive approval includes a review of potential disruption and benefits so that a business decision can be made by those responsible. Key personnel who are part of the test planning can be positioned in advance of the test in order to monitor performance metrics and to call a halt to testing if a genuine disruption occurs as a result.

The simplest test method is a tabletop exercise. A tabletop is usually performed in a conference room or other location around the "table," where key personnel are presented with a scenario and then work through the plan verbally. This is usually the first step for a new plan and can identify missing pieces in the plan or steps that need greater detail. The next step may be a walk-through where key personnel move to the appropriate locations and verbally verify the steps, sometimes even performing some parts of the plan. While developing a plan, regular tabletops and walk-throughs can help flesh out a more robust plan, identify incorrect assumptions, and even test logistics. A tabletop or walk-through can also be useful for new members of the team to assist them in learning their responsibilities under the plan.

A more substantial test is a simulation. Like a fire drill or a shelter-in-place activity, a disaster is simulated, and the plan is exercised while normal operations continue. A simulation is more robust and detailed than a walk-through, with personnel performing certain steps simulating their response to a disaster, which may include actual work like moving to an alternate facility or spinning up cloud resources that would need to be provisioned in the event of a disaster.

The next level of testing is a parallel test. Care must be taken not to disrupt normal business operations when performing a parallel test, which requires key personnel and workforce members to perform the steps needed in case of a disaster. More than simulating the steps, they actually perform the steps to ensure that they can accomplish the critical business processes using the actions documented in the plan. Processing happens in parallel with the still-running primary systems, and parallel testing can be useful to ensure that systems are able to handle current workloads or produce expected outputs. The output of the parallel test can be compared to outputs from actual production environments to identify any gaps.

The most robust level of testing is a full cutover test. In this test, the actual steps to be taken in a disaster are performed. The primary system is disconnected, and the business attempts to run critical functions. This is a high-risk test, as the critical functions may fail, so only the most mature organizations and BC/DR teams should attempt a full cutover test.

Summary

Moving to the cloud is a business decision, often driven by the financial change of shifting from capital expense to operating expense. Cloud environments offer native high availability and resiliency at a price that is attractive to businesses of all types. They also provide capabilities not available to many organizations, such as active-active configuration without the need to fully build out multiple data centers. To achieve these benefits, a customer must have an understanding of the key infrastructure pieces of a cloud environment, architect systems that take advantage of these features, and configure the features correctly. The customer must also understand the shared security responsibility between the CSP and the customer. Finally, a customer must understand how to properly configure and use the cloud resources they purchase to ensure that appropriate controls are in place to secure the process and data.

Chapter 4

Cloud Application Security

Organizations that migrate to cloud environments often assume that the cloud provider handles security tasks. This is partially true, but the cloud consumer still has a vital role to play, especially if a cloud environment is used for developing or hosting applications. Often, security focuses only on the controls associated with identity and access management (IAM), networking, and infrastructure components. But if the application software running on these components is insecure, then the organization's data is also insecure. This chapter will discuss the processes needed to secure the software through the application development lifecycle.

Advocate Training and Awareness for Application Security

Secure software development begins with the development of a culture of security and the implementation of a secure software development lifecycle (SSDLC). The SSDLC is similar to governance documents like security policies and should define requirements and processes for the organization to securely develop software. A secure culture is not developed through occasional efforts but through regular, deliberate action. The three parts identified by the Software Assurance Forum for Excellence in Code (SAFECode) are executive support and engagement, program design and implementation, and program sustainment and measurement. Training and awareness are important parts of developing a security culture and of developing secure cloud applications.

Cloud Development Basics

According to the Cloud Security Alliance (CSA) and SAFECode, the development of collective responsibility is essential but can be challenging when building a safety-conscious application development program. This effort can be broken down into three parts.

- **Security by design:** This implies that security is part of every step in the process, not simply an activity that occurs after an application is built or a reactive response to an identified flaw. Security requirements should be documented along with all other system requirements at the beginning of development, and adequate attention must be paid to ensuring that the system meets those requirements. Various models exist to help design these processes, such as the Building Security In Maturity Model (BSIMM).

- **Shared security responsibility:** The idea is that security is the responsibility of everyone from the most junior member of the team to senior management. No one should say that security is not their responsibility—instead, it is recognized that security is the result of individual responsibility and trust. The shared responsibility model in cloud computing is a similar concept, where both the provider and customer have explicitly defined responsibilities and must work effectively together.

- **Security as a business objective:** Organizations that have a compliance-driven approach to security can sometimes see it as nothing more than a roadblock. However, a security incident can cause significant or even fatal disruption to an organization's operations. Security controls help to prevent or avoid these risks, so understanding security risks and ensuring that they are mitigated should be a key business objective, similar to customer satisfaction or revenue.

Each of these basic concepts requires a clear understanding of organizational culture, security vulnerabilities, and organizational vision and goals. Without an organization-wide understanding of security and proper resources, software development and application security in the cloud are unlikely to be successful.

Common Pitfalls

One of the most common pitfalls related to cloud security is a lack of understanding the responsibility for securing the cloud. Even though major cloud service providers (CSPs) publish their shared security model, it is common to find cloud consumers who believe that all aspects of IT are outsourced to the cloud provider—including security. Ensuring that organizational leaders are aware of what responsibility the organization retains is a crucial step in avoiding a dangerous mentality of ignoring security risks.

Once leaders are aware of the need for proper security, another pitfall awaits. Inadequate support from senior management for cloud application security initiatives will lead to inadequate resources and wasted effort. Efforts to instill a security culture are unlikely to be successful unless senior leadership supports these efforts—through their approval and adherence to security policy as well as funding and staffing security initiatives that are part of organizational goals.

The next pitfall is failing to understand organizational culture. Even companies in the same industry have very different cultures. Building and sustaining a security culture requires careful planning that recognizes an organization's existing culture and employs sound change management tactics to introduce security into the culture. In addition, program-level efforts must be reviewed regularly to ensure that they remain aligned with business objectives and cultural realities. For example, a culture that places high value on speed and efficiency is unlikely to embrace security processes, like approval of new cloud services, that add significant delays.

Another resource-related pitfall is staffing. The size of an organization may limit the number of security experts due to competing hiring needs or even resources available for security practitioner salaries. These experts may then serve as resources to multiple development processes rather than as a member on one team. If the organization is large, development teams may use security experts as resources or may include security experts as team members. In either situation, it can be challenging to ensure that the development of security-aware applications will be consistent across the organization.

Organizations that do not implement a framework for secure software development will also cause difficulties. A mature organization will have a well-defined process that integrates security as part of each step. The lack of a framework or process leads to ad hoc security and does not support a security-aware organization.

Finally, in times of budget constraints, the training budget is often a first target for budget cuts. It is easy to cut training without immediate impact; however, a security-conscious organization should find ways to continue security awareness training and secure development practices. Switching from instructor-led training (ILT) to computer-based training (CBT) is one such strategy. CBT may be somewhat less effective, but it still provides useful training at a reduced cost and helps achieve a better cost-benefit outcome than eliminating training entirely.

Additional security training options include subscriptions to online security courses, as well as online asynchronous and synchronous training. Each of these options eliminates travel expenses and is typically lower cost than live, in-person training. One other option is to bring the trainer to the work location. If a large number of people need the same training, bringing the trainer to you rather than sending the people to training can be cost-effective. These options can keep training active while trimming the budget.

Common Cloud Vulnerabilities

Common cloud vulnerabilities include data breaches, data integrity, insecure application programming interfaces (APIs), and denial-of-service (DoS) attacks. The broadly network-accessible nature of the cloud and need to exchange data between networked systems introduces some specific vulnerabilities into cloud computing. Any time an application is accessed or transmits data over the Internet, it is doing this in a hostile environment.

There are several organizations that provide information on security threats, including the Cloud Security Alliance (CSA), the SANS Institute, and the Open Web Application Security Project (OWASP). They publish research on top threats in cloud computing and related technologies, and offer routinely updated content on general, cloud, and application security topics. The following sections contain examples of the risks from each organization and further reference materials.

CSA Top Threats to Cloud Computing

For the past several years, the CSA Top Threats Working Group (`cloudsecurityalliance .org/research/working-groups/top-threats`) has published the top threats to cloud computing. The number of threats varies, and the publications are entertainingly named based on the number of threats. In 2016 to 2018, it was the Treacherous 12, and from 2019 to the present it is the Egregious 11. These lists provide security practitioners with a framework for reviewing cloud computing and cloud application security risks. Here is an example of the top four threats identified in 2020's Egregious 11:

- Data breaches
- Misconfiguration and inadequate change control
- Lack of cloud security architecture and strategy
- Insufficient identity, credential access, and key management

None of these threats should be surprising. Protection of data, which may be put at risk through misconfiguration, poor access control, and other failures, tops the list. The top items on the list also suggest that cloud security needs to become more mature in many organizations. For organizations utilizing other CSA resources, like the cloud controls matrix (CCM), this can be a useful resource for identifying and mitigating cloud security risks.

OWASP Top 10

The OWASP Top 10 (owasp.org/www-project-top-ten) is a periodically updated list and features the top threats in web application security. The most recent version was released in 2021, and the list is updated approximately every three years. The top 10 security risks lead to a variety of issues that include data breach, data integrity, and DoS attacks, and the list is ideally suited for developers, engineers, and architects who need to account for these threats when designing systems. Essentially, each item of the CIA triad can be affected by one or more of these risks. The following were the top four in 2021:

- Broken access control
- Cryptographic failures
- Injection
- Insecure design

The most disturbing thing about this list is that the items on the list rarely change—many of the items have been on the list for many years and simply change order over time. This indicates that the prevalence of these vulnerabilities remains high, although new items have entered the list as technology evolves. For example, some vulnerabilities like cross-site scripting (XSS) have been combined into broader categories such as injection vulnerabilities.

New categories have also been created to mirror technology trends like the increased use of distributed system components. The OWASP Top 10 is especially useful for organizations that design or build their own applications in cloud environments. With a focus on shifting security activities into the software development lifecycle (SDLC), engineers should be aware of these vulnerabilities and ensure that system designs avoid them whenever possible.

SANS CWE Top 25

The Top 25 (cwe.mitre.org/top25/archive/2021/2021_cwe_top25.html) is a list of the most dangerous software weaknesses. It is similar in scope to the OWASP Top 10 and is designed for a highly technical engineering audience. The list has been updated annually for the past several years and pulls data from the common vulnerabilities and exposures (CVEs) reported to the national vulnerability database (NVD).

The NVD captures data about known vulnerabilities in information systems and software products. Because these are real-life, existing flaws, the CWE Top 25 is a measure of the actual weaknesses that are prevalent in software products. The top four in 2021 were:

- Out-of-bounds write
- Improper neutralization of input during web page generation (cross-site scripting)
- Out-of-bounds read
- Improper input validation

The Top 25 list is useful when architecting secure software and provides a good starting point for designing testing methodologies. Because it is broadly measuring reported software vulnerabilities, it also includes legacy, noncloud systems. Organizations that are entirely cloud-native may find that some weaknesses are less applicable to cloud applications, but the general principles of secure software development remain largely the same.

Describe the Secure Software Development Life Cycle Process

A software development lifecycle (SDLC) refers to all the activities necessary to identify what requirements a system must meet and then design, build, test, and operate the system. Security is not inherently a part of the SDLC, so the concept of a secure SDLC (SSDLC) evolves the lifecycle to incorporate security activities throughout the entire process. When looked at on a timeline, system development moves from left to right over time, so the concept of an SSDLC is often known as "shifting left." Rather than security activities occurring at the end of the lifecycle, key security activities are incorporated from the very beginning.

An SDLC has several phases, and there are different models with more or fewer phases. In general, the steps of an SDLC include requirements, design, development, testing, deployment, and operations and maintenance (O&M). In the SSDLC, these phases are enhanced to include specific security-focused tasks relevant to each phase to allow security by design. For example, during requirements gathering, specific security requirements should be documented, such as the need for the system to support encryption of data at rest.

There are many resources for implementing an SSDLC. These include the Microsoft security development lifecycle (SDL), which can be found here: `microsoft.com/en-us/securityengineering/sdl`. Other frameworks include the NIST Secure Software Development Framework and the OWASP Software Assurance Maturity Model (SAMM), detailed in this section.

NIST Secure Software Development Framework

Similar to the popular NIST Cybersecurity Framework (CSF), the NIST Secure Software Development Framework (SSDF) defines and describes secure software development practices (csrc.nist.gov/publications/detail/sp/800-218/final). This framework is useful for developing secure traditional IT systems, as well as Industrial Control Systems (ICS), IoT systems, and cyber-physical systems (CPS).

The SSDF can be adapted to existing SDLCs, supports the use of modern software development techniques such as agile, and leverages guidelines and standards from other organizations.

The SSDF is organized into these four groups:

- **Prepare the organization:** This includes people, processes, and technology.
- **Protect the software:** Protect it from tampering and unauthorized access.
- **Produce well-secured software:** This means software with minimal vulnerabilities.
- **Respond to vulnerabilities:** This includes preventing them in future releases.

OWASP Software Assurance Maturity Model

The OWASP SAMM can be used to assess the current state of secure development using an existing SDLC and to identify improvements that increase the maturity of these practices. It is ideal for organizations with well-established SDLC methodologies and processes and is useful for defining the current state as well as key activities to move to a desired state within the existing SDLC practices.

The SAMM (owaspsamm.org) consists of domains subdivided into security practices, which are used to measure software security maturity and develop actionable plans to improve the SSDLC capability. The domains and practices include the following:

- **Governance:** Strategy and Metrics, Policy and Compliance, Education and Guidance
- **Design:** Threat Assessment, Security Requirements, Security Architecture
- **Implementation:** Secure Build, Secure Deployment, Defect Management
- **Verification:** Architecture Assessment, Requirements-driven Testing, Security Testing
- **Operations:** Incident Management, Environment Management, Operational Management

SAMM provides assessment tools and guidance to improve an organization's security posture and supports the development of secure software and systems.

Business Requirements

Mature software development shops utilize an SDLC because it saves money and supports repeatable, quality software development. Studies have been conducted that show that the later in the development phase issues are found, the more expensive it is to fix those issues.

Adding security to the SDLC benefits secure software development, because security issues that are discovered after a system is developed can be costly or even impossible to fix. Minimizing the number of flaws that make it into a final system is a more cost-effective approach than trying to mitigate security risks after the system goes live.

While the SSDLC adds some up-front cost to the development of new software applications and the modification of existing applications, identifying security vulnerabilities early will lower overall development costs. The expected return is software solutions that are more secure against attack, reducing the exposure of sensitive business and customer data. Bolting on security after the coding or deployment phases simply increases the cost of that security while limiting its effectiveness.

However, an SSDLC is fully successful only if the integration of security into an organization's existing SDLC is required for all development efforts. Only when secure development is a requirement of a business will security by design occur consistently.

Business requirements capture what the organization needs its information systems to do. Functional requirements can include parameters like supporting up to 1,000 concurrent users logged in, which in turn support business requirements like all users being able to access a system during the workday to perform their assigned duties. In addition to these functional requirements, the organization must also consider security, privacy, and compliance objectives that must be met.

For example, a system that processes healthcare data is likely to have legal and regulatory requirements for protecting data. This will drive system requirements such as encryption of data at rest and in transit, role-based access control to ensure that only authorized users can view information, and data retention schedules and supporting infrastructure such as cloud backups. Requirements are an essential part of all SDLCs, and ensuring that these requirements include security objectives is a key trait of a more mature SSDLC.

Phases and Methodologies

There are many models for SDLCs, from linear and sequential approaches, such as waterfall, to interactive and incremental approaches, such as spiral, agile, and most recently DevOps, which increase the speed and frequency of deployment.

There are several primary stages to any SDLC. If these stages incorporate explicit security-focused practices, like documenting security requirements and documenting acceptance criteria for security testing, the organization has created an SDLC that considers security from the very beginning, creating an SSDLC. The generally accepted SDLC stages are as follows:

- **Requirements:** This phase includes all parts of the planning and can include feasibility studies, as well as gathering business, functional, and security requirements.

- **Design:** The design step starts as a high-level design and gets increasingly detailed as this stage progresses. The design must address all requirements, including security requirements, that were identified in the prior phase. Design can also include the design of test cases that will be used to determine if the system is fit for use. Test cases should be tied to specific requirements identified in the requirements stage and should be designed to simulate both expected and unexpected use of the system to identify any errors, flaws, or functions that do not meet the requirements.

- **Development:** The coding phase is the creation of the software components as well as the integration or build of the entire solution. This can involve custom development of all elements of the system, as well as the use of commercial off-the-shelf (COTS) software and cloud services. During development, unit testing is generally performed as various parts of the system are completed or integrated.

- **Testing:** This phase is the initial testing of the solution built, as well as more focused testing that occurs to validate the solution before the final phase. This should include testing of all use cases and traceability of how test outcomes map back to requirements. For example, if the system must provide protection for data in transit, then all interfaces where data leaves the system over a network should be tested to verify that encryption is in place and operational.

- **Deployment:** Deployment is the work associated with the initial release of the software. Part of the effort in this stage is to ensure that default configurations conform to security requirements and best practices, including configuration of application programming interfaces (APIs) and any identity and access management (IAM). These steps reduce the risk of credential compromise and also protect the processes for account creation, maintenance, and deletion. Deployment is also where hardening measures are taken, to ensure that system components are installed in a secure manner. For example, if a cloud storage service is to be used in the system, it should be configured with only the minimum necessary access permissions. It is a good practice to consider each service that is approved for use by a business and create a standard configuration guide for each of those services to ensure a secure configuration for each service that adheres to company standards.

- **O&M:** This is usually the longest phase in the lifecycle, as it encompasses everything that happens after the release of a software solution. This stage includes all operational, monitoring, and maintenance needs of the solution, including ongoing security activities like logging, access reviews, and incident response.

Each phase of the SDLC can be divided into ever finer phases with associated security activities to make an SSDLC. The steps presented here capture the general flow of most SDLC methodologies. Organizations may choose a predefined methodology, such as the NIST SSDF, or choose to build one customized to their specific operations. At each step, security tasks and practices are an important part of the overall solution. Following these steps leads to a consistent and repeatable process for designing and delivering secure software.

Different SDLC methodologies exist, from traditional models like the waterfall to more modern approaches like Agile and DevOps. The choice of a methodology, similar to the choice of an SSDLC framework, may be dictated by an organization's existing development practices as well as the types of products or services the organization delivers.

Waterfall

The waterfall methodology mimics a stepped waterfall, where the development project moves along once all processes have been completed within each step. Traditional waterfalls are very rigid regarding this—all requirements must be documented before system design begins. A modified waterfall methodology allows for some flexibility if the project needs to step back to an earlier phase. Although waterfall was not initially designed to be iterative, organizations can iterate system development using a waterfall methodology by focusing only on a subset of requirements during each cycle of the development lifecycle.

Waterfall traditionally contains phases for requirements, design, implementation, testing, deployment, and maintenance. The rigor of the waterfall can be a security benefit, as all requirements must be documented before development begins. However, the inflexibility of the model can make it difficult to make changes to the software once development has begun. Iterative and more flexible models, like Agile, have evolved to address the complex and dynamic nature of requirements by facilitating faster and more flexible development.

Agile

Agile software development emerged in the early 21st century and focuses on key principles designed to increase the speed and consistency of software delivery. The Agile Manifesto lays out these principles (`agilemanifesto.org/principles.html`), which provide organizations with a framework for designing development processes.

Although not a development methodology itself, Agile software development practices aligned with the principles follow similar SDLC phases as discussed previously. Instead of gathering all requirements before development can begin, Agile development can begin on the existing documented requirements. Once the system is delivered, additional requirements are elicited, and the development lifecycle iterates to incorporate new or changed functionality to meet those requirements.

This iterative approach is a great security benefit offered by Agile development. As requirements change, the organization can change a system to meet those with more flexibility. Given the speed of change and evolving cyber threats, this agility can be beneficial to security, as updates to address new vulnerabilities or flaws can be delivered faster. Agile also prioritizes speed and efficiency, with a focus on automation. This offers an excellent opportunity to inject security into the SDLC; as code moves through the development pipeline, automated testing is performed. If the testing includes security tests such as static code analysis, then this automated process can be run repeatedly, providing more frequent security testing.

Because of its iterative nature, Agile focuses on a smaller set of requirements for each development cycle or sprint. With limited developer resources, this can lead to prioritization issues when addressing requirements. High-profile user requirements may be prioritized over security requirements, meaning the system is at increased risk until a future development cycle occurs to address the security requirements.

Apply the Secure Software Development Life Cycle

The SSDLC is a collection of best practices focused on embedding security practices throughout each stage or phase of a standard SDLC, with the goal of ensuring that security is not treated as an afterthought. Applying an SSDLC process requires dedicated effort to identify appropriate security activities at each phase of the SDLC, starting with requirements gathering and continuing through to deployment and maintenance. An SSDLC requires a change of mindset by not only development teams but also the entire organization. A true SSDLC does not treat security as a one time activity performed when a system has been developed.

Identifying security requirements and potential issues or flaws early on in the process can reduce the resources needed to address these flaws. Building a system that meets security requirements is almost always more cost effective than adding security to an already-designed system. For example, ensuring that a system is designed with a database that supports encryption is likely to be less expensive than designing controls like complex monitoring strategy for a system with sensitive data that does not support encryption.

Having an SSDLC is beneficial only if it is implemented and used consistently. The SSDLC should be complemented by traditional security activities, such as penetration tests and internal audit or compliance reviews. The SSDLC shifts security activities away from the security team, which usually lacks direct responsibility for system development. Instead, developers and engineers responsible for designing and building information systems must address security concerns as part of the activities they perform. Additionally, some standards and regulations, such as the General Data Protection Regulation (GDPR), Payment Card Industry Data Security Standard (PCI DSS), ISO 27001, and others mandate data security safeguards that must be incorporated in the development process.

Cloud-Specific Risks

Cloud-specific vulnerabilities identified by the CSA Egregious 11 can lead to violations of one of more of the CIA triad requirements of confidentiality, integrity, and availability. Breaches, compromises, or unauthorized exposure of data can lead to legal and regulatory violations. For example, a breach of payment card data can lead to an organization losing its ability to process payment card transactions, which is likely to have a catastrophic effect on revenue. At the least, a well-publicized data breach can lead to a loss of reputation, loss of new business, and market share. Loss of data integrity and availability can have similar consequences.

Risks beyond those discussed by the CSA will exist for specific companies at different levels of security maturity, in various industries, and in different geographic locations.

Security practitioners should work to identify the organization-specific requirements that they face, such as specific geographic privacy legislation or industry-specific requirements for the type of data they are processing. Cloud-specific challenges that can cause issues include the easy cross-border transfer of data in cloud environments, as well as the issues associated with the organization losing direct control over their infrastructure when it is provided by a CSP.

Any organization using computing should analyze cloud-specific risks that affect the organization's data and information systems. As discussed in the previous section, the choice of a framework for the SSDLC will be guided by other standards already in use. For a cloud-native organization, the CSA Egregious 11 can be useful when addressing cloud-specific risks in software development. In an organization with a mix of cloud and legacy, on-premises infrastructure, frameworks like the OWASP Top 10 may be more appropriate as they contain less cloud-specific guidance.

While there are many risks present in cloud computing, the CSA Egregious 11 (`cloudsecurityalliance.org`) is a good summary of cloud-specific risks. The CSA Top Threats working group has published the Egregious 11 as well as a deep dive that provides additional examples, clarifications, and mitigation options for each of the identified threats. A high-level explanation of each of the 11 is presented here, along with specific examples of flaws or vulnerabilities in cloud applications that highlight these vulnerabilities.

- **Data breaches:** Confidential and restricted data should, as the name implies, remain confidential. This can include sensitive personal information or intellectual property, and data breaches are primarily an attack against confidentiality. They can lead to fines, legal or contractual liabilities, and a loss of customer trust. During requirements gathering, the types of data to be handled must be documented, as well as associated protection mechanisms like access controls or encryption. These controls should be thoroughly tested to ensure that they achieve an appropriate level of risk mitigation based on the sensitivity and value of the data.

- **Misconfiguration and inadequate change control:** Software can offer the most secure configuration options, but if it is not properly set up, then the resulting system will have security issues. Misconfigurations at deployment or inadequate procedures for controlling changes can result in systems with security vulnerabilities even if security was designed in—a secure facility where the front door is left unlocked can be less secure than a facility where basic security hygiene is observed. At deployment the organization must ensure that all security-relevant settings are properly configured. As part of change control, the organization should analyze any proposed changes for security impacts, and verify that deployed changes do not result in a degradation of system security.

- **Lack of cloud security architecture and strategy:** As organizations migrate to the cloud, it is easy to overlook security. After all, cloud computing has significant advantages for an organization's finances, but it is dangerous to overlook the security implications of migrating to the cloud. Ironically, the initial cost savings the cloud offers can be quickly offset by sprawling cloud deployments. A coherent security architecture for cloud computing should comprise well-documented shared-responsibility items, as well as organization-specifics for proper cloud usage given the organization's unique business processes and data needs. ISO 27001 clearly identifies the need for coherent strategy and executive support for a security program, and this concept applies equally to cloud computing.

- **Insufficient identity, credential, access, and key management:** Cloud computing offers many benefits over legacy computing environments, but it can also introduce additional complexity. In a traditional on-premises environment all systems may be able to talk directly to a single identity and access management (IDAM) service on the same network, but cloud resources that exist in different CSP environments lack this capability. This can easily lead to problems like user exhaustion creating and remembering passwords, and issues related to logging and monitoring if user access logs are spread across disparate systems. A key part of a cloud security strategy must be a well-architected IDAM strategy, and the importance of encryption in cloud environments necessitates a robust approach to key and secret management.

- **Account hijacking:** As the name implies, this risk relates to attackers gaining access to and abusing valid user credentials to gain access. Administrative and service accounts are a high-value target as they often have broad access within an environment, and the broad network accessibility of cloud services makes these attacks easier since a stolen set of credentials can be used anywhere an attacker has Internet access. Safeguards against account hijacking are similar to the practices in privileged access management (PAM), including practices like separate administrative credentials, increased use of MFA, more robust auditing, and awareness and training to help users of these accounts avoid common risks like phishing.

- **Insider threat:** Insider threats can come from malicious sources, like disgruntled employees, or nonmalicious sources, like careless or overworked employees who make mistakes. Insiders do not need to gain access to an environment to cause issues and may have a higher level of access than an outsider could gain, which makes these risks high impact. Ensuring adequate training and security awareness to avoid careless mistakes is essential, and additional practices like robust auditing or break-the-glass procedures for gaining access to emergency administrative privileges can help safeguard against these types of risks.

- **Insecure interfaces and APIs:** Cloud computing offers services in novel ways, such as accessing systems using APIs and managing virtual infrastructure using a web-based console. Improperly securing these interfaces can lead to new vulnerabilities that were not present in legacy computing environments; organizations moving to the cloud may be unaware of these risks. Since these interfaces are accessible via the Internet, additional security measures may be required if they expose sensitive systems or data. Controls against insecure interfaces include the use of strong authentication for any access, such as MFA for console users or key-based authentication for API access. An SSDLC for cloud applications must include interface testing, due to the heavy reliance on APIs in cloud computing, and specific attention should be paid to testing the security of these interfaces.

- **Weak control plane:** The control plane refers to the elements of a cloud system that enable cloud environment configuration and management. A weak control plane is one in which the system architect or controller has limited oversight or control capabilities, which can lead to a loss of data confidentiality, system availability, or data integrity. CSPs typically provide the control plane in the form of a web app or command-line interface. Additionally, most CSPs offer security reference architectures that specify how to properly secure the cloud environment and control plane, including practices such as adequately segregating environments for production data from environments used for development or testing.

- **Metastructure and applistructure failures:** This risk can be difficult to comprehend, since metastructure and applistructure refer to entirely virtualized concepts in the cloud with few examples in the legacy, on-premises world. At a high level, these concepts refer to the operational capabilities that CSPs make available, such as standard computing images and APIs for accessing various cloud services. If the CSP has inadequately secured these interfaces, any resulting solutions built on top of those services will inherit these weaknesses. Cloud customers have little capability to directly address these risks, since the CSP bears the responsibility. Instead, cloud security practitioners should look for evidence that a CSP has implemented their own SSDLC and conducted testing against their service offerings to validate the security of the cloud service. This might include API security testing, penetration testing, or verification of cloud services against third-party standards.

- **Limited cloud usage visibility:** Using a CSP can help an organization realize cost savings, but the use of a service provider also removes the organization's visibility into how its systems are operated. CSA breaks this threat down into two sub items: unsanctioned app use and sanctioned app misuse. Unsanctioned use refers to the practice of shadow IT, where organizational users acquire and use cloud services without official approval, leading to loss of data control and visibility. Sanctioned app misuse refers to the use of approved services for nonapproved purposes, such as storing sensitive data in a cloud service that is not approved for data of that classification. Security training and governance can be effective safeguards, and some security tools like data loss prevention (DLP) and data flow tools can help augment visibility into cloud service usage.

- **Abuse and nefarious use of cloud services:** Cloud computing makes massive computing power much more affordable. While this is an advantage for organizations looking to save money, it is also advantageous to attackers, who can now access massive computing power at a cost-effective rate. This computing power can be put to nefarious uses, such as launching distributed denial-of-service (DDoS) attacks, conducting phishing campaigns, or hosting malicious content. CSPs are largely responsible for implementing controls that mitigate these risks. All organizations should be evaluating changes that cloud computing has brought to the threat landscape. For example, DDoS attacks that were financially impossible a few years ago might be possible now with rented cloud computing capacity. This can increase the likelihood of a DDoS attack, which should in turn drive additional investment in risk mitigations.

Threat Modeling

Threat modeling allows security practitioners to identify potential threats and security vulnerabilities and is often used as an input to risk management. When applied to software development, threat modeling can help with prioritizing secure development activities. For example, an Internet-facing application will face different threats than one only used internally by an organization—any attacker in the world can reach the first one, while a much smaller number of users will have access to the second.

There are numerous frameworks for threat modeling, but they all share similar characteristics. As with many aspects of application security, OWASP has a reference page that details how these models can be applied to achieve an SSDLC: owasp.org/www-community/ Threat_Modeling. All threat models allow security teams to identify potential threats and break them down into different elements, which can be used to assess the threat and design mitigations.

The process of conducting threat modeling will vary based on the framework chosen. No single model is appropriate for all organizations, as the business processes, geographic locations, and risks faced will vary based on the organization's unique circumstances. When designing a threat modeling program, it is important to choose a model that aligns to the organization's specific operations. For example, the PASTA model can be applied to organizations with blended computer- and human-based information processing, while STRIDE includes elements that are more applicable to electronic information systems. Once a model has been chosen, a security practitioner should seek out adequate training, reference material, or consulting applicable to the specific model to ensure that it is properly applied.

STRIDE

The STRIDE name is a mnemonic for the categories of threats it identifies and was originally developed by Microsoft to identify and classify security threats against software. The categories are as follows:

- **Spoofing:** This is an attack in which a user or system account is used to falsify an identity, such as user Jane Singh calling the help desk pretending to be Shelley Doe and asking for a password reset. Mitigations can include strong passwords and MFA as access controls, as well as digital signatures for software or communications.

- **Tampering:** This attack is primarily against the integrity of data and involves maliciously changing data. Strong access controls can be a preventative control, while logging, monitoring, and auditing can be effective reactive controls.

- **Repudiation:** This is not really a type of attack, but a weakness in system design. If a user can repudiate an action, it means they can deny having taken that action, and no evidence exists to contradict this assertion. Effective logging and digital signatures can be effective tools for enforcing nonrepudiation, which supports the security goal of accountability.

- **Information disclosure:** This threat incorporates any type of attack that allows information to be accessed by unauthorized parties. This is commonly known as a data breach, and controls like encryption, DLP, and access controls can be effective in preventing unintended disclosure.

- **Denial of service (DoS):** Attacks that result in a DoS are associated with a loss of availability, where attackers either prevent legitimate users from accessing a system or take the system offline altogether. Controls that work against DoS can include system redundancy, high availability architecture, and DoS mitigation services that help to absorb malicious network traffic.

- **Elevation of privilege:** This type of attack is also known as privilege escalation and involves an attacker gaining privileged access from an unprivileged account. This may exploit system weaknesses that do not enforce proper access controls or system functions that accept user input without validating it. Strong access controls and input sanitization are effective countermeasures.

DREAD

The DREAD model provides a quantitative threat assessment to assist with prioritizing remediation based on the numeric value associated with each threat. Once threats have been identified, the DREAD mnemonic provides a series of questions to ask that help rank the threat.

- **Damage:** If the threat is realized, how much damage would it cause to the organization?
- **Reproducibility:** How easily can an attack be replicated?
- **Exploitability:** Do the attackers need extraordinary resources, or is it a simple attack to perpetrate?
- **Affected users:** How many users will be affected by the threat if it is exploited?
- **Discoverability:** How easily can this vulnerability be found by an attacker? Note that although security through obscurity is not a sound security practice, it is nonetheless true that easy-to-find vulnerabilities are likely to be exploited first due to the lower effort required.

PASTA

PASTA is an acronym for Process for Attack Simulation and Threat Analysis, and it presents a set of seven steps for performing risk-based threat analysis. PASTA focuses on integrating security and business objectives when performing threat modeling and provides security teams with a way to leverage some existing work such as business impact analysis (BIA). The following are the steps of the PASTA methodology:

- **Define objectives:** Key business objectives as well as security and compliance requirements are defined in this stage, along with a BIA to identify high-priority systems and processes.
- **Define technical scope:** Technical boundaries are defined in this step, and once defined, all assets included in those boundaries must be documented. This should include any

infrastructure that needs to be protected, such as hosts, devices, applications, network protocols, and data assets.

- **Application decomposition:** Threat models can be challenging due to the overwhelming number of components in modern applications. Breaking them down into smaller units and defining the flow of data and communications allows for simpler analysis.

- **Threat analysis:** Threat analysis relies on information inputs, such as logs from security monitoring tools or threat intelligence sources. The goal of this step is to identify the most likely attack vectors against the system.

- **Vulnerability analysis:** Once threats are identified, vulnerabilities that exist in the system must be identified and correlated to the previously identified threats. Risk requires a vulnerability and exploit by a threat, so this combination represents the risks faced by the system.

- **Attack modeling:** Modeling and simulating attacks using the identified threats and vulnerabilities allows for analysis of the likelihood and impact of the threat-vulnerability pairs.

- **Risk and impact analysis:** Once the threats, vulnerabilities, and risks are documented, the BIA is updated with the findings. The identified risks must also be prioritized for treatment based on their criticality and potential impact to the organization's operations.

ATASM

ATASM is an acronym for a series of process steps to perform threat modeling, rather than a threat model itself. As such, it can be used in combination with a threat model like STRIDE, DREAD, or PASTA when analyzing threats, and it provides a framework for developing or maturing the process of threat modeling inside the organization. The steps that make up ATASM include the following:

- **Architecture:** Threat modeling begins with an analysis of the system's architecture to ensure that the participants in the thread model can enumerate potential attacks and threats. This must include technology components and system functions, as well as the assets that require protection. This helps provide a link between asset inventory, threat modeling, and risk management.

- **Threats:** The next step is to list all possible threats, threat actors, and their goals. This includes the methods they might use and what objectives they seek to achieve, e.g., phishing for credentials to gain unauthorized system access.

- **Attack surfaces:** An attack surface is any part of a system that is exposed to attack. Attacks that do not have a viable surface are less likely to be exploited and should be prioritized lower than attack surfaces that are exposed. For example, a system that is not connected to the Internet and requires physical presence in a facility for access is more likely to be attacked by a malicious insider than script kiddies on the Internet.

- **Mitigations:** This step analyzes existing mitigations in place, their effectiveness, and any risks that are not adequately mitigated. For systems just beginning development, all risks may be present, unless the system will inherit controls that are already in place within the organization. Systems that already exist may need a more detailed analysis of existing mitigations, since some controls are likely to be in place already.

The ATASM framework was developed by security professional Brook Schoenfield, who has blogged about the framework, applications to system and cloud application security, and other topics. Additional details about ATASM can be found here: `brookschoenfield .com/?page_id=341`.

Avoid Common Vulnerabilities during Development

Common cloud vulnerabilities are well-known and documented in lists like the OWASP Top 10 and CSA Egregious 11. Avoiding them can be achieved in several ways. Like all risk mitigations, a layered approach combining multiple types of controls is a best practice. These controls include the following:

- **Training and awareness:** Training for developers is critical, because they make decisions about how to design and implement system components. If a developer is unaware of flaws like injection attacks and codes an application with one of these flaws, the system is at risk. Training and awareness targeted at these audiences is a useful countermeasure, such as OWASP Top 10 awareness and training on how to avoid these vulnerabilities in the specific coding languages used by the organization.

- **Documented process:** The SSDLC should be well documented and communicated to all members of the team responsible for designing, developing, and operating a system. This is similar to security policies, which must be well understood by users if they are to be followed.

- **Test-driven development:** Ensuring that security requirements are met can be challenging, but focusing on meeting acceptance criteria can be one way of simplifying the task. Having well-defined test cases for security requirements can help avoid vulnerabilities such as Top 10 flaws, since developers know that testing will be conducted against those criteria.

Secure Coding

The practice of designing systems and software to avoid security risks is a proactive risk mitigation step. As in many areas of security, there are standards and organizations designed to mature these practices, such as OWASP. Since these security practices are designed by external parties, they may not be a guaranteed fit for an individual organization, but by tailoring the practices identified in one of these standards, any organization can build a secure coding capability.

OWASP

The OWASP project contains a wide variety of secure coding resources, including a series known as "Cheat Sheets" that are targeted to developers and engineers: `cheatsheetseries .owasp.org`. These provide quick, targeted guidance for specific security practices related to development and span topics like access control, HTML security, and cloud-specific topics like container and API security.

There are also technology-agnostic quick-reference guides that provide guidance on topics like building and implementing secure development. This includes a Secure Coding Practices reference with 13 practices that organizations need to achieve for secure coding, such as addressing input validation, cryptographic practices, and database security.

ASVS

OWASP publishes an Application Security Verification Standard (ASVS), which is useful for testing activities related to secure coding. The ASVS contains guidance for performing tests of application security, as well as categories of control objectives. It is frequently used by security testers as a way to categorize their findings; e.g., a lack of SSDLC documentation is a security failure of Control Objective 1, Architecture, Design, and Threat Modeling.

The ASVS contains 14 of these control objectives, which cover topics ranging from development processes to system configuration and handling of user-supplied data. The standard and supporting materials are available on the OWASP website: `owasp.org/ www-project-application-security-verification-standard`.

SAFECode

SAFECode is an industry forum devoted to software security and includes organization partners like Adobe, Microsoft, VMware, and Veracode. Its purpose is to facilitate sharing best practices and lessons learned with a goal of publishing information that any organization can use to improve secure software development. This includes providing information on processes and practices needed to achieve secure software development.

Organizations can take advantage of a number of different resources published by SAFE-Code. These range from secure development practices like building a DevSecOps function and hardware-based security tools to the tools and resources needed to build a secure development culture as well as a software security program.

Like other standards, the SAFECode resources are designed to be broadly applicable, so organizations should identify standards that are relevant to their businesses and then apply tailoring to modify the standard guidance to apply specifically to the organization's unique activities and development practices. The full list of resources can be found at `safecode.org`.

Software Configuration Management and Versioning

The purpose of software configuration management (SCM) and versioning is to manage software assets, and it focuses on maintaining the integrity of critical information system components. A loss of integrity could result in unexpected or unwanted system behavior, such as an access control module failing to adequately restrict access, which could in turn lead to a loss of data confidentiality if unauthorized users gain access to sensitive data. This practice can be challenging as software is almost always developed by teams, whose members may be geographically dispersed and work asynchronously. Multiple people may be making changes to both the config and source code files. Properly managing all of this is essential to ensure that changes are current and accurate, and the final software product contains the correct versions of all source code.

Properly managed SCM can make rolling back changes possible, so if a loss of integrity does occur, it is possible to restore the system to a known good state. Versioning can also maintain copies of the configuration and software for deployment to different machines and operating system versions, which can be useful in a disaster scenario if manual recovery is needed. Version control can also be a critical element of a compliance program, as system configurations may be unique to meet various customer, geographic, or regulatory framework requirements.

A key role of SCM occurs at deployment and during O&M release management for system updates and patches. Without formal SCM tools and processes, it is possible for incorrect software versions to be released. This can be a costly error, exposing the organization to reputational, operational, regulatory, and contractual issues.

SCM also allows for configuration audits and reviews by providing the artifacts necessary to verify whether processes are being followed. Compliance with requirements may be related to an organization's policies, regulatory requirements, or contractual obligations. The evidence generated during SCM processes, such as version checking before deployment and well-documented rollback plans, supports the ability to quickly and accurately perform audits.

SCM and versioning should be common practices in all software development environments and can be implemented along with other configuration management processes and tools like a configuration management database (CMDB). It may be possible to federate the CMDB with both on-premises and cloud-based solutions, which enables tracking of SCM regardless of where the software is deployed. Organizations that are cloud-native may not require a federated CMDB if their entire infrastructure is in the cloud.

Similar to SSDLC choices, each organization will need to decide how to implement configuration management. It is as important to perform configuration management on premise as it is for software development in the cloud, and each organization's mix of on-premises and cloud infrastructure will be different. In general, the SCM program must support versioning, provide assurance that the correct versions of various software modules are being deployed during a release, and allow for auditing of the entire lifecycle to support the implementation of an SSDLC.

Apply Cloud Software Assurance and Validation

Software assurance defines the level to which software is free from vulnerabilities and operates as intended. This assurance is a level of confidence and not an absolute measurement, as the absence of errors cannot be proven. We can also test how well the application or software meets the defined requirements. Regardless, there is always a possibility that a software solution will exhibit unintended behaviors as well, so methods like an SSDLC are useful. They help organizations with a number of tasks related to producing quality software, such as designing security into the software solution from the beginning and testing to ensure that security goals are met, the software functions as designed, and the system is capable of meeting the defined requirements.

There are multiple types of testing designed to determine if various aspects of the software fulfill requirements. There are also different approaches to testing, which can be used at various phases of the SSDLC or to test specific aspects of a system, like how new changes impact existing functionality. Some aspects of testing are unlikely to involve security teams, but security-specific testing is an area where security practitioners will need to work closely with development teams. It is also important to remember that even if all tests pass, the result is only a confidence level as to the security of the software system—new vulnerabilities or flaws are always possible, so other controls like ongoing security monitoring are necessary to further reduce these risks.

Functional and Non-functional Testing

Functional testing is used to test that the functional specifications of the system, linked to system requirements, are met. The execution of a robust set of test cases, linked to functional requirements, will create a level of confidence that the software operates as intended.

There are many ways to test software, but there are some well-defined categories of testing that are defined by the goal of the tests performed. The primary categories of testing that lead up to functional testing are unit testing, integration testing, and usability testing.

- **Unit testing:** This is testing by a developer on a single unit, often a function or module, that is developed as part of a larger system. All paths through the function module should be tested.

- **Integration testing:** As modules are combined, integration testing ensures that the modules work together. These modules may be developed by the organization or may be acquired software such as operating systems that integrate to provide a full application. As additional modules are added, we get ever closer to functional testing.

- **Usability testing:** This testing uses customers in a production-like environment to get feedback on the interaction between the user and the system.

As the modules are tested and then are integrated (and tested) and the user's feedback is obtained and incorporated into the system, we get to the point where we are ready to perform functional testing on the entire system. When conducting functional testing, there are important considerations that include the following:

- **Testing must be realistic:** Many development shops have Dev, Test, Stage, and Prod environments. These environments are called *lanes* in some organizations. The Dev, or development, environment can be set up to suit the developers' needs. However, for the greatest assurance, the Test and Stage environments should be set up as closely as possible to the Prod environment. In many cases, the Test and Stage environments will have live data or older copies of live data to ensure that functional requirements are met.

Once development is complete, the application moves to the Test environment for testing. Upon successful testing, the application will move to the Stage environment for configuration management and potentially additional testing. Once the next release cycle occurs, the software in the Stage environment moves into production. Any environment with live data (current or older) must be protected as well as the Prod environment to prevent data loss.

- **Acceptance:** Testing must be sufficient to guarantee that the application service meets the requirements of the customer and the organization (sometimes they are the same). This means that testing must be designed to exercise all requirements.

- **Bug free:** Testing must be sufficient to have reasonable assurance that there are no major bugs in the software. If there are any remaining bugs, they need to be small, rare, and inconsequential.

Once the system passes functional testing, it is ready to follow a QA process to deploy the system. Once deployed, enhancements and bugs will lead to further development, which should follow the organization's SSDLC processes. This leads to another form of testing, which is regression testing.

Regression testing is done during the maintenance phase of software development to ensure that modifications to the software application (for example, to fix bugs or enhance the software) do not reduce current functionality, add new vulnerabilities, or reintroduce previous bugs and vulnerabilities that have been fixed.

By contrast, *non-functional testing* covers aspects of the system that are not directly related to the system's primary functions. For example, an online shopping application would undergo functional testing for features like user search, shopping cart management, and purchasing, since these are the main functions of a shopping app.

Non-functional requirements for the system might include support for encrypted connections, so users can safely share payment card information. This would be part of a system's security testing. The ability of the system to handle anticipated traffic volume is also important and is often done as part of load or capacity testing. Other non-functional testing can include compatibility testing across different platforms, as well as documentation testing to ensure that system documentation is properly updated when new functions or modules are released.

Testing is the way we obtain the confidence or assurance that our software is free of vulnerabilities and functions as required and designed. Testing allows for quality assurance. Adequate testing is important. This requires that adequate time be allocated to conduct testing to find, fix, and test again in an iterative process. In addition, automated testing tools can improve the efficiency and completeness of testing. In a continuous integration/continuous deployment (CI/CD) environment, automated testing becomes a required feature.

Security Testing Methodologies

Security testing is conducted to provide assurance that the organization's security strategy and architecture are followed and that all security requirements have been met. There are various methodologies for conducting software testing, and the approach will depend on several factors. The type of applications used by an organization will be one factor, as analyzing source code for entirely COTS-based software is likely impossible. Similarly, an organization utilizing only software as a service (SaaS) will be restricted from performing certain types of tests by the CSP, as the testing activity could disrupt other customers of the SaaS platform.

Test Types

Testing is usually one of three types. The key difference between them is the amount of knowledge available to the tester, which can be used to simulate different threat types. For example, a complete outsider is unlikely to have access to source code for a custom-built application, but a developer employed by the organization would have such access. The types of testing are as follows:

- **White-box testing:** Tests the internal structures of the software. This requires access to the software at the source code level and may also include testing of the full application. Static application security testing is a form of white-box testing.

- **Gray-box testing:** Tests a system with some limited information about the application. The tester does not have access to the code but will have knowledge of things such as algorithms, internal system architecture like IP addresses or hostnames, and some details about the application such as user documentation. It is primarily used in integration and penetration testing.

- **Black-box testing:** Tests a system with no knowledge of the code, algorithms, or architecture. This simulates a complete outsider with no internal knowledge. Dynamic application security testing is a form of black-box testing.

Application Testing

There are common tests used in security testing. These happen at different stages of the development process and perform testing on different targets. Application testing methods include the following:

- **Static Application Security Testing (SAST):** This test performs a static analysis of source code. Source code is usually available for internally developed software. Static testing will not find all vulnerabilities, but it is a good initial test to eliminate common vulnerabilities in source code. This is a form of white-box testing, since access to source code is required. SAST tests can be run prior to deployment once a testable amount of code is available and can be run throughout the remaining steps in the SSDLC. SAST tools are often integrated with other tools used by developers, so the output is easily accessible and understood by those who need to fix the issues.

- **Dynamic Application Security Testing (DAST):** This tool is used primarily as a web application vulnerability scanner. It is a form of black-box testing. DAST is known for having poor risk coverage, unclear reporting, and slow performance, so in most cases it is not adequate as a single testing control. When used, it should be used as early in the development process as practical, typically when a system is undergoing functional testing. Once an application is deployed, a DAST may not provide sufficient coverage but can be a useful continuous monitoring tool for production applications.

- **Interactive Application Security Testing (IAST):** IAST is newer than SAST and DAST and provides a gray-box testing approach. IAST provides an agent within an application and performs real-time analysis of real-time application performance, detecting potential security issues. It can also be used to analyze code as well as runtime behavior, HTTP/HTTPS traffic, frameworks, components, and back-end connections. IAST can be used at every phase of the SSDLC.

Another tool often discussed with SAST, DAST, and IAST is Runtime Application Self-Protection (RASP). RASP is less a test and more of a security tool but is often integrated with IAST tools. RASP runs on a server and works whenever the application is running. RASP intercepts all calls to and from the application and validates all data requests. The application can be wrapped in RASP, which provides autonomous capabilities to respond to unusual application behavior. If the RASP agent detects suspicious activity, it can take actions like terminating an offending user's session or shutting down the application. In a layered defense, this is an additional layer and should not replace secure development and testing.

Security testing provides assurance that the software has been developed securely. While SAST and DAST may have their place, if you could use only one security testing tool, IAST would be the best choice. Many evolving cloud-based computing options, such as microservices and serverless architectures, face testing-related challenges. If there is no traditional server on which to install an agent, performing some security tests is impossible. In these cases, compensating controls must be deployed, such as a web application firewall (WAF) that can intercept and block suspicious requests to the application.

Code Review and Manual Testing

Code review is a form of testing that can be useful before software is finished and ready for more robust, automated testing tools. *Code peer reviews* are performed by peer developers who read through the code looking for mistakes, like asking another writer to proofread an essay. Some automation is built into developer tools as well to spot common mistakes, similar to spell-check functions in a word processor. As the developer writes code, incorrectly used functions, missing punctuation marks, and the like are highlighted for the developer's awareness. Depending on the programming language and development tools, these automated reviews may even be able to highlight security issues, such as the use of insecure or deprecated functions, API calls, etc., and suggest more secure or up-to-date options.

Code reviews may be performed at various stages of the development process but are best used when the code to be reviewed is of manageable size. Peer reviews are often performed when a developer finishes their assigned work and the trigger for review can be automated by the tools in the CI/CD pipeline. When Kathy checks in her code, the ticket she is working on progresses to Raj for review. If the code contains errors, the ticket is reassigned to Kathy with notes for correcting the issues; otherwise, the code progresses to the next step of the pipeline.

Manual testing refers to any type of testing that is not performed by an automated platform. This can include both security and nonsecurity testing. Performing tests manually is typically more expensive than automated testing, but it also has advantages. An automated tool might identify an individual module that does not properly implement user authentication, but if the system relies on a single sign-on (SSO), then this missing functionality may not be an actual security risk. Manual testing can also help overcome limitations of automated platforms, such as deviating from programmed workflows to test application functionality in unique circumstances.

A Smiley Face Crashed the App

Manual testing allows for human creativity, which users and cyberattackers will certainly use. In this author's experience, an application with very robust testing and quality assurance began to experience unexplained crashes and data integrity issues in the database. The app was designed to send a text survey to customers via SMS, and it expected standard responses like "Satisfied" or a number from 1–10.

However, as text messaging evolved, users began to include emoji characters with their responses, and the computer representation of emoji is different from standard characters and numbers. Neither the app nor the database could properly handle this data, and the automated testing platform had only been programmed to send numbers, letters, and standard symbols, so all automated tests indicated the app was functioning correctly. Discovering the bug required creative thinking to try other, unexpected inputs and observing the impact they had on the app.

While more expensive, manual testing can be a vital part of both application security and application quality assurance. As with other tools, the costs must be balanced against the benefits offered. In most cases, a combination of automated and manual testing allows the organization to get the benefits of each, such as performing manual penetration testing once a year along with automated vulnerability scanning weekly to identify known vulnerabilities.

Software Composition Analysis

Modern software relies on a number of components to function, many of which come from open source software (OSS) projects. One of the OWASP Top 10 items deals with software components that have known vulnerabilities—known as *dependencies*, these components can introduce vulnerabilities into the finished application.

Software Composition Analysis (SCA) aims to provide visibility into software dependency risk. SCA tools identify all dependencies in the application and provide an inventory. Most offer some additional capabilities, such as identifying out-of-date dependencies or those with known vulnerabilities. Manual investigation may be required to determine if a dependency vulnerability translates to a vulnerability in a finished application.

For example, if an online transaction module accidentally exposes credit card numbers, most organizations would hurry to apply updates. However, if an organization is only using the module to collect customer shipping information and not credit cards, then the vulnerability has no impact on that organization.

An emerging concept in the field of tracking software dependencies is known as the software bill of materials (SBOM). As the name implies, this is a bill of materials that lists all the components in a finished software product. There are standard formats for exchanging this data, some of which include the ability to include authenticity information such as a digital signature. For systems with high integrity requirements, this allows for verification that the software has not been maliciously altered. More information on SBOM can be found here: cisa.gov/sbom.

Quality Assurance

In a traditional development process, quality assurance (QA) was the testing phase. Separate from the development team, QA was the check before deployment that ensured that requirements were met and that the code was bug-free. QA was also part of the configuration management process, testing patches prior to deployment. In many organizations, that remains the role of QA.

The role of QA is significantly expanded in a DevOps or DevSecOps team, where QA is part of the process and is embedded throughout the development process. QA at this point isn't about the application service developed. Instead, QA is centered on service delivery of the software development function. QA occurs at each phase, ensuring continuous improvement and quality tracking. Testing is tied to both functional and security requirements developed in the requirements phase and specified by the security architecture and strategy. Because of the speed of modern DevOps, automated testing is heavily used, providing more frequent but potentially limited security testing capabilities.

For QA to be effective, further functional and requirements testing should be performed. QA should be involved in load testing, performance testing, stress testing, and vulnerability management. They may be a key part of tracking any identified security flaws from testing activities like SAST, DAST, or penetration testing.

In some DevOps environments, it is the QA team that pushes out the code once testing is completed. That team is responsible for ensuring that the code delivered to the customer through the cloud environment is quality code, defect-free, and secure. The QA team then takes a pivotal role in developing and delivering secure software and systems and is the final gate in the process of developing and delivering software.

Abuse Case Testing

Use cases are designed to test whether a system meets a defined requirement; e.g., a user logs in and must provide a username, password, and MFA code to gain access. Abuse cases are used to test the opposite of expected behavior. For example, what if a user put a SQL statement into the "password" field instead of their legitimate password? Would the application reject the input, maintaining security, or would it execute the SQL query and potentially lose confidentiality, integrity, or availability?

Abuse cases, sometimes known as misuse cases, are a key part of penetration testing and application security testing. Legitimate users may only perform functions in the expected manner, but attackers are unlikely to follow rules, since their objective is to circumvent those rules. Abuse case testing helps determine whether an application maintains security and responds correctly to unexpected inputs, behaviors, or attack attempts.

Use Verified Secure Software

The only type of software that a security-conscious organization should use is software that has been verified as secure. Verification generally comes from a third party that will perform testing on software and validate that it has no discernable vulnerabilities. When there are no verified secure options, a customer must do their own due diligence to ensure security. In this section, we will discuss some major components of secure software.

Securing Application Programming Interfaces

APIs provide a standardized way to access features or capabilities that a system offers. Unlike the user interface, which is accessed by an end user, APIs are typically accessed by other systems, some of which may be requesting data on behalf of an end user. These functions are exposed as endpoints, and many modern APIs are web-based and use standard HTTPs to communicate. Their modularity makes them popular in modern web and cloud applications, so securing them is important as they are likely to handle critical data.

API development and deployment in custom applications requires the same SSDLC as other software development projects. API functionality should be well documented in requirements, including security requirements such as supporting encryption. The requirements should also specify the methods used in the API to monitor access. API access monitoring is often done through authentication or keys. If not securely developed, a custom API can be vulnerable, leading to the compromise of the system it fronts. Deployment should focus on API configuration and automate the monitoring of that configuration.

APIs can control access to software or application services in a SaaS solution, to back-end services in a PaaS solution, or even to computing, storage, and other infrastructure components in an IaaS solution. For each of these, an approved API is important to ensure security to the system components with which we are interacting. In addition, when possible, enforcing the use of APIs to create a minimum number of methods for accessing an application service simplifies monitoring and protection of these application services.

A CSP or other vendor will provide an API or services that allow the use of an API. It is important to use the APIs as defined and to configure them carefully. An organization can develop approved configurations for APIs used commonly within that customer's organization, and policy can enforce the use of those standard configurations. Just as with cloud solutions, there is often shared responsibility for the security of APIs, so part of an SSDLC should include testing the configuration of any dependency applications and verifying the system configuration properly enforces API security.

In addition, vulnerability scanning of APIs can test the adherence to standards and can provide assurance that known vulnerabilities do not exist. It is impossible of course to ensure that unknown vulnerabilities such as zero-day vulnerabilities do not exist, so API testing should be supplemented with logging and monitoring to detect these threats.

Supply-Chain Management

There are two parts to supply chain risk management. First, it can refer to the needs of a CSP and potentially the customer to use third parties to provide services. For example, the CSP may rely on other vendors to provide services used by their customers. Management of this supply chain is a form of vendor risk management. When creating relationships with these vendors, both operational and security concerns should be addressed.

Additionally, traditional supply chain management is moving increasingly to the cloud. As the life of many organizations is tightly coupled with their supply chain management, the risks of cloud computing are important to consider. However, as the supply chain becomes increasingly global and sourcing of goods requires primary and secondary sources, cloud computing increases the reach and benefit of supply chain management. Cloud computing can optimize infrastructure to provide operational and financial benefits.

In recent years, supply chain risk has become an increasingly common theme. An earthquake in one country will affect the availability of a resource in another. Large-scale cyberattacks like the SolarWinds hack can impact critical infrastructure. A global pandemic leads to shortages worldwide. Even a simple problem, like a ship blocking the Suez Canal, can interrupt the global supply in unexpected ways.

One crucial part of supply chain risk management is assessing risk, which is similar to performing internal security risk assessments. Vendors may be assessed directly, where the organization performs a direct audit or assessment of the vendor's security posture. This is often done by sending the supplier a questionnaire, and several cloud-based SaaS providers exist to facilitate this information-gathering process.

Organizations with hundreds or thousands of customers may be incapable of supporting that volume of work. A third-party audit report is one solution. The audit report can be shared with customers as a method of assuring the security of data and systems that the organization provides. Common audits for this type of assurance include the Service Organization Controls (SOC) 2, Type II report, as well as ISO 27001 certifications.

Third-Party Software Management

The use of third-party software adds additional risk. A third party may have limited access to your systems but will often have direct access to some portion of your data. If this is sensitive data, a careful review is necessary and should involve the vendor management office (VMO) if your organization has one. Specific language regarding security should be part of every vendor contract.

The typical issues that are addressed include the following:

- Where in the cloud is the software running? Is this on a well-known CSP, or does the provider use their own cloud service?

- Is the data encrypted at rest and in transit, and what encryption technology is used?

- How is access management handled?

- What event logging can you receive?

- What auditing options exist?

In addition to basic security questions, a review of the third-party SOC-2 report, recent vulnerability scans and penetration tests, and security and privacy policies will provide an assessment of the security maturity of the organization and whether you should entrust them with your sensitive data. While you may delegate some processes, you cannot delegate responsibility for your data.

Licensing is another risk present to an organization using third party-supplied software. Software is typically licensed for use, and the terms of the license specify how the organization may utilize the software. One example is how many users can use the software. Some licenses apply to a "site," which is often the entire organization; all users at the "site" can use the software. Other licenses are based on the number of users, such as one license per user or bands like 100–500 users.

Licenses may also specify how software may be used. Some software can be freely used and integrated into other software products, but some free and open-source software (FOSS) licenses prohibit the use of free tools in any for-profit system. License management may be integrated with the organization's SCA process to ensure that any software dependencies are being used in accordance with their license terms.

Validated Open-Source Software

All software, including open-source software (OSS), must be validated in a business environment. Some argue that open-source software is more secure because the source code is available to review, and many eyes are upon it. However, large and complex solutions are not simple to review, and the way OSS is integrated into any new application can introduce new vulnerabilities. Adequate validation testing is required and may be achieved through sandbox testing, vulnerability scans, and third-party verification.

While it is true that more eyes on a problem can result in better security outcomes, the transparent nature of OSS code is not an absolute guarantee of security. Well-known OSS projects like OpenSSL and Apache have contained serious vulnerabilities, and any systems that depended on these projects were impacted by the vulnerabilities. OSS must follow the same risk-based steps of verification that commercial software undergoes.

When using OSS, there are steps you can take to validate this resource. The easiest method is to use well-known and well-supported products in the OSS space. For example, there are many versions of Linux available for use, but not all versions are equal. A well-supported version with a proven track record is preferable to a less known and less supported version.

One method for validation that can be used would be to perform code analysis on the open-source code. The advantage of OSS is that the code is available, so SAST tools can be used to find security vulnerabilities in the code. Since not all vulnerabilities are tied to code flaws, IAST can be used in conjunction with SAST to identify other issues like system misconfiguration. An agent runs on the application server and analyzes traffic and execution flow to provide real-time detection of security issues.

These methods can also be utilized together. You can use a well-known and well-supported OSS, perform SAST to reveal initial vulnerabilities, and then implement IAST for real-time detection of additional security issues.

One element of SBOM is the ability to verify the integrity of software dependencies incorporated into a final system. This may be useful in deploying secure systems, as it provides assurance that the dependencies deployed in a system match the authentic copies distributed by the authors. A security breach in any part of the software supply chain can cause vulnerabilities in applications, so validating that authentic OSS modules are incorporated into an application is important.

Comprehend the Specifics of Cloud Application Architecture

The traditional application architecture is a three-tier client-server module. In cloud computing, we have some additional choices. These include microservices, serverless, cloud-native, and cloud-based architectures.

The microservice application designs a complex architecture as a collection of services and data. This follows an old software engineering principle of cohesion. Each microservice performs a single business function. Each microservice uses the appropriate language and tools for development and can be combined as needed to provide a complex system. Microservices application architectures are a natural for containers running on virtual machines or physical machines, so they are well suited to the cloud. Container management is managed through services like Kubernetes (K8s) or Docker.

A cloud-native architecture is for applications deploying to the cloud. The applications exploit the cloud computing delivery model and can be run in any type of cloud (public, private, community, or hybrid) and allow organizations to focus on specialized development tasks rather than generalized IT management. A cloud-native architecture can deploy in a DevOps and a CI/CD process and can use microservices and containers.

Serverless environments use an event-driven architecture. Events trigger and communicate between decoupled services. Unlike traditional environments that remain running even when no processing is happening, serverless computing activates only the needed functions when they are triggered. This can present a security challenge, since a nonrunning service cannot be monitored. Because they are serverless, these architectures scale well using a REpresentational State Transfer (REST) API or event triggers. Security controls discussed in this section, such as an API gateway, can be used to perform security monitoring of the system activity.

Cloud-based architectures are well suited to building and deploying web applications. Using an API Gateway, a secure API is a front door to web applications that provide access to data and business logic. These may be utilized by other systems for communicating or can be used in other user-facing applications to provide access to data and functions across different systems.

Considering these cloud architectures, there are a number of tools and services that can support the security needs of both new software solutions and legacy devices. These services provide enhanced security and deal directly with common security issues. They are key ways to implement security protections for common risks, such as encryption services that protect data at rest or in motion to ensure the confidentiality of the data or network security services that provide traffic monitoring and alerting.

Supplemental Security Components

Supplemental security components provide service to your cloud environment, and most are designed to solve specific security concerns. For example, database monitoring works to ensure the integrity of databases by blocking malicious transactions, while XML firewalls support application services by analyzing XML messages. Organizations must have an accurate inventory of cloud functions or features in use and select these supplemental components based on the security risk analysis for each.

Web Application Firewall

A web application firewall (WAF) protects HTTP/HTTPS applications from common attacks. A WAF can protect any web application, whether deployed to users over the Internet or accessed internally on an intranet. The WAF can be a physical hardware device, a software device, or a virtualized device suitable for deployment in a cloud network. Some cloud service offerings incorporate a WAF in their service offerings, which can simplify configuration as applications deployed to that cloud can also configure their own WAF rules as part of deployment.

A WAF monitors HTTP requests, such as GET and POST, and compares them to predefined rules that describe normal, allowable system functions. A WAF may look for specific signatures or apply heuristics. By filtering HTTP/HTTPS traffic, a WAF helps protect against SQL injection, cross-site scripting (XSS), cross-site forgery, and other attacks. The WAF specifically addresses attacks on application services and external sources.

The WAF differs from an intrusion detection system (IDS), which monitors specific traffic patterns on a network. A WAF works at the application level and focuses on specific web application traffic and is often employed as a proxy, with one or more websites or web applications protected behind the WAF.

Database Activity Monitoring

Database activity monitoring (DAM) refers to a set of tools that supports the identification and reporting of fraudulent or suspicious behavior in a database. Applications and users typically follow routine patterns when accessing a database, such as accessing one record at a time. Unusual or unexpected requests can be detected and generate an alert for investigation, or the DAM may even block suspicious transactions to prevent an attack. As with any automated system, false positives can occur, so ensuring that the DAM is properly tuned and does not interfere with normal system operations is important.

The real-time monitoring may use, but is independent of, native DBMS auditing and logging tools. DAM analyzes and reports on suspicious activity and alerts on anomalies, and database audit logs provide information needed to detect such anomalies. In addition to monitoring applications and protecting from web attacks, DAM also provides privileged user monitoring. DAM tools can be deployed inline to monitor traffic like a WAF or IDS and may be used as a tool for detecting operational issues by generating alerts when services are disrupted.

Like other services, there are third-party vendors that provide DAM services, and CSPs provide services that are configured for their database offerings. These monitor database usage, privileged or administrative use, data discovery, data classification, and other database needs. Some DAM toolsets also provide assistance in compliance to contractual and regulatory requirements such as PCI DSS, HIPAA, and GDPR, by monitoring and controlling access to the regulated data.

Like all services provided by third parties and CSPs, the tools change over time, adding breadth and functionality. As with other tools, not all DAM solutions will provide optimum support for cloud-based architectures. Similarly, cloud-native DAM solutions may not offer any support for on-premises applications, so it is important to properly document the use case and select a tool that offers appropriate coverage.

Extensible Markup Language Firewalls

While beneficial for application integration, security is a concern when deploying Extensible Markup Language (XML) services. XML provides a standard way to exchange data between applications and provide context. XML tags define what each data element is, and a schema is used to define what data elements are supported by the system.

XML firewalls work at the application layer to protect XML-based applications and APIs over HTTP, HTTPS, and other messaging protocols. XML messaging and APIs between these services are an area of security concern, and XML-based vulnerabilities have appeared in the OWASP Top 10 in the past. An XML firewall can solve this problem, by monitoring all requests made. As an XML firewall must inspect traffic, they are generally implemented as proxies and stand in front of the web application or API server. An XML firewall can implement complex security rules and may perform its scanning when XML requests are translated from the sending system to the receiving system utilizing Extensible Stylesheet Language Transformations (XSLT).

A number of common web-based attacks can be launched through XML. These attacks include SQL injection and cross-site scripting (XSS). This is done through misuse of input fields and can be prevented through data validation and verification on input fields and schema verification. The use of an XML firewall can support the security needs of an application but should not be a substitute for developing secure software and systems. Instead, it should be an added level of protection. An XML firewall can benefit legacy code that was not designed with security. This becomes a compensating control until the development and deployment of a secure system. By dropping inappropriate traffic, it can also decrease the likelihood of DoS attacks.

Application Programming Interface Gateway

An API gateway monitors traffic to your application backend services, which are exposed as API endpoints. The services provided by an API gateway include rate limiting, access logging, and authorization enforcement. For secure computing, there should be limited doors into your application service. For example, some SaaS providers provide an API to access your account from your PC, Apple device, or Android device. These gateways control the way a user accesses and interacts with the SaaS solution, and they allow securing and monitoring traffic to the SaaS tool. API gateways provide authentication and key validation services that control who may access the service, enforcing confidentiality and integrity of data.

Amazon Web Services (AWS) provides this service through Amazon API Gateway. AWS provides both RESTful for serverless computing and WebSocket APIs for real-time communication. Google Cloud provides an API gateway for REST APIs to provide serverless computing and a consistent and scalable interface, while Azure API management provides a REST-based API for legacy systems. Essentially, all CSPs provide an API to allow the customer to monitor and control access to data and services to their workforce, partners, and customers in a way that provides a layer of protection and access control.

There are numerous commercial WAF solutions in addition to the CSP offerings, and it is common to find WAF bundled with other solutions or services. For example, network proxy providers like Cloudflare and Akamai provide an API gateway, since their proxy solutions provide an ideal chokepoint for implementing security monitoring. Organizations with a multi-cloud strategy or mix of different SaaS providers should investigate whether distributed WAFs or a single WAF support their risk mitigation needs.

Cryptography

Cryptography is a key technology for protecting sensitive data in the cloud. Encryption is the first line of defense for data confidentiality and provides a method of access control data crucial in cloud environments. Encryption requires the use of keys, and only users or systems with keys can read data. In the cloud, where physical control over IT infrastructure is given up, this allows users of cloud services to prevent other cloud tenants or the CSP from accessing their data.

There are three primary data states where encryption can be implemented: data at rest, data in motion, and key management.

Encryption for data at rest is a standard practice for all sensitive information. Many CSP services offer encrypted storage as a standard option. Some CSPs provide APIs that allow encryption to be added to any CSP service or customer application, and CSPs generally provide encryption options for their storage and database services. Some of these offerings utilize a CSP-managed key, but for high-security applications a user-generated and controlled key is needed.

Data-in-motion encryption is accomplished in standard ways including TLS, HTTPS, and VPNs. The ability to work with standard secure data transmission methods is supported across major CSPs and software like operating systems and web browsers. For securing data in transit between CSP data centers, the larger CSPs can accommodate data transfer without ever transiting the public Internet. However, this promise of not transiting the Internet does not necessarily mean that data is transiting a trusted network. Even when staying off the Internet, encrypted data transmission should be expected and may require proper configuration under the shared responsibility model.

Since encryption relies on keys, the generation, management, and secure sharing of those keys is a crucial practice. The major CSPs all provide key management services (KMS) as do some third-party vendors. Organizations must make a risk-based decision regarding a KMS. Solutions exist to allow the CSP to manage the keys, but for sensitive data it is preferable that the customer use their own KMS to improve key security. This can be achieved using an on-premises KMS solution, or utilizing a cloud-based KMS that is under the control of the customer and can be integrated with the CSP's solution, typically leveraging an API. This provides a separation of duties between the service managing the encrypted data and the service managing encryption keys.

Sandboxing

A sandbox is an environment with restricted connectivity and restricted functionality. Sandboxes provide security benefits by isolating potentially dangerous workloads, such as development environments, malware research, or untrusted applications. Cloud computing offers relatively simple sandboxing functionality, as new virtual instances can be created and isolated from all other services.

Sandboxes can be crucial in the SSDLC, by allowing developers to perform needed activities that might damage systems or data if done in a production environment. Code testing also benefits from an isolated environment like a sandbox. Any problems generated, such as a vulnerability that leads to a denial of service, will not impact anything outside the sandbox. This is also a suitable environment for developers new to cloud application development to try or test services provided by cloud providers without interfering with data integrity or confidentiality in the production application. This is a safe way to learn about and test cloud tools and services.

Sandboxes provide an environment for evaluating the security of code without impacting other systems. For example, many email security solutions open attachments in a virtual sandbox environment to perform security checks and scans. If the attachment is malicious, the sandbox contains the damage, but if it is benign, the user is allowed to open the attachment locally. Sandboxes can also be used for security testing activities like malware analysis or system security tests that could be harmful if performed in a live production environment.

Sandboxing is a common application security approach. Most desktop and mobile operating systems implement sandboxing for local applications, and many cloud-native architectures implement the concept as part of virtual machine (VM) isolation. When a new VM instance is created, it is isolated from communicating with anything else unless explicitly authorized, and network sandboxes can be created with virtual private clouds (VPCs), which isolate resources created inside them from other resources in the CSP.

Application Virtualization and Orchestration

Virtualization of infrastructure is an essential core technology for cloud computing, and there are several approaches to application orchestration and virtualization. One approach is microservices, which are small and independent services that communicate to share and handle data. Communication is typically API-based, and the microservices are specialized to perform a limited set of functions.

An application that is broken down into microservices is not truly virtualized, but deploying the various microservices needed requires coordination and orchestration. The microservices that make up an application can be updated independently, but orchestrating those updates is critical to ensure that needed functionality is not broken or removed.

Application virtualization through containers allows an application to be packaged with all dependencies together and deployed on any system that supports the container technology used. This makes applications more portable since they are not specifically tied to the underlying system architecture and may be useful for implementing a multi-cloud strategy.

Containers provide a method for implementing security control, since they can be subject to strict configuration management and patch management and offer an automated and repeatable build process.

Container technology and orchestration typically require a combination of tools. Docker is one popular containerization platform, while Kubernetes is a popular orchestration platform. The orchestration tool provides the ability to manage container resources, manage configurations, and monitor the configuration of containers to ensure that they align with organization policies.

Containers do not come without a cost. The containerization technology used must be properly configured, and as a software system it is important to ensure that it is properly patched. If the technology is compromised, so is the container; while the container platform provides a single point of implementing security controls, it can also be a single point of failure if a vulnerability exists. Any orchestration software must also be configured and patched.

Separate from container orchestration, cloud orchestration allows a customer to manage their cloud resources centrally in an efficient and cost-effective manner. This is especially important in a multi-cloud environment. Management of the complexity of corporate cloud needs will only increase as more computing workloads move to the cloud. Cloud orchestration allows the automation of workflows and management of accounts and the deployment of cloud applications, containerized applications, and services in a way that manages cost and enforces corporate policy in the cloud. The major CSPs offer orchestration tools that work within their cloud environment, and third-party tools can be used for orchestrating complex, multi-cloud workloads.

Applications can be "containerized" as well, and this is often implemented as part of mobile device management (MDM). In this case, the container creates an isolated environment on a user's device where the application can run and over which the organization has control. This is often used for segregating organizational data from user data in a bring-your-own-device (BYOD) environment. The container can be configured to follow specific access controls like using a VPN, restrict transfer of data to nonapproved apps, and even provide the organization with remote data wiping capabilities for lost or stolen devices.

Design Appropriate Identity and Access Management Solutions

Identity and access management (IAM) solutions encompass a range of processes and tools designed for controlling access. IAM begins with the provisioning of users, including the creation of credentials like a username and password, as well as authorizing systems and data access for the newly created user. IAM solutions also support the ongoing maintenance of access, such as adding and deleting access when a user changes roles or auditing access granted to users to ensure that it follows principles of least privilege and minimum necessary access. Users who no longer require access, due to either a role change or leaving the organization, should have their access deprovisioned, which is another critical function of an IAM solution.

IAM solutions also perform identification and authentication functions for users and accounts, which is crucial to controlling access to systems. Once a user has asserted their identity and been authenticated, the IAM solution may also provide information about that user's authorization. Authorization determines which resources an authenticated user can access, and depending on the access controls, authorization decisions may be handled by the IAM or by the system the user is accessing. Access controls may be role-based or attribute-based, and the choice will be defined by what type of access is needed and what capabilities the IAM solution provides. Since passwords are commonly used as an authentication mechanism, some IAM solutions offer password management as part of the feature set.

There are a variety of options for cloud-based IAM. This section will discuss the methods of authentication available and the security issues that exist with each of these. In addition to these tools, a variety of protocols exist to facilitate IAM functions, including OAuth2, Security Assertion Markup Language (SAML), Lightweight Directory Access Protocol (LDAP), etc. Some protocols are more appropriate for specific types of applications and environments. For example, OAuth2 was developed to provide authorization with web applications and mobile devices, while SAML is an XML-based authentication service well-suited for authentication across systems. Both are appropriate for complex, distributed applications like cloud computing, whereas LDAP is designed to work well with directory services, like

Active Directory (AD), which are typically associated with legacy or on-premises environments. Which protocol is used varies by authentication provider and use and is a choice determined by each organization.

Federated Identity

Federated identity, sometimes known as federated identity management (FIM), is related to single sign-on (SSO). In a federated identity setup, a particular digital ID allows access across multiple systems—the various systems that rely on the digital ID provider are federated with that provider. In a FIM system, a user has a single digital ID and authentication credentials, which grant access to applications across both cloud and on-premises resources.

Federation allows SSO for systems across multiple organizations and is often used for sharing resources with partners or other organizations. These may be subsidiaries of the same company, multiple CSPs, cloud vendors, or multiple organizations.

Although it provides benefits, there are security risks to FIM. The primary issue is that once someone compromises a digital ID in a federated system, the ID is compromised on all systems that are federated. This makes the security of the IAM itself a critical concern, and typical controls include increased access control to the IAM itself, as well as robust monitoring for malicious use. Although a compromised FIM account can be a serious security risk, the ease of revoking access across federated systems is a security benefit. Instead of disabling access to multiple systems, security responders can simply disable an account in the FIM tool, cutting off an attacker's access across all federated systems.

Other drawbacks to identity federation are similar to SSO. The level of trust between systems owned by multiple organizations may not be the same as between systems of a single organization. Just as with any other system interconnection, the organization must assess the risk of federating identity management with another organization's systems. Additionally, no organization controls the system protection across all organizations or the evaluation of all users in each organization, which can lead weak access controls in one organization to impact others.

Identity Providers

An identity provider (IdP) can be a CSP service or a service acquired from a third party. Many identity as a service (IDaaS) providers exist, and in a multi-cloud environment these may be the best choice since they are platform agnostic and designed for easy integration across different CSPs. Identity providers do not replace other cloud security tools, such as a Cloud Access Security Broker (CASB), but work together to provide a layered security defense based on user, system, and account identity management. The IdP is a key part of the IAM solution, ensuring that users are identified and authenticated. Authorization and monitoring of access may be provided by other tools like a CASB or application-specific audit logging and a log analysis tool.

The major CSPs provide IAM services, including Azure Active Directory (Azure AD), AWS Identity and Access Management, and Google Cloud Identity and Access Management.

There are also many third-party choices for identity management. Each organization should evaluate its cloud strategy and choose an IdP to match it. For example, an organization that is cloud native with multiple SaaS providers will likely benefit from an IDaaS solution, while an organization with on-premises Microsoft infrastructure and Azure-based cloud resources might find Azure AD to be the best tool, since it is well-designed for the existing infrastructure. As with all security tools, the choice of an IdP should be done with business objectives and requirements in mind.

Single Sign-on

Single sign-on (SSO) allows access to all authorized systems that fall under a single IAM system and only require users to assert an identity and authenticate once. The user can move freely between systems without having to reauthenticate each time, similar to a theme park where visitors can purchase a ticket to enter and move freely about the park without waiting in line to buy another ticket.

An SSO is a centralized resource and can be a single point of failure. It is important to monitor all access within an SSO system, since a compromised account can be used to gain access to all systems that integrate with the SSO. Availability is also a key concern for the SSO, since the system being unreachable will lead to users locked out of all integrated applications.

The primary advantage of an SSO is limiting the number of credentials a user must manage, which can be used to increase the strength of access controls like passphrases. Instead of remembering 10 passwords, a user is required to remember only one, so the organization can more easily ask for increased complexity. In the event of an account compromise, the centralized nature of an SSO also makes recovery easier—only one set of credentials must be changed to block an attacker from further access. The SSO allows for simpler central monitoring and access maintenance as well. When each system implements its own IAM functions, monitoring is more complex, and if a user's access must be modified or removed, the increased complexity can lead to errors or oversights.

SSO evolved with a focus on simplifying internal access management, but extending SSO across systems controlled by other organizations is an example of federation. Federation increases the risk caused by a compromised identity, as the number of systems that may be compromised is greater. However, it also offers a more powerful response to compromised accounts, with decreased complexity required in responding to the compromise. Just as with a FIM, an SSO should be a crucial part of continuous monitoring, and incident response procedures should be developed and documented for responding to malicious activity.

Multifactor Authentication

Multifactor authentication (MFA) adds a level of security to standard authentication, by requiring users to provide additional proof of their identity. Two-factor authentication (2FA) and MFA are often used interchangeably. 2FA requires two authentication factors, while MFA requires two or more, so 2FA is a subset of MFA.

Authentication is performed when users provide something that confirms their identity, known as factors. The factors are categorized by types:

- **Type 1, Something you know:** This includes answers to security questions, identification of previously selected photos/pictures, PINs, passphrases, and passwords.

- **Type 2, Something you have:** Examples include a hardware token, smartphone, or a card, such as a debit card or smart card. Authentication is achieved when the user proves they have possession, such as by presenting the card or entering a code generated by a hardware token or authenticator app.

- **Type 3, Something you are:** This category generally refers to biometrics, which are measurements of biological characteristics such as fingerprints, facial recognition, or iris scans. Of the three, these are the most challenging to do reliably and at a reasonable cost, although the prevalence of fingerprint and facial geometry hardware on modern smartphones has increased the viability of biometric authentication.

A fourth authentication factor is beginning to emerge: characteristics of the user request. Factors such as signing in from a previously used device are part of this authentication decision. If a user signs in from the same trusted device every day, the use of that device provides some assurance of the user's identity. The same user credentials entered from a new device or different location, however, indicate a potential security risk. If the user has received a new laptop, the access is legitimate, but if the user's account has been compromised, then it is beneficial to deny access. These types of policy-based authentication schemes can be used to require additional MFA steps for suspicious access, providing a balance between irritating normal users with cumbersome logins and protecting sensitive accounts.

Some solutions described as MFA are simply multiple instances of the same factor, which is not true MFA. An example is when a system requires a user ID, a password, and the answer to a security question—these are all things you know. This is single-factor authentication since it relies on only Type 1 factors; to be true MFA, another factor such as the user's IP address (Type 4) or sign-in from a trusted device (Type 2) must be added.

One use of MFA is to limit the potential damage caused by a compromised account in an SSO or federated system, and MFA deployed here is a compensating control for the risk of a single compromised account granting access to multiple systems. If, when moving from one federated system to another or one federated resource to another, a token is required from something you have, then the ease of SSO or federation is decreased slightly while increasing security. The method chosen will be a balanced decision based on available options, the cost of available options, the value of the asset being protected, and the organization's risk tolerance.

Another approach would be to simply require a token from a device periodically throughout the day, for example, every two hours. This limits the time a compromised identity can be used. The additional burden of authenticating two to three times a day may be an acceptable price to pay to limit the damage of a compromised identity in a federated or SSO environment.

Cloud Access Security Broker

A CASB is an important addition to cloud security and helps to solve challenges related to multiple systems with varying access control models and abilities. A CASB sits between the cloud application or server and the users and may be software- or hardware-based. The CASB monitors activity, enforces security policies, and mitigates security events through identification, notification, and prevention. A part of a layered security strategy, a CASB is not meant to replace firewalls, IDS/IPS systems, or similar security systems. Instead, a CASB is meant to enhance the security provided by these other devices.

A CASB that provides security must be in the line of communication that users follow to reach the application. In on-premises architecture this type of task was easy, with a single network inside a facility where monitoring tools could be attached. Multi-cloud organizations with distributed teams will find this task more complicated, since a user in an office and a user working from home will take different paths to reach cloud-based resources. Architecting and deploying an appropriate CASB solution requires deep knowledge of the environment and use cases, such as support for remote work and need to access one or more cloud environments.

CASBs may be agent-based or agentless, referring to a software agent deployed on computing devices. In either case, they must be inline on the communications paths in order to function as a preventative control. There are also out-of-band CASBs that receive copies of cloud traffic for security analysis, which can be deployed as a reactive control since they do not have the ability to proactively block traffic. These are somewhat analogous to an IPS and an IDS. The inline CASB analyzes requests and enforces policy, like an IPS, blocking suspicious activity when detected. An API-based, out-of-band CASB monitors for violation and analyzes cloud traffic and can generate alerts once suspicious activity has occurred.

Agent-based CASBs may face pushback from users in BYOD organizations. When the user owns the device, it may not be possible to install an agent on the device, and not all CASBs support the wide variety of mobile devices and platforms. Similar to antimalware agents, an agent-based CASB may impact device performance such as speed or battery life. When the organization owns the devices, an agent-based approach can be more effective, and containerized apps may provide a way to implement security controls on BYOD without as much impact.

An agentless CASB typically uses an API on the cloud resources to inspect all traffic to and from that resource, granting the CASB access to logs of activity for analysis. This allows access to all cloud resources to be monitored regardless of endpoint ownership and regardless of cloud service, so long as an API is available. Agentless CASBs can be quickly deployed and more easily maintained but lack the proactive detection and response capabilities of an agent-based solution.

Secrets Management

Secrets are a special subset of credentials, most often associated with nonhuman accounts, systematic access to systems, or privileged account credentials. Examples include API encryption keys, used for system-to-system communication, digital certificates used to verify the identity of a remote host, and SSH keys used by system administrators when performing their administrative functions.

Secrets can be used to gain access to systems, so protecting them is just as vital as providing robust control over user credentials like passwords. Since many of these secrets grant highly privileged access, additional controls may be necessary, similar to the practices of privileged access management (PAM). Just as with PAM, there are two fundamental areas of concern when managing risks associated with secrets.

- **Generation:** Secrets are used to control access, so a secret that is easily guessed is inherently insecure. In cloud environments secrets are often generated via automated processes, such as a CI/CD pipeline that must provision infrastructure as part of system deployment. In these cases, the secret generation must be done using only approved methods and securely distributed to the necessary infrastructure. Elasticity in the cloud can create additional security challenges for secrets—new hosts can be dynamically created in response to demand. However, these new hosts will require secrets in order to authenticate, so a secrets management tool, whether provided by the CSP or a third-party solution, is critical.

- **Secure storage:** Secrets must be stored so they can be retrieved when needed, but should also be secured against unauthorized access. Bad practices, like hard-coding secrets into source code or storing them in insecure locations like code repositories, can lead to unauthorized access. The secrets management tool should provide integration capabilities so that development tools and cloud services can securely access secrets.

The overall practice of secrets management deals with authenticating requests that use nonhuman credentials, such as API keys or digital certificates. It is a key element of an access control program, since most applications provide access capabilities for more than just human users. Modern distributed applications rely heavily on system-to-system communication using APIs, and cloud computing applications make extensive use of them as well, so proper generation, secure storage, and logging of secrets use are crucial.

Summary

Securing cloud applications requires security throughout the application's lifecycle, from the beginning of development to ongoing maintenance to final disposition. The first step is to choose to develop secure applications and implement appropriate policies, procedures, and job aids to support development teams. Without this focus on building security from the start, it will likely be more difficult and expensive to secure the resulting application.

Once the decision is made to build secure applications, an SSDLC must be adopted and training provided on secure software development, as well as the tools and processes used by the organization to implement the SSDLC practices. This begins with well-documented requirements for any system or application, proper development practices following secure coding guidelines, and finally assurance and validation activities to ensure that developed solutions are secure.

Once secure software is developed, it also requires mechanisms to ensure that the verified software is distributed securely. Integrity of the application code is essential to proper system security; otherwise, maliciously modified code could be distributed to users. Finally, the software solutions must be deployed using the organization's overall security architecture. Dependent upon the organization, this may include security tools such as API gateways, XML firewalls, web application firewalls, DAM, IAM, CASB, and other tools as necessary. These tools monitor the applications in use, with the ability to respond to potentially malicious behavior and potentially prevent malicious use.

Chapter 5

Cloud Security Operations

Cloud security operations comprise a mix of old and new practices for understanding, mitigating, and monitoring security risks in an organization's cloud environments. Old practices include standard activities that apply to legacy or on-premises IT, such as legal and regulatory compliance management, as well as novel activities like orchestrating cloud infrastructure by writing virtual machine (VM) definitions instead of physically installing new hardware and software.

Key to cloud security operations are the two main roles in cloud computing: the cloud service provider (CSP) and the cloud consumer. The CSP and consumer share responsibilities for securely operating and using the cloud, respectively, and require clearly defined, agreed-upon objectives documented in contracts and service level agreements (SLAs).

Build and Implement Physical and Logical Infrastructure for Cloud Environment

It is important to bear in mind that many aspects of secure cloud operations will be handled by the CSP and therefore may be largely invisible to the cloud consumers. As security professionals, it is critical to understand the importance of both the provider and consumer roles; particularly important is including adequate oversight of the CSP in third-party security risk management activities. From the CSP's perspective, proper isolation controls are essential due to the multitenant nature of the cloud, as well as appropriate capacity, redundancy, and resiliency to ensure that the cloud service meets the availability requirements that customers demand.

Hardware-Specific Security Configuration Requirements

In public cloud deployments, hardware configuration will be handled by the CSP rather than the cloud consumer. Obviously, private and community clouds will require the security practitioner to properly configure and secure hardware, and in some cases, public clouds may offer a virtual private cloud (VPC) option, where some of these elements are configurable by the consumer. The rules for *hardening*, or securely configuring, systems in cloud environments are the same as they are for on-prem systems, though the methods may be different.

There are several targets for hardening hardware, including the following:

- **TPM:** The Trusted Platform Module (TPM) is a dedicated module included in a computing system with specialized capabilities for cryptographic functions, sometimes referred to as a *cryptographic coprocessor*. Unlike an HSM, it is usually a physical component of the system hardware and cannot be added or removed at a later date. It has dedicated components including a processor, persistent storage memory, and volatile memory for performing cryptographic processing, and it is used to support cryptographic functions and enable trust in a computing system.

- The TPM typically provides a number of services related to cryptography, including random or pseudorandom number generators, asymmetric key generation, and hash generators. TPMs are often used for highly secure storage of limited data as well, such as the cryptographic keys used in full disk encryption solutions like Microsoft BitLocker.

- TPMs are often used to form roots of trust, since they are highly specialized and secured. For example, a hash of hardware component versions installed in a system can be relied upon if it is digitally signed by the TPM. This hash can be compared with a hash of the current system state to determine if any changes have been made, allowing for the verification of a system's hardware integrity.

- TPMs are implemented in a variety of form factors. Dedicated hardware may be used to provide tamper resistance or tamper evidence. Integrated and firmware TPMs may be included as part of another chipset or run in a dedicated trusted execution environment of a specific chip but are generally less resistant to tampering.

- Virtual TPMs are part of the hypervisor and provided to VMs running on a virtualization platform. Since this is a software solution, it cannot implement the same level of tamper resistance as a hardware-based TPM. The hypervisor is responsible for providing an isolated or sandboxed environment where the TPM executes, which is separate from the software running inside a particular VM. This isolated environment must implement robust access controls to block inappropriate access to the TPM.

- A definition of TPM is provided in ISO/IEC 11889, which specifies how various cryptographic techniques and architectural elements are to be implemented. It consists of four parts including an overview and architecture of the TPM, design principles, commands, and supporting routines (code). An industry consortium known as the Trusted Computing Group publishes a specification for TPMs, which currently stands at version 2.0.

- **HSM:** A hardware security module (HSM) is a dedicated piece of hardware designed to support and perform cryptographic functions. It is a stand-alone module that can be added to a computing system, often as an expansion card or physically connected using a cable, port, or network interface. This allows the HSM to be added later for enhanced security and allows for upgrades of the HSM if needed for enhanced security.

  - The HSM performs many of the same functions as a TPM, including secure storage of cryptographic keys, encryption and decryption functions, and cryptographic-based authentication functions. They can also generate data needed for cryptographic functions, such as pseudorandom numbers.

- Common uses for HSMs include generation and storage of asymmetric key pairs in a public key infrastructure (PKI), generation and authorization of financial information including encryption of account information, cryptocurrency wallet security, and securing records in Domain Name System Security Extensions (DNSSEC).

- Because of the lack of physical control over cloud computing infrastructure, major cloud vendors offer virtual HSMs that can be created inside a consumer's cloud environment. Once the virtual cloud HSM is installed, it can be used for the standard cryptographic functions; as with other cloud services, one of the major advantages is an abstraction of the underlying hardware. The HSM functions are presented as a service that all servers or other cloud resources can utilize, typically by making an API call to the cloud HSM.

- For cloud consumers with very high security requirements, some CSPs offer the ability to integrate a physical HSM that is managed by the consumer on their own premises. This allows customers to generate and securely store their own cryptographic keys that can be used to encrypt data or control access to resources in the cloud, making it nearly impossible for other cloud tenants or the CSP staff to access the consumer's data. This approach adds expense and complexity but can be useful for organizations with significant concerns regarding cloud security.

Storage Controllers

Storage controllers are hardware implemented to, as their name implies, control storage devices. This may involve a number of functions including access control, assembly of data to fulfill a request (for example, reconstructing a file that has been broken into multiple blocks and stored across disks), and providing users or applications with an interface to the storage services. Several standards exist including iSCSI and Fibre Channel/Fibre Channel over Ethernet (FCoE). These are storage area network (SAN) technologies that create dedicated networks for data storage and retrieval. Security concerns for SANs are much the same as for regular network services, including proper access control, encryption of data in transit or at rest, and adequate isolation/segmentation to address both availability and confidentiality.

Network Configuration

For public cloud consumers, the majority of network configuration is likely to happen in a software-defined network (SDN) management console rather than via hardware-based network device configuration. It is the responsibility of the CSP to manage the underlying physical hardware including network controller devices such as switches and network interface cards (NICs). Concerns for this physical hardware include the following:

- Providing adequate physical and environmental security for ingress and egress points to the facility such as point of presence (POP) rooms where ISP connectivity is established. This includes physical access control devices such as locks, adequate and redundant electrical power, and appropriate environmental controls like cooling to deal with the heat generated by these devices.

- Designing for resiliency and redundancy of network infrastructure is essential, due to the heavy reliance on virtualization in cloud environments. A single network cable being unplugged or severed can lead to thousands of hosts losing connectivity. The obvious advantage to virtualization is that a redundant network connection is also shared, so dual NICs and ISP connections can be easily shared by hundreds or even thousands of hosts. Performing single point of failure (SPOF) analysis is crucial for the CSP to ensure that they meet requirements for availability.

- Establishing flexible and scalable network architecture is key. In physical terms, creating a LAN requires physically interconnecting users to a single switch. In SDNs, this same functionality needs to be available without physically changing any device connections. The CSP's network must provide sufficient physical connectivity and support software-defined virtual local area networks (VLANs) through the use of 802.1Q VLAN tags.

- CSPs must provide appropriate security capabilities for the virtualized and distributed environment. Many traditional security tools rely on techniques like monitoring traffic via a switched port analyzer (SPAN) or mirror port, which sends a copy of all traffic to the monitoring device. Inter-VM network communication on a virtualized host generally does not leave the physical hardware and traverse network connections and could therefore bypass monitoring tools that rely on mirroring. VM-specific tools exist to overcome this limitation, and secure configuration of hypervisors must be enforced to ensure that they provide appropriate monitoring capabilities.

- CSPs may have business drivers to allow for customer-managed network security controls. Many public clouds offer a virtual private cloud (VPC), which is essentially a sandboxed area within the larger public cloud dedicated to use by a specific customer. These take the form of a dedicated VLAN for a specific user organization, which means other cloud tenants are blocked from accessing resources in the VPC since they are not members of the same VLAN.

Installation and Configuration of Virtualization Management Tools

Virtualization management tools require particular security and oversight measures as they are essential to cloud computing. Without these in place, compromising a single management tool could lead to further compromise of hundreds or thousands of VMs and data. Tools that fall into this category include VMware vSphere, for example, as well as many of the CSP's administrative consoles that provide configuration and management of cloud environments by consumers.

Best practices for these tools will obviously be driven in large part by the virtualization platform in use and will track closely to practices in place for other high-criticality server-based assets. Vendor-recommended installation and hardening instructions should always be followed and possibly augmented by external hardening standards such as Center for

Internet Security (CIS) Benchmarks or Defense Information Systems Agency (DISA) Security Technical Implementation Guides (STIGs). Other best practices include the following:

- **Redundancy:** Any critically important tool can be a single point of failure (SPOF), so adequate planning for redundancy should be performed. High availability and duplicate architecture will likely be appropriate due to the nature of these tools.

- **Scheduled downtime and maintenance:** Patching is crucially important for virtualization management tools, as is routine maintenance. Downtime may not be acceptable, so these tools may be patched or taken offline for maintenance on a rotating schedule with migration of live VMs to prevent loss of service.

- **Isolated network and robust access controls:** Access to virtualization management tools should be tightly controlled, with adequate enforcement of need-to-know restrictions and least privilege to ensure that authorization is not excessive to a user's job function. Where possible, isolated networks, communication channels, or encryption should be utilized, such as a VPN or dedicated administrative network.

- **Configuration management and change management:** These tools and the infrastructure that supports them should be placed under configuration management to ensure that they stay in a known, hardened state. When changes are necessary, formal change management should be utilized to ensure that the impact of any changes is understood and new risks adequately mitigated.

- **Logging and monitoring:** Logging activities can create additional overhead, which may not be appropriate for all systems. Highly critical assets like virtualization management tools are likely to warrant the extra operational overhead and should be configured to log all activity.

Virtual Hardware–Specific Security Configuration Requirements

The cloud's heavy reliance on virtualization and multitenancy creates a new risk of data breaches when multiple users share a single piece of hardware. In a nonvirtual environment, it is comparatively difficult to leak data between systems, but a VM shares physical hardware with potentially hundreds of other machines.

The biggest issue related to virtual hardware security is the enforcement, by the hypervisor, of strict segregation between the guest operating systems running on a single host. The hypervisor acts as a form of reference monitor by mediating access by the various guest machines to the physical resources of the hardware they are running on and, in some cases, inter-VM network communication. Since most hypervisors are proprietary and produced by software vendors, there are two main forms of control a CCSP should be aware of:

- **Configuration:** Ensure that the hypervisor has been configured correctly to provide the minimum necessary functionality, such as disallowing inter-VM network communications if not required or ensuring that virtualization tools like guest snapshots are encrypted.

- **Patching:** This control applies for any software. Monitor vulnerabilities disclosed that impact the virtualization tools in use by your organization, and ensure that all patches are applied in a timely manner.

Virtual hardware is highly configurable and, especially in general-purpose environments like platform as a service (PaaS) or infrastructure as a service (IaaS) public cloud offerings, may not be configured for security by default. It is the responsibility of the cloud consumer to properly configure the cloud environment to meet their specific needs, such as segmenting networks and configuring network access controls to permit only appropriate host-to-host communications. Particular concerns for virtual network security controls include the following:

- **Virtual private cloud (VPC):** This is essentially a carved-out section of a public cloud dedicated to use by a particular customer. Similar to the way a VPN creates a virtual connection over the public Internet, a VPC gives the customer a greater level of control, including managing private nonroutable IP addresses and control over inter-VM communication, such as allowing only specific hosts in a middleware VPC to communicate on specific ports to databases in a database VPC. VPCs are essentially a hybrid of the public and private cloud models designed to balance cost savings of the public cloud with greater security in a private cloud.

- **Security groups:** In clouds, a security group is similar to an access control list (ACL) for network access. Security groups can be configured to control access to various elements of the cloud environment, and then new VMs instantiated have the security group applied to manage their network access.

A partial security concern related to virtual hardware configuration is the amount of virtual hardware provisioned. Many tools will allow the user to specify quantities, such as amount of memory, speed, and number of processing cores, as well as other attributes such as type of storage for a VM. Availability is obviously one concern—sufficient quantities of these virtual resources must be provisioned to support the intended workload. From a business perspective, these virtual resources should not be overprovisioned, however, because they do have associated costs.

An emerging trend in cloud environments is the provisioning of hardware using definition files, referred to as *infrastructure as code.* These definition files are read by the CSP and used to specify virtual hardware parameters and configurations, simplifying the process of setting up and configuring the environment. In many organizations, this changes the old paradigm of developers writing code and operations personnel configuring the hosts, because developers can package infrastructure definitions with their application code. This requires adequate training for developers to ensure that they understand the business needs, security requirements, and configuration options available to them.

The ability to deploy infrastructure using a definition file enables a feature of cloud computing known as *autoscaling.* Resources deployed in the cloud environment can be monitored for utilization, and as resources reach their limit, additional resources are automatically added. For example, a web server hosting an online ordering app may come under increased traffic when a celebrity endorses a product; in an autoscaling cloud environment, new instances of the web server are spun up automatically to deal with the increased traffic. *Serverless computing* is another feature of cloud computing that can support availability. Serverless environments like Azure Functions and AWS Lambda allow developers to deploy their application code without specifying server resources required. When the application is run—for example, a customer wants to place an order—the CSP provides sufficient resources to handle that demand, supporting availability. The cloud consumer pays for the resources only when they are running the particular application, saving costs.

Installation of Guest Operating System Virtualization Toolsets

Toolsets exist that can provide extended functionality for various guest operating systems including Unix, Linux, and Microsoft Windows. These toolsets provide specific or enhanced capabilities for a particular operating system (OS), such as support for additional devices, driver software, or enhanced interactivity. In a public cloud, these toolsets will typically be provided by the CSP; if a customer requires functionality that depends on a particular OS toolset, it is up to the customer to verify if the CSP can support it before using that provider's cloud.

When managing your own virtualization environment, installing these toolsets should follow the concept of minimum necessary functionality. If a virtualization cluster will not be running virtual Windows servers, then the Windows OS toolset does not need to be installed. The personnel responsible for the virtualization cluster need to understand the business requirements and build the solution appropriately.

Operate Physical and Logical Infrastructure for Cloud Environment

Cloud computing has shifted many responsibilities for managing physical and logical infrastructure away from the users of the corresponding services. When organizations hosted their own infrastructure, it was essential to have adequate processes to assess risks and provision adequate security controls to mitigate them, but in the cloud, many of these tasks are the responsibility of the cloud provider instead. However, the consumers must still be aware of the risks inherent in using the cloud. It is essential for a CCSP to understand these matters to adequately assess cloud services and doubly important if the organization is providing a cloud service. In the case of a private cloud host or a security practitioner working for a CSP, these controls will be directly under the purview of the organization.

Configure Access Control for Local and Remote Access

In most instances, access to cloud resources will be done remotely, so adequate security controls must be implemented in the remote administrative tools implemented to support these functions. A CCSP should be familiar with the following protocols for supporting remote administration:

- **Secure Shell (SSH):** As the name implies, this standard provides a secure way for an administrator to access and manipulate a remote system. This is often achieved by interacting with a local command-line interface (CLI), which sends commands to the remote host for execution. SSH can be configured to implement encryption using either symmetric (shared) or asymmetric (public/private key pair) cryptography. In both cases, cryptography is used for both protection of data via encryption and authentication of users based on the assumption that a user has maintained control of their key. Only users with the appropriate key(s) will be granted access.

- **Remote Desktop Protocol (RDP):** RDP was initially a technology specific to Microsoft Windows but is now widely available across Windows, macOS, Linux, and mobile operating systems including iOS and Android. A typical session requires both an RDP server, which provides remote access and control to the machine it is running on, and an RDP client through which the user interacts with the remote machine. Security features available in RDP include encryption of data in transit, user authentication, and bandwidth management to ensure that remote desktop sharing and interaction are adequate to support user interactions. As a key element of the Windows OS as well as remote access, RDP functionality is often a target of hackers, so it is critical to maintain up-to-date versions as part of patch management.

  Access to RDP can be controlled in a variety of ways. As a Microsoft standard, Active Directory is often utilized for identification and authentication, and the RDP standard also supports smart card authentication.

- **Virtual network computing (VNC):** This may be considered analogous to RDP and is often implemented for remote access and control of Unix- or Linux-based systems where RDP is not native.

In situations where local administration is being performed, a secure Keyboard Video Mouse (KVM) switch may be utilized. This is a device that allows access to multiple hosts using a single set of human interface peripherals such as a keyboard, mouse, and monitor—a user does not need to have multiple keyboards on their desk physically attached to different computers.

A basic KVM allows the user to switch their peripherals to interact with various computers; a secure KVM adds additional protections for highly secured environments that primarily address the potential for data to leak between the various connected systems. Attributes of secure KVMs include the following:

- **Isolated data ports:** The physical construction ensures that each connected system is physically isolated from others.

- **Tamper-evident or tamper-resistant designs:** Secure KVMs may be manufactured to make physical tampering extremely difficult or impossible without destroying vital hardware, such as permanently soldered circuit boards or components. They may also implement tamper-evident stickers/labels that make it obvious if the KVM has been opened because the sticker is torn.

- **Secure storage:** KVMs may implement a buffer to store data, but switching between connected systems causes any data in the buffer to be erased. The buffer may additionally have only limited capacity, which reduces the usefulness but also reduces the amount of data that could potentially be leaked.

- **Secured firmware:** The software required by the KVM to run may often be fixed—it can't be changed without rendering the unit inoperable—or require signed firmware updates from the original manufacturer. Both are designed to prevent tampering.

- **Physical disconnects:** A KVM typically contains buttons on the front that allow the user to switch between the various connected systems. A physical disconnect physically breaks the connection between each system when a new system button is pressed, preventing data leaks from the currently connected system to the next system being connected.

- **USB port and device restrictions:** KVMs typically offer USB ports that are used to connect the peripherals being shared. Highly secured KVMs may implement restrictions on the type of USB devices that can be connected, such as allowing keyboards and mice but blocking mass storage devices, as a way to restrict what a malicious user can do if they gain physical access.

All CSPs provide remote administrative access to cloud users via an administrative console. In AWS this is known as the Management Console, in Azure as the Portal, and in Google Cloud as the Cloud Console. All three offer a visual user interface (UI) for interaction that allows for the creation and administration of resources including user accounts, VMs, cloud services such as compute or storage, and network configurations. These functions are also available via CLI tools, most of which call APIs to perform these same administrative functions manually and which enable automation such as creating resources based on infrastructure as code definition files.

The CSP is responsible for ensuring that access to these consoles is limited to properly authenticated users, and in many cases, the CSPs restrict access to consumer resources entirely. For example, it is possible for a user in Azure to create a VM and remove all network access from it, effectively locking themself out as well. Even Microsoft cannot reconfigure that VM, because allowing that level of access to consumer resources is incredibly risky. By contrast, the cloud consumer is responsible for implementing appropriate authorization and access control for their own members in accordance with access management policies, roles, and rules. Because of the highly sensitive nature and abilities granted by these consoles, they should be heavily isolated and protected, ideally with multifactor authentication. All use of the admin console should be logged and should be routinely reviewed as a critical element of a continuous monitoring capability. Access to the UI or CLI functions is a key area for personnel security and access control policies, similar to any system or database admin position in an on-prem environment.

Secure Network Configuration

One aspect of cloud services is their broad network accessibility, so it is virtually impossible to find a cloud security concern that does not in some way relate back to secure network connectivity. Several protocols and concepts are important to understand as they relate to securing networks and the data transmitted.

Virtual Local Area Networks

VLANs were originally designed to support the goal of availability by reducing contention on a shared communications line. They do so by isolating traffic to just a subset of network hosts, so all hosts connected to the VLAN broadcast their communications to each other but not to the broader network. Communication with other VLANs or subnets must go through a control device of some sort, often a firewall, which offers confidentiality and integrity protections by enforcing network-level access control. For example, in a multitiered application architecture, the web servers will traditionally be isolated from database servers in separate VLANs, and the database layer will implement much more restrictive access controls.

VLAN network traffic is identified by the sending device using a VLAN tag, specified in the IEEE802.1Q standard. The tag identifies the VLAN that the particular data frame belongs to and is used by network equipment to determine where the frame will be distributed. For example, a switch will not broadcast frames tagged VLAN1 to devices connected to VLAN2, alleviating congestion. Firewalls that exist between the two VLANs can make decisions to allow or drop traffic based on rules specifying allowed or denied ports, protocols, or sender/recipient addresses.

An extension of VLAN technology specific to cloud computing environments is the virtual extensible LAN (VXLAN) framework. It is intended to provide methods for designing VLANs utilizing layer 2 protocols onto layer 3; effectively, it allows for the creation of virtual LANs that may exist across different data centers or cloud environments. VXLAN is more suitable than VLANs for complex, distributed, and virtualized environments due to limitations on the number of devices that can be part of a VLAN, as well as limitations of protocols designed to support availability of layer 2 devices such as Spanning Tree Protocol (STP). It is specified in RFC 7348.

From the standpoint of the cloud consumer, network security groups (NSGs) are also a key tool in providing secure network services and provide a hybrid function of network traffic isolation and filtering similar to a firewall. The NSG allows or denies network traffic access based on a list of rules such as source IP, destination IP, protocol, and port number. Virtual resources can be segmented (isolated) from each other based on the NSGs applied to them. For example, a development environment may allow inbound traffic only from your organization's IP addresses on a broad range of ports, while a production environment may allow access from any IP address but only on ports 80/443 for web traffic. Resources in the development environment could also be prevented from communicating with any resources in production to prevent an attacker from pivoting.

Transport Layer Security

Transport Layer Security (TLS) is a set of cryptographic protocols that provide encryption for data in transit, and it replaced a previous protocol known as Secure Sockets Layer (SSL). The current version of TLS is 1.3; versions below this either are considered less secure or have demonstrated compromises. TLS provides a framework of supported cryptographic ciphers and keylengths that may be used to secure communications, and this flexibility ensures broad compatibility with a range of devices and systems. It also means the security practitioner must carefully configure their TLS-protected systems to support only ciphers that are known to be secure and disable older options if they have been compromised.

TLS specifies a handshake protocol when two parties establish an encrypted communications channel. This comprises these three steps:

1. The client initiates a request with a ClientHello message. This provides a list of cipher suites and TLS version it supports.

2. The server (if configured properly) chooses the highest-supported TLS version and cipher suite and communicates that choice to the client, along with the server's certificate containing a public key.

3. Depending on the cipher suite chosen, the client and server may then exchange other data, including a pre-master secret key used to negotiate a session key. The session key is utilized to encrypt all data that is to be shared.

TLS can be used to provide both encryption of data and authentication/proof of origin, as it relies on digital certificates and public key cryptography. In many cases, such as publicly available web apps, one-way authentication is used for the client's browser to authenticate the server it is connecting to, such as an online banking application. In *mutual authentication*, both client and server (or server and server) are required to exchange certificates. If both parties trust the issuer of the certificates, they can mutually authenticate their identities. Some high-security or high-integrity environments require mutual authentication before data is transmitted, but the overhead makes it largely infeasible for all TLS encryption (imagine the PKI required to authenticate every Internet user, web app, and IoT device on the planet).

Dynamic Host Configuration Protocol

Dynamic Host Configuration Protocol (DHCP) enables computer network communications by providing IP addresses to hosts that dynamically join and leave the network. The process of dynamically assigning IP addresses is as follows:

1. A DHCP server running on the network listens for clients.

2. When a new client machine joins a network, it sends out a DHCPDISCOVER request on UDP port 67, to which the DHCP server responds with a DHCPOFFER on port 68.

3. The client responds with a DHCPREQUEST indicating it will use the address assigned, and the server acknowledges with a DHCPACK.

An easy mnemonic to remember this DHCP process is DORA for Discover, Offer, Request, Acknowledge. As with many network protocols, security was not originally part of the DHCP design. The current DHCP version 6 specifies how IPSec can be utilized for authentication and encryption of DHCP requests. An improperly configured DHCP server can lead to denial of service if incorrect IP addresses are assigned or, worse, can be used in a man-in-the-middle attack to misdirect traffic.

Domain Name System and DNS Security Extensions

Imagine how difficult it would be if you were required to remember every company's and person's IP address to send them data. Human-readable addresses like www.isc2.org are used instead, but these need to be converted to a machine-readable IP address. DNS does this by a process known as *resolving*.

1. A user initiates a network communication using a fully qualified domain name (FQDN). This might be done by entering a URL into a web browser or sending an email to a particular domain.

2. The user's machine queries a Domain Name System (DNS) resolver service on UDP port 53, which provides the IP address associated with the FQDN. The user's machine uses this information to address the communications and carry out the user's action—for instance, loading a web page or sending an email.

DNS operates using records, definitive mappings of FQDNs to IP addresses, which are stored in a distributed database across zones. DNS queries are facilitated by DNS servers sharing information from time to time, known as *zone transfers*, which enable resolution of client requests without having to iterate a request.

DNS Attacks

As with many network protocols, DNS was originally designed without security in mind, which leaves it open to attack. *Cache poisoning* is an attack where a malicious user updates a DNS record to point an FQDN to an incorrect IP address. One way of doing this is to initiate a zone transfer, which by default does not include authentication of the originator. This poisoned record causes users to be redirected to an incorrect IP address, where the attacker can host a malicious phishing site, malware, or simply nothing at all to create a denial of service.

DNS spoofing is another attack against DNS. In this case, an attacker spoofs a DNS service on a network with the goal of resolving a user's requested FQDN to an attacker-controlled IP address. Some attacks against DNS also abuse graphical interfaces instead of the underlying infrastructure. This can be achieved using characters that appear identical to users, such as zero and the letter *o*, sending users to an illegitimate site.

DNS Security Extensions (DNSSEC) is a set of specifications primarily aimed at reinforcing the integrity of DNS. It achieves this by providing for cryptographic authentication of DNS data using digital signatures. This provides proof of origin and makes cache poisoning and spoofing attacks more difficult if users cannot create a proper digital signature for their DNS data. It does not provide for confidentiality, since digital signatures rely on publicly decryptable information, nor does it stop attacks using graphically similar domain names, as these may be legitimate records registered with an authoritative DNS zone.

Virtual Private Network

Resources inside a network can be protected with security tools like firewalls and access controls, but what happens if users are not on the same network? A VPN gives external users the ability to virtually and remotely join a network, gaining access to resources hosted on that network and benefiting from the security controls in place. This security is achieved by setting up a secure tunnel, or encrypted communication channel, between the connecting host and the network they want to join. On the target network, there is often a VPN device or server that authenticates the user connecting and mediates their access to the network.

Commonly used to provide remote workers access to in-office network resources, VPNs can also be useful in cloud architectures to safely share data between offices, cloud environments, or other networks. These are often implemented at the edge of networks to allow secure communication between any hosts on connected networks and are called *site-to-site* or *gateway-to-gateway* VPNs.

There are a variety of VPN protocols and implementations that a CCSP should be familiar with, such as the following:

- **OpenVPN:** This is an open-source VPN built on encryption in the OpenSSL project, which can be deployed and run on your own infrastructure, as well as commercial service options. These consist of packages that can be easily deployed in cloud environments as a virtual VPN server. OpenVPN can be used to establish site-to-site VPN connectivity and provides client-server functionality across a wide variety of Linux and Unix operating systems, as well as several versions of the Windows and macOS operating systems. Details can be found at openvpn.net.

- **Internet Key Exchange v2 and IPSec (IKEV2/IPSec):** This protocol utilizes the Security Associate (SA) features of IPSec to establish the encrypted communications channel. Public keys are exchanged, and Diffie–Hellman is used to independently calculate the shared session key. It is widely built into Microsoft products and Apple iOS devices, which may simplify deployment as no additional software is required.

- **SSL VPN:** Although the use of SSL has largely been replaced with TLS, these are still commonly referred to as SSL VPNs. These are often implemented in a browser due to ubiquitous support for TLS encryption and can provide remote connectivity for users without requiring the installation of additional software. This ubiquity is also a potential downside, as a user might be connecting from any Internet-connected machine, which may lack standard security software, be missing patches, or have malware installed. In this case, compensating controls such as tightly restricted access for SSL VPN users or some form of network access control (NAC) may be required.

Software-Defined Perimeter

A software-defined perimeter (SDP) is an emerging concept driven by the decentralized nature of cloud applications and services, which have upended the traditional model of a network with a perimeter (secure boundary). Since cloud applications may reside in data centers anywhere in the world, and users may also be connecting from anywhere in the world, it is no longer possible to define a perimeter.

1. One or more SDP controllers are created, which are connected to an authentication service to enforce access control.

2. Accepting SDP hosts are brought online and authenticate to the SDP controllers. By default, accepting hosts do not accept communication from any other host.

3. Initiating SDP hosts connect to the SDP controllers for authentication and can request access to resources on an accepting host. The SDP controller makes authorization decisions and provides details to both the initiating and accepting hosts. These details include authorization and encryption policies to establish a VPN.

4. A mutual VPN is established between the initiating and accepting hosts, and the user is able to interact with the resource.

For further reference, see the CSA SDP site: `cloudsecurityalliance.org/research/working-groups/software-defined-perimeter`.

Operating System Hardening through the Application of Baselines

Hardening is the configuration of a machine into a secure state. Common hardening practices include changing default credentials, locking/disabling default accounts that are not needed, installing security tools such as anti-malware software, configuring security settings available in the OS, and removing or disabling unneeded applications, services, and functions.

Prior to virtualization, the process of hardening an OS was often a manual task; once a system's hardware was installed, an administrator had to manually install and configure the OS and any application software. The advent of virtualization introduced machine images, which are essentially templates for building a VM. All VMs created from the same image will have the same settings applied, which offers dual benefits of efficiency and security. Of course, the image cannot remain static—patches and other security updates must be applied to the image to ensure that new VMs remain secure. Existing VMs must also be updated independently of the image, which is a concern of patching and configuration management disciplines.

A modern OS has thousands of configuration options, so to speed this up, an organization may choose to create or use a baseline configuration. Baselines are simply a documented, standard state of an information system, such as access control requiring multifactor authentication, vulnerable services such as File Transfer Protocol (FTP) disabled, and nonessential services such as Windows Media Player removed. Each of these configuration options should match a risk mitigation (security control objective).

This baseline and corresponding documentation may be achieved in a number of ways.

- **Customer-defined VM image:** A customer spins up a VM and configures it to meet their specifications. Virtualization tools allow you to create an image from an existing machine, and from then on, this image may be used to create secure VMs. This option may also be built on top of one of the other options in this list. For example, an organization might use a CIS Benchmark as a starting point, tailor it to their specific needs, and create an image from that. This is similar to word processing software that allows you to create a template from an existing document.

- **CSP-defined images:** CSPs may offer one or more of the following as a PaaS solution: popular operating systems like Microsoft Windows and various Linux distributions, databases and big data tools, or virtualization platforms like Hyper-V and VMware. These images often incorporate the latest patches and may have some security configuration already applied, but they should always be evaluated for appropriateness against the organization's own security needs and tailored where needed.

- **Vendor-supplied baselines:** Microsoft, VMware, and some Linux creators offer configuration guidelines for their products that point out specific security options and recommended settings. As with any external source, it is imperative that the organization evaluate the recommendations against their own needs.

  DISA STIGs: The U.S. Defense Information Systems Agency (DISA) produces baseline documents known as Security Technical Implementation Guides (STIGs). These documents provide guidance for hardening systems used in high-security environments and, as such, may include configurations that are too restrictive for many organizations. They are available for free and can be tailored, obviously, and also cover a broad range of OS and application software. Many configuration and vulnerability management tools incorporate hardening guidance from the STIGs to perform checks.

  STIGs and additional information can be found here: `public.cyber.mil/stigs/downloads`.

  NIST checklists: The National Institute of Standards and Technology (NIST) maintains a repository of configuration checklists for various OS and application software. It is a free resource.

  The NIST Checklist repository (which also includes access to DISA STIGs) can be found here: `nvd.nist.gov/ncp/repository`.

  CIS Benchmarks: The Center for Internet Security (CIS) publishes baseline guides for a variety of operating systems, applications, and devices, which incorporate many security best practices. These can be used by any organization with appropriate tailoring and are also built into many security tools such as vulnerability scanners.

  More information can be found here: `www.cisecurity.org/cis-benchmarks`.

Availability of Stand-Alone Hosts

Stand-alone hosts are isolated, dedicated hosts for the use of a single tenant. These are often required for contractual or regulatory reasons, such as processing highly sensitive data like healthcare information. The use of nonshared resources carries obvious consequences related to costs. A CSP may be able to offer secure dedicated hosting similar to colocation, which still offers cost savings to the consumer due to shared resources including physical facilities and shared resources like power and utilities. A CCSP will need to gather and analyze the organization's requirements to identify whether the costs of stand-alone hosting are justified. In some CSPs, the use of virtual private resources may be an acceptable alternative with lower costs, due to the use of shared physical infrastructure with strong logical separation from other tenants.

Availability of Clustered Hosts

Clusters are a grouping of resources with some coordinating element, often a software agent that facilitates communication, resource sharing, and routing of tasks among the cluster. Clustered hosts can offer a number of advantages, including high availability via redundancy, optimized performance via distributed workloads, and the ability to scale resources without disrupting processing via addition or removal of hosts to the cluster. Clusters are a critical part of the resource pooling that are foundational to cloud computing and are implemented in some fashion for most resources needed in modern computing systems including processing, storage, network traffic handling, and application hosting.

The cluster management agent, often part of hypervisor or load balancer software, is responsible for mediating access to shared resources in a cluster. *Reservations* are guarantees for a certain minimum level of resources available to a specified virtual machine. The virtualization toolset or CSP console is often where this can be configured, such as a certain number of compute cores or RAM allocated to a VM. A *limit* is a maximum allocation, while a *share* is a weighting given to a particular VM that is used to calculate percentage-based access to pooled resources when there is contention.

Maintenance mode refers to the practices surrounding the routine maintenance activities for clustered hosts. Although taking a system offline primarily impacts availability, there are considerations for all three elements of the confidentiality, integrity, availability (CIA) triad related to maintenance mode.

- **Confidentiality**: Many live migration tools transmit data in cleartext due to the operational overhead incurred by trying to encrypt all the data related to a running OS and applications. If this is the case, compensating controls may be required for the migration, especially if the live migration data will be transmitted across untrusted network segments.

- **Integrity**: During maintenance mode, customers are not able to access or get alerts regarding the environment's configuration. The CSP's change management process needs to include robust integrity controls such as change approvals and documentation, and systems should still generate logs when in maintenance mode to support after-the-fact investigation if needed.

- **Availability**: Maintenance usually involves taking a system offline, which is obviously counter to the goal of availability. To meet obligations for uptime and availability, the CSP should migrate all running VMs or services off a cluster prior to entering maintenance mode. Most virtualization toolsets automate this process, which is referred to as *live migration*. In some limited cases, a CSP may also take a service completely offline; in these cases, all consumers must be made aware of the outage beforehand, either through ad hoc communication or through a published maintenance window. SLAs should be documented that take into account the need for both routine and emergency maintenance tasks.

High Availability

Availability and uptime are often used interchangeably, but there is a subtle difference between the terms. Uptime simply measures the amount of time a system is running. In a cloud environment, if a system is running but not reachable due to a network outage, it is not available. Availability encompasses infrastructure and other supporting elements in addition to a system's uptime; *high availability* (HA) is defined by a robust system and infrastructure to ensure that a system is not just up but also available. It is often measured as a number of 9s, for example, five nines or 99.999 percent availability. This equates to approximately five minutes of downtime per year and should be measured by the cloud consumer to ensure that the CSP is meeting SLA obligations.

Organizations can implement multiple strategies to achieve HA. Some, detailed in the following sections, are vendor-specific implementations of cluster management features for maintaining system uptime. Other strategies include redundancy of infrastructure such as network connectivity and utilities. The Uptime Institute publishes specifications for physical and environmental redundancy, expressed as tiers, that organizations can implement to achieve HA.

- Tier 1 involves no redundancy and the most amount of downtime in the event of unplanned maintenance or an interruption.

- Tier 2 provides partial redundancy, meaning an unplanned interruption will not necessarily cause an outage.

- Tiers 3 and 4 provide N+1 and 2N+1 levels of redundancy, which results in increased availability. Tier 3 allows for planned maintenance activities without disruption, but an unplanned failure can still cause an outage. Tier 4 is known as fault-tolerant, meaning it can withstand either planned or unplanned activity without affecting availability. This is achieved by eliminating all single points of failure and requires fully redundant infrastructure such as dual commercial power feeds and dual backup generators. This redundancy provides very high availability but also comes at a higher cost.

Distributed Resource Scheduling

Distributed Resource Scheduling (DRS) is the coordination element in a cluster of VMware ESXi hosts, which mediates access to the physical resources and provides additional features supporting high availability and management. It is a software component that handles the resources available to a particular cluster, the reservations and limits for the VMs running on the cluster, and maintenance features.

DRS maintenance features include the ability to dynamically move running VMs from one physical hardware component to another without disruption for the end users; this is obviously useful if hardware maintenance needs to be performed or additional capacity is added to the cluster and the workload needs to be rebalanced. This supports the element of rapid elasticity and self-service provisioning in the cloud by automating dynamic creation and release of resources as client demands change.

DRS can also handle energy management in physical hardware to reduce energy consumption when processing demands are low and then power resources back up when required. This enables cost savings for both the CSP and consumer, as hardware that is not actively being used does not consume energy.

Microsoft Virtual Machine Manager and Dynamic Optimization

Similar to VMware's DRS, Microsoft's Virtual Machine Manager (VMM) software handles power management, live VM migration, and optimization of both storage and compute resources. Hosts (servers) and storage capacity can be grouped into a cluster; options available to configure in the VMM console include the movement of VMs and virtual hard disks between hosts to balance workloads across available resources.

Storage Clusters

Storage clusters create a pool of storage, with the goal of providing reliability, increased performance, or possibly additional capacity. They can also support dynamic system availability by making data available to services running anywhere—if a data center in one part of the country fails and web hosts are migrated to another data center, they can connect to the same storage cluster without needing to be reconfigured. There are two primary architectures for storage clusters.

- Components in a *tightly coupled* cluster are often all provided by the same manufacturer, and updates or expansion must come from that same manufacturer. The advantage of a tightly coupled cluster is generally better performance due to the division of data into deterministic blocks. When a file is written to such a storage cluster, it is broken down into blocks that are faster to read and write to disks than the entire file. This is especially relevant if the data is to be mirrored, as writing multiple copies of a long file will take longer than duplicating blocks, and blocks can be written across multiple nodes or disks simultaneously.

- *Loosely coupled* storage offers more flexibility and lower cost at the expense of performance. Components can usually be added using any off-the-shelf parts, but the use of file-level storage means operations will be slower.

Availability of Guest Operating Systems

The availability of a guest OS in a CSP's environment is generally the consumer's responsibility, as the CSP only provides a base image. Once a VM is created in IaaS, the CSP no longer has direct control over the OS, while in PaaS the CSP maintains control. In the software as a service (SaaS) model, the consumer only needs to plan for availability of the data their organization puts into the app.

Ensuring the availability of guest OSs in a cloud environment may involve planning for backup and restoration, which will be similar to traditional on-prem backup and recovery planning, or it may involve utilizing cloud-specific features to design resiliency into the system. Details of these two approaches are presented here:

Backup and recovery: This is a more traditional method that assumes a system will be built, may be interrupted, and will then need to be recovered. In virtualized cloud infrastructure, this might involve the use of snapshots, which are provided by virtualization toolsets. Snapshots typically capture the state of a VM's primary storage, random access memory (RAM), and software configurations, which can be used to re-create the VM— at the point of the snapshot—on another physical host. Obviously, this approach could involve loss of data between the snapshot creation and the failure, as well as the time required to manually create the new VM instance.

As with all backup and restoration activity, there are concerns across all three CIA triad elements. Backup integrity should be routinely tested to ensure recovery, and the backups should not be stored on the same physical hardware as the primary systems since this single point of failure could impact availability. Snapshots will contain data with the same sensitivity level as the systems they are made from, so adequate access controls and other measures to enforce confidentiality are required.

Resiliency: Building resiliency is achieved by architecting systems to handle failures from the outset rather than needing to be recovered. One example is using a clustered architecture with live migration; in this case, if a physical hardware failure is detected, all running VMs are transferred to another physical host, with little or no interruption to the users.

Many cloud services also have resiliency options built in, such as worldwide data replication and availability zones or regions that can transfer running apps or services transparently in the event of a failure. The cloud consumer is responsible for choosing and configuring these resiliency options, and in some cases will need to make trade-offs. For example, some CSPs offer database encryption that makes it harder to perform data replication. In traditional on-prem architecture, building such a resilient app would have been cost prohibitive for all but the largest organizations, but the inherent structure of cloud computing makes this type of resiliency broadly available.

Manage Physical and Logical Infrastructure for Cloud Environment

Although many elements of physical and logical infrastructure in cloud environments will be under the direct control of the CSP, it is essential for cloud consumers and the CCSP practitioner to be aware of these practices. In some cases, there will be shared responsibilities that both parties are required to perform, and in others, the consumer must adequately understand these practices and conduct oversight activities like SLA reviews to ensure that security objectives are being met.

Access Controls for Remote Access

Remote administration is the default for a majority of cloud administrators from both the CSP and the consumer side. Tools including Remote Desktop Protocol (RDP), used primarily for Windows systems, and Secure Shell (SSH), used primarily on Unix and Linux systems, must be provisioned to support this remote management.

Secure remote access is a top-level priority in many security frameworks due to the highly sensitive nature of operations it entails and its inherent exposure to attacks. Remote access often relies on untrusted network segments for transmitting data, and in a cloud environment, this will entail users connecting via the Internet. Physical controls that could prevent unwanted access in a data center will be largely missing in a cloud as well; not that the CSP is ignoring physical security controls, but the inherently network-accessible nature of the cloud means most administrative functions must be exposed and are therefore susceptible to network-based threats.

There are a number of concerns that should be addressed to reduce the risk associated with remote access, including the following:

- **Session encryption:** Remote access always requires additional security because it happens outside an organization's perimeter, and cloud-based applications often do away with secure perimeters altogether. Data transmitted in remote access sessions must be encrypted using strong protocols such as TLS 1.3 and should implement cryptographic best practices such as session-specific cryptographic keys, which reduce the possibility of replay attacks.

- **Strong authentication:** Users performing remote administration present higher risk to the organization, so more robust authentication is appropriate for these users. This may be combined with cryptographic controls such as a shared secret key for SSH, assuming the user retains control over their key, as well as the use of two or more authentication factors for multifactor authentication (MFA), such as a one time code or hardware key.

- **Separate privileged and nonprivileged accounts:** A general best practice for administrative users is the use of a dedicated admin account for sensitive functions, and a standard user account for normal functions such as daily web browsing or email. This approach offers two benefits: first, it reduces threats related to phishing by reducing the likelihood that a user's admin account credentials will be stolen, and second, it allows the organization to implement more stringent controls on the admin account without creating undue overhead for the user's daily business account. In many cloud environments, this is implemented by default, as a user's credentials to log in to the cloud admin console are separate from their main email or computer login.

- **Enhanced logging and reviews:** This is also a general best practice not specific to cloud remote access. All admin accounts should be subject to additional logging and review of activity, as well as more frequent review of permissions.

- **Use of identity and access management tool:** Many CSPs offer identity and access management tools specific for their environments, and third-party identity as a service (IDaaS) providers also exist, which offer the ability to manage logical access controls across cloud and on-prem applications. Many of these offer easy management of the previously discussed controls for administrator accounts, such as enhanced logging or more stringent password requirements. Examples of IDaaS tools include offerings from companies such as Okta, Microsoft Azure AD, Ping, and Auth0.

- **Single sign-on (SSO):** Two of the major CSPs also offer productivity software: Google Workspace and Microsoft's 365 product line (previously known as Office 365). Both platforms enable users to log into other services using their company accounts, similar to the option in many consumer services to log in with a Facebook or Gmail account. This reduces the burden on users to remember passwords and simplifies administration of user access by reducing the number of accounts. Many IDaaS solutions also offer the ability to function as an SSO provider.

Operating System Baseline Compliance Monitoring and Remediation

A hardened OS implements many of the security controls required by an organization's risk tolerance and may also implement security configurations designed to meet the organization's compliance obligations. Once built, however, these systems do need to be monitored to ensure that they stay hardened. This ongoing monitoring and remediation of any noncompliant systems must be part of the organization's configuration management processes, designed to ensure that no unauthorized changes are made, any unauthorized changes are identified and rolled back, and changes are properly approved and applied through a change control process.

Monitoring and managing OS configuration against baselines can be achieved in a number of ways. Some are similar to legacy, on-prem techniques, while newer methods are also emerging, including the following:

- **Use of a configuration management database (CMDB) and CM audits:** The organization's CMDB should capture all configuration items (CIs) that have been placed under configuration management. This database can be used for manual audits as well as automated scanning to identify systems that have drifted out of their known secure state. For example, an auditor performing a manual audit could pull the registry file from a sample of Windows servers and compare the entries against the configuration baseline values. Any systems that deviate from the baseline should be reconfigured, unless a documented exception exists. Automated configuration and vulnerability scanners can also perform this task on a more routine basis, and any findings from these scans should be treated using standard vulnerability management processes.

- **Organization-wide vulnerability scanning:** System-specific vulnerability and configuration scans should be complemented by the organization's broader vulnerability management policy. For example, insecure services such as FTP may be disallowed on all organization systems, and a vulnerability scanner can easily identify a server responding to FTP requests. This vulnerability indicates a system that does not conform to baseline configuration and that requires immediate remediation action.

- **Immutable architecture:** This is an evolving solution to the problem of systems that, over time, can drift away from baseline configurations. Immutable architecture is unchangeable but short lived. In cloud environments, it is possible to tear down all virtual infrastructure elements used by an old version of software and deploy new virtual infrastructure quite simply; in traditional architecture, this process would be much more difficult and time-consuming. Immutable architecture can address baseline monitoring and compliance by limiting the amount of time a host can exist in a noncompliant state; the next time the application is deployed, the old host is torn down, and a new VM is built from the standard baseline image.

Patch Management

Maintaining a known good state is not a static activity, unfortunately. Today's hardened system is tomorrow's highly vulnerable target for attack, as new vulnerabilities are discovered, reported, and weaponized by attackers. Patch management involves identifying vulnerabilities in your environment, applying appropriate patches or software updates, and validating that the patch has remediated the vulnerability without breaking any functionality or creating additional vulnerabilities.

Information needed to perform patch management can come from a variety of sources, but primary sources include vendor-published patch notifications, such as Microsoft's Patch Tuesday, as well as vulnerability scanning of your environment. Patch management processes will vary depending on the cloud service model you are using.

- For SaaS environments, the consumer has almost no responsibilities, as applying patches is the CSP's purview. Verifying that patches are being applied according to established SLAs is a recommended practice for the consumer organization, and maintaining oversight on this metric is important. Additionally, some SaaS offerings provide staggered or on-your-own schedule patching, especially for custom software. In these models, the consumer may have the option to apply patches/updates immediately or apply to a small sample of users for testing purposes. In this case, the consumer must understand the shared responsibility and take appropriate action.

- For IaaS and PaaS, it is usually the consumer's exclusive responsibility to apply patches to existing infrastructure. Hardware-based patches will likely be handled by the CSP, who is also likely to maintain up-to-date templates, used for PaaS VMs. Once a consumer creates a VM from a PaaS template the CSP retains responsibility for patching the OS, while the consumer is responsible for patching any applications installed on the VM.

Patch management tools exist that can help to identify known software vulnerabilities and the state of patching across an organization's system, such as Windows Server Update Services (WSUS). Such tools can also be used to orchestrate and automate patch application, though in some cases automation may not be desirable if a patch has operational impacts. There are plenty of patches and updates from major companies that caused unknown issues when installed, including turning otherwise functional hardware into bricks! A generic patch management process ought to incorporate the following:

- **Vulnerability detection:** This may be done by security researchers, customers, or the vendor. A software flaw, bug, or other issue that could be exploited drives the need for a patch.

- **Publication of patch:** The vendor provides notice, either through a standard update mechanism or through ad hoc communication such as press releases, circulating details to information sharing and analysis centers (ISACs), or other means. Consuming organizations ought to have subscriptions to relevant information sources for their industry and infrastructure. In other words, if an organization uses Red Hat Linux exclusively, the IT and security teams ought to be subscribed to relevant data feeds from Red Hat to receive notice of vulnerabilities and patches.

- **Evaluation of patch applicability:** Not all users of software will need to apply all patches. In some cases, there may be features or functions that are not in use by an organization, meaning the patched vulnerability has no real impact. As a general best practice, all applicable patches should be applied unless there is a known functionality issue with the patch.

- **Test:** Most patches should be tested in a limited environment to identify any potential functionality issues before being broadly deployed; patches designed to close highly critical vulnerabilities may be treated as an exception, since the vulnerability they remediate is riskier than the potential for an outage.

- **Apply and track:** Assuming a patch does have negative functionality impacts, the organization must identify all systems that require the patch and then plan for and track the deployment to ensure that it is applied to all systems. In many organizations, there will be a key security metric worth tracking. Patches should have timeframes for application based on their criticality; for example, critical patches must be applied within seven days of release. This service level helps the organization measure and track risk and associated remediation efforts.

 NOTE VMs present a particular challenge for patching efforts. As discussed, one of the features in many virtualization tools is the ability to power down a VM when it is not needed, but this can have the unintended consequence of leaving systems unpatched. The organization should have compensating controls, such as powering on all VMs when patches are deployed or performing checks when a VM is first powered on to detect and apply any missing patches.

- **Rollback if needed:** Not all patching goes smoothly, so a rollback plan is essential. Virtualization makes this incredibly easy, as a snapshot can be created before the patch is applied, but that step must be part of the deployment process.

- **Document:** Patched software represents a changed system baseline; the new, patched version of software is the new known good state. Systems used to track this, such as the CMDB, need to be updated to record this official change and new expected configuration.

Evolving cloud architectures are introducing new ways of managing patching, which offers significant advantages if applied correctly.

- The use of infrastructure as code, where system architecture is documented in a definition file used by the CSP to spin up virtual infrastructure, offers a way for organizations to utilize a CSP's patched template files. These definition files are often used to create virtual infrastructure in PaaS environments and should always make use of the latest patched version of the platforms in question.

- Immutable architecture, which is created each time a system is deployed and then torn down when the next deployment occurs, can also help prevent the spread of old systems with unpatched software. This relies on infrastructure as code and should be configured to always make use of the latest, patched infrastructure elements.

- Software composition analysis (SCA) is a concern for applications built with open-source software components, many of which provide highly reusable elements of modern applications such as data forms or code libraries. Since this type of software is included in many applications, SCA tools identify flaws/vulnerabilities in these included pieces of the application. This represents a merging of application security and patch management and is a key automation point for security in application development. Identifying vulnerabilities in these included functions and ensuring that the latest, patched versions are in use by your application is a critical part of both development processes and patch management.

Equifax Data Breach

In 2017, credit monitoring company Equifax suffered a massive data breach that affected more than 140 million people, primarily in the United States but in other countries as well. The company maintains highly sensitive personal information used in financial decision making, and this information was exposed due to an unpatched software flaw in a web application server. The vulnerability had been published and a patch provided by the software vendor, but it was not properly applied throughout the Equifax environment. This unpatched software vulnerability allowed attackers to break in and steal data; estimates of the costs associated with this breach top $1 billion, including fines, lawsuits, and an overhaul of the company's information security program!

Source: www.bankinfosecurity.com/equifaxs-data-breach-costs-hit-14-billion-a-12473

Performance and Capacity Monitoring

Monitoring is a critical concern for all parties in cloud computing. The CSP should implement monitoring to ensure that they are able to meet customer demands and promised capacity, and consumers need to perform monitoring to ensure that service providers are meeting their obligations and that the organization's systems remain available for users.

The majority of monitoring tasks will be in support of the availability objective, though indicators of an attack or misuse may be revealed as well, such as spikes in processor utilization that could be caused by cryptocurrency mining malware. Alerts should be generated based on established thresholds, and appropriate action plans initiated in the event of an event or disruption. Monitoring is not necessarily designed to detect incidents, however. It is also critical for CSPs to measure the amount of services being used by customers so they can be billed accurately.

Infrastructure elements that should be monitored include the following:

- **Network:** Cloud computing is, by design, accessible via networks, so it is essential to monitor their performance and availability. Bandwidth utilization, link state (up or down), and number of dropped packets are examples of metrics that might be captured.

- **Compute:** Though traditionally defined as CPU utilization, often measured in cores or number of operations, compute can also include other forms of processing such as GPUs, field-programmable gate arrays (FPGA), or even service calls to an API or microservices architecture, where the service is billed based on the number of requests made.

- **Storage and memory:** Data storage and memory are often measured in terms of total amount used, but other measures also exist such as number of reads and writes (input output operations, or IOPS), as well as speed of data access. Speed is a critical measure for many cloud services that are priced based on data retrieval, allowing cloud consumers to realize cost savings by storing infrequently needed data in a slower environment, while keeping essential data more quickly accessible in a more expensive environment.

Regardless of what is being monitored and who performs it, adequate staffing is critical to make monitoring effective. Just as reviews make log files impactful, appropriate users of performance data are also essential. If a metric is captured but the cloud consumer never reviews it, they run the risk of a service being unavailable with no forewarning or paying for services that were not actually usable. CSPs also face risks of customers complaining, customers refusing to pay, and loss of reputation if their services are not routinely available.

Hardware Monitoring

Although cloud computing relies heavily on virtualization, at some point physical hardware is necessary to provide all the services. Monitoring this physical hardware is essential, especially for availability as hardware failures can have an outsized impact in virtualization due to multiple VMs relying on a single set of hardware.

Various tools exist to perform physical monitoring, and the choice will depend on the hardware being used as well as organizational business needs. Similar to capacity monitoring, all hardware under monitoring should have alert thresholds and response actions if a metric goes outside expected values, such as automated migration of VMs from faulty hardware or an alert to investigate and replace a faulty component. Hardware targets for monitoring may include the following:

- **Compute hardware and supporting infrastructure:** The CPU, RAM, fans, disk drives, network gear, and other physical components of the infrastructure have operating tolerances related to heat and electricity. Monitoring these devices to ensure that they are within tolerance is a critical aspect of ensuring availability; a CPU that overheats or a power supply that sends too much wattage can shorten the lifespan of a component or cause it to fail altogether. Fan speed can also be used as an indicator of workload; the harder a system is working, the more heat it produces, which causes fans to spin faster.

   Some devices also include built-in monitoring, such as hard drives that support self-monitoring, analysis, and reporting technology (SMART). SMART drives monitor a number of factors related to drive health and can identify when a failure is imminent. Many SSDs also provide reporting when a set number of sectors have failed, which means the drive is reaching the end of its useful life. Especially in large environments, storage tools like storage area networks (SAN) will include their own health and diagnostic tools; the information from these should be integrated into the organization's continuous monitoring strategy.

- **Environmental:** All computing components generate heat and are generally not designed for use in very wet environments or in direct contact with water. Monitoring environmental conditions including heat, humidity, and the presence of water can be critical to detecting issues early.

The types of monitoring tools in use will depend on a number of factors. Many vendors of cloud-grade hardware such as SAN controllers or virtualization clusters include diagnostic and monitoring tools. The usefulness of these built-in tools may be limited if your organization's measurement needs require data that is not captured, in which case a third-party tool may be required.

In general, hardware monitoring will be the purview of the CSP and not the consumer, as the CSP is likely to retain physical control of hardware. Data center design and infrastructure management are entire fields of endeavor largely outside the scope of the CCSP, but it is obviously important for a CSP to have appropriately skilled team members. The Uptime Institute (uptimeinstitute.com/tiers) is one resource that provides guidance and education on designing and managing infrastructure; another is the International Data Center Authority (www.idc-a.org).

Configuration of Host and Guest Operating System Backup and Restore Functions

There is a clear delineation of responsibility between the CSP and consumer when it comes to configuring, testing, and managing backup and restoration functions in cloud environments. In SaaS cloud models, the CSP retains full control over backup and restore and will often be governed by SLA commitments for restoration in the event of an incident or outage.

In the PaaS model, there will be backup and restoration responsibilities for both the consumer and the CSP, especially for VMs. The CSP is responsible for maintaining backup and restoration of the host OS and any hypervisor software and for ensuring the availability of the system in line with agreed-upon service levels.

Backup and recovery of individual VMs in IaaS are the responsibility of the consumers and may be done in a variety of ways. This might include full backups, snapshots, or definition files used for infrastructure as code deployments. Regardless of which backup method is utilized, a number of security considerations should be taken into account.

- Sensitive data may be stored in backups, particularly in snapshot functions that do not support the same access controls or encryption as the OS they are created from. In this case, access to snapshots and need-to-know principles must be considered when designing the backup plan.

- Snapshots and backups may be created on the same physical hardware as the running VMs, which violates a core principle of data backups: physical separation. As a best practice, these should be stored on different hardware (if possible) or in a different availability zone to ensure that an incident affecting the main environment does not also impact the backup data.

- Integrity of all backups should be verified routinely to ensure that they are usable. Snapshots or backups should also be updated as system changes occur, especially patches or major configuration changes. Disaster recovery (DR) and business continuity (BC) exercises may be used as formal testing of backup and recovery capabilities, and many organizations conduct such exercises annually. Depending on the frequency of these exercises, additional testing may be appropriate to ensure that backup and restoration capabilities are adequate in the event a recovery is needed. Some backup systems provide for automated testing of every backup, and manual recovery tests can also be useful.

Configuration of resiliency functions, such the use of automatic data replication, failover between availability zones offered by the CSP, or the use of network load balancing, will always be the responsibility of the consumer. The CSP is responsible for maintaining the capabilities that enable these options, but the consumer must architect their cloud environment, infrastructure, and applications appropriately to meet their own resiliency objectives.

Network Security Controls

Cloud environments are inherently network accessible, so the security of data in transit between the consumer and the CSP is a critical concern, with both parties sharing responsibility for architecting secure networks. CSPs must ensure that they adequately support the networks they are providing in the cloud service environment, and consumers are responsible, in some cloud service models, for architecting their own secure networks using a combination of their own tools and those provided by the CSP.

One major concern related to network security is the ability of some tools to function in a cloud paradigm. The early days of virtualization brought challenges for many security tools that relied on capturing network traffic as it flowed across a switch; the devices were attached to a SPAN or mirror port on the switch and received a copy of all traffic for analysis. VMs running on the same physical host did not need to send traffic outside the host to communicate, rendering tools listening for traffic on a switch useless. Complex software-defined networks (SDNs) that can span multiple data centers around the world likely require more advanced solutions, and security practitioners must be aware of these challenges.

Firewalls

Firewalls are most broadly defined as a security tool designed to isolate and control access between segments of a network, whether it is an internal network and the public Internet or even between environments such as an application with highly sensitive data and other internal apps. Firewalls operate by inspecting traffic and making a decision whether to forward the traffic (allow) or drop it (deny) and are often used to isolate or *segment* networks by controlling what network traffic is allowed to flow between segments. There are a variety of firewall types.

- **Static packet or stateless:** These are the original type of firewall, designed to inspect network packets and compare them against a ruleset. For example, the firewall might see TCP destination port 23 (Telnet) in a packet's headers and decide to drop the packet since Telnet is an insecure protocol. Static firewalls operate quickly but can struggle with complex situations like voice over IP (VoIP) and videoconferencing where a call is initiated on one port, but the actual call traffic is exchanged on a different port negotiated for that communication session.

- **Stateful:** These are an evolution of static firewalls and offer the ability for the firewall to understand some context regarding communication (known as a *state*). For example, the firewall might allow traffic on a random high-number port from a particular host if it had also seen previous traffic on port 20/21 (FTP). Since FTP clients often negotiate a custom port to be used for a specific file transfer, this traffic makes sense in the context of previous traffic; without the previous traffic on port 20, the firewall would block the traffic on the high-number port. In this case, the firewall has more intelligence and flexibility to make decisions, but with a higher processing overhead and cost.

- **Web application firewall (WAF) and API gateway:** These are a highly specialized form of network access control devices that are designed to handle specific types of traffic, unlike a generic firewall that can handle any network traffic. WAFs and API gateways allow for the analysis of traffic destined specifically for a web application or an application's API and can be useful in detecting more complex attacks such as SQL injection, which could not be identified by looking at raw network traffic. These devices apply a set of rules to HTTP conversations and look for anomalous interactions with the application.

- **Security groups:** In SDNs, it can be difficult or impossible to locate specific infrastructure elements of the network. For example, a globally load-balanced application may exist in several data centers all over the world, and it would be a headache to place firewalls at the edge of each data center's network. Security groups (also called *network security groups*, or NSGs) are an abstraction layer that allows a consumer to define protections required, and the CSP's infrastructure deploys appropriate virtualized resources as needed. In the previous example, a cloud consumer defines a set of allowed traffic for the application, and the CSP's hardware and software will be configured uniquely for each data center to implement those rules. This is a similar concept to infrastructure as code, where hardware variations between data centers are abstracted and presented to the consumer in a virtual, self-serve manner.

- **Next-generation firewalls (NGFW):** Although more of a marketing term than a unique type of firewall, NGFWs combine multiple firewall functions into a single device, such as a stateful firewall and API gateway. Many NGFWs also include other network security protections such as intrusion detection or VPN services.

Firewalls may be hardware appliances that would traditionally be deployed by the CSP, or virtual appliances that can be deployed by a cloud consumer as a VM. Host-based firewalls, which are software-based, are also often considered a best practice in a layered defense model. In the event a main network firewall fails, each host still has some protection from malicious traffic, though all devices obviously need to be properly configured.

There are a number of cloud-specific considerations related to firewall deployment and configuration, such as the use of security groups for managing network-level traffic coupled with host-based firewalls to filter traffic to specific hosts. This approach is an example of *microsegmentation*, which amounts to controlling traffic on a granular basis—often at the level of a single host. In a cloud environment, an NSG might block traffic on specific ports from entering a DMZ, and then the host firewalls would further restrict traffic reaching a host based on ports or protocols. Traditional firewall rules may also be ineffective in a cloud environment, which necessitates these new approaches. In an autoscaling environment, new hosts are brought online and dynamically assigned IP addresses. A traditional firewall would need its ruleset updated to allow traffic to these new hosts; otherwise, they will not be able to handle traffic at all. The newly created resources can be automatically placed into the proper security group with no additional configuration required.

Intrusion Detection/Intrusion Prevention Systems (IDS/IPS)

As the name implies, an intrusion detection system (IDS) is designed to detect a system intrusion when it occurs. An intrusion prevention system (IPS) is a bit of a misnomer, however—it acts to limit damage once an intrusion has been detected. The goal in both cases is to limit the impact of an intrusion, either by alerting personnel to an intrusion so they can take remedial action or by automatically shutting down an attempted attack.

An IDS is a passive device that analyzes traffic and generates an alert when traffic matching a pattern is detected, such as a large volume of unfinished TCP handshakes. IPS goes further by taking action to stop the attack, such as blocking traffic from the malicious host with a firewall rule, disabling a user account generating unwanted traffic, or even shutting down an application or server that has come under attack.

Both IDS and IPS can be deployed in two ways, and the deployment method as well as location are critical to ensure that the devices can see all traffic they require to be effective. A network-based intrusion detection system/intrusion prevention system (NIDS/NIPS) sits on a network where it can observe all traffic and may often be deployed at a network's perimeter for optimum visibility. Similar to firewalls, however, NIDS/NIPSs may be challenged in a virtualized environment where network traffic between VMs never crosses a switch. A host-based intrusion detection system/intrusion prevention system (HIDS/HIPS) is deployed on a specific host to monitor traffic. While this helps overcome problems associated with invisible network traffic, the agents required introduce processing overhead, may require licensing costs, and may not be available for all platforms an organization is using.

Honeypots and Honeynets

Honeypots and honeynets can be useful monitoring tools if used appropriately. They should be designed to detect or gather information about unauthorized attempts to gain access to data and information systems, often by appearing to be a valuable resource. In reality, they contain no sensitive data, but attackers attempting to access them may be distracted or deflected from high-value targets or give up information about themselves such as IP addresses.

In most jurisdictions, there are significant legal issues concerning the use of honeypots or honeynets, centered around the concept of *entrapment*. This legal concept describes an agent inducing a person to commit a crime, which may be used as a defense by the perpetrator and render any attempt to prosecute them ineffective. It is therefore imperative that these devices never be set up with an explicit purpose of being attractive targets or designed to "catch the bad guys."

Vulnerability Assessments

Vulnerability assessments should be part of a broader vulnerability management program, with the goal of detecting vulnerabilities before an attacker finds them. Many organizations will have a regulatory or compliance obligation to conduct vulnerability assessments, which will dictate not only the schedule but also the form of the assessment. An organization with an annual PCI assessment requirement should be checking for required configurations and vulnerabilities related to credit cardholder data, while a medical organization should be checking for required protected health information controls and vulnerabilities.

Vulnerability scanners are an often-used tool in conducting vulnerability assessments and can be configured to scan on a relatively frequent basis as a detective control. Human vulnerability assessments can also be utilized, such as an internal audit function or standard reviews like access and configuration management checks. Even a physical walk-through of a facility to identify users who are not following clean desk or workstation locking policies can uncover vulnerabilities, which should be treated as risks and remediated.

A more advanced form of assessments an organization might conduct is penetration or pen testing, which typically involves a human tester attempting to exploit any vulnerabilities identified. Vulnerability scanners typically identify and report on software or configuration vulnerabilities, but it can be difficult to determine if a particular software vulnerability could actually be exploited in a complex environment. The use of vulnerability scanners and pen testers may be limited by your CSP's terms of service, so a key concern for a CCSP is understanding the type and frequency of testing that is allowed.

Management Plane

The management plane is mostly used by the CSP and provides virtual management options analogous to the physical administration options a legacy data center would provide, such as powering VMs on and off or provisioning virtual infrastructure for VMs such as RAM and storage. The management plane will also be the tool used by administrators for tasks such as migrating running VMs to different physical hardware before performing hardware maintenance.

Because of the functionality it provides, the management plane requires appropriate logging, monitoring, and access controls, similar to the raised floor space in a data center or access to domain admin functions. Depending upon the virtualization toolset, the management plane may be used to perform patching and maintenance on the virtualization software itself. Functionality of the management plane is usually exposed through an API, which may be controlled by an administrator from a command line or via a graphical interface.

A key concept related to the management plane is *orchestration*, or the automated configuration and management of resources. Rather than requiring an administrator to individually migrate VMs off a cluster before applying patches, the management plane can automate this process. The admin schedules a patch for deployment, and the software comprising the management plane coordinates moving all VMs off the cluster, preventing new VMs from being started, and then enters maintenance mode to apply the patches.

The cloud management *console* is often confused with the cloud management *plane*, and in reality, they perform similar functions and may be closely related. The *management console* is usually a web-based console for use by the cloud consumer to provision and manage their cloud services, though it may also be exposed as an API that customers can utilize from other programs or a command line. It may utilize the management plane's API for starting/stopping VMs or configuring VM resources such as RAM and network access, but it should not give a cloud consumer total control over the entire CSP infrastructure. The management plane's access controls must enforce minimum necessary authorization to ensure that each consumer is able to manage their own infrastructure and not that of another customer.

Implement Operational Controls and Standards

IT service management (ITSM) frameworks consist of operational controls designed to help organizations design, implement, and improve IT operations in a consistent manner. They can be useful in speeding up IT delivery tasks and providing more consistent oversight, and they are also critical to processes where elements of security risk management are implemented. Change management is one example; it helps the organization to maintain a consistent IT environment that meets user needs and also implements security controls such as a change control board where the security impact of changes can be adequately researched and addressed.

The two standards that a CCSP should be familiar with are ISO 20000-1 (not to be confused with ISO 27001) and ITIL (formerly an acronym meaning Information Technology Infrastructure Library). Both frameworks focus on the process-driven aspects of delivering IT services to an organization, such as remote collaboration services, rather than focusing on just delivering IT systems like an Exchange server. In ITIL, the set of services available is called a *service catalog*, which includes all the services available to the organization.

Both frameworks start with the need for policies to govern the ITSM processes, which should be documented, well understood by relevant members of the organization, and kept up-to-date to reflect changing needs and requirements. ISO 20000-1 and ITIL emphasize the need to deeply understand user needs and also focus on gathering feedback to deliver continuous service improvement. Stated another way, those in charge of IT services should have a close connection to the users of the IT system and strive to make continual improvements; in this regard, it is similar to the Agile development methodology.

Change Management

Change management is concerned with keeping the organization operating effectively, even when changes are needed such as the modification of existing services, addition of new services, or retirement of old services. To do this, the organization must implement a proactive set of formal activities and processes to request, review, implement, and document all changes.

Many organizations utilize a ticketing system to document all steps required for a change. The first step is initiation in the form of a change request, which should capture details such as the purpose of the proposed change, the owner, resources required, and any impacts that have been identified, such as downtime required to implement the change or impacts to the organization's risk posture.

The change then goes for a review, often by a change control or change advisory board (CCB or CAB). This review is designed to verify whether the proposed change offers business benefits/value appropriate to its associated costs, understand the impact of the change and ensure that it does not introduce unacceptable levels of risk, and, ideally, confirm that the change has been properly planned and can be reversed or rolled back in the event it is unsuccessful. This step may involve testing and additional processes such as decision analysis, and it may be iterated if the change board needs additional information from the requestor.

Once a change has been approved, it is ready for the owner to execute the appropriate plan to implement it. Since many changes will result in the acquisition of new hardware, software, or IT services, there will be a number of security concerns that operate concurrently with the change, including acquisition security management, security testing, and the use of the organization's certification and accreditation process if the change is large enough. In the event a change is not successful, fallback, rollback, or other restoration actions need to be planned to prevent a loss of availability.

Not all changes will be treated the same, and many organizations will implement different procedures based on categories of changes.

- **Low-risk:** These are changes that are considered unlikely to have a negative impact and are therefore pre-authorized to reduce operational overhead. Examples include application of standard patches, addition of standard assets to address capacity (for example, deploying a standard server build to provide additional processing capability), or installation of approved software that is not part of a standard baseline but is required for a particular job function.
- **Normal changes:** These changes require the full change management request-review-implement process. They will typically follow a routine schedule based on the meeting schedule of the change board.

Automating Change Management

In the case of a continuous integration/continuous deployment (CI/CD) software development environment, change reviews may be automated when new code is ready for deployment, particularly security testing such as code analysis. The goal of this automation is to reduce operational overhead while still adequately managing the risk associated with the change (in this case, new software).

- **Emergency changes:** Things happen unexpectedly, and the process of requesting, testing, and receiving approval for a change may require too much time. For changes required to resolve an incident or critical security concern, formal procedures should be utilized to implement the change as needed to address the incident and document all details related to the change. Depending on the organization, a faster or less cumbersome change control decision process may be utilized; for example, only one CCB member approval is required, or the change may be reviewed and approved retroactively.

Continuity Management

Continuity is concerned with the availability aspect of the CIA triad and is a critical consideration for both cloud customers and providers. Continuity management addresses the reality that, despite best efforts and mitigating activities, sometimes adverse events happen. How the organization responds should be planned and adequate resources identified prior to an incident, and the business continuity policy, plan(s), and other documentation should be readily available to support the organization's members during an interruption.

It is essential for both cloud customers and providers to do the following:

- **Identify critical business functions and resources:** This is usually accomplished by conducting a business impact assessment (BIA), which assists the organization to understand its essential assets and processes. For a customer, this may be business-critical applications, while for the provider, it will be the infrastructure and other resources required to deliver the cloud services. The BIA is a structured method of identifying what impact a disruption of critical business functions poses to the organization, as well as the resources necessary to recover a minimum level of functionality.

- **Prioritize recovery:** Not all systems or assets can be recovered all at once, so it is essential that the organization develop a prioritization of critical processes that are essential to the continued functioning of its operations and identify which assets are essential to those processes. The set of ordered steps should also be documented to ensure that dependencies are documented and restored in the correct order, for example, that power to a facility is restored before any information systems can be operated in it.

- **Plan continuity:** This will entail identifying continuity capabilities such as automated failovers, as well as understanding relevant cloud offerings and how they are to be used. In some cases, the cloud will function as a backup for an organization's on-prem infrastructure, while in other cases, the cloud's availability features will be utilized, such as different availability regions around the world, automatic duplication of data to multiple sites, etc. The cloud customer is responsible for understanding the availability features of their chosen cloud provider and properly architecting their cloud applications to meet continuity requirements.

- **Document plans and procedures:** Issues that cause a loss of availability are often high-stress situations, such as a natural disaster. In these instances, it is preferable to have employees working from a previously prepared set of instructions rather than trying to think and respond on the fly. Decision makers and standard processes/tools may be unavailable, so appropriate alternatives should be documented.

Training is also critical in high-stress continuity situations. Members with key responsibilities should receive training to ensure that they are aware of what they need to do in an emergency, rather than trying to make crucial decisions under duress.

There are a variety of standards related to continuity management; these may be useful to the organization in planning, testing, and preparing for contingency circumstances. Many legal and regulatory frameworks mandate the use of a particular standard depending on an organization's industry or location. The CCSP should be aware of the relevant framework for their industry; the following are some key frameworks:

- **NIST Risk Management Framework and ISO 27000:** Since both frameworks focus on information security concerns, both deal with business continuity and disaster recovery (BCDR), terms that fall under the larger category of *continuity management*. In the NIST framework, a family of controls called contingency planning is specified depending on the system's risk profile, while the ISO 27002 framework specifies information security aspects of business continuity management.

- **Health Insurance Portability and Accountability Act (HIPAA):** Healthcare data in the United States is governed by this standard, which mandates adequate data backups, disaster recovery planning, and emergency access to healthcare data in the event of a system interruption.

- **ISO 22301:2019 Security and resilience — Business continuity management systems:** This specifies the requirements needed for an organization to plan, implement and operate, and continually improve the continuity capability. This includes adequate support from leadership within the organization, planning resources for managing continuity, and steps to implement/operate the program such as conducting a BIA, exercising contingency plans, and monitoring the capability's effectiveness.

Information Security Management

The goal of an information security management system (ISMS) is to ensure a coherent organizational approach to managing information security risks; stated another way, it is the overarching approach an organization takes to preserving the confidentiality, integrity, and availability (the CIA triad) of systems and data in use. The operational aspects of an ISMS include standard security risk management activities in the form of security controls such as encryption, as well as supporting business functions required for the organization to achieve risk management goals like formal support and buy-in from management, skills and training, and adequate oversight and performance evaluation.

Various standards and frameworks exist to help organizations implement, manage, and, in some cases, audit or certify their ISMS. Most contain requirements to be met in order to support goals of the CIA triad, as well as best practices for implementation and guidance on proper use and operation of the framework. While many security control frameworks exist, not all are focused on the larger operational task of implementing an ISMS. Payment Card Industry Data Security Standard (PCI DSS), for example, focuses specifically on securing cardholder data that an organization is processing. Frameworks that focus on both security controls as well as the overall ISMS functions include the following:

- **ISO 27000 series:** The ISO 27001 standard provides a set of requirements for an organization's ISMS. It is often confused with ISO 27002, which is the code of practice for information security controls, due to the inclusion of the 27002 set of controls as an appendix to 27001. The two are interrelated, because 27001 sets out the high-level requirements an organization must meet to provide leadership for, plan, implement, and operate an ISMS.

  - ISO 27002 provides a set of controls and implementation guidance, broken down by domains such as Asset Management and Cryptography. 27001 and 27002 provide a road map for an organization to understand its security risk posture and implement appropriate security controls to mitigate and manage those risks.

  - There are additional ISO standards that provide guidance on implementing and managing security controls in cloud-specific environments. ISO 27017 is a "Code of practice for information security controls based on ISO/IEC 27002 for cloud services," and ISO 27018 is a "Code of practice for protection of personally identifiable information (PII) in public clouds acting as PII processors." Both documents enhance/extend the guidance offered in ISO 27002 controls to deal with particular security risk challenges in cloud implementation.

- ISO 27701 is also relevant to cloud security environments where personally identifiable information (PII) is being handled. 27701 extends the ISMS guidance in 27001 to manage risks related to privacy, by implementing and managing a privacy information management system (PIMS). As many privacy regulations require security controls and risk management, this standard will be relevant to a CCSP whose organization acts as a data owner or processor.

- **NIST RMF, SP 800-53, and CSF:** Although it uses different terminology, the NIST Risk Management Framework (RMF) specified in Special Publication (SP) 800-37, "Risk Management Framework for Information Systems and Organizations: A System Lifecycle Approach for Security and Privacy," has the same objective as the ISO-defined ISMS: identifying information security risks and applying adequate risk mitigations in the form of security controls. SP 800-37 provides the guidance for creating the organization's risk management framework and points to NIST SP 800-53, "Security and Privacy Controls for Federal Information Systems and Organizations," for the control requirements and implementation guidance.

  While the NIST RMF and SP 800-53 standards are mandated for use in many parts of the U.S. federal government, they are free to use for any organization. The NIST Cybersecurity Framework (CSF) was originally designed to help private-sector critical infrastructure providers design and implement information security programs; however, its free-to-use and relatively lightweight approach have made it a popular ISMS tool for many nongovernment organizations.

- **AICPA SOC 2:** The Service Organization Controls (SOC 2) framework has seen wide adoption among cloud service providers for a variety of reasons, primarily the relatively lightweight approach it provides as well as the use of a third party to perform audits, which provides increased assurance for business partners and customers. While not as robust as the ISO and NIST frameworks, SOC 2 contains Trust Services Criteria (TSC), which cover organizational aspects including Security, Availability, Processing Integrity, Confidentiality, and Privacy. The Common Criteria apply to all organizations and contain similar requirements to other frameworks: executive support and buy-in, assessment and treatment of risks, monitoring of controls, and implementation guidance. The other TSCs such as availability may be implemented at the discretion of the organization; typically, an organization's service offering will drive which TSCs are chosen.

Continual Service Improvement Management

Most ITSM models include some form of monitoring capability utilizing functions such as internal audit, external audit and reporting, or the generation of security metrics and management oversight of processes via these metrics. The organization's IT services, including the ISMS and all related processes, should be monitored for effectiveness and placed into a cycle of continuous improvements. The goals of this continuous improvement program should be twofold: first to ensure that the IT services (including security services) are meeting the organization's business objectives and second to ensure that the organization's security risks remain adequately mitigated.

One critical element of continual service improvement includes elements of monitoring and measurement, which often take the form of security metrics. Metrics can be tricky to gather, particularly if they need to be presented to a variety of audiences. It may be the case that business leaders will be less interested in deeply technical topics, which means the metrics should be used to aggregate information and present it in an easily understood, actionable way.

For instance, rather than reporting a long list of patches and Common Vulnerabilities and Exposures (CVEs) addressed (undoubtedly an important aspect of security risk management), a more appropriate metric might be the percentage of machines patched within the defined timeframe for the criticality of the patch; for example, 90 percent of machines were patched within seven days of release. Acceptable values should also be defined, which allows for key performance indicators (KPIs) to be reported. In this example, the KPI might be red (bad) if the organization's target is 99 percent patch deployment within seven days of release—a clear indicator to management that something needs their attention.

There are other sources of improvement opportunity information as well, including audits and actual incidents. Audits may be conducted internally or externally, and findings from those audits can be viewed as improvement opportunities. Actual incidents, such as a business interruption or widespread malware outbreak, should be concluded with a lessons learned or postmortem analysis, which provides another source of improvement opportunities. The root cause of the incident and any observations made during the recovery can be used to improve the organization's IT security services.

Incident Management

It is important to understand the formal distinction between *events* and *incidents* as the foundation for incident management.

- **Events** are any observable item, including routine actions such as a user successfully logging into a system, a file being accessed, or a system being unavailable during a scheduled maintenance window. Many routine events will be logged but do not require any additional actions.

- **Incidents,** by contrast, are events that both are unplanned and have an adverse impact on the organization. Incidents typically require investigation and remedial action by some combination of IT, operations, and security personnel. Examples of incidents include unexpected restart of a system, ransomware preventing users from accessing a system, or a loss of network connectivity to a cloud service.

All incidents should be investigated and remediated as appropriate to restore the organization's normal operations as quickly as possible and to minimize adverse impact to the organization such as lost productivity or revenue. This resumption of normal service is the primary goal of incident management.

Not all incidents will require participation by the security team. For example, a spike in new user traffic to an application after a marketing campaign goes live, which leads to a partial loss of availability, is an operational issue and not a security one. A coordinated denial-of-service attack by a foreign nation-state, however, is an incident that requires participation by both IT and security personnel to successfully remediate.

All organizations require some level of incident management capability, that is, the tools and resources needed to identify, categorize, and remediate the impacts of incidents. This capability will revolve around an incident management plan, which should document the following:

- Definitions of incident types, such as internal operational incidents, security incidents, and cloud provider incidents.

- The incident response team (IRT) personnel. Note that the composition of this team will be dependent upon the type of incident, but an incident response coordinator should always be appointed to assess the situation and identify the requisite team members on a per-incident basis.

- Roles and responsibilities for the IRT personnel in each incident type. This should include roles internal to the organization, as well as responsibilities of external stakeholders such as law enforcement, business partners or customers, and the cloud provider if the incident may affect them.

- Resources required such as operations or security management tools to facilitate detection and response, such as a security information and event management (SIEM) or IDS, and required personnel.

- Incident management processes following a logical lifecycle from detection of the incident to response to restoration of normal service. The response coordinator should determine relevant response requirements, including the following:

  - Communications appropriate to the specific incident, both internal and external, with stakeholders including customers, employees, executive management, law enforcement, regulatory bodies, and possibly the media

  - Any required breach or privacy law notifications, if the incident involved PII or other regulated data

A variety of standards exist to support organizations developing an incident response capability, including the ITIL framework, NIST Special Publication 800-61, "Computer Security Incident Handling Guide, and ISO 27035, Security incident management." All standards implement a lifecycle approach to managing incidents, starting with planning before an incident occurs, activating the response, and following the documented steps, and ending with reporting on the results and any lessons learned to help the organization better mitigate or respond to such incidents in the future. Figure 5.1 shows an example of the NIST SP 800-61 lifecycle and a description of the activities.

FIGURE 5.1   NIST incident response lifecycle phases

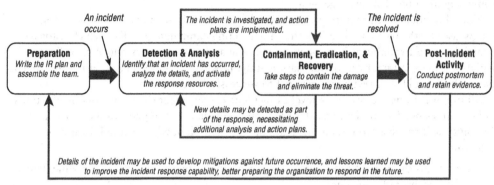

Source: Adapted from NIST SP 800-61

The CCSP's role in developing the capability is, obviously, the responses required for security incidents, while other stakeholders from IT or operations will provide input relevant to their responsibilities. All incident response frameworks emphasize the importance of planning ahead for incidents by identifying likely scenarios and developing response strategies before an incident occurs, as incidents can be a high-stress situation and ad hoc responses are less preferable than preplanned, rehearsed responses.

As with all aspects of cloud service use, there are shared responsibilities between the CSP and the consumer when responding to incidents. For many incidents, the CSP will not be involved; for example, an internal user at a consumer organization breaches policies to misuse company data. This does not impact the CSP; however, some incidents will require coordination, such as a denial-of-service attack against one consumer, which could impact other consumers by exhausting resources. The CSP could also suffer an incident, like an outage of a facility or theft of hardware resources, which must be reported to consumer organizations and may trigger their incident management procedures. The major CSPs have dedicated incident management teams to coordinate incident responses, including resources designed to provide notice to consumers such as a status page or dedicated account managers. Your incident planning must include coordination with your CSPs, and you should be aware of what capabilities are and are not available to you. Many CSPs forbid physical access to their resources during an incident response unless valid law enforcement procedures, such as obtaining a warrant, have been followed.

In addition to managing incidents with the CSPs involvement, incident management processes should take into account the difference between first- and third-party incidents. A first-party incident is one that happens internally, such as an employee stealing information or a server being infected with malware. A third-party incident is one that affects another organization like a contractor or vendor. Some incidents could be operational only, such as a vendor being hit by ransomware that prevents them from providing services, while others may be security related like a data breach at a contractor that exposes the data of the contractor's customers. In this case, the incident response plan should include information such as points of contact and steps needed to coordinate the incident response with the third party. This should include any legal or regulatory obligations the organization must meet in the event of a data breach, such as reporting to regulators or impacted customers.

Another important aspect of the organization's incident management capability is the proper categorization and prioritization of incidents based on their impact and criticality. Incident management seeks to restore normal operations as quickly as possible, so prioritizing incidents and recovery steps is critical. This is similar to the risk assessment process where risks are analyzed according to their impact and likelihood; however, since incidents have already occurred, they are measured by the following:

- **Criticality/impact:** The effect the incident will have on the organization, often measured as low/moderate/high/critical.

- **Urgency:** The timeframe in which the incident must be resolved to avoid unwanted impact. For example, unavailable systems that do not impact life, health, or safety will always be less urgent than systems that do impact these factors; therefore, they should be prioritized lower for resolution.

Many organizations utilize a P score (P0–P5) to categorize incidents. Members of the incident response team use this score to prioritize the work required to resolve an incident. For example, a P5 or low-priority item may be addressed as time permits, while a P0, which equates to a complete disruption of operations, requires that all other work be suspended. In many organizations, a certain priority rating may also be a trigger for other organizational capabilities, such as the invocation of a business continuity or disaster recovery plan if the incident is sufficiently disruptive to normal operations.

Problem Management

In the ITIL framework, problems are the causes of incidents or adverse events, and the practice of problem management seeks to improve the organization's handling of these incidents. Problems are, in essence, the root cause of incidents, so problem management utilizes root-cause analysis to identify the underlying problem or problems that lead to an incident and seeks to minimize the likelihood or impact of incidents in the future; it is therefore a form of risk management.

Identified problems are tracked as a form of common knowledge, often in a known issues or known errors database. These document an identified root cause that the organization is aware of, as well as any shared knowledge regarding how to fix or avoid them. Examples might include a set of procedural steps to follow when troubleshooting a particular system, or a *workaround*, which is a temporary fix for an incident. Workarounds do not mitigate the likelihood of a problem occurring but do provide a quick fix, which supports the incident management goal of restoring normal service as quickly as possible. Problems are risks to the organization, and if the workarounds do not provide sufficient risk mitigation, then the organization should investigate a more permanent solution to resolve the underlying cause.

Release Management

The last few years have seen an enormous shift from traditional release management practices due to widespread adoption of Agile development methodologies. The primary change is the frequency of releases due to the increased speed of development activities in continuous integration/continuous delivery, often referred to as a CI/CD pipeline. Under this model, developers work on small units of code and merge them back into the main branch of the application's code as soon as they are finished.

Inherent in a CI/CD pipeline is the concept of automated testing, which is designed to more quickly identify problems in an easier-to-solve way. Running tests on only small units of code being integrated makes it easier for the developers to identify where the problem is and how to fix it. From the user's perspective, they get access to new features more quickly than waiting for a monolithic release and, ideally, get fewer bugs due to the faster feedback to developers that automated testing offers.

Release management activities typically comprise the logistics needed to release the changed software or service and may include identifying the relevant components of the service, scheduling the release, and post-implementation reviewing to ensure that the change was implemented as intended, i.e., that the new software or service is functioning as intended. The process has obvious overlap with change management processes.

In the Agile methodology, the process of release management may not involve manual scheduling, instead relying on the organization's standard weekly, monthly, or quarterly release schedule. For organizations using other development methodologies, the process for scheduling the deployment might require coordination between the service provider and consumers to mitigate risks associated with downtime, or the deployment may be scheduled for a previously reserved maintenance window during which customer access will be unavailable.

The release manager must perform a variety of tasks after the release is scheduled and before it occurs, including identifying whether all changes to be released have successfully passed required automated tests as well as any manual testing requirements. Other manual processes such as updating documentation and writing release notes may also be part of the organization's release management activities. Once all steps have been completed, the release can be deployed and tested and is ready for users.

Deployment Management

In more mature organizations, the CD in CI/CD stands for continuous deployment, which automates the process of release management to deliver a truly automatic CI/CD pipeline. Once a developer has written their code and checked it in, an automated process is triggered to test the code, and if all tests pass, it is integrated and deployed automatically to users. This has the advantage of getting updated software and services deployed to users quickly and offers security benefits as well. For example, automated testing is typically less expensive than manual testing, making it feasible to conduct more tests and increase the frequency in complement to the organization's manual testing plans.

Even organizations with continuous deployment may require some deployment management processes to deal with deployments that cannot be automated, such as new hardware or software. In this case, the release management process should develop a set of deployment steps including all required assets, dependencies, and deployment order to ensure that the deployment process is successful.

One recent technology development supporting this trend of more frequent deployment is *containerization*, which packages application code and non-OS software the application requires into a container. Containers can be run on any computing platform regardless of underlying hardware or operating system, so long as container software such as the Docker Engine is available. The container software makes the resources of the computing environment available in response to the requirements of the containerized applications when they run, similar to the way virtualization makes hardware resources available to a virtualized guest OS.

Containers offer advantages of portability. In other words, they can be run on any OS and hardware platform with container software, as well as availability advantages over traditional infrastructure due to requiring fewer pieces of software to run. Continuous deployment pipelines often make use of containers, as they provide more flexibility and can speed development.

Deployment scheduling for noncontinuous environments may follow a set schedule such as a routine maintenance window or be deployed in a phased approach where a small subset of users receive the new deployment. This phased approach can offer advantages for riskier deployments such as large operating system updates, where unexpected bugs or issues may be encountered. Rolling out updates to a subset of the user pool reduces the impact of any bugs in the release, and the organization has more opportunity to find and correct them. Organizations may also choose not to push deployments but instead allow users to pull the updated software/service on their own schedule. This is the model many consumer OSs follow, where an update is made available and users are free to accept or delay the update at their discretion. This is advantageous for uptime as a user may not want to restart their machine in the middle of an important task, though it does lead to the problem of software never being updated, which means vulnerabilities fixed by that update are also not addressed.

Immutable Infrastructure

Cloud services have significantly shifted the way many organizations build their information system environments. In traditional models, a physical location with utilities had to be built, appropriate equipment like servers and routers installed, and then operating systems and application software installed on top of that hardware. Once installed, software was placed into an operations and maintenance cycle where new patches or features were installed, but often the basic infrastructure was untouched for years, due to the time and cost involved. You wouldn't go out and build a whole new data center just to apply a minor patch! This led to sometimes "stale" assets such as hardware or software that hadn't been updated or that had drifted away from a secure configuration, which can introduce major vulnerabilities.

In cloud environments where all resources exist as virtual pools, there are fewer limitations on building virtual infrastructure, tearing it down, and rebuilding it. This gives rise to the idea of immutable architecture, which is built as needed, remains in a consistent state in line with a validated image during its (rather short) useful life, and then is destroyed and replaced by a new version when the system is next deployed. This helps overcome the problem of assets becoming stale by ensuring that systems with up-to-date patches are always deployed and by blocking the infrastructure from being changed, which is why it's called immutable, which means unchangeable.

Configuration Management

Configuration management (CM, not to be confused with change management, which is also abbreviated CM) comprises practices, activities, and processes designed to maintain a known good configuration of something. *Configuration items* (CIs) are the things that are placed under configuration control and may be assets such as source code, operating systems, documentation, or even entire information systems.

Changes to CIs are usually required to go through a formal change process designed to ensure that the change does not create an unacceptable risk situation, such as introducing a vulnerable application or architecture. Part of the change management process must include updating the CMDB to reflect the new state of the services or components after the change is executed. For example, if a particular host is running Service Pack 1 (SP1) of an OS and a major upgrade to SP2 is performed, the CMDB must be updated once the change is completed successfully.

IT service CM may include hardware, software, or the cloud services and configurations in use by a consumer organization, while the CSP would also need to include configurations of the service infrastructure as well as the supply chain used to provide the services.

In many organizations, a formal CMDB will be used to track all CIs, acting as a system of record against which current configurations may be compared in order to detect systems that have gone out of line with expected configurations. The CMDB can also be useful for identifying vulnerabilities. As a source of truth for systems and software versions running in the organization, it is possible to query the CMDB to identify software running in the organization that contains a newly disclosed vulnerability. Furthermore, the CMDB can be useful to support audits by acting as a source of population data to allow auditors to choose a subset of systems to review. If the CMDB is not updated after changes are made, the organization is likely to face audit findings stemming from failure to properly follow processes.

Due to the type of information contained in a CMDB, such as version numbers, vendor information, hardware components, etc., it can also be used as the organization's asset inventory. Many tools that provide CMDB functionality can also be used to automatically detect and inventory systems, such as by monitoring network records to identify when a new system joins or by integrating with cloud administrative tools and adding any new cloud services that are invoked to the CMDB.

Checklists or baseline are often mentioned in discussions of CM, primarily as starting points or guidance on the desired secure configuration of particular system types. Configuration checklists are often published by industry or regional groups with specific guidance for hardening of operating systems like Windows, macOS, and various Linux distributions, as well as the hardening of popular applications such as Microsoft Office and collaboration tools. In many cases, the vendors themselves publish security checklists indicating how their products' various security settings can be configured. In all cases, these checklists are usually an input to an organization's CM process and should be tailored to meet the organization's unique needs.

Infrastructure as Code

Similar to immutable architecture, which supports configuration management security goals for cloud consumers by preventing unwanted changes, infrastructure as code can help organizations ensure that known good versions of infrastructure are deployed. This might include specially hardened OS or applications, network configurations, or other elements of infrastructure.

Infrastructure as code is a form of virtualization whereby system configuration information is written as a definition file that can be used by the cloud service to create machines with particular settings, rather than manual hardware and software configuration. In this way, developers can specify their application's needed infrastructure, and all instances will be configured according to that definition, ensuring that properly patched and configured systems are deployed automatically without the need for human intervention. While it's possible human error might occur in writing a definition file, it's less likely than an error in a mundane repetitive task like building and deploying servers.

Service Level Management

In the ITSM view of IT as a set of services, including information security, there is a function for defining, measuring, and correcting issues related to delivery of the services. In other words, performance management is a critical part of ITSM. This is closely related to the process of continual service improvement, and in fact, the same metrics are likely to be used by the organization to determine if services are meeting their defined goals.

Service level management rests on the organization's defined requirements for a service. The most common service level many cloud organizations encounter is availability, often expressed as a percentage of time that a system can be reached and utilized, such as 99.9 percent. A service with a 99.9 percent availability level must be reachable approximately 364.64 days per year; put another way, the system can only be down for less than 24 hours each year. Examples of other service levels that may be managed include number of concurrent users supported by a system, durability of data, response times to customer support requests, recovery time in the event of an interruption, and timeframes for deployment of patches based on criticality.

A key tool in managing service levels is the service level agreement (SLA), which is a formal agreement similar to a contract, but focused on measurable outcomes of the service being provided. This measurement aspect is what makes SLAs critical elements of security risk mitigation programs for cloud consumers, as it allows them to define, measure, and hold the cloud provider accountable for the services being consumed.

SLAs require routine monitoring for enforcement, and this typically relies on metrics designed to indicate whether the service level is being met. Availability metrics are often measured with tools that check to see if a service can be reached. For example, a script may run that checks to see if a website loads at a particular address. The script may run once an hour and log its results; if the SLA is 99.9 percent, then the service should not be down for more than nine hours in a given year. If the service level is not met, the SLA should define penalties, usually in the form of a refund or no obligation for the consumer to pay for the time the service was unavailable.

Defining the levels of service is usually up to the cloud provider in public cloud environments, though there is obviously a need to meet customer demands in order to win business. Requirements should be gathered for cloud service offerings regardless of the deployment model, and customer feedback should also be gathered and used as input to the continual service improvement. The metrics reported in SLAs are a convenient source of input to understand if the services are meeting the customers' needs.

Availability Management

In cloud environments, the ability of users to reach and make use of the service is incredibly important, so the provider must ensure that adequate measures are in place to preserve the availability aspect of the relevant services. Availability and uptime are often used synonymously, but there is an important distinction. A service may be "up"—that is, reachable but not available—meaning it cannot be used. This could be the case if a dependency like the access control system is not available, so users can get to a login page for the cloud service but no further.

Due to the expansive nature of availability management, it is critical to view this as a holistic process. Factors that could negatively impact availability include many of the same concerns that an organization would consider in business continuity and disaster recovery, including loss of power, natural disasters, or loss of network connectivity.

There are additional concerns for providing a service that meets the agreed-upon service levels, including the issue of maintenance. Some cloud service providers exclude periods of scheduled maintenance from their availability guarantees. For example, a system will be available 99 percent of the time with the exception of the third Saturday of each month. This gives defined timeframes to make changes that require a loss of availability, as well as some flexibility for unexpected events or emergency maintenance outside the normal schedule.

Many of the tools that make cloud computing possible provide integral high availability options. For example, many virtualization tools support automatic moving of guest machines from a failed host in the event of an outage, or provide for load balancing so that sudden increases in demand can be distributed to prevent a denial of service. Many cloud services are also designed to be highly resilient, particularly PaaS and SaaS offerings that can offer features such as automatic data replication to multiple data centers around the world, or concurrent hosting of applications in multiple data centers so that an outage at one does not render the service unreachable.

Cloud consumers have a role to play in availability management as well. Consumers of IaaS will, obviously, have the most responsibility with regard to availability of their cloud environment, since they are responsible for virtually everything except the physical facility. PaaS and SaaS users will need to properly architect their cloud solutions to take advantage of their provider's availability options. For example, some cloud providers offer automatic data replication for cloud-hosted databases, but there may be configuration changes required to enable this functionality. There may be other concerns as well, such as data residency or the use of encryption, which can complicate availability; it is up to the cloud consumer to gather and understand these requirements and to configure their cloud services appropriately.

Capacity Management

In ITSM, one of the core concerns of availability is the amount of service capacity available compared with the amount being subscribed to. In a simple example, if a service has 100 active users but only 50 licenses available, that means the service is over capacity and 50 users will face a denial-of-service condition. In this simple example, the service is oversubscribed, meaning there are more users than capacity. The service provider must be able to predict, measure, and plan for adequate capacity to meet its obligations; failure to do so could result in financial penalties in the form of SLA enforcement.

As users, we are aware of the negative impacts resulting from a lack of system resources—irritating situations such as a spinning hourglass or beach ball when our desktop computer's RAM capacity is exceeded. While a minor irritant for individual users, this situation could prove quite costly for a business relying on a cloud service provider's infrastructure. Any service that is being consumed should be measurable, whether it is network bandwidth, storage space, processing capability, or availability of an application. Measured service is one of the core elements of cloud computing, so metrics that illustrate demand for the service are relatively easy to identify.

Cloud service providers must take appropriate measures to identify the service capacity they need to provision. These measures might include analysis of past growth trends to predict future capacity, identifying capacity agreed to in SLAs, or even analysis of external factors such as knowing that a holiday season will cause a spike in demand at certain customers like online retailers. Monitoring of current services, including utilization and demand, should also be part of the analysis and forecasting model.

In some cases, cloud service providers and their customers may be willing to accept a certain amount of oversubscription, especially as it could offer cost savings. To extend the previous example, assume the service provider offers 50 licenses and the business has 100 users split between the United States and India. Given the time zone difference between the two countries, it is unlikely that all 100 users will try to access the system simultaneously, so oversubscription does not present an issue.

If the consumer does require concurrent accessibility for all 100 users, then they must specify that as an SLA requirement. The provider should then utilize their capacity management processes to ensure that adequate capacity is provisioned to meet the anticipated demand.

Support Digital Forensics

Digital forensics, broadly, is the application of scientific techniques to the collection, examination, and interpretation of digital data. The primary concern in forensics is the integrity of data, as demonstrated by the chain of custody. Digital forensics is a field that requires very particular skills and is often outsourced to highly trained professionals, but a CCSP must be aware of digital forensic needs when architecting systems to support forensics and how to acquire appropriate skills as needed to respond to a security incident.

Digital forensics in cloud environments is complicated by a number of factors; some of the very advantages of cloud services are also major disadvantages when it comes to forensics. For example, high availability and data replication mean that data is stored in multiple locations around the world simultaneously, which complicates the identification of a single crime scene. Multitenant models of most cloud services also present a challenge, as there are simply more people in the environment who must be ruled out as suspects. The shared responsibility model also impacts digital forensics in the cloud. As mentioned previously, most CSPs do not allow consumers physical access to hardware or facilities, and even with court orders like a warrant, the CSPs may have procedures in place that make investigation, collection, and preservation of information more difficult. This is not to frustrate law enforcement but is a predicament caused by the multitenant model; allowing investigation of one consumer's data might inadvertently expose data belonging to other consumers. Investigation of one security incident should, as a rule, not be the cause of other security breaches!

Forensic Data Collection Methodologies

In legal terminology, *discovery* means the examination of information pertinent to a legal action. E-discovery is a digital equivalent comprising steps including identification, collection, preservation, analysis, and review of electronic information. There are two important standards a CCSP should be familiar with related to e-discovery.

- **ISO 27050:** ISO 27050 is a four-part standard within the broader ISO 27000 family of information security standards.
  - Part 1, "Overview and concepts," defines terms and requirements for organizations to consider when planning for and implementing digital forensics to support e-discovery.
  - Part 2, "Guidance for governance and management of electronic discovery," offers a framework for directing and maintaining e-discovery programs, with correlation to other elements of the 27000 framework for managing information security.

- Part 3, "Code of practice for electronic discovery," provides detailed requirements for achieving e-discovery objectives in alignment with the standard, including evidence management and analysis.
- Part 4, "Technical readiness," is under development as of 2020 and is designed to provide more discrete guidance on enabling various systems and architectures to support digital forensics.

- **Cloud Security Alliance (CSA) Security Guidance Domain 3: Legal Issues: Contracts and Electronic Discovery:** This standard is part of the CSA's freely available guidance related to cloud security and covers legal issues, contract requirements, and special issues raised by e-discovery.

  - Legal Issues details concerns related to privacy and data protection and how moving data to the cloud can complicate an organization's legal obligations. Examples include data residency, where laws may restrict the geographic locations that data may be stored in, as well as liability issues when a CSP is acting as a data processor.
  - Contract Considerations lists concerns and recommendations for dealing with common contract issues related to security and privacy. These include performing adequate due diligence on any CSP vendors and their practices, ensuring that contractual obligations are properly documented, and performing ongoing monitoring of the CSP and services to ensure that they do not exceed the organization's changing risk tolerance.
  - Special Issues Raised by E-Discovery details a number of critical concerns both CSPs and consumers must consider when choosing and architecting cloud solutions. These include possession, custody, and control of data; in short, outsourcing processing of data to a CSP does not absolve the cloud consumer of legal responsibility for the security of that data. Other issues include challenges related to discovery itself, as data may exist in multiple locations or multiple pieces (data dispersion), as well as issues related to privacy in a multitenant environment if one tenant is subject to legal action. In addition, there may be tools like bit-by-bit analysis or data replication that may be impossible in cloud environments, as these tools make use of hardware features that are not present in a virtualized cloud environment.
  - The full document may be accessed here: `cloudsecurityalliance.org/ artifacts/csa-security-guidance-domain-3-legal-issues-contracts- and-electronic-discovery`.

When legal action is undertaken, it is often necessary to suspend some normal operations such as routine destruction of data or records according to a defined schedule. In this case, a process known as *legal hold* will be utilized, whereby data is preserved until the legal action is completed. Provisions for legal hold, such as extra storage availability and proper handling procedures, must be part of contracts and SLAs, and during legal proceedings, the cloud consumer should have easy access to appropriate points of contact at the CSP to facilitate e-discovery or other law enforcement requirements.

The process of collecting evidence is generally a specialized activity performed by experts, but security practitioners should be aware of some steps, especially those performed at the beginning before a forensics expert is brought in.

- Logs are essential. All activities should be logged including time, person performing the activity, tools used, system or data inspected, and results.

- Document everything, including physical or logical system states, apps running, and any physical configurations of hardware as appropriate.

- Some data is volatile and requires special handling. In a traditional computer system, RAM is often a particular concern for forensics, because it requires constant power to retain data. In cloud architectures where VMs may be spun up on demand or microservices run only as long as needed to perform a particular task, identifying any ephemeral data or services and preserving them may be critical.

- Whenever possible, work on copies of data or images of systems, as simple actions like opening a folder or file can overwrite or change critical elements of the evidence, leading to a loss of integrity and possible destruction of evidence.

- Verify integrity often and follow standard procedures. Incident response plans will often be the first set of steps leading into an investigation where evidence is required, and they should incorporate checks for integrity of evidence and handling such as hashing and verifying physical custody records.

Evidence Management

When handling evidence, the *chain of custody* documents the integrity of data, including details of time, manner, and person responsible for various actions such as collecting, making copies, performing analysis, and presenting the evidence. Chain of custody does not mean that the data has not been altered in any way, as it is often necessary to make changes such as physically collecting and moving a piece of hardware from a crime scene to a lab. Instead, chain of custody provides a documented, reliable history of how the data has been handled, so if it is submitted as evidence, it may be relied upon. Adequate policies and procedures should exist, and it may be appropriate to utilize the skills of trained forensic experts for evidence handling.

The scope of evidence collection describes what is relevant when collecting data. In a multitenant cloud environment, this may be particularly relevant, as collecting data from a storage cluster could inadvertently expose data that does not belong to the requesting party. Imagine that two competing companies both utilize a CSP, and Company A makes a request for data relevant to legal proceedings. If the CSP is not careful about the evidence collected and provided to Company A, they may expose sensitive data about Company B to one of their competitors!

Evidence presented to different audiences will follow different rules. For example, an industry regulator may have a lower integrity threshold for evidence, as they are not able to assess criminal penalties for wrongdoing. A court of law, however, will have higher constraints as the stakes are higher—they have the power to levy fines or possibly imprison individuals. Evidence should possess these five attributes to be useful.

- **Authentic:** The information should be genuine and clearly correlated to the incident or crime.

- **Accurate:** The truthfulness and integrity of the evidence should not be questionable.

- **Complete:** All evidence should be presented in its entirety, even if might negatively impact the case being made (it is illegal in most jurisdictions to hide evidence that disproves a case).

- **Convincing:** The evidence should be understandable and clearly support an assertion being made; for example, this particular person accessed this particular system and copied this particular file for which they were not authorized.

- **Admissible:** Evidence must meet the rules of the body judging it, such as a court, which may rule out evidence such as hearsay (indirect knowledge of an action) or evidence that has been tampered with.

Collect, Acquire, and Preserve Digital Evidence

There are four general phases of digital evidence handling: collection, examination, analysis, and reporting. There are a number of concerns in the first phase, collection, which are essential for a CCSP. Evidence may be acquired as part of standard incident response processes before the need for forensic investigation and criminal prosecution have been identified, so the incident response team needs to handle evidence appropriately in case a chain of custody needs to be demonstrated. Proper evidence handling and decision making should be a part of the incident response procedures and training for team members performing response activities.

There are a number of challenges associated with evidence collection in a cloud environment, including the following:

- **Control:** Using a cloud service involves loss of some control, and different service models offer varying levels of access. SaaS models typically offer little to no visibility outside a consumer's data or app instance, so investigating network security failures may be impossible as the CSP does not disclose them. On the other hand, IaaS gives an organization complete control over their virtualized network security but may stop short of any physical network data that might be pertinent to an investigation. Evidence that is inaccessible is obviously a challenge to an investigation; proper contract terms should be in place with any CSP to support an organization's likely investigation needs.

- **Multitenancy and shared resources:** Evidence collected while investigating a security incident may inadvertently become another data breach in a multitenant environment, if the evidence collected includes information that does not belong to the investigating organization. This can also cause problems of attribution—was a particular incident caused by a malicious attacker or by the accidental action of another tenant?

- **Data volatility and dispersion:** Cloud environments support high availability of data, which often requires novel data storage techniques like *sharding*, which is breaking data into smaller pieces and storing multiple copies of each piece across different data centers. Reconstructing that data could be an error-prone process, lowering the believability when evidence is presented, and may involve multiple legal frameworks and jurisdiction issues when data is stored across multiple countries. Other positive features of cloud computing such as live VM migration can complicate evidence gathering as well. When a VM can move to anywhere in the world virtually instantaneously, it may be hard to prove that a specific set of actions carried out by a specific person occurred in a specific place, leading to evidence that is worthless for prosecution.

Preparing for Evidence Collection

There are a number of important steps the organization should take prior to an incident that can support investigations and forensics. These can be built into several processes the organization is likely to perform for other security objectives, including the following:

- **Logging and monitoring:** All apps, systems, and infrastructure should generate audit trails, which should be forwarded to a secure, centralized logging tool such as a syslog server or a SIEM platform. These tools should have unique access controls so that insiders cannot easily cover their tracks by deleting or altering logs, which also increases the work factor for an attacker by requiring multiple sets of compromised credentials to pull off an attack and cover the evidence. Regular reviews of logs for suspicious activity or automated correlation and alerting should be performed to identify potentially suspicious activity.

- **Backup and storage:** Evidence often needs to be compared against a baseline to show how malicious activity caused changes. Adequate backups are useful to show how a system was configured before an incident to prove that a particular activity was the cause of an incident.

- **Baselines and file integrity monitoring:** The known good state of a system is useful for comparison to an existing system when an investigator is trying to determine if malicious activity has occurred. Deviations from the baseline or files that have been changed can be indicators of an attack, or they could be the sign of poorly implemented change management and configuration management practices. If all intentional changes made by the organization are properly documented, it makes spotting unintended or malicious changes much easier.

- **Data and records retention:** Most organizations have some requirement to retain records for a specific period of time dictated by business needs or legal/regulatory requirements. These records may be a useful source of information in an investigation. At the end of that retention period, data is generally destroyed, but the retention policy should also have clear requirements and procedures for placing a legal hold on records that may be pertinent, thereby preventing their destruction until the investigation is complete.

Evidence Collection Best Practices

Although forensics experts may perform significant amounts of evidence collection, security practitioners must be aware of some best practices, including the following:

- When collecting evidence, it is best to utilize original physical media whenever possible, as copies may have unintended loss of integrity. Note that this applies only to collection; the best practice for analysis is to always use verified copies to preserve the original evidence. As mentioned, collecting physical evidence in the cloud may not be possible, though cyber-forensic tools such as Netscout are emerging that ease collection of digital forensic evidence, and some CSPs offer digital forensics services using their own tools and staff. In exceptional circumstances where physical evidence must be collected, it is likely the CSP will require that law enforcement be involved, particularly an agency with international jurisdiction. Even then, there is no guarantee; in a well-publicized case, *Microsoft Corp. v. United States*, Microsoft challenged a U.S. Department of Justice warrant for data stored in an Irish data center, which Microsoft claimed was outside U.S. jurisdiction. The case was ultimately rendered moot by passage of the Clarifying Lawful Overseas Use of Data Act (U.S. Cloud Act), but new laws being written for specific circumstances like this are exceedingly rare.

- Verify integrity at multiple steps by using hashing, especially when performing operations such as copying files. Calculate original and copy hashes and compare them to ensure that they match.

- Follow all documented procedures, such as the use of a dedicated evidence custodian for collection, logging of activities performed, leaving systems powered on to preserve volatile data, etc. These procedures should be documented in the organization's incident response plan.

- Establish and maintain communications with relevant parties such as the CSP, internal legal counsel, and law enforcement for guidance and requirements.

Evidence Preservation Best Practices

Once evidence has been collected, it must be adequately preserved to support a variety of goals: maintain the chain of custody, ensure admissibility, and be available for analysis to support the investigation. Preservation activities and concerns should cover the following:

- **Adequate physical security:** Most of us are familiar with TV police shows where an evidence locker is used. In the best-case scenario, the detectives must check out evidence following a documented procedure; in the worst-case scenario, the evidence has been removed with no documentation, leading to a criminal getting away with their actions. Digital evidence must be stored on physical media, which requires adequate physical protections, similar to a data center, and should also be subject to integrity tracking similar to a library book: documenting who checked out the evidence at what time and additionally documenting the actions taken such as copying data.

- **Physical and environmental maintenance:** Since evidence is stored on physical media, it may require environmental maintenance such as temperature and humidity controls, as well as available power to preserve data. Battery replacement or charging will be especially important for mobile devices.

- **Blocking interference:** Computing systems have access to a wide variety of wireless communications media including Bluetooth and Wi-Fi and may also try to communicate with the outside world via wired connections. Forensic analysts and evidence handlers need to adequately shield evidence-containing devices from this interference. To block wireless communications during analysis, the use of a Faraday cage, which blocks electromagnetic signals, is a best practice. For transporting mobile devices, a Faraday bag is recommended; in both cases, this can prevent these devices from being remotely wiped or reset. Workstations and other devices should be analyzed using a physically air-gapped network to prevent similar activities.

- **Working from copies:** Unlike evidence collection where use of originals is preferred, examination and analysis activities should be performed on copies of data and devices wherever possible, with frequent integrity comparisons to ensure that the copy being analyzed matches the original. Tools such as virtualization are useful here, as they can create an exact copy (image) of a system for analysis. Where copies are not available, tools such as write blockers should be used; these devices allow for read-only access to devices and prevent writing to them. Even the simple act of connecting a drive to a modern OS causes files such as a search index to be written, which could destroy or damage data that the investigator needs.

- **Document everything:** Remember that the chain of custody does not mean data or a system has not been changed at all, but defensibly documents the who, what, how, why, and when of changes. Checking evidence out for analysis, calculating hashes for comparison, and making copies for analysis are examples of actions that should be documented.

Manage Communication with Relevant Parties

Adequate coordination with a variety of stakeholders is critical in any IT operation, and the move to utilize cloud computing resources coupled with an increasingly regulated and dispersed supply chain elevates the priority of managing these relationships. Communication is a cornerstone of this management; providing adequate and timely information is critical. While this may be a skillset fundamental to project managers rather than security practitioners, it is worth understanding the importance of effective communication and supporting it whenever possible.

Effective communication should possess a number of qualities. The contents, nature, and delivery of communications will drive many decisions, which can be elicited using a series of questions about the information to be conveyed.

- **Who?** The intended audience will determine the contents of a communication, such as the level of technical detail included or amount of information. In security incidents, communications to the general public may be reviewed by the organization's legal department to avoid any admission of culpability or exposing sensitive information.

- **What?** The goal of the communication must be met by the contents. For example, reports to investors and business partners would contain different sets of details, as partners are likely to be under an NDA, but the general public is not. If the message does not clearly answer the question "So what?" it is likely the audience will not find it terribly useful.

- **Why?** The purpose of the communication should be clear, and the intended audience should be able to make immediate use of it. We are all familiar with technical error messages that provide less-than-helpful details of an internal memory error at a specific register address, but that does not help the average user to carry on with their work.

- **When?** Is the communication timely? If a data breach happened two years ago and the organization knew but did not report it, the information is likely to be useless as users will already have been targeted for identity theft scams. Furthermore, the communication is likely to cause reputational harm, as the organization could be accused of covering up the incident rather than reporting it in a timely fashion.

There are a number of stakeholders or constituents with whom an organization is likely to communicate regarding IT services, organizational news and happenings, and emergency information. Establishing clear methods, channels, and formats for this communication is critical.

Vendors

Few organizations exist in a vacuum; the modern supply chain spans the globe, and regulatory oversight has begun to enforce more stringent oversight of this supply chain. It is therefore essential that an organization and its security practitioners understand the supply chain and establish adequate communications.

The first step in establishing communications with vendors is an inventory of critical third parties on which the organization depends. This inventory will drive third-party or vendor risk management activities in two key ways. First, some vendors may be critical to the organization's ongoing functioning, such as a CSP whose architecture has been adopted by the organization. Second, some vendors of goods and services may provide critical inputs to an organization like a payment card processor whose service supports the organization's ability to collect money for its goods or services.

Communication with critical vendors should be similar to internal communications due to the critical role these vendors play in the business. If a vendor incident is likely to impact an organization's operations, the organization ought to have well-established communications protocols to receive as much advance notice as possible. If a consumer notices an incident such as loss of availability of a vendor's service, there should be adequate reporting mechanisms to raise the issue and resolve it as quickly as possible.

Many vendor communications will be governed by contract and SLA terms. When a CSP is a critical vendor, there should be adequate means for bidirectional communication of any issues related to the service, such as customer notices of any planned outages or downtime, emergency notifications of unplanned downtime, and customer reporting for service downtime or enhancements. In many cases, this will be done through a customer support channel with dedicated personnel as well as through ticketing systems, which creates a trackable notice of the issue, allowing all parties to monitor its progress.

Customers

As cloud consumers, most organizations will be the recipients of communications from their chosen CSPs. While this might seem to imply there are no responsibilities other than passively receiving information from and reporting issues to the CSP, consumers do have a critical accountability: defining SLA terms. Levels of communication service from the CSP should all be defined and agreed upon by both parties, such as speed of acknowledging and triaging incidents, required schedule for notification of planned downtime or maintenance, days/times support resources are available, and even the timeframe and benchmarks for reporting on the service performance. SLAs may be generic and standardized for all customers of a CSP or may be highly specific and negotiated per customer, which offers more flexibility but usually at greater cost.

Shared Responsibility Model

A key source of information to be communicated between CSPs and their customers is the responsibility for various security elements of the service. The CSP is solely responsible for operational concerns like environmental controls within the data center, as well as security concerns like physical access controls. Customers using the cloud service are responsible for implementing data security controls, like encryption, that are appropriate to the type of data they are storing and processing in the cloud. Some areas require action by both the provider and customer, so it is crucial for a CCSP to understand which cloud service models are in use by the organization and which areas of security must be addressed by each party. This is commonly referred to as the *shared responsibility* model, which defines who is responsible for different aspects of security across the different cloud service models. The generic model in Table 5.1 identifies key areas of responsibility and ownership in various cloud service models.

TABLE 5.1   Cloud Shared Responsibility Model

Responsibility	IaaS	PaaS	SaaS
Data classification	C	C	C
Identity and access management	C	C/P	C/P

Responsibility	IaaS	PaaS	SaaS
Application security	C	C/P	C/P
Network security	C/P	P	P
Host infrastructure	C/P	P	P
Physical security	P	P	P

C = Customer, P = Provider

A variety of CSP-specific documentation exists to define shared responsibility in that CSP's offerings, and a CCSP should obviously be familiar with the particulars of the CSP their organization is utilizing. The following is a brief description of the shared responsibility model for several major CSPs and links to further resources:

Amazon Web Services (AWS): Amazon identifies key differences for responsibility "in" the cloud versus security "of" the cloud. Customers are responsible for data and configuration in their cloud apps and architecture, while Amazon is responsible for shared elements of the cloud infrastructure including hardware, virtualization software, environmental controls, and physical security.

More information can be found here: aws.amazon.com/compliance/shared-responsibility-model.

Microsoft Azure: Microsoft makes key distinctions by the service model and specific areas such as information and data and OS configuration. Customers always retain responsibility for managing their users, devices, and data security, while Microsoft is exclusively responsible for physical security. Some areas vary by service model, such as OS configuration, which is a customer responsibility in IaaS but a Microsoft responsibility in SaaS.

More information can be found here: docs.microsoft.com/en-us/azure/security/fundamentals/shared-responsibility.

Google Cloud Platform (GCP): Google takes a different approach with a variety of shared responsibility documentation specific to different compliance frameworks such as ISO 27001, SOC 2, and PCI DSS. The same general rules apply, however: customer data security is always the customer's responsibility, physical security is always Google's responsibility, and some items are shared depending on what service offerings are utilized.

More information can be found here: cloud.google.com/security.

Partners

Partners will often have a level of access to an organization's systems similar to that of the organization's own employees but are not directly under the organization's control. Communication with partners will be similar to communication with employees, with initial steps required when a new relationship is established, ongoing maintenance activities throughout the partnership, and termination activities when the partnership is wound down. Each of these phases should deliver clear expectations regarding security requirements.

- **Onboarding:** During onboarding, a partner is introduced to the organization, and two important processes must be executed: third-party or vendor due diligence activities to assess the partner prior to sharing data or granting access, and communication of security requirements through contracts, SLAs, or other documentation. Elements of the organization's security program may be shared with the partner such as security policies and training.

- **Management:** Once a partner has been onboarded, the organization's ongoing security efforts must include any partner activities. This should include managing access and permissions, auditing and oversight activities, and processes such as incident response and disaster recovery testing.

- **Offboarding:** When a partnership ends, the organization must follow procedures to terminate access and communicate any security requirements relevant to the termination, such as reminders of nondisclosure requirements and the return of any assets the partner might have.

Regulators

There are a vast array of regulatory bodies governing information security, and most of them have developed cloud-specific guidance for compliant use of cloud services. In the early days of cloud computing, security practitioners often faced significant unknowns when moving to the cloud, but as the cloud became ubiquitous, regulators delivered clear guidance, and CSPs moved quickly to deliver cloud solutions tailored to those compliance requirements. A CCSP is still responsible for ensuring that their cloud environment is in compliance with all regulatory obligations applicable to their organization.

The main component of regulatory communication regarding the cloud is monitoring incoming information regarding regulatory requirements in the cloud. For example, the implementation of GDPR in the European Union (EU) forced many organizations to make architectural decisions regarding their cloud applications. GDPR's restrictions on data leaving the geographic boundaries of the EU mean many organizations need to implement additional privacy controls to transfer data out of the EU, otherwise they must host their applications in an EU-based data center. The CCSP should subscribe to feeds and be aware of regulatory changes that impact their organization's use of the cloud.

Similar to monitoring incoming cloud requirements, a CCSP may also be required to report information to regulatory bodies regarding their organization's state of compliance. For example, U.S.-based companies with GDPR privacy requirements may be required to communicate to the U.S. Department of Commerce on the status of privacy compliance under the U.S. Privacy Shield framework. CCSPs should be aware of regulatory reporting requirements specific to their organization and ensure that required documentation, artifacts, audits, etc., are communicated in a timely fashion.

Other Stakeholders

Communications may not be a primary job responsibility of a CCSP, but important details of security risk management work may need to be shared. Working with appropriate personnel in the organization will be crucial to ensure that information is communicated in a timely manner and with relevant details for each audience, such as the following:

- **Public:** Details of security incidents are the most obvious category, especially if the breach could affect security or privacy. In this case, adequately trained public relations (PR) professionals as well as legal personnel should be consulted and may handle communications with input from the security team.

- **Security researchers:** Increasingly, security experts are performing research on a specific organization's apps and services, with the goal of responsibly disclosing their findings before an attacker can exploit them. Organizations should have a method for receiving and responding to this type of communication, often via a publicly documented security email address. Getting details from a researcher, following up if more information is required, and in some cases paying a bounty for the discovered bug may all be ongoing communications that need to be handled.

- **Investors:** In many countries, formal communication with investors is required on a regular basis, such as quarterly business filings, annual financial statements, or unusual business activities such as a merger. Security posture, incidents, and compliance may all be relevant to some investors, and due to legal requirements, certain security details may be required.

- **Crisis communication:** An incident that causes significant disruption or disturbance such as a natural disaster may require communications to multiple stakeholder groups at once. Internal employees, business partners, investors, and the general public may all be impacted by a business disruption; in this case, the organization's communications personnel should have documented procedures, and security practitioners should look to these personnel for guidance on what information may be required.

Manage Security Operations

Security operations represent all activities undertaken by an organization in monitoring, maintaining, and generally running their security program. This may include continuous oversight of security systems to identify anomalies or incidents, as well as an organizational unit to house concerns related to security processes like incident response and business continuity. A large percentage of security process and procedure documentation will be attached to this function, and these processes should also be the target of continuous improvement efforts.

As in many security topics, an ISO standard exists that may be useful for security practitioners conducting security operations: ISO 18788, "Management system for private security operations — Requirements with guidance for use." A word of caution: this document contains a great deal of material not applicable to cybersecurity or infosec concerns, as the numbering might imply (it is not part of the 27000 series). One extraneous topic is implementing and managing a private security force with authorization to use force; however, it also provides a business management framework for understanding the organization's needs, guidance on designing strategic and tactical plans for operating security programs, and applying a risk management approach. It also suggests a standard plan, do, check, act framework for implementing and improving security operations.

Security Operations Center

The security operations center (SOC) is an organizational unit designed to centralize a variety of security tasks and personnel at the tactical (mid-term) and operational (day-to-day) levels of the organization. While security strategy may rely on input from top leaders such as a board of directors, department secretary or minister, or the C-suite executives, SOC personnel are responsible for implementing steps required to achieve that strategy and maintain daily operations. Building and running a SOC in a traditional, all on-prem environment is basically building a monitoring and response function for IT infrastructure. Extending these concepts to the cloud may require some trade-offs, as the CSP will not offer the same level of access for monitoring that an on-prem environment does.

It is also important to note that there will be at least two SOCs involved in cloud environments. The CSP should run and manage their own SOC focused on the elements they control under the shared responsibility model such as infrastructure and physical security, while consumers should run their own SOC for their responsibility areas, chiefly data security when using the cloud.

The CISO Mind Map published by security author Rafeeq Rehman, found at rafeeqrehman.com/?s=mindmap, provides a more information-security-centric view of security operations than ISO 18788. Updated each year, the Mind Map details the items that a CISO's role should cover; the largest element of the job responsibilities is security operations, which is broken down into three main categories. This provides a strong framework for responsibilities the SOC should undertake, including the following:

- **Threat prevention:** This subcategory includes preventative controls and risk mitigations designed to reduce the likelihood of incidents occurring. These include adequate network security, vulnerability and patch management programs, application security (appsec), information system hardening, and maintenance activities for common security tools such as PKI.

- Threat prevention in the cloud will involve similar activities such as keeping an adequate asset inventory and utilizing it to detect vulnerabilities and fix them via patching, particularly when using IaaS. In some PaaS and virtually all SaaS, vulnerability and patch management will be the responsibility of the CSP. Implementing network security in the cloud requires adequate selection and deployment of cloud-appropriate tools like firewalls and intrusion detection tools; many traditional tools do not work in virtualized networks or rely on capabilities like mirroring network traffic from a SPAN port on a switch to inspect traffic, which is not available in a virtual cloud network. SOC operations need to be able to access that data and integrate it with monitoring tools, often through the use of API.

- **Threat detection:** Detecting threats requires tools, processes, and procedures, such as log capture/analysis/correlation, which is often achieved with a SIEM tool. Other capabilities include real-time monitoring tools such as data loss/leak prevention (DLP) tools and network security solutions like IDS/IPS, anti-malware, and firewalls. Some security testing processes also fall in this category such as red (offensive) and blue (defensive) team exercises.

  - The general process of running the SOC falls into this category, covering topics such as resource management and training. Adequately trained personnel and robust procedures are essential to the success of a security program. Because of the tools in use, there will be architectural management concerns as well; chief among them is ensuring that the tools in use adequately monitor the infrastructure. As many organizations migrate to the cloud, legacy tools designed to monitor and defend a single network become obsolete since they do not scale to a globally accessible cloud environment.

  - Building out a SOC for cloud operations may require the use of different monitoring tools, as many legacy tools are designed to be deployed on a physical network to monitor traffic and events. That capability is not available in a virtualized, cloud network, and given the use of a CSP's resources, many organizations implement additional encryption to protect data. This has the downside of often rendering data invisible to monitoring tools. CSPs offer a number of built-in security monitoring and alerting tools, such as Azure Sentinel and AWS Amazon GuardDuty, which can be used as stand-alone programs or integrated with SOC monitoring tools using an API.

  - No security program is foolproof, so detecting threats and incidents is critical. Ideally, threats should be proactively identified by the organization via threat hunting *before* an attacker exploits them. If an attacker finds and exploits an unknown vulnerability, this function also provides incident detection capabilities that can reactively identify an incident that would be handled by the third function.

- **Incident management:** Once an incident has occurred, the SOC will often serve as the main point of coordination for the incident response team (IRT). This subcategory will house many of the functions previously discussed, such as developing incident response capabilities, handling communications like regulator and customer notifications, and handling forensics.

- Two particular threats stand out for extra attention in this category. The first is data breach preparation, which encompasses the majority of incident response planning activities, business continuity planning, logging and monitoring functions, and the recently included cyber risk insurance. Insurance represents a form of risk transfer, which helps to shift the impact of a risk from the organization to another party, in this case the organization's insurer. Many cyber risk insurance plans also offer access to useful incident handling specialties such as data breach and privacy lawyers, forensic experts, and recovery services.

- The other threat explicitly called out is one that has grown in recent years: ransomware. Attackers are exploiting encryption to lock users out of information systems until a ransom is paid, so preparing for or preventing one of these attacks is critical. Preventative steps can include file integrity monitoring, designed to detect unwanted changes such as ransomware encrypting files or even the malware being installed. Planning for recovery is also crucial beforehand, with adequate business continuity, disaster recovery, and backup plans being the primary implementations for ransomware recovery.

- As discussed in the incident management section of this chapter, coordination between the CSP and consumer will be essential for incident response and handling and is a key difference from on-prem environments.

A SOC is typically made up of security analysts, whose job involves taking incoming data and extracting useful information, and security engineers who can keep operations running smoothly. There may be overlap with operations personnel, and in some organizations, the SOC may be combined with other operational functions. Common functions that may be performed in the SOC are the following:

- **Continuous monitoring and reporting:** All the security tools implemented by an organization require at least some level of ongoing oversight by a human being. The SOC will typically centralize relevant data into a dashboard, which may be projected on large screens in the SOC physical office or available as a web page so all members can see vital information. In addition to SOC members, certain information may be reported to other members of the organization in the form of metrics or incident reports.

- **Data security:** The SOC should have the ability to perform monitoring across any environments where sensitive data is being stored, processed, or transmitted. This can be used to ensure that data is being adequately protected in various states across all stages of its lifecycle. Threat hunting and vulnerability management functions in the SOC should look for risks to data, such as improperly configured cloud storage environments or insecure data transmission when users are connecting with SaaS applications.

  Alert prioritization: Not all alerts are critical, require immediate attention, or represent imminent harm to the organization. SOC functions related to log management should include definitions to assist in prioritizing alerts received from various sources such as monitoring tools, as well as defined procedures for taking action on alerts.

Loss of commercial power at a facility is an alert worth monitoring but may not be a major incident if backup power is available and the power is likely to be restored quickly. If the organization is experiencing exceptional operations, such as retail during a major holiday, then the organization may choose to preemptively declare a business interruption and shift processing to an alternate facility. Detecting and triaging incidents, up to and including declaration of an interruption or disaster, is a logical function for the SOC to perform due to the type of data they work with.

- **Incident response:** SOC personnel are uniquely situated to detect and respond to anomalous activity such as an interruption or incident and as such are often the core constituent of an incident response team. Skills and expertise such as digital forensics, whether internal to the team or via third-party services, may be a logical fit on this team as well. At the conclusion of an incident response, this team is also well suited to perform root-cause analysis and recommend remedial actions.

- **Compliance management:** The SOC is likely to have information that is quite crucial to managing the organization's compliance posture. Although compliance functions may be implemented elsewhere in the organization to avoid conflict of interest, critical information monitored by the SOC can be useful, such as server configurations, results of routine vulnerability scans, and crucial risk management activities like business continuity.

As always, there are two key perspectives for the SOC. CSPs will likely need a robust SOC function with 24/7/365 monitoring of the environment. While such a capability will be expensive, the cost is likely justified by requirements of the cloud consumers and can be shared among this large group. Cloud consumers may operate a SOC for their own operations, which will include any on-prem IT services as well as their cloud services and environments. This may require the use of some legacy tools deployed to more traditional cloud services such as IaaS or PaaS, newer tools designed to monitor services such as SaaS (for example, access management or encryption tools), or even the use of CSP-provided monitoring capabilities.

As an example, the major CSPs offer security incident reporting services that customers can log in to if an incident affects them. They also offer the following public status pages that list operational information for public-facing services:

- **AWS Service Health Dashboard:** `status.aws.amazon.com`

- **Microsoft Azure status:** `status.azure.com/en-us/status`

- **Google Cloud Status Dashboard:** `status.cloud.google.com`

One crucial decision to be made when designing a SOC is the use of internal resources or outsourcing the function (build versus buy). As previously mentioned, the CSPs can likely justify the cost of robust SOC resources due to cost sharing among customers and the requirements those customers will impose. A small organization with only cloud-based architecture may decide to outsource their security operations and monitoring, as many services provide dedicated support for specific cloud platforms at a lower cost than building the same function internally. These are known as managed security services providers (MSSPs). Like most business decisions, this will be a trade-off between control and cost and should be made by business leaders with input from security practitioners. A CCSP should understand the cloud architecture and communicate any risks the organization might assume by utilizing a third-party SOC.

Monitoring of Security Controls

Monitoring of security controls used to be an activity closely related to formal audits that occur relatively infrequently, sometimes once a year or even once every three years. A newer concept is known as *continuous monitoring*, which is described in the NIST SP 800-37 Risk Management Framework (RMF) as "Maintaining ongoing awareness to support organizational risk decisions." Information that comes from an audit conducted more than a year ago is not ongoing awareness. Instead, the RMF specifies the creation of a continuous monitoring strategy for getting near real-time risk information.

Real-time or near real-time information regarding security controls comprises two key elements: the status of the controls and any alerts or actionable information they have created. Network resources are at risk of attacks, so network security controls like IDS are deployed. Continuous monitoring of the IDS's uptime is critical to ensure that risk is being adequately mitigated. A facility to view any alerts generated by the device, as well as personnel and processes to respond to them, is also crucial to the organization's goal of mitigating security risks; if the IDS identifies malicious network activity but no action is taken to stop it, the control is not effective.

A longer-term concern for monitoring security controls and risk management is the suitability of the current set of tools. As organizations evolve, their infrastructure will likely change, which can render existing tools ineffective. The SOC should be charged with ensuring that it can monitor the organization's current technology stack, and a representative should be part of change management or change control processes. Migrating a business system from on-prem hosting to a SaaS model will likely have a security impact with regard to the tools needed to monitor it, and the change board should ensure that this risk is planned for as part of the change.

In general, the SOC should have some monitoring capabilities across all physical and logical infrastructure, though detailed monitoring of some systems may be performed by another group. For example, a physical access control system dashboard may be best monitored by security guards who can perform appropriate investigation if an alarm is triggered. Some organizations run a network operations center (NOC) to monitor network health, and NOC engineers would be best suited to manage telecommunications equipment and ISP vendors. However, an operational incident in either of these two systems, such as a break-in or loss of ISP connectivity, could be an input to the SOC's incident management function. Several controls that might be particularly important for SOC monitoring include the following:

- **Network security controls:** This includes traditional devices (or their virtual equivalents) such as network firewalls, web app firewalls (WAF), and IDS/IPS. The SOC should be able to see if devices are functioning, alerts such as suspicious activity or problems, and trends such as volume of dropped packets on a firewall or activity on a honeypot system. These could be indicators of a potential attack and are best dealt with proactively. Services may be included in the SOC monitoring as well, especially if used to achieve critical risk mitigation objectives like identity management (ID as a service, or IDaaS) or cloud application orchestration via platforms like Kubernetes.

- **Performance and capacity:** All IT services have performance requirements and capacity limitations. While the cloud can theoretically offer benefits with both, the process may not be entirely automated. Some cloud service offerings are simply cloud-based, virtualized versions of legacy services. In these cases, there can be capacity constraints if the organization's usage grows; for example, a PaaS database may run out of storage as usage grows. Core services like storage, network bandwidth, and compute capacity should be monitored. Many of these will also be SLA metrics that the organization should monitor, so this function can achieve two objectives.

- **Vulnerability assessments:** Vulnerability scanners can be configured to run on a defined frequency, either time- or trigger-based. Unlike audit frameworks in the past, which included a vulnerability scan once a year during audit, organizations implementing continuous monitoring should seek to define more frequent scan schedules. Time-based schedules should be made to balance any operational overhead, such as system performance slowdown, with user needs—often achieved by running scans outside of normal business hours. Trigger-based scans can be set up to conduct scans when certain activities occur, such as a new version of an application being deployed to the production environment. These can often be useful in achieving real-time risk visibility, as the scan is conducted at the same time a new attack surface is created. Vulnerability assessments may be conducted from an internal or external perspective to simulate what vulnerabilities a trusted insider or malicious outsider might be able to find and exploit.

Log Capture and Analysis

NIST SP 800-92, "Guide to Computer Security Log Management," defines a log as "a record of the events occurring within an organization's systems and networks" and further states that "Many logs within an organization contain records related to computer security . . . including security software, such as antivirus software, firewalls, and intrusion detection and prevention systems; operating systems on servers, workstations, and networking equipment; and applications." These logs of internal activity can unfortunately be overwhelming for humans to attempt to meaningfully review due to the sheer number of events generated by modern information systems. Security information and event management (SIEM) tools offer assistance.

SIEM tools provide a number of functions useful to security, namely, the following:

- **Centralization:** It would be impossible for a human to navigate all the log files of individual hosts in even a moderately complex information system. There may be database, middleware, and web servers each with a corresponding log file, not to mention application logs for the software running on each of those systems. A SIEM provides the ability to centralize all log data. Logs are forwarded or sent to the SIEM tool from the system they originate on; this may be done as a native function of the system or rely on an agent installed that copies log files and sends them to the SIEM. This can also be used to enforce a key access control for log data. Users with credentials to monitored systems may be able to delete or change logs on those systems but can be easily denied permission to the SIEM tool.

- **Normalization:** Log files generated by disparate systems may contain data that is similar but not exactly the same. One system may generate log files with a user's ID, like jsmith, while another utilizes the user's email address, like john.smith@company.com. This makes it harder to analyze the data, so SIEM platforms can transform data to a common format, such as the use of UTC for timestamps to avoid issues with time zones, or the use of consistent field names like Timestamp instead of Event Time.

- **Correlation and detection:** Once data has been centralized and normalized, the SIEM can better support detection of suspicious events. This is often done by comparing activities in the log with a set of rules, such as a user's location. If a user typically accesses a system every day from their desk on the corporate network, then that user suddenly logging on from another country halfway around the world is suspicious. Some SIEM platforms incorporate more complex detection methods like artificial intelligence, which uses learning models to identify potentially suspicious activity or weed out false positives.

  Correlation refers to discovering relationships between two or more events; in this example, if the user has suddenly logged in from a new location, accessed email, and started downloading files, it could indicate compromised credentials being used to steal data. It could also indicate that the user is attending a conference and is getting some work done in between sessions, but the organization should still perform checks to verify. If travel is a common situation, the organization might also integrate data from an HR or travel reservation system to correlate travel records for a certain user with their activity accessing data from a particular country. If the user is not known to be traveling in that country, the activity is highly suspicious.

  Other sources of information could include external information like threat intelligence or CSP status feeds, which can be relevant in investigating anomalies and categorizing them as incidents. Major CSPs offer monitoring capabilities in their platforms as well, and this data may be critical for investigating anomalies.

- **Alerting:** Once suspicious activity is detected, the SIEM should generate an alert, and a SOC analyst should follow a documented procedure to review and take action on the alert. Many SOCs will utilize a system for handling this process, such as an IT ticketing system that generates work tickets in a queue for analysts to take action on. The activities related to each ticket are captured along with details such as who is working on it, steps taken, and artifacts from the process like investigation logs.

PaaS and SaaS in particular can pose issues for logging and monitoring, as the logs themselves may not be visible to the consumer. CSPs typically don't share internal logs with consumers due to the risk of inadvertently exposing customer details, so these services may be a black hole in the organization's monitoring strategy. Solutions have been designed that can address this, such as the cloud access security broker (CASB), which is designed to log and monitor user access to cloud services. These can be deployed inline to a user's connection to cloud services or collect information via API with cloud services. The CASB can monitor access and interaction with applications; for example, user Alice Doe logged into Dropbox at 12:30, and uploaded file `Super Secret Marketing Data.xlsx` at 12:32. Dropbox as a CSP may not share this data with consumers, but the CASB can help overcome that blind spot.

Log Management

NIST SP 800-92 details critical requirements for securely managing log data, such as defining standard processes and managing the systems used to store and analyze logs. Because of their critical nature in supporting incident investigations, logs are often a highly critical data asset and worthy of robust security mechanisms. These may include the following:

- High-integrity storage media such as write once, read many (WORM), which allows a definitive copy of the data to be written just once. This prevents tampering with log files after they are written to disk, but allows for analysis.

- Restricted access to only SOC personnel, as logs may contain highly sensitive information. This could include details of internal system configuration, as well as sensitive information being processed if an application or database error contains pieces of the sensitive data.

- Capacity monitoring and rotation to ensure adequate storage space. Logs grow quite quickly, and allocating sufficient space for logs is essential. Maintaining all data readily available may be cost-prohibitive, so some log files may be stored offline if appropriate or rotated (written over) after a set period of time.

- Retention and secure deletion when logs are no longer needed. Log files should be part of the organization's retention schedule and should be in compliance with applicable legal and regulatory obligations and are also critical to reconstruction of historical events as needed for incident investigations. Because of the possibility of highly sensitive data, secure destruction methods should be defined for log data.

- Proper configuration of logging functions on all systems. Many systems and apps provide configuration options for what data is written to log files based on the value of the information. Informational alerts, such as a server synchronizing its clock with a time-server, may not be of much value. Events like a user successfully logging in, entering the wrong credentials, or changing their password would be of more value, as they provide evidence of the organization's access controls at work. The *clipping level* defines which categories of events are and are not written to logs, such as user authentication events, informational system notices, or system restarts.

- Testing and validation of log data to ensure that integrity is not compromised. Log data collected, especially on a centralized tool like a SIEM, should be periodically validated against the originals to ensure that it is being transmitted without alteration. It should not be possible to alter data being forwarded to the centralized platform, and any attempts to tamper with or disable the forwarding functionality should result in an alert so corrective action can be taken.

Incident Management

An *incident* is any unplanned event that actually does or has the ability to reduce the quality of an IT service. In security terms, reducing the quality is synonymous with impacting any element of the CIA triad. As an example, an event could be a loss of commercial power at a data center. If the organization has been notified that the power company is performing maintenance and is able to continue running with backup generators, then this is merely an event. The IT services provided by the data center can continue uninterrupted. If, instead, the power is cut unexpectedly and the facility must switch to backup power, this could cause systems to be unresponsive or lose data during the transition to backup power. This is an obvious negative impact to data integrity and system availability.

Incident management or incident response (IR) exists to help an organization plan for incidents, identify them when they occur, and restore normal operations as quickly as possible with minimal adverse impact to business operations. This is referred to as a capability, or the combination of procedures and resources needed to respond to incidents, and generally comprises three key elements.

- **Incident response plan (IRP):** The IRP (sometimes known as an *incident management plan*) is a proactive control designed to reduce the impact of an incident. It defines structure for the processes to be used when responding to an incident, which allows team members to respond in a quick and orderly fashion. People are often in high-stress situations when an outage or interruption occurs, and having a plan with detailed scenarios and response steps can provide better decision-making and response outcomes. The IRP should include detailed, scenario-based response procedures for team members to follow, which are based on incidents that the organization is likely to face. For example, an IT consulting firm is unlikely to face a major attack on an industrial control system (ICS) but is likely to fall victim to phishing attacks. The IRP should include detailed instructions on how to identify a phishing campaign, prevent the message from propagating, and provide cleanup or remediation steps for users who have fallen victim, such as immediately locking user accounts until investigation can be conducted.

- **Incident response team (IRT):** The IRP should detail the personnel needed to respond to incidents. This team is likely to be dynamic based on the type of incident; for example, a small malware infection is likely to require help-desk technicians to assist, while a data breach of PII will require legal counsel to assist with data breach notifications. All members of the IRT should be trained on their responsibilities *before* an incident occurs, and a designated coordinator must be appointed to lead the incident response effort. This coordinator should be empowered to dynamically assemble a team based on the incident, up to and including overriding conventional job duties for the duration of the incident. IRT members should also have dedicated communication protocols in place, such as a phone tree or instant messaging group, allowing them to receive information on incidents in a timely manner.

- **Root-cause analysis:** Once an incident has been resolved, the IRT should perform a root-cause analysis, document these findings, and offer suggestions for preventing the incident in the future. Some incidents, such as natural disasters, may be unavoidable, but the organization may be able to implement proactive measures to reduce their impact, such as relocating staff ahead of a forecastable natural disaster. Incident response plans and procedures should also be updated as appropriate to help the organization better respond in the future to incidents of a similar nature.

Incident Classification

To ensure that an incident is dealt with correctly, it is important to determine how critical it is and prioritize the response appropriately. Each organization may classify incidents differently, but a generic scheme plots Urgency against Impact. These are assigned values from Low, Medium, or High, and incidents that are High priority are handled first. The following are descriptions and examples of these criteria:

- **Impact:** How much or how significantly does the incident degrade IT services? An issue with identity management that forces users to try logging in multiple times before successfully accessing a system is irritating but has a minor effect on operations. A data center being completely unreachable due to cut network cables means a complete loss of the business function and should be dealt with before other issues.

- **Urgency:** How soon does the organization need resolution? An outage on a system for internal staff social information like team sporting events is unlikely to be critical and can wait for restoration if a mission-critical system is also suffering an outage.

Incident classification criteria and examples should be documented for easy reference. The IRP should contain this information, and it is also advisable to include it in any supporting systems like incident trackers or ticketing systems. These ratings are subjective and may change as the incident is investigated, so the IR coordinator should ensure that critical information like prioritization is communicated to the team.

Incident Response Phases

The organization's IRP should include detailed steps broken down by phases. At a high level, there are activities to be conducted prior to an incident and after an incident occurs; namely, planning the IR capability and the actual execution of a response when an incident is detected. There are a number of IR models that contain slightly different definitions for each phase, but in general they all contain the following:

- **Prepare:** Preparation is the phase where the IR capability's foundation is established. During this phase, the IRP and IRT should be documented, training given to IRT members, and adequate detection abilities implemented.

- **Detect:** To be effective, the IR capability requires the ability to detect and draw attention to events that could negatively impact the organization's operations. This is most often in the form of the organization's continuous monitoring tools, which can identify anomalous activity and alert SOC personnel trained to analyze, prioritize, and initiate response procedures. Other methods of detection can include noncontinuous monitoring activities like routine audits, user-reported issues such as unexpected application or system behavior, and even external entities like security researchers.

Security researchers or malicious actors may draw attention to a vulnerability they have discovered or, worse, exploited, in which case the organization must take steps to investigate if the claim is true and take appropriate action. Organizations are also beginning to subscribe to external intelligence feeds from third-party services that can provide advance alert of an incident, such as compromised user credentials showing up on the dark web, or adjacent domains being registered that might be used in a phishing attack.

As soon as an incident is detected, it must be documented, and all actions from the point of detection through to resolution should be documented as well. Initial analysis or triage of incidents, prioritization, members of the IRT called upon to deal with the incident, and plans for implementing recovery strategies should be documented. As discussed in the section on digital forensics, it may be the case that a seemingly simple incident evolves into a malicious act requiring criminal charges. In this case, as much evidence as possible, handled correctly, will be crucial and cannot be created after the fact.

Investigation will begin as the IRT starts to gather information about the incident. This can be as simple as attempting to reproduce a user-reported app issue to determine if it is only affecting that user or is a system-wide issue. This is a key integration point to the practice of digital forensics. As soon as it appears, the incident may require prosecution or escalation to law enforcement, and appropriately trained digital forensics experts must be brought in.

Notification may also occur during this stage, once the incident is properly categorized. In many cases, this will be done to satisfy legal or compliance obligations, such as U.S. state privacy laws and the EU GDPR, which require notification to authorities within a certain timeframe after an incident is detected. Appropriate communication resources like legal counsel or public relations personnel may be required on the IRT to handle these incidents.

- **Respond:** Once the organization has been alerted to an incident, its IR capability is activated, and an appropriate remediation must be developed. In most incidents, the overriding concern during the response phase should be containing the incident—that is preventing it from causing further damage. In some cases, gathering information about the attack may be required, during which time the incident continues to occur; in this case, the extra information gained must be more valuable than the damage caused by the ongoing attack.

Once sufficient information is gathered, a containment strategy must be formulated and implemented. This should follow the documented scenario-based responses in the IRP whenever possible—for example, responding to a ransomware attack by isolating any affected machines and working to establish how the malware was installed. Once this is ascertained, deploying techniques for preventing other machines from being affected may be more important than recovering data on machines that have already been compromised. These types of decisions should be made by qualified personnel with as much information as possible at their disposal.

Notification is typically handled as part of incident detection, and formal reporting is an ongoing task that starts after the initial notification. In simple cases, the report may comprise a single document at the resolution of an incident with the particulars, while in other cases, ongoing reporting of a dynamic situation will be required. As you may have seen during high-profile data breaches at public organizations, initial reporting is made on the incident with information available at that moment, even if it is estimated. As the investigation proceeds, updated reports are delivered to convey new information. The IR coordinator, along with appropriate communication resources on the IRT, is responsible for creating and disseminating all required reporting to appropriate stakeholders.

During the response phase, additional information should be gathered and documented regarding the incident. This may include details of any external attacker or malicious insider who might be responsible and should be conducted in accordance with the digital evidence handling previously discussed.

- **Recover:** This phase may actually be started as soon as the detection phase and continue until the cause of the incident is completely eradicated and normal operations have resumed. Actions like changing a password for a user who responded to a phishing email or following documented procedures like restarting a server for unexpected app behavior can be recovery actions.

  Eradication of the underlying cause is also a critical element of the recovery. This may include actions such as replacing faulty hardware, blocking a specific IP address or user from accessing a resource, or rebuilding compromised systems from known good images. Containment prevents the incident from spreading further, while eradication removes the immediate cause of the incident. It may be the case that neither prevents the problem from reoccurring in the future, which is a part of post-incident activities.

  Recovery and eradication end when the organization returns to normal operations. This is defined as the pre-incident service level delivered using standard procedures.

- **Post-incident:** Once normal operations have resumed, the IRT should ensure that all documentation from the incident is properly created and stored. Lessons learned from conducting the response should be gathered and used to improve the incident response process itself. Finally, the organization should conduct a root-cause analysis to identify any underlying causes and appropriate steps to prevent the incident from recurring in the future.

Incident response is designed to help the organization restore normal operations quickly, but there are situations when this will be impossible. In these cases, the incident may need to be upgraded to an *interruption*, which is an event whose impact is significant enough to disrupt the organization's ability to achieve its goals or mission. A few users with malware infections on their workstations is an incident that can likely be handled by normal IT resources, but an outbreak affecting all critical systems and a large percentage of users is likely to require more resources.

In such cases, the IR coordinator may be empowered to declare an interruption or disaster, which invokes processes like BCDR. Similar to IR, there should be clear plans in place to guide the organization's response, such as emergency authorization to buy new equipment outside of normal purchasing processes or invocation of alternate procedures like using a third party to process information. The IR coordinator should be aware of their role and responsibilities in these plans, including the process for declaring and notifying appropriate members of the BCDR team to take over.

Cloud-Specific Incident Management

As discussed, the migration to a third-party CSP can introduce additional complexity to an organization. When planning for incident management, the CSP must be considered as a critical stakeholder. Appropriate points of contact should be documented and reachable in the event of an incident, such as a service delivery or account manager who can support the organization's incident response and recovery. An incident at the CSP should be communicated to all the CSP's consumers, and the CSP may be required to provide specific information in the case of regulated data or negligence. Even if a data breach is the fault of the CSP, the consumer who is the data controller is still legally liable on several counts, including notifying affected individuals and possible fines.

Communication from a consumer to the CSP may be critical, especially if the incident has the ability to affect other CSP customers. Additionally, some options for performing incident management, such as rebuilding compromised architecture, will be different in the cloud environment. It is possible to rapidly redeploy completely virtual architecture to a known good state in the cloud; the same task in a traditional data center environment could take significant time.

Incident Management Standards

There are three standards that can guide a security practitioner in designing and operating an incident management capability.

- **Carnegie Mellon University Software Engineering Institute (SEI)—Incident Management Capability Assessment:** SEI publishes a variety of capability maturity models, which can be useful for organizations assessing how robust their procedures are currently and identifying opportunities for future improvement. This model is freely available and utilizes categories to break down essential activities, including Prepare, Protect, Detect, Respond, and Sustain. Within each category are subcategory activities designed to help the organization proactively build the IR capability, respond when incidents occur, and continuously improve the capability.

    You can find the technical report document at `resources.sei.cmu.edu/asset_files/TechnicalReport/2018_005_001_538866.pdf`.

- **NIST SP 800-61, Computer Security Incident Handling Guide:** This NIST standard is also freely available and breaks incident handling down into four high-level phases: Preparation, Detection and Analysis, Containment Eradication and Recovery, and Post-Incident Activity. It focuses on creating incident handling checklists designed to speed response times and is a useful guide for organizations in the U.S. federal government or those following other NIST standards such as the RMF or using NIST SP 800-53 as a security control framework.

  You can find NIST SP 800-61 here: `csrc.nist.gov/publications/detail/ sp/800-61/rev-2/final`.

- **ISO 27035:** As with all ISO standards. there are several documents in this standard, including Part 1: Principles of Incident Management, Part 2: Guidelines to Plan and Prepare for Incident Response, and Part 3: Guidelines for ICT Incident Response Operations. The standard is similar to other frameworks including a phased approach broken down into pre-, during-, and post-incident steps. Unlike other frameworks, these documents are not freely available. The steps are most closely aligned with the security controls framework and implementation approach outlined in the rest of the ISO 27000 standard.

Summary

Cloud security operations, like all other security practices, must be anchored by two key principles: operations must be driven by the organization's business objectives or mission, and they must preserve the confidentiality, integrity, and availability of data and systems in the cloud. Operations is a far-reaching topic covering the selection, implementation, and monitoring of physical and logical infrastructure, as well as security controls designed to address the risks posed in cloud computing.

There are a variety of standards that can assist the CCSP in implementing or managing security controls for cloud environments. These cover major objectives such as access control, securing network activity, designing operational control programs, and handling communications. Choosing the correct standard will be driven by each organization's location, industry, and possibly costs associated with the various standards. All programs implemented should have feedback mechanisms designed to continuously improve security as risks evolve.

Also key is an understanding of the shared responsibility model. CSPs will perform the majority of work related to physical infrastructure, though cloud consumers may need physical security for infrastructure that connects them to cloud computing. Logical infrastructure is a more equally shared responsibility: in non-SaaS models, the CSP runs the underlying infrastructure, but consumers have key responsibilities in securing the logical infrastructure in their virtual slice of the cloud.

Chapter 6

Legal, Risk, and Compliance

The cloud offers companies and individuals access to vast amounts of computing power at economies of scale made possible only by distributed architectures. However, those same distributed architectures can bring a unique set of risks and legal challenges to companies due to the geographic distribution of the cloud infrastructure. The cloud, similar to the Internet, allows data to flow freely across national borders and facilitates storage and processing in data centers worldwide. Determining what laws apply to cloud computing environments is an ongoing challenge. The cloud service provider (CSP) can be based in one country, operate data centers across multiple countries, and serve customers in even more countries. In this situation there may be overlapping legal requirements, which introduces risk, and using a third-party CSP can introduce additional risks.

Articulating Legal Requirements and Unique Risks within the Cloud Environment

Legal and compliance requirements are more complex for cloud computing than they were for traditional on-premises information systems. With data and compute power spread across countries and continents, international disputes have dramatically increased. Various countries and regions have taken differing approaches to governing data privacy, intellectual property protection, and law enforcement methods. These types of disputes existed before cloud computing, but the transborder data flow and processing enabled by the cloud emerged before legal frameworks were written to deal with these scenarios. To prepare for these challenges, a cloud security professional must be aware of the legal requirements and unique risks presented by cloud computing architectures.

Conflicting International Legislation

Using distributed cloud services provides benefits for redundancy and data integrity and can even offer performance benefits by moving information systems closer to the end users. This can, however, lead to physical infrastructure, business operations, and customers that are all governed by completely separate and sometimes conflicting laws.

For example, the European Union (EU) is governed by a data privacy law known as the General Data Protection Regulation (GDPR), which is a wide-ranging law. A Brazilian company that handles or stores data of EU citizens is obligated to comply, even though they are not based in the EU. Further complicating matters, each EU member state has its own privacy laws—although they align with GDPR, there can be subtle variations, such as time-frames and procedures for reporting security breaches to the member state data protection authority.

Although cloud security practitioners are not expected to be legal professionals as well, it is important to be aware of the various laws and regulations that govern cloud computing. Laws can introduce risks to a business, such as fines, penalties, or even a loss of the ability to do business in a certain place. It is important to identify such risks and make recommendations to mitigate them just like any other risk.

As an example, GDPR forbids the transfer of data to countries that lack adequate privacy protections; a mitigation to avoid a GDPR fine might involve building an application instance in an EU cloud region and preventing transfer of the data outside the EU. However, some countries require companies operating in that country to respond to law enforcement actions, such as a warrant to turn over data. In this situation, the GDPR restriction on data transfers might be violated in order to comply with another country's legal requirements.

Because of the international nature of cloud offerings and customers, cloud practitioners must be aware of multiple sets of laws and regulations and the risks introduced by conflicting legislation across jurisdictions. These conflicts may include the following:

- Copyright and intellectual property law, particularly the jurisdictions that companies need to deal with (local versus international) to protect and enforce their IP protections

- Safeguards and security controls required for privacy compliance, particularly details of data residency or the ability to move data between countries, as well as varying requirements of due care in different jurisdictions

- Data breaches and their aftermath, particularly breach notification

- International import/export laws, particularly technologies that may be sensitive or illegal under various international agreements

Craig Mundie, the former chief of Microsoft's research and strategy divisions, explained it in these terms:

> People still talk about the geopolitics of oil. But now we have to talk about the geopolitics of technology. Technology is creating a new type of interaction of a geopolitical scale and importance. . . . We are trying to retrofit a governance structure which was derived from geographic borders. But we live in a borderless world.

In simple terms, a cloud security practitioner must be familiar with a number of legal arenas when evaluating risks associated with a cloud computing environment. This does not mean, however, that they must be legal experts. As with many aspects of security, legal compliance requires collaboration; in this case, legal counsel should be part of the evaluation of any cloud-specific risks, legal requests, and the company's response to these.

Evaluation of Legal Risks Specific to Cloud Computing

The cloud offers computing capabilities that were unheard of a decade ago. CSPs can offer content delivery options to host data within a few hundred miles of almost any human being on Earth, offer novel architectures like microservices, and make computing power cheaper than it has ever been. Customers are not limited by political borders when accessing services from cloud providers, but this flexibility introduces a new set of risks. Legal, regulatory, and compliance risks in the cloud can be significant for certain types of data or industries.

Storing or processing data in multiple countries introduces legal and regulatory challenges. Cloud computing customers may be impacted by one or more of the following:

- **Differing legal requirements:** For example, state and provincial laws in the United States and Canada have different requirements for data breach notifications, such as timeframes. In addition, there are federal laws governing certain types of privacy data in these countries, which have separate breach reporting requirements. In building out incident response plans, security practitioners must account for the types of data they handle and the location of their users, as well as ensure that any incident communications procedures meet these legal reporting obligations.

- **Different legal systems and frameworks in different countries:** In some countries there is clear, written legislation in place, while in others legal precedent is more important. *Precedent* refers to the judgments in past cases and is subject to change over time with less advance notice than updates to legislation. Security practitioners will need to get input from legal counsel to ensure that the different types of legal systems and evolving requirements are understood and to take appropriate action to help the organization respond accordingly.

- **Conflicting laws:** The EU GDPR and the U.S. Clarifying Lawful Overseas Use of Data (CLOUD) Act can leave an organization in a legal mess. GDPR forbids transfer of EU citizen data without adequate protections, while the CLOUD Act requires U.S.-based companies to respond to legal requests for data regardless of where the data is physically located. Simply locating physical infrastructure in another country is not enough to avoid potential legal consequences in this scenario—different corporate structures may be required to avoid the risk of one country's law enforcement action leading to legal issues in another.

Legal Frameworks and Guidelines

Cloud security practitioners should be aware of the legal frameworks that affect the cloud computing environments. The following frameworks are the products of multinational organizations working together to identify key priorities in the security of information systems and data privacy.

The Organisation for Economic Co-operation and Development

The Organisation for Economic Co-operation and Development (OECD) guidelines lay out privacy and security guidelines. (See www.oecd.org/sti/ieconomy/privacy-guidelines.htm.) The OECD guidelines are echoed in European privacy law in many instances. The basic principles of privacy in the OECD include the following:

- **Collection limitation principle:** There should be limits on the collection of personal data as well as consent from the data subject.

- **Data quality principle:** Personal data should be accurate, complete, and kept up-to-date.

- **Purpose specification principle:** The purpose of data collection should be specified, and data use should be limited to these stated purposes.

- **Use limitation principle:** Data should not be used or disclosed without the consent of the data subject or by the authority of law.

- **Security safeguards principle:** Personal data must be protected by reasonable security safeguards against unauthorized access, destruction, use, or disclosure.

- **Openness principle:** Policies and practices about personal data should be freely disclosed, including the identity of data controllers.

- **Individual participation principle:** Individuals have the right to know if data is collected on them, access any personal data that might be collected, and obtain or destroy personal data if desired.

- **Accountability principle:** A data controller should be accountable for compliance with all measures and principles.

In addition to the basic principles of privacy, there are two overarching themes reflected in the OECD: first, a focus on using risk management to approach privacy protection, and second, the concept that privacy has a global dimension that must be addressed by international cooperation and interoperability. The OECD council adopted guidelines in September 2015, which provide guidance in the following:

- **National privacy strategies:** Privacy requires a national strategy coordinated at the highest levels of government. Security practitioners should be aware of the common elements of national privacy strategies based on the OECD suggestions and work to help their organizations design privacy programs that can be used across multiple jurisdictions. Additionally, they should help their organization design a privacy strategy using business requirements that deliver a good cost-benefit outcome.

- **Data security breach notification:** Both the relevant authorities and the affected individuals must be notified of a data breach. CCSPs should be aware that multiple authorities may be involved in notifications and that the obligation to notify authorities and individuals rests with the data controller.

- **Privacy management programs:** These are operational mechanisms to implement privacy protection. A CCSP should be familiar with the programs defined in the OECD guidelines.

Asia-Pacific Economic Cooperation Privacy Framework

The Asia-Pacific Economic Cooperation Privacy Framework (APEC) is an intergovernmental forum consisting of 21 member economies in the Pacific Rim. The full framework text is available here: `apec.org/Publications/2017/08/APEC-Privacy-Framework-(2015)`. The goal of this framework is to promote a consistency of approach to information privacy protection. This framework is based on nine principles.

- **Preventing harm:** An individual has a legitimate expectation of privacy, and information protection should be designed to prevent the misuse of personal information.

- **Collection limitation:** Collection of personal data should be limited to the intended purposes of collection and should be obtained by lawful and fair means with notice and consent of the individual. As an example, an organization running a marketing operation should not collect Social Security or national identity numbers, as they are not required for sending marketing materials.

- **Notice:** Information controllers should provide clear and obvious statements about the personal data that they are collecting and their policies around use of the data. This notice should be provided at the time of collection. You are undoubtedly familiar with the banners and pop-ups in use at many websites to notify users of what data is being collected.

- **Use of personal information:** Personal information collected should be used only to fulfill the purposes of collection and other compatible or related purposes except: a) with the consent of the individual whose personal information is collected; b) when necessary to provide a service or product requested by the individual; or c) by the authority of law and other legal instruments, proclamations, and pronouncements of legal effect.

- **Integrity of personal information:** Personal information should be accurate, complete, and kept up-to-date to the extent necessary for the purposes of use.

- **Choice and consent:** Where appropriate, individuals should be provided with clear, prominent, easily understandable, accessible, and affordable mechanisms to exercise choice in relation to the collection, use, and disclosure of their personal information.

- **Security safeguards:** Personal information controllers should protect personal information that they hold with appropriate safeguards against risks, such as loss or unauthorized access to personal information or unauthorized destruction, use, modification, or disclosure of information or other misuses.

- **Access and correction:** Individuals should be able to obtain from the personal information controller confirmation of whether the personal information controller holds personal information about them, and have access to information held about them, challenge the accuracy of information relating to them, and have the information rectified, completed, amended, or deleted.

- **Accountability:** A personal information controller should be accountable for complying with measures. Companies must identify who is responsible for complying with these privacy principles.

General Data Protection Regulation

The EU GDPR is perhaps the most far-reaching and comprehensive set of laws ever written to protect data privacy. Full details can be found at `gdpr.eu/what-is-gdpr`. Within the EU, the GDPR mandates privacy for individuals, defines companies' duties to protect personal data, and prescribes punishments for companies violating these laws. GDRP fines for violating personal privacy can be massive at 20 million euros or 4 percent of global revenue (whichever is greater). For this reason alone, security practitioners must be familiar with these laws and the effects that they have on any company operating within, housing data in, or doing business with citizens of these countries in the 27-nation bloc. GDPR came into force in May 2018 and incorporated many of the same principles of the previous EU Data Protection Directive.

GDPR formally defines many roles related to privacy and security, such as the data subject, controller, and processor. The *data subject* is defined as an "identified or identifiable natural person," or, more simply, a person. There is a subtle distinction between a data controller and a data processor, which recognize that not all organizations involved in the use and processing of personal data have the same degree of responsibility.

- A *data controller* under GDPR determines the purposes and means of processing personal data.

- A *data processor* is the body responsible for processing the data on behalf of the controller.

In cloud environments, the data controller is often the cloud customer, while the data processor is the CSP. The cloud customer provides services to their customers and utilizes the CSP's infrastructure to process the data. Both the controller and processor have responsibilities to ensure that privacy data is adequately protected, but the data controller retains most legal liability. If the CSP suffers a data breach, the data controller is likely to be fined if they cannot prove they took adequate steps to mitigate the risk associated with a CSP breach. This drives security decisions such as encrypting all data stored in the cloud, which reduces the impact of unauthorized access.

 Keep in mind that privacy does not equal data security, and sometimes the two ideals are at odds.

The GDPR is a massive set of regulations that covers almost 90 pages of details and requires significant effort to achieve compliance. Security practitioners must be familiar with the broad areas of the law if it applies to their organization, but ultimately organizations should consult an attorney to identify requirements. Legal counsel or an outside auditor may also be needed to ensure that operations are compliant. GDPR encompasses the following main areas:

- **Data protection principles:** If a company processes data, it must do so according to seven protection and accountability principles.

- **Lawfulness, fairness, and transparency:** Processing must be lawful, fair, and transparent to the data subject.

- **Purpose limitation:** The organization must process data for the legitimate purposes specified explicitly to the data subject when it was collected.

- **Data minimization:** The organization should collect and process only as much data as absolutely necessary for the purposes specified.

- **Accuracy:** The organization must keep personal data accurate and up-to-date.

- **Storage limitation:** The organization may store personally identifying data for only as long as necessary for the specified purpose.

- **Integrity and confidentiality:** Processing must be done in such a way as to ensure appropriate security, integrity, and confidentiality (for example, by using encryption).

- **Accountability:** The data controller is responsible for being able to demonstrate GDPR compliance with all of these principles.

- **Data security:** Companies are required to handle data securely by implementing appropriate technical measures and to consider data protection as part of any new product or activity.

- **Data processing:** GDPR limits when it is legal to actually process user data. There are very specific instances when this is allowed under the law.

- **Consent:** Strict rules are in place for how a user is to be notified that data is being collected.

- **Personal privacy:** The GDPR implements a litany of privacy rights for data subjects, which gives individuals far greater rights over their data that companies collect. This includes the rights to be informed, access, rectify, restrict, and obtain, and the well-known "right to be forgotten," which allows the end user to revoke consent and request deletion of all personal data.

Additional Legal Frameworks

Cloud services have added complexity to well-established legal frameworks that were put into place before cloud computing was developed. The CSP is a vital third party to many organizations, but one that introduces complexity to existing security and privacy risk mitigation. As a service provider, legal liability usually does not transfer to CSPs; instead, the cloud consumer is responsible for evaluating if a service provider offers adequate security controls. These evaluations are often done in light of laws or regulations that govern data security, such as the following:

- **Health Insurance Portability and Accountability Act (HIPAA):** This 1996 U.S. law regulates the privacy and control of health information data. It mandates privacy, security, and breach notification, as well as strict management of third parties processing healthcare data through contracts known as business associate agreements (BAAs).

- **Payment Card Industry Data Security Standard (PCI DSS):** This is an industry standard for companies that accept, process, or receive payment card transactions. The network accessibility of cloud services has actually made PCI DSS compliance easier, as large third-party processors can offer their services to smaller organizations. This shifts the burden of PCI DSS compliance to the processor, who has more scale and resources available.

- **Privacy Shield:** The United States lacks a federal-level privacy law comparable to the EU GDPR, so companies with EU citizen data face hurdles when transferring that data from the EU to the United States. Various frameworks have existed to address this problem, such as Safe Harbor and Privacy Shield (the most current). However, all have run into legal issues due to disclosures regarding how the U.S. government handles data on non-U.S. citizens. This unsettled legal environment requires security practitioners and legal counsel to continuously evaluate the legality and potential risks associated with data transfers.

- **Sarbanes-Oxley Act (SOX):** This law was enacted in 2002 and sets requirements for U.S. public companies to protect financial data when stored and used. It is intended to protect shareholders of the company as well as the general public from accounting errors or fraud within enterprises. This act specifically applies to publicly traded companies and is enforced by the Securities and Exchange Commission (SEC). It is applicable to cloud practitioners in particular because it specifies what records must be stored and for how long, internal control reports, and formal data security policies.

Laws and Regulations

The cloud represents a dynamic and changing environment, and monitoring/reviewing legal requirements is essential to staying compliant. All contractual obligations and acceptance of requirements by contractors, partners, legal teams, and third parties should be subject to periodic review. When it comes to compliance, words have very specific meanings, which impact how security programs must be defined and implemented. For example, many security practitioners treat *law* and *regulation* as interchangeable terms. However, there are very different consequences, and therefore very different risks, associated with noncompliance.

Understanding the compliance requirements that your organization is subject to is vital for a security practitioner. The outcome of noncompliance can vary greatly, including imprisonment, fines, litigation, loss of a contract, or a combination of these. To understand this landscape, it is helpful to recognize the difference between data protections required by laws, regulations, or contractual obligations:

- **Statutory requirements** are required by law.
  - Country-level laws such as HIPAA in the United States, GDPR and associated member state laws like the German Bundesdatenschutzgesetz, and the Personal Information Protection and Electronic Documents Act (PIPEDA) in Canada
  - Industry-specific laws, such as the Family Education Rights and Privacy Act (FERPA) in the United States that deals with privacy rights for students
  - State, provincial, or regional data privacy laws, such as the Personal Information Protection Act (PIPA) in British Columbia, Canada, or the Stop Hacks and Improve Electronic Data Security (SHIELD) Act in New York

- **Regulatory requirements** may also be required by law, but refer to rules issued by a regulatory body that is appointed by a government entity. In this case, the guidance does not come from the legislation itself but from a regulatory body that interprets the law and issues rules, requirements, or guidance on compliance.

  - In the United States, legal requirements exist for the security of sensitive data handled by contractors to the U.S. government. For example, the Federal Information Security Modernization Act (FISMA) requires government agencies to implement security programs. The actual guidance for these programs is published by the National Institute of Standards and Technology, such as the security control catalog in NIST Special Publication 800-53. These controls have evolved to govern the security and privacy controls in cloud environments as part of the Federal Risk and Authorization Management Program (FedRAMP).

  - At the state level, several states use regulatory bodies to implement their cybersecurity requirements. One example is the New York State Department of Financial Services (NY DFS) cybersecurity framework for the financial industry (23 NYCRR 500).

  - There are numerous international requirements dealing with cloud legal requirements, including APEC and GDPR. Member states of these international blocs may implement their laws and regulations aligned to these standards, but with some variations such as reporting timeframes.

- **Contractual requirements** are required by a legal contract between private parties. These are not laws, and breaching these requirements cannot result in imprisonment, but can result in financial penalties, litigation, and termination of contracts. PCI DSS is a common example: to process payment card transactions, the payment card issuers require compliance with the standard. Vendor risk management programs often specify a set of security controls or a compliance framework that must be implemented by a vendor, such as Service Organization Controls (SOC), Generally Accepted Privacy Principles (GAPP), Center for Internet Security (CIS) Critical Security Controls (CSC), or the Cloud Security Alliance (CSA) Cloud Controls Matrix (CCM). The organizations that publish these standards do not mandate compliance, but contracts with business partners do. In this case, the organization must provide evidence of compliance or risk losing business with that partner.

It is vital to consider the legal and contractual issues that apply to how a company collects, stores, processes, and ultimately deletes data. Few companies or entities can ignore the need for compliance with national and international laws, since noncompliance can result in loss of the ability to do business. Perhaps not surprisingly, company officers have a vested interest in complying with these laws. Laws and regulations are specific in who is responsible for the protection of information, and many laws identify penalties for individuals who knowingly support noncompliance. Federal laws like HIPAA spell out that senior officers within a company are responsible for (and liable for) the protection of data. International regulations like GDPR and state regulations such as NYCRR 500 identify the role of a data protection officer or chief information security officer and outline their culpability for negligence that leads to a data breach.

As a cloud consumer, security practitioners are responsible for identifying all legal, regulatory, and contractual obligations, and ensuring that the CSP is able to meet those requirements. If not, using the CSP's services or infrastructure introduces significant risks. No matter who is hosting data or services, the data controller (usually the cloud customer) is ultimately accountable for effective security controls, privacy protections, and compliance with legal, regulatory, and compliance obligations.

eDiscovery

When a crime is committed, law enforcement or other agencies may perform eDiscovery using forensic practices to gather evidence about the crime that has been committed, which can be used to prosecute the guilty parties. eDiscovery is defined as any process in which electronic data is pursued, located, secured, and searched with the intent of using it as evidence in a civil or criminal legal case. In a typical eDiscovery case, computing data might be reviewed offline, with the equipment powered off or viewed with a static image, or online with the equipment powered on and accessible.

In the cloud environment, almost all eDiscovery cases will be done online due to the nature of distributed computing and the difficulty in taking those systems offline, though some offline analysis is also possible. Virtual machine (VM) images or snapshots may be analyzed without powering on the VM itself. Forensics, especially cloud forensics, is a highly specialized field that relies on expert technicians to perform the detailed investigations required for discovery while not compromising the potential evidence and chain of custody. Not all security practitioners will possess this set of skills, so it is important to identify where in-house resources can perform certain actions and where highly trained external resources are required. This may involve the use of dedicated digital forensics and incident response (DFIR) personnel or law enforcement.

eDiscovery Considerations and Challenges in the Cloud

Cloud computing's essential characteristics add significant complexity to eDiscovery. A SaaS app in the cloud distributed across 100 countries is exponentially more complex to investigate than a simple server cluster in a traditional data center. An organization investigating an incident may lack the ability to compel the CSP to turn over vital information needed to investigate, or the information may be housed in a country where jurisdictional issues make the data more difficult to access. Even if information is available, it may not be sufficient to support the investigation, and maintaining a chain of custody is more difficult since there are more entities involved in the process.

When considering a cloud vendor, eDiscovery should be considered as a security requirement during the selection and contract negotiation phases. Once a CSP is chosen, it's important to proactively gather information that might be relevant in an investigation or discovery situation. This includes contact information, escalation procedures, and any relevant stakeholders to such a process. This type of information may logically fit into an incident response plan or similar documentation.

Data residency and system architecture are other important considerations for eDiscovery in the cloud and can be handled proactively when designing or deploying a system or business process. For example, if a platform is likely to receive law enforcement requests to hand over data, that data should not be stored in a country that restricts the organization's ability to honor such a request. Distributed cloud services can reduce availability risks by providing global replication and failover abilities but can introduce additional legal risks due to competing laws and jurisdictions.

Cloud security practitioners must inform their organizations of any risks and required due care and due diligence related to the use of cloud computing. This may involve working with legal counsel to identify requirements, documenting the steps needed and steps taken to meet those requirements, and also performing oversight functions like audits and assessments to measure compliance. This can make the process of eDiscovery easier by ensuring that the organization is prepared in the event of a discovery process, rather than finding itself unable to conduct necessary activities to investigate.

eDiscovery Frameworks

DFIR practitioners working in a cloud environment can utilize a variety of frameworks and tools to conduct investigations. Some of these include proactive practices similar to traditional on-premises investigations, such as identifying vital data, logging it, and centralizing it in a platform where analysis can take place. CSPs may not preserve essential data for the required period of time to support historical investigations or may not even log data relevant to support an investigation. This shifts the burden of recording and preserving potential evidence onto the consumers, who must identify and implement their own data collection. For example, the CSP is unlikely to log application-level data related to microservices usage, such as whether the user-requested action completed successfully or was terminated. The CSP is concerned only with whether the microservice was available and the length of time it was used, which is critical for CSP billing.

Frameworks designed to assist with planning for eDiscovery include some cloud-specific guidance, as well as more general guidance for any information system. These include the following:

- **ISO 27050:** This standard is applicable to any information system and deals with practices and procedures needed to collect data, perform analysis, and present the findings of analysis to support investigations or theories. It is not cloud-specific but covers many common tasks associated with digital forensics that are applicable in any environment.

- **Cloud Security Alliance (CSA):** Although they do not provide a specific cloud forensics and eDiscovery framework, CSA has done a cross-mapping of relevant ISO standards for cloud computing environments. This includes several key practices that extend forensics to cloud computing and can be accessed here: downloads.cloudsecurity-alliance.org/initiatives/imf/Mapping-the-Forensic-Standard-ISO-IEC-27037-to-Cloud-Computing.pdf.

- **NIST:** Common issues and solutions needed to address DFIR in cloud environments are the focus of NISTIR 8006, "Cloud Computing Forensic Science Challenges," which can be found here: csrc.nist.gov/publications/detail/nistir/8006/final.

Forensics Requirements

Digital forensics and eDiscovery requirements for many legal controls are greatly complicated by the cloud environment. Unlike on-premises systems, it can be difficult or impossible to perform physical search and seizure of cloud resources such as storage or hard drives. ISO/IEC and CSA provide guidance to cloud security practitioners on best practices for collecting digital evidence and conducting forensics investigations in cloud environments.

As discussed, DFIR is a highly specialized field within security and should be performed only by qualified personnel. Untrained or unskilled personal performing forensics run the risk of destroying or altering evidence, which renders it useless for investigation and prosecution. All security practitioners should be familiar with the following standards, even if they do not specialize in forensics:

- **Cloud Security Alliance:** The CSA Security Guidance Domain 3: Legal Issues: Contracts and Electronic Discovery highlights some of the legal aspects raised by cloud computing. This provides cloud security practitioners with guidance on negotiating contracts with cloud service providers in regard to eDiscovery, searchability, and preservation of data.

- **ISO/IEC 27037:2012:** This provides guidelines for the handling of digital evidence, which include the identification, collection, acquisition, and preservation of data related to a specific case.

- **ISO/IEC 27041:2015:** This provides guidance on mechanisms for ensuring that methods and processes used in the investigation of information security incidents are "fit for purpose." Cloud consumers and security practitioners should pay close attention to the sections on how vendor and third-party testing can be used to assist with assurance processes.

- **ISO-IEC 27042:2015:** This standard is a guideline for the analysis and interpretation of digital evidence. Security practitioners can use these methods to demonstrate proficiency and competence with an investigative team.

- **ISO/IEC 27043:2015:** The security techniques document covers incident investigation principles and processes. This can help a security practitioner build processes for various types of investigations, including unauthorized access, data corruption, system crashes, information security breaches, and other digital investigations.

Understand Privacy Issues

The Internet age has brought with it an unprecedented amount of information flow. Everything from financial transactions to academic research to cat videos can be shared around the world. However, not all of this data is equally valuable. Some categories of information can be used to cause real-world harm if they fall into the wrong hands. Private information is of particular importance, because in many cases tampering with or stealing this data can have serious consequences to the subject of the information. These consequences may include identity theft, discrimination, or even death in cases where unpopular or illegal speech or viewpoints is involved.

Privacy is defined as the state of being free from observation by others, and it is often discussed alongside security. The two fields are not the same, however. Privacy is often codified into laws and regulations as an individual's right, which organizations must uphold when they collect, store, or process the individual's information. Security practitioners often implement security controls as part of privacy compliance, such as encryption to reduce the impact of a data breach or incident response procedures that include mandatory reporting to victims of a data breach.

Data that is considered private is also often useful for identifying an individual, meaning the data can be associated with a single person or entity. This can lead to situations where a point of data in a larger data set makes the difference between private data, which needs protection, and sensitive data, which might warrant some protection but does not carry the risk of fines or legal penalties. Information about a medical procedure is not generally considered sensitive, but if the patient's insurance number is associated with the procedure records, it can now be used to uniquely identify an individual and their health condition. In many jurisdictions that information is regulated by privacy laws.

Difference between Contractual and Regulated Private Data

It is important to understand what types of data an organization is processing, where it is being processed, and any associated requirements such as contractual obligations. In any cloud computing environment, the legal responsibility for data privacy and protection rests with the cloud consumer, who may enlist the services of a cloud service provider (CSP) to gather, store, and process that data. The data controller is always responsible for ensuring that the requirements for protection and compliance are met, whether the data is processed in on-premises systems or a cloud solution. When third parties like a CSP are involved, it is important to ensure that contracts with the CSP stipulate data privacy, security, and protection requirements.

There are a number of terms that describe data that requires protection, and the specific types of data may have unique protection requirements. It is essential to understand what type of data is being handled, such as personally identifiable information (PII). This is a widely recognized classification of data that is almost universally regulated. PII is defined by the NIST standard 800-122 as follows:

> "any information about an individual maintained by an agency, including
> (1) any information that can be used to distinguish or trace an individual's
> identity, such as name, social security number, date and place of birth,
> mother's maiden name, or biometric records; and (2) any other information
> that is linked or linkable to an individual, such as medical, educational,
> financial, and employment information."

While NIST is a U.S. body, the definition of PII is similar to other standards and frameworks, such as GDPR. Different frameworks explicitly identify certain data points that may be unique, but in general any information that can be used to uniquely identify an individual is considered PII. Security practitioners should be aware of the types of data their organization handles and associated regulatory or contractual obligations.

Protected health information (PHI) is a U.S.-specific subset of PII and is codified under HIPAA. Data that relates to a patient's health, treatment, or billing for medical services that could identify a patient is PHI. When this data is electronically stored, it must be adequately secured by controls such as unique user accounts for every user, strong passwords and MFA, least privilege-based access controls, and auditing all access and changes to a patient's PHI data.

Table 6.1 summarizes types of private data and how they differ.

TABLE 6.1   Types of Private Data

Data Type	Definition
Personally identifiable information (PII)	Personally identifiable information is information that, when used alone or with other relevant data, can identify an individual. PII may contain direct identifiers, such as name or address that can identify a person uniquely. It may also include indirect or quasi-identifiers such as place of birth, date of birth, etc., which could be combined with other quasi-identifiers to successfully recognize an individual.
	PII is legally defined in and regulated by numerous privacy laws, and additional PII data elements may be defined in contracts along with required protections.
Protected or personal health information (PHI)	PHI includes medical histories, test and laboratory results, mental health conditions, insurance information, and other data that a healthcare professional collects to identify an individual and determine appropriate care.
	In the United States, PHI is explicitly identified in and regulated by HIPAA. Covered entities, which store or handle PHI, are defined in the law, and any third parties they do business with are also required to safeguard the information. These requirements are passed on to the third parties via business associate agreements (BAAs), which are contractual requirements for handling any PHI that is shared.
Payment data (PCI DSS)	Bank and credit card data used by payment processors in order to conduct point-of-sale transactions.
	Payment data is governed by contracts with payment card issuers such as Mastercard and Visa. To accept and process payment card transactions, merchants must agree to implement the required protections specified in PCI DSS.

Regulated Private Data

The biggest differentiator between contractual and regulated data is that the requirements to protect regulated data flow from legal and statutory requirements. Both PII and PHI data are subject to regulation, and the disclosure, loss, or altering of these data can subject a company (and individuals) to statutory penalties including fines and imprisonment. Organizations can be fined for mishandling or failing to protect private data under laws like HIPAA or GDPR, and in some cases individuals may also be held accountable if they are found to be negligent.

Regulations are put into place by governments and government-empowered agencies to protect entities and individuals from risks. In addition, they force providers and processors to take appropriate measures to ensure that protections are in place while identifying penalties for lapses in procedures and processes. In some industries, the regulators also perform audit and oversight functions to ensure that organizations are meeting their regulatory obligations. Security practitioners must understand their regulatory environment and work to implement the required controls and facilitate any oversight activities by regulators.

One of the major differentiators between contracted and regulated privacy data is in breach reporting. A data breach of regulated data (or unintentional loss of confidentiality of data through theft or negligence) is covered by regional and country laws around the world. As an example, in some U.S. states there are financial penalties for data breaches and no requirement to report to state regulators, while in others there are very specific timeframes for reporting. Knowing the overlapping requirements and ensuring that policies and procedures are adequate to meet those requirements will require collaboration between the security team and others in the organization, such as the legal team. The International Association of Privacy Professionals (iapp.org) publishes several guides that highlight privacy regulations and requirements across different countries.

There are several risks associated with regulated privacy data. Obviously a breach can lead to severe consequences for individuals — some information could be used by malicious parties to perform identity theft or extortion. A large dating site serving people who wanted to have extramarital affairs suffered a data breach of its user information, and individuals were blackmailed to prevent their use of the service from being publicized. Sadly, some of the affected individuals committed suicide rather than face embarrassment. From an organizational standpoint, fines and penalties are another major privacy regulation risk. As an example, the ridesharing company Uber was forced to pay $148 million in fines to the state of California for a 2016 data breach and associated cover-up of the incident.

Contractual Private Data

Contractual obligations to safeguard data can be used as a method to enforce data safeguards throughout a supply chain, such as with a HIPAA BAA for subprocessors. This method can also be used to provide safeguards for data that does not have a legal or regulatory need for protection but is nonetheless valuable. Examples include business confidential information, intellectual property, and other nonpublic information that an organization creates or uses.

Contracts are used to provide governance for relationships with third parties, such as vendors, service providers, and business partners. They are relevant to security professionals, because they provide a way to communicate the requirements for handling this data and also provide some risk mitigation if a breach occurs. Contracts are similar to nondisclosure agreements, which identify the types of data being shared, required safeguards, and legal measures that may be pursued if either party fails to meet the specified agreement.

A contractual obligation can be a proactive mitigation, similar to security policies that define approved data handling activities, as well as a reactive mitigation. If either party breaches the contract, methods such as the right to pursue legal action are specified in the contract.

The major difference between contractual and regulated private data is the level of control the organization can exert. Regulatory frameworks often specify the exact controls that must be in place, while organizations are free to write and negotiate their own contracts. As with other areas, this is a critical point of collaboration between the security team and other departments, such as legal or contract management.

Components of a Contract

Outsourcing to a CSP does not transfer risk away from the cloud consumer, as they remain the data owner and must ensure that it is adequately protected. Key elements of contracts to enforce security should be defined based on the data owner's responsibilities and include the following:

- **Scope of data processing:** The CSP must have a clear definition of the permitted forms of data processing. For example, data collected on user interactions for a cloud customer should not be used by the CSP to inform new interface designs, unless the data subjects have given explicit consent for this.

- **Subcontractors:** It is important to know exactly where all processing, transmission, storage, and use of data will take place and whether any part of the process might be undertaken by a subcontractor to the cloud service provider. If a subcontractor will be used in any phase of data handling, it is vital that the customer is contractually informed of this development. The contract should bar the CSP from using any unapproved subcontractors.

- **Deletion of data:** How data is to be removed or deleted from a cloud service provider is important and helps protect against unintentional data disclosure. Cloud environments make physical destruction of storage media difficult, so contracts must spell out methods for secure data deletion if that is a service provided by the CSP. Due to the nature of the cloud, this may be handled by the consumer organization with a method such as cryptoshredding, which is easier to implement.

- **Data security controls:** If data requires a level of security controls when it is processed, stored, or transmitted, that same level of security control must be ensured in a contract with a cloud service provider. Ideally, the level of data security controls would exceed what is required (as is often the case for cloud service providers). Typical security controls include encryption of data while in transit and while at rest, access control and auditing, layered security approaches, and defense-in-depth measures.

- **Physical location of data:** Many privacy frameworks specify where data can be stored or processed, and this requirement must be passed on to any data processors to ensure compliance. Contract clauses specifying the methods, locations, and approved purposes for data transfer or storage should be included. Many CSPs shift this responsibility to the customer by offering a variety of geolocated services and allowing the customer to choose those in a region or geography that matches their compliance needs.

- **Return or surrender of data:** It is important to include termination agreements and requirements, such as specifying what the CSP is and is not allowed to do with data after termination of a contract.
- **Audits:** Right to audit clauses should be included to allow a data owner or an independent consultant to audit compliance with the agreed-upon security practices. In practice, most CSPs do not allow all customers to perform their own audits, but instead publish security and privacy documentation such as ISO 27001 or SOC 2 Type II reports for all customers. If these audits identify a weakness or deficiency that increases risk, the contract should specify that the customer can terminate the contract with no penalties.

Country-Specific Legislation Related to Private Data

An individual's right to privacy, and therefore their right to have their data handled in a secure and confidential way, varies widely by country and culture. The global nature of the cloud and many services, such as social media apps, means that organizations face a much broader range of privacy compliance obligations. As a result, security practitioners need to be aware of the broad range of statutory and regulatory obligations around data privacy. These are based on the citizenship of a data subject, rather than the location of the organization's operations, and govern many aspects such as the jurisdiction for any legal proceedings.

There are many different attitudes and expectations of privacy in countries around the world. In some more authoritarian regimes, the data privacy rights of the individual are almost nonexistent. In other societies, data privacy is considered a fundamental right. Security practitioners handling privacy data should be aware of these requirements and seek qualified legal opinion on how these requirements govern their organization's operations.

There are hundreds of country- and region-specific privacy laws and regulations, and an exhaustive analysis is outside the scope of this reference guide. The first task that a security practitioner should perform when addressing privacy is identifying all relevant laws and regulations that govern the data their organization handles. Legal firms that specialize in international privacy laws exist, and should be engaged as needed to provide the necessary guidance.

The European Union (GDPR)

The 27-member EU has one of the most robust privacy frameworks in the world. The right to personal and data privacy is strictly regulated and actively enforced in Europe, and it is enshrined into European law in many ways. In Article 8 of the European Convention on Human Rights (ECHR), a person has a right to a "private and family life, his home and his correspondence," with some exceptions. Some additional types of private data under the GDPR include information such as race or ethnic origin, political affiliations or opinions, religious or philosophical beliefs, and information regarding a person's sex life or sexual orientation.

In the European Union, PII covers both facts and opinions about an individual. Individuals are guaranteed certain privacy rights as data subjects. Significant areas of Chapter 3 of the GDPR (see gdpr.eu/tag/chapter-3) include the following on data subject privacy rights:

- The right to be informed
- The right of access
- The right to rectification
- The right to erasure (the so-called right to be forgotten)
- The right to restrict processing
- The right to data portability
- The right to object
- Rights in relation to automated decision making and profiling

Australia

Australian privacy law was originally published in 1988, with a revision in 2014 and republication with minor updates in 2021. It provides a solid foundation of privacy rights similar to GDPR, and the updates were designed to address evolving privacy rights driven by GDPR as well as issues associated with international data transfers and cloud computing. The foundational principles can be found at oaic.gov.au/privacy/australian-privacy-principles, while the full Privacy Act can be found here: legislation.act.gov.au/a/2014-24/default.asp.

Under the Australian Privacy Act, organizations may process data belonging to Australian citizens offshore, but the transferring entity (the data owner) must ensure that the receiver of the data holds and processes it in accordance with the principles of Australian privacy law. As discussed in the previous section, this is commonly achieved through contracts that require recipients to maintain or exceed the data owner's privacy standards. An important consequence under Australian privacy law is that the entity transferring the data out of Australia remains responsible for any data breaches by or on behalf of the recipient entities, meaning significant potential liability for any company doing business in Australia under current rules.

The United States

Data privacy laws in the United States generally date back to fair information practice guidelines that were developed by the precursor to the Department of Health & Human Services (HHS). (See Ware, Willis H. (1973, August). "Records, Computers and the Rights of Citizens," Rand. Retrieved from www.rand.org/content/dam/rand/pubs/papers/2008/P5077.pdf.) These principles include the following concepts:

- For all data collected, there should be a stated purpose.
- Information collected from an individual cannot be disclosed to other organizations or individuals unless specifically authorized by law or by consent of the individual.
- Records kept on an individual should be accurate and up-to-date.

- There should be mechanisms for individuals to review data about them, to ensure accuracy. This may include periodic reporting.

- Data should be deleted when it is no longer needed for the stated purpose.

- Transmission of personal information to locations where "equivalent" personal data protection cannot be assured is prohibited.

- Some data is too sensitive to be collected (such as sexual orientation or religion) unless there are extreme circumstances.

Perhaps the defining feature of U.S. data privacy law is its fragmentation. There is no overarching law regulating data protection in the United States. In fact, the word *privacy* is not included in the U.S. Constitution. However, there are now data privacy laws in each of the 50 states as well as U.S. territories.

There are few restrictions on the transfer of PII or PHI out of the United States, a fact that makes it relatively easy for companies to engage cloud providers and store data in other countries. The Federal Trade Commission (FTC) and other regulatory bodies do hold companies accountable to U.S. laws and regulations for data after it leaves the physical jurisdiction of the United States. U.S.-regulated companies are liable for the following:

- Personal data exported out of the United States

- Processing of personal data by subcontractors based overseas

- Projections of data by subcontractors when it leaves the United States

Several important international agreements and U.S. federal statutes deal with PII. The Privacy Shield agreement is a framework that regulates the transatlantic movement of PII for commercial purposes between the United States and the European Union. Federal laws worth review include HIPAA, GLBA, SOX, and the Stored Communications Act, all of which impact how the United States regulates privacy and data. At the state level, it is worth reviewing the California Consumer Protection Act (CCPA), the strongest state privacy law in the nation.

U.S. CLOUD Act

After multiple requests for electronic evidence led to lengthy court battles regarding jurisdiction, the United States passed the CLOUD Act. This provided a framework for bilateral agreements between countries in support of law enforcement requests for access to data. In one well-known case, Microsoft received a legal request to hand over data that was stored in European data centers, but due to privacy regulation in the EU, the company was unable to honor the request.

Under the CLOUD Act, U.S. law enforcement agencies and any counterparts in a corresponding country with an agreement in place can issue requests for data. CSPs may honor these requests without fear of violating privacy regulations. This solves some of the problems that cloud computing creates by allowing easy flow of data across national borders. The full text of the law and supporting resources can be found here: `justice.gov/dag/cloudact`.

Privacy Shield

Unlike the GDPR, which is a set of regulations that affect companies doing business in the EU or with citizens of the EU, Privacy Shield is an international agreement between the United States and the European Union that allows the transfer of personal data from the European Economic Area (EEA) to the United States by U.S.-based companies. Organizations can pursue a certification of their privacy practices under the framework, which enables them to demonstrate sufficient protections to allow for data processing in the United States.

This agreement replaced the previous safe harbor agreements, which were invalidated by the European court of justice in October 2015. The Privacy Shield agreement faces ongoing legal challenges in EU courts due to nonexistent federal level privacy laws in the United States that govern data belonging to non-U.S. citizens, and the agreement was partially struck down in 2020. Organizations with existing obligations may continue to operate under the framework but should seek legal guidance to stay informed of the changing requirements.

Adherence to Privacy Shield does not make U.S. companies GDPR-compliant, but it allows the company to transfer personal data out of the EEA into infrastructure hosted in the United States. Under Privacy Shield, organizations self-certify to the U.S. Department of Commerce and publicly commit to comply with the seven principles of the agreement. Those seven principles are as follows:

- **Notice:** Organizations must publish privacy notices containing specific information about their participation in the Privacy Shield Framework; their privacy practices; and the use, collection, and sharing of EU residents' data with third parties.

- **Choice:** Organizations must provide a mechanism for individuals to opt out of having personal information disclosed to a third party or used for a different purpose than that for which it was provided. Opt-in consent is required for sharing sensitive information with a third party or its use for a new purpose.

- **Accountability for onward transfer:** Organizations must enter into contracts with third parties or agents who will process personal data for and on behalf of the organization, which require them to process or transfer personal data in a manner consistent with the Privacy Shield principles.

- **Security:** Organizations must take reasonable and appropriate measures to protect personal data from loss, misuse, unauthorized access, disclosure, alteration, and destruction, while accounting for risks involved and nature of the personal data.

- **Data integrity and purpose limitation:** Organizations must take reasonable steps to limit processing to the purposes for which it was collected and ensure that personal data is accurate, complete, and current.

- **Access:** Organizations must provide a method by which the data subjects can request access to and correct, amend, or delete information the organization holds about them.

- **Recourse, enforcement, and liability:** This principle addresses the recourse for individuals affected by noncompliance, consequences to organizations for noncompliance, and means for verifying compliance.

The Health Insurance Portability and Accountability Act of 1996

The HIPAA legislation of 1996 defined what comprises personal health information, mandated national standards for electronic health record keeping, and established national identifiers for providers, insurers, and employers. Under HIPAA, PHI may be stored by cloud service providers provided that the data is protected in adequate ways. Under HIPAA there are separate rules for privacy, security, and breach notification, as well as specifications for how these requirements flow down to third parties. HIPAA-covered entities are those organizations that collect or generate PHI, while their third parties are known as business associates and must enter into a formal agreement that defines their obligations for safeguarding the PHI.

The Gramm-Leach-Bliley Act (GLBA) of 1999

This U.S. federal law requires financial institutions to explain how they share and protect their customers' private information. GLBA is widely considered one of the most robust federal information privacy and security laws, but it is very narrowly targeted to financial services firms. This act consists of three main sections.

- The Financial Privacy Rule, which regulates the collection and disclosure of private financial information

- The Safeguards Rule, which stipulates that financial institutions must implement security programs to protect such information

- The Pretexting provisions, which prohibit the practice of pretexting (accessing private information using false pretenses)

The act also requires financial institutions to give customers written privacy notices that explain their information-sharing practices. GLBA explicitly identifies security measures such as access controls, encryption, segmentation of duties, monitoring, training, and testing of security controls.

The Stored Communication Act of 1986

The Stored Communication Act (SCA), enacted as Title II of the Electronic Communication Privacy Act, created privacy protection for electronic communications such as email or other digital communications stored on the Internet. In many ways, this act extends the Fourth Amendment of the U.S. Constitution—the people's right to be "secure in their persons, houses, papers, and effects, against unreasonable searches and seizures"—to the electronic landscape. It outlines that private data is protected from unauthorized access or interception (by private parties or the government).

State-Level Laws

The United States is made of up at least 51 smaller governments, one for each of the 50 states and Washington, D.C., which governs some of its own affairs. The federal government provides services and legislation for affairs between states and on issues that are not state-specific, such as regulating PHI. All states have enacted some privacy legislation, and in the wake of GDPR some states have begun to implement privacy laws with similar requirements.

As with the multitude of international privacy laws, competent legal counsel should be engaged to identify any and all state-specific security and privacy requirements that must be met. States like California, with the California Consumer Privacy Act (CCPA), and New York's SHIELD Act provide a robust set of privacy rights, protections, and defined terms.

One major difference between the various state-level laws is the means of recourse made available to data subjects. Some states provide what is known as a private right to action, meaning an organization can be sued by an individual who feels the company violated their privacy rights. In states where a collective right to action is provided, some organization can pursue legal action against an organization for violating privacy laws. This may be an attorney general or other designated office within the state government, but individual data subjects cannot sue the organization directly. Risks associated with legal action should be assessed carefully—a single individual lawsuit is unlikely to have a large impact, and a state government with relatively lax enforcement is also unlikely to pose a significant risk. However, a state with strict enforcement is much more likely to pursue action, raising the likelihood and possibly impact of any legal action.

Jurisdictional Differences in Data Privacy

Cloud computing resources enable global placement of infrastructure for processing and storing data, which brings with it challenges related to complying with overlapping, and often conflicting, privacy laws. Different laws and regulations may apply depending on the location of the data subject, the data collector, the cloud service provider, subcontractors processing data, and the company headquarters of any of the entities involved. Security practitioners must be aware of these challenges and ensure that their risk assessments adequately capture these risks. Mitigation activities should be implemented to ensure compliance, and consultation with legal professionals during the construction of any cloud-based services is essential.

Legal concerns can prevent the utilization of a cloud services provider, add to costs and time to market, and drive changes to the technical architectures required to deliver services. Nevertheless, it is vital to never replace compliance with convenience when evaluating services, as this increases risks. In 2020, the video conferencing service Zoom was found to be engaged in the practice of routing video calls through servers in China in instances when no call participants were based there. This revelation caused an uproar throughout the user community and led to the abandonment of the platform by many customers out of privacy concerns: see `theguardian.com/uk-news/2020/apr/24/uk-government-told-not-to-use-zoom-because-of-china-fears`. In this case, the impact was mainly reputational, as customers abandoned the platform because their data would certainly not enjoy the same privacy protections within China compared to other nations. While lost business can be hard to quantify, many privacy frameworks impose fines or other regulatory action for noncompliance.

Standard Privacy Requirements

With so many concerns and potential harm from privacy violations, entrusting data to a CSP can be daunting. Fortunately, there are industry standards that address the privacy aspects of cloud computing for customers. International organizations such as ISO/IEC have codified privacy controls for the cloud. Adherence to the privacy requirements outlined by ISO 27018 enable cloud customers to trust their providers.

ISO 27018 was published in July 2014 as a component of the ISO 27001 standard and was most recently updated in 2019. Security practitioners can use the certification of ISO 27000 compliance as assurance of adherence to key privacy principles, and CSPs can publish details of their ISO certification to provide assurance to their customers. Major cloud service providers such as Microsoft, Google, and Amazon maintain ISO 27000 compliance, which include the following key principles:

- **Consent:** Personal data obtained by a CSP may not be used for marketing purposes unless expressly permitted by the data subject. A customer should be permitted to use a service without requiring this consent.

- **Control:** Customers shall have explicit control of their own data and how that data is used by the CSP.

- **Transparency:** CSPs must inform customers of where their data resides and any subcontractors that might process personal data.

- **Communication:** Auditing should be in place, and any incidents should be communicated to customers.

- **Audit:** Companies must subject themselves to an independent audit on an annual basis.

Privacy and security concerns can generate conflict when monitoring is used to inspect network traffic or system usage. Organizations may have a legitimate need to observe what their users are doing, for example to identify users who violate policy by visiting inappropriate websites or sending protected data outside the organization's control. Monitoring tools can be useful, but the privacy rights of the users may conflict with this monitoring. In some jurisdictions, providing notice that a system is monitored is sufficient, while in others it is illegal to perform monitoring without a specific, documented reason. It is important to ensure that the monitoring strategy does not create a breach of privacy protections the users are entitled to.

Generally Accepted Privacy Principles

Generally Accepted Privacy Principles (GAPP) is a framework of privacy principles originally published by a task force of professional accountants in the United States and Canada. It is now widely incorporated into the SOC 2 framework as an optional criterion, meaning organizations that pursue a SOC 2 audit can include their privacy controls if appropriate based on the type of services they provide. Similar to ISO 27018, which is an optional extension of the controls defined in ISO 27002, the privacy criteria in SOC 2 provide objectives, which can be met by an organization's security controls. An audit of these controls results in a report that can be shared with customers or potential customers, who can use it to assess a service provider's ability to protect sensitive data.

GAPP is a set of standards for the appropriate protection and management of personal data. There 10 main privacy principles grouped into the following categories:

- **Management:** The organization defines, documents, communicates, and assigns accountability for its privacy policies and procedures.

- **Notice:** The organization provides notice of its privacy policies and procedures. The organization identifies the purposes for which personal information is collected, used, and retained.

- **Choice and consent:** The organization describes the choices available to the individual. The organization secures implicit or explicit consent regarding the collection, use, and disclosure of the personal data.

- **Collection:** Personal information is collected only for the purposes identified in the notice provided to the individual.

- **Use, retention, and disposal:** The personal information is limited to the purposes identified in the notice the individual consented to. The organization retains the personal information only for as long as needed to fulfill the purposes or as required by law. After this period, the information is disposed of appropriately and permanently.

- **Access:** The organization provides individuals with access to their personal information for review or update.

- **Disclosure to third parties:** Personal information is disclosed to third parties only for the identified purposes and with implicit or explicit consent of the individual.

- **Security for privacy:** Personal information is protected against both physical and logical unauthorized access.

- **Quality:** The organization maintains accurate, complete, and relevant personal information that is necessary for the purposes identified.

- **Monitoring and enforcement:** The organization monitors compliance with its privacy policies and procedures. It also has procedures in place to address privacy-related complaints and disputes.

Standard Privacy Rights under GDPR

GDPR codifies specific roles, such as a data controller and data subject, as well as rights and responsibilities for each role. Specifically, the rights of the data subject are enumerated and must be met by any data collector or processor. These rights are outlined in Chapter 3 of the GDPR ("Rights of the Data Subject") and consist of 12 articles detailing those rights:

- Transparent information, communication, and modalities for the exercise of the rights of the data subject

- Information to be provided where personal data are collected from the data subject

- Information to be provided where personal data have not been obtained from the data subject
- Right of access by the data subject
- Right to rectification
- Right to erasure ("right to be forgotten")
- Right to restriction of processing
- Notification obligation regarding rectification or erasure of personal data or restriction of processing
- Right to data portability
- Right to object
- Automated individual decision making, including profiling
- Restrictions

The complete language for the GDPR data subject rights can be found at `gdpr.eu/tag/chapter-3`.

Privacy Impact Assessments

Assessing the impact of systems and business processes is a familiar task—a business impact assessment (BIA) is a crucial element of performing continuity and resilience planning. Similarly, a privacy impact assessment (PIA) is designed to identify the privacy data being collected, processed, or stored by a system, and assess the effects that a breach of that data might have. Several privacy laws explicitly require PIAs as a planning tool for identifying and implementing required privacy controls, including GDPR and HIPAA.

Conducting a PIA typically begins when a system or process is being evaluated, though evolving privacy regulation often necessitates assessment of existing systems. The first step is to define a scope of the PIA, such as a single system or an organizational unit. Once the scope is defined, the types of data collected and data flow throughout the target system must be documented. These are critical for the next phase, which is analysis, since the types of data often dictate the required protections.

For example, a system that handles sensitive personal data like health records or financial transactions is regulated by privacy legislation that mandates specific security controls. The culmination of the PIA process is a documented impact assessment detailing the information in use, consequences of a breach or mishandling of the data, and required controls. These may include identifying a data or system owner and assigning them responsibility for ensuring that required controls are implemented, choosing technologies that offer required security capabilities, and architecting systems to meet the requirements. From a cloud security perspective, this may drive decisions about which CSP to use, which specific services can or cannot be used, and even whether the proposed system is appropriate for cloud hosting at all.

Methods of gathering information when conducting the PIA can include questionnaires and interviews with relevant staff, such as system architects, administrators, or even project leaders. Diagrams of systems, networks, or data flows can be created and are a useful tool when defining what data is being handled and where it exists during different lifecycle phases. This dictates the type and manner of controls implemented—for example, a system that does not archive data will not need any controls in place for data retention. Some regulatory frameworks mandate retention, however, so understanding if the data in question is regulated by one of these frameworks is an essential part of the analysis.

The IAPP has published guides and resources related to privacy efforts like PIAs. More details on the functioning and creation of PIA processes can be found here: `iapp.org/resources/article/privacy-impact-assessment`.

Understanding Audit Process, Methodologies, and Required Adaptations for a Cloud Environment

The word *audit* can be daunting, as many IT professionals have undergone audits that can feel invasive, and in the context of government taxing agents an audit is never a pleasant experience. Complexity and uncertainty can make the process highly unpleasant, and the rigorous and time-consuming processes that must be followed exactly are error prone. However, audits are an essential part of verifying compliance and effectiveness of security controls. A well-architected audit strategy and security controls that are properly designed to provide necessary information proactively can make audits much less burdensome.

Auditing in a cloud environment presents additional challenges when compared to traditional on-premises requirements. This section will detail some of the controls, impacts, reports, and planning processes for a cloud environment and how these preparations may differ from noncloud environments. It is important for cloud security professionals to work in concert with other key areas of the business to successfully navigate the journey to and in cloud computing. Since the cloud and IT services are utilized by and affect the whole organization, it is vital to coordinate efforts with legal counsel, compliance, finance, and executive leadership.

A key element of a well-designed audit strategy is a security control framework that helps the organization map their internal controls to a variety of compliance frameworks. Auditors are looking for evidence of compliance, so controls that are aligned with the relevant compliance obligations make the task much easier. There are multiple control sets that can be used to achieve this purpose, such as the CSA Cloud Controls Matrix (CCM) and the Secure Control Framework (SCF). The frameworks can be found at `cloudsecurityalliance.org/research/cloud-controls-matrix` and at `securecontrolsframework.com`. Both frameworks identity key security controls and activities, as well as compliance framework mappings that show how the controls satisfy compliance objectives.

Internal and External Audit Controls

Audits help organizations communicate important details of their security and privacy controls, including the adequacy of control design and whether the controls are in place and achieving the desired level of risk mitigation. External auditors provide a trusted source of information that allows this information to be communicated with outside parties; CSPs can engage a third-party auditor to conduct a review and share that report with potential customers to earn new business. The auditor in this case is unbiased, so the level of trust in the report is higher than with an internal auditor, whose job security rests on the results of the report.

Internal audit and compliance does have a key role to manage and assess risk for both CSPs and cloud customers. External audits perform a vital function in evaluating controls but are typically expensive and happen relatively infrequently. An internal audit function can provide more continuous monitoring of control effectiveness and also brings more inside knowledge of the organization's operations. This can uncover issues that an outsider might miss, and the more frequent review schedule allows the organization to catch and fix any issues before they show up on a formal audit report.

An internal auditor acts as a "trusted advisor" as an organization takes on new risks. In general, this role works with IT to offer a proactive approach with a balance of consultative and assurance services. An internal auditor can engage with relevant stakeholders to educate the customer about cloud computing risks, such as security, privacy, contractual clarity, business continuity planning (BCP) and disaster recovery planning (DRP), compliance with legal and jurisdictional issues, etc. They fulfill this role both proactively, when projects begin, and also reactively, as they conduct audits of existing systems or processes and report on any weaknesses.

An internal audit can also mitigate risk by examining cloud architectures to provide insights into an organization's cloud governance, data classifications, identity and access management effectiveness, regulatory compliance, privacy compliance, and cyber threats. While more frequent audit schedules can create an operational burden, the rapidly evolving nature of cloud computing means that risks can change significantly in a short period of time. Waiting for the next annual external audit may allow risks to exist for much longer than desirable.

It is a best practice for an internal auditor to maintain independence from both the cloud customer and the cloud provider, even though they may be employed by one of these organizations. The auditor is not "part of the team" but rather an independent entity who can provide facts without fear of reprisal. To achieve this, most internal audit teams report to a different executive than their IT counterparts. Controls in place around the audit function typically focus on this separation of duties and minimizing potential for conflict of interest.

Security controls may also be evaluated by external auditors, and in many compliance frameworks the engagement of a third-party, unbiased auditor is required. An external auditor, by definition, is not employed by but does work on behalf of the firm being audited. This is similar to financial audits, which require an objective third-party auditor to review financial statements. External auditors are generally barred from offering advisory services due to the potential conflict of interest, so controls in place for selecting and interacting with the auditors must account for this requirement.

Other controls that should be in place for audits include the following:

- **Timing:** When audits must be conducted will likely be driven by business requirements, especially legal and regulatory frameworks that require reporting on or before a specific date. Contractual obligations may also drive this decision, as new customers may require proof of security controls within a specific timeframe after signing a contract. Audits happen regularly; these requirements are often gathered once, and then a recurring schedule is set based on them—for example, providing an initial SOC 2 Type II report to a new customer within 18 months of signing the contract, and then annually thereafter.

- **Requirements for internal/external audit:** Some legal and regulatory frameworks require the use of an independent auditor, while others are explicit in requiring a competent third-party auditor. Understanding these requirements is crucial to designing an audit approach. Even if an organization must engage an external auditor, internal audits can be used to perform spot checks or continuous monitoring that complements the external auditor's work.

Impact of Audit Requirements

The requirement to conduct audits can have a large procedural and financial impact on a company. In a cloud computing context, the types of audits required are impacted largely by a company's business sector, the types of data being collected and processed, and the variety of laws and regulations that these business activities subject a company to. In addition, customer requirements can be a significant driver, especially for organizations providing SaaS that is built on another CSP's infrastructure. While some elements of the security program are covered by the infrastructure CSP's controls and audit reports, the SaaS provider is responsible for implementing controls over their activities and providing an audit report showing how they are implemented.

Some entities operate in heavily regulated industries subject to numerous auditing requirements, such as banks or critical infrastructure providers. Others may be data processors with international customers, such as big tech companies like Apple, Facebook, Google, and Microsoft. This significantly increases the scope and complexity of the audit program, due to overlapping and sometimes conflicting requirements.

The dynamic and quickly evolving nature of cloud computing demands changes to processes associated with audits. For example, auditors must rethink some traditional methods that were used to collect evidence needed during an audit. As an example, consider the problems of data storage, virtualization, and dynamic failover.

- Is a data set representative of the entire user population? Cloud computing allows for the relatively easy distribution of data to take advantage of geographic proximity to end users, so obtaining a representative sample may be difficult since the data and system architecture can be dispersed.

- Physical servers are relatively easy to identify and locate. Virtualization adds a layer of challenge in ensuring that an audited server is, in fact, the same system over time.

- Dynamic failover presents an additional challenge to auditing operations for compliance to a specific jurisdiction. A system that is operating under normal conditions in a particular region can be compliant with legal obligations, but a disaster that causes failover to another region could be a violation of the regulatory requirements.

Identify Assurance Challenges of Virtualization and Cloud

The cloud is made possible by virtualization technologies. Abstracting the physical servers that power the cloud from the virtual servers that provide cloud services allows for the necessary dynamic environments that make cloud computing powerful and cost-effective. Furthermore, the underlying virtualization technologies that power the cloud are changing rapidly. Even a seasoned systems administrator who has worked with VMware or Microsoft's Hyper-V may struggle with understanding the inherent complexity of mass scalable platforms such as AWS, Google, or Azure cloud.

Migrating from on-premises to cloud hosting fundamentally changes the practice of risk management, which presents challenges to gaining the necessary assurance that controls are in place and reducing risk to an acceptable level. An on-premises system audit can be conducted by an organization using their own personnel. That same audit is likely impossible in a cloud environment for a number of reasons. CSPs rarely allow customers to perform their own audits of the CSP's facilities, and even if an auditor could gain access, finding the specific physical hardware hosting a cloud system may be impossible. This means that assurance must come from third-party-issued reports rather than direct observation, shifting the process to more of a supply chain or vendor risk management activity.

Depending on the cloud architecture employed, a cloud security professional must perform multiple layers of auditing. Elements of both the hypervisor and VMs themselves must be inspected to obtain assurance during the audit. It is vital for the auditor to understand the architecture that a cloud provider is using for virtualization and ensure that both hypervisors and virtual host systems are hardened and up-to-date. Change logs are especially important in a cloud environment to create an audit trail as well as an alerting mechanism for identifying when systems may have been altered in inappropriate ways by accidental or intentional manners.

Because of the shared responsibility model, some elements of auditing will be shared by the CSP and the cloud customer. Audits of controls over the hypervisor will usually be the purview of the CSP, since they control and manage the relevant hardware. VMs deployed on top of that hardware are usually under the direct control of the cloud customer, so assurance activities must be performed by either customer personnel or their third-party auditor. This is more complicated than auditing an on-premises environment where one organization has complete control over the infrastructure. Audit standards, as discussed in the next section, have evolved to deal with this complexity by specifying which controls are owned by the audited organization, and which are inherited from another provider.

Types of Audit Reports

Any audit, whether internal or external, will produce a report focused either on the organization or on the organization's relationship with an outside entity or entities. In a cloud relationship, oftentimes the ownership of security controls designed to reduce risk resides with a cloud service provider. An audit of the cloud service provider can identify if there are any gaps between what is contractually specified and what controls the provider has in place.

SOC, SSAE, and ISAE

The American Institute of CPAs (AICPA) provides a suite of audit and assurance standards that are widely used to report on controls in place at a service organization, such as a CSP. This includes standards for auditors to use when conducting audit activities, as well as specifics for report formats and details that customers can use to understand the risks associated with using a CSP's services. The various report types are detailed in Table 6.2.

TABLE 6.2   AICPA Service Organization Control (SOC) Reports

Report	Users	Concerns	Details Required
SOC 1	User entities and the CPAs that audit their financial statements	Effect of the controls at the service organization on the user entities' financial statements	Systems, controls, and tests performed by the service auditor and results of tests
SOC 2	Broad range of users who need detailed information and assurance about controls at a service organization	Security, availability, and processing integrity of the systems the service organization uses to process users' data and the confidentiality and privacy of the information processed by these systems	Systems, controls, and tests performed by the service auditor and results of tests
SOC 3	Broad range of users who need information and assurance about controls but do not have the need for detailed information provided in a SOC 2 report	Security, availability, and processing integrity of the systems the service organization uses to process users' data and the confidentiality and privacy of the information processed by these systems	Referred to as a "Trust Services Report," SOC 3 reports are generally used and can be freely distributed, unlike SOC 2, which usually requires nondisclosure

Table source: Adapted from AICPA SOC Reports

The differences between the SOC reports are as follows:

- **SOC 1:** These reports deal mainly with financial controls and are intended to be used primarily by CPAs who audit an entity's financial statements. Business partners may find these reports useful to gauge the financial stability of partner organizations, but this is usually an operational risk rather than a security risk concern.

- **SOC for Service Organizations: Trust Services Criteria (SOC 2):** This is a report on "Controls at a Service Organization Relevant to Security, Availability, Processing Integrity, Confidentiality, or Privacy." These reports are intended to meet the needs of a broad range of users who need detailed information and assurance about the controls at a service organization relevant to security, availability, and processing integrity of the systems the service organization uses to process users' data and the confidentiality and privacy of the information processed by these systems. Put simply, a SOC 2 report can show customers how well a CSP's controls are designed and whether they are operating as intended to reduce risk. These reports can play an important role in the following:

  - Organizational oversight
  - Vendor management programs
  - Internal corporate governance and risk management processes
  - Regulatory oversight

    There are two types of reports for these engagements:

  - **Type I:** Report on the fairness of the presentation of management's description of the service organization's system and the suitability of the design of the controls to achieve the related control objectives included in the description as of a specified date. Type I reports are only a review of control design but do not test the effectiveness of controls; as such they provide less assurance regarding the service provider's ability to safeguard data.

  - **Type II:** Report on the fairness of the presentation of management's description of the service organization's system and the suitability of the design and operating effectiveness of the controls to achieve the related control objectives included in the description throughout a specified period. When conducting a Type II audit the auditor performs tests of the controls, so the report provides greater assurance that the provider is effectively addressing risks.

- **Service Organization Controls 3 (SOC 3):** SOC 3 reports are considered general use and can be freely distributed, as sensitive details that are captured in a SOC 2 Type II have been removed. These contain only the auditor's general opinions and nonsensitive data, unlike a SOC 2 which usually contains sensitive system and business process details. A SOC 3 may be shared publicly, while most organizations require a nondisclosure agreement (NDA) in order to access a SOC 2 report.

  AICPA definitions of SOC controls can be found at the following locations:

- **SOC 1:** `aicpa.org/interestareas/frc/assuranceadvisoryservices/aicpasoc1report.html`

- SOC 2: `aicpa.org/interestareas/frc/assuranceadvisoryservices/aicpa-soc2report.html`
- SOC 3: `aicpa.org/interestareas/frc/assuranceadvisoryservices/aicpa-soc3report.html`

The Statement on Standards for Attestation Engagements (SSAE) is a set of standards defined by the AICPA to be used when conducting audits and generating SOC reports. The most current version (SSAE 18) was made effective in May 2017 and added additional sections and controls to further enhance the content and quality of SOC reports. It is primarily used by auditors when conducting SOC audits rather than service providers or customers.

The International Auditing and Assurance Standards Board issues the International Standard on Assurance Engagements (ISAE). This is similar to the AICPA and SSAE standards, but there are some differences between the two standards. A security professional should always consult the relevant business departments to determine which audit report(s) will be used when assessing cloud systems. Although SOC 2 is a standard defined by a U.S. body, it has become something of a de facto global standard. Although cloud computing is global, the major CSPs are U.S.-based and implemented these standards for other large tech companies that are also U.S.-based. The ISAE 3402 standard is roughly equivalent to the SOC 2; the major CSPs offer audit reports for both. As a cloud provider or customer, it is important for a security practitioner to understand the relevant types of reports they need to either consume from their CSPs or provide to their customers.

CSA

The Security Trust Assurance and Risk (STAR) certification program from CSA can be used by cloud service providers, cloud customers, or auditors and consultants to demonstrate compliance to a desired level of assurance. STAR consists of two levels of certification, which provide increasing levels of assurance to customers:

- **Level 1:** Self-assessment is a complimentary offering that documents the security controls provided by the CSP, which helps customers assess the security of cloud providers they currently use or are considering using.
- **Level 2:** Third-party audit requires the CSP to engage an independent auditor to evaluate the CSP's controls against the CSA standard. This can be done as a stand-alone report or incorporated into other audits such as SOC 2 or ISO 27001. The controls are evaluated against the CSA CCM objectives, and the audit report is then submitted to the CSA registry for customers to access.

Since CSA is an industry group comprising cloud providers and major customers, it is focused specifically on cloud computing security risks and controls. A Level 1 STAR is a weak form of assurance, as an organization's self-assessment is not as rigorous as a third-party audit conducted by a trained, qualified auditor. More details on the registry and assurance requirements can be found at `cloudsecurityalliance.org/star`.

Restrictions of Audit Scope Statements

Audit scope statements are an essential part of an audit report. They provide the reader with details on what was included in the audit and what was not—if the reader is using a service that was not included in the scope of the audit, then the report provides nothing useful for making a risk decision. Learning to read audit reports and extract these important details is key to gaining assurance regarding the security controls in place at a CSP or other service provider.

Determining the scope of an audit is usually a joint activity performed by the organization being audited and their auditor. Several frameworks, such as SOC 2 and ISO 27001, include guidance on defining the scope of the audit, specifying which parts of the organization and services are included. The final scope is documented by the auditor in the resulting report and should be used by any consumers when determining if the services they are evaluating have been audited.

An audit scope statement generally includes the following information:

- Statement of purpose and objectives

- Scope of audit and explicit exclusions

- Type of audit

- Security assessment requirements

- Assessment criteria and rating scales

- Criteria for acceptance

- Expected deliverables

- Classification (for example, secret, top secret, public, etc.)

Any audit must have parameters set to ensure that the efforts are focused on relevant areas that can be effectively audited. Setting these parameters for an audit is commonly known as the *audit scope restrictions*. Why limit the scope of an audit? Audits are expensive endeavors that can engage highly trained (and highly paid) content experts. The auditing of systems can affect system performance and, in some cases, require the downtime of production systems.

Large organizations with multiple service offerings may also restrict the scope of an audit to a specific service or set of services for a variety of reasons. A newly created service may not have all relevant controls implemented, so an audit is largely useless until the service is complete and controls are implemented. In other cases, it may be a deliberate decision to exclude certain services from being audited, as the cost of implementing controls and auditing to verify their effectiveness is too high relative to the revenue the service generates.

Scope restrictions are of particular importance to security professionals. They can spell out the operational components of an audit, such as the acceptable times and time periods (for example, days and hours of the week), types of testing that will be conducted, and which systems or services are to be audited. Carefully crafting scope restrictions can ensure that production systems are not adversely impacted by an auditor's activity, and it is vital to ensure that systems that customers need assurance for are included in the scope. Scoping can also be a means of controlling costs related to compliance. For example, an audit on HIPAA compliance should only include systems that handle PHI; otherwise, the auditor will charge for time spent auditing systems that should have no valid reason to be audited.

Gap Analysis

As a precursor to a formal audit process, an organization may find a gap analysis a useful starting point. Gap analyses lack the rigor of a formal audit and can be a quick check of compliance, which is useful for organizations preparing to undergo a formal audit for the first time. They can also be useful when assessing the impact of changes to regulatory or compliance frameworks, which introduce new or modified requirements. A gap analysis identifies where the organization does not meet these changed requirements and provides important information to help remediate thee gaps.

The main purpose of a gap analysis is to compare the organization's current practices against a specified framework and identify the gaps between the two. These may be performed by either internal or external parties, and the choice of which to use will be driven by the cost and need for objectivity. If a gap analysis is being performed against a business function, the first step is to identify a relevant industry-standard framework to compare business activities against. In information security, this usually means a standard such as ISO 27002 (best-practice recommendations for information security management). Another common comparison framework used as a cybersecurity benchmark is the NIST cybersecurity framework.

A gap analysis can be conducted against almost any business function, from strategy and staffing to information security. The common steps generally consist of the following:

- Establishing the need for the analysis and gaining management support for the efforts.

- Defining scope, objectives, and relevant frameworks.

- Identifying the current state of the department or area (which involves the evaluation of the department to understand current state, generally involving research and interviews of employees).

- Reviewing evidence and supporting documentation, including the verification of statements and data.

- Identifying the "gaps" between the framework and reality. This highlights the risks to the organization.

- Preparing a report detailing the findings and getting sign-off from the appropriate company leaders.

Since a gap analysis provides measurable deficiencies and, in some cases, needs to be signed off by senior leadership, it can be a powerful tool for an organization to identify weaknesses in their efforts for compliance. It is also useful as a planning and prioritization tool, as any identified gaps can be evaluated against known risks. The gaps that correspond to risks should be prioritized first, since closing them also supports the organization's overall security risk management strategy.

Audit Planning

Any audit, whether related to financial reporting, compliance, or cloud computing security risk management, must be carefully planned and organized. This helps ensure that the results of the audit are relevant to the organization and contain useful information that can be used to help the organization improve on any identified weaknesses or deficiencies.

The audit process can generally be broken down into four phases, starting with audit planning. During this phase, the organization must perform several tasks, including the following:

- **Document and define audit program objectives:** This process must be a collaborative effort and begins with internal planning to determine what systems or processes are to be audited and what standards are to be used. In many scenarios, this will be done many months before the audit, since time is required to implement controls that are required by the chosen standard.

- **Gap analysis or readiness assessment:** A mock or mini audit, usually performed by internal personnel, can be useful in assessing the organization's ability to successfully undergo a full audit. In the process of implementing security and compliance controls, it is possible to overlook key tasks, and the changing nature of an organization can also render existing controls ineffective. Identifying and fixing these issues before a formal audit helps to ensure that the audit report does not contain unfavorable findings.

- **Define audit objectives and deliverables:** Once the organization is ready to undergo an audit, it is important to identify the expected outputs from the audit. These may include a report that can be shared with customers, data to be shared with leadership, and action items for security or compliance teams to address, among others. Many audit frameworks dictate the deliverables, such as a SOC 2 Type II, which always results in a SOC 2 report, or FedRAMP, which results in an authorization to operate (ATO).

- **Identifying auditors and qualifications:** Compliance and audit frameworks usually specify the type of auditor required, such as a partially independent internal auditor or completely independent third-party auditor. Frameworks that rely on third-party auditors often specify a standard and issue credentials to auditors authorized to perform specific types of audits, such as a CPA who can perform a SOC audit. Security practitioners must ensure that they engage an auditor with appropriate skills, credentials, and training.

- **Identifying scope and restrictions:** Once the auditor is chosen, they will usually work with the organization to define a scope and any restrictions or exclusions. This might include scoping the audit to just a set of systems or organizational units and is usually documented formally in the audit report. This allows consumers of the report to understand whether the systems or services they are accessing have been audited and whether any issues or deficiencies exist.

Once the audit planning process is completed, the actual work of the audit begins. After planning, there are three major phases of an audit, which include the following activities:

- **Audit fieldwork:** This involves the actual work the auditors perform to gather, test, and evaluate the organization. This includes examining evidence, interviewing organization personnel, and testing controls.

- **Audit reporting:** The report writing begins as the auditors conduct their fieldwork, as they capture notes and any findings. The formal audit report is typically provided in a draft form to allow the organization to challenge any incorrect information. Once agreed upon, the final audit report is issued.

- **Audit follow-up:** Various activities may be conducted after the audit, including addressing any identified weaknesses. Some auditors will perform retesting of fixed controls and issue an update or addendum to an audit report to indicate the organization's actions that addressed the original finding. This is useful, as consumers of the audit report will naturally ask what the organization has done to address identified findings, since they represent risks.

In many organizations, audit is a continuous process. This is often structured into business activities to provide an ongoing view into how an organization is meeting compliance and regulatory goals. As part of the audit planning process, scheduling and coordinating these audits can be challenging but is essential to prevent audits from adding too much operational overhead. Cloud security practitioners can utilize audits as a way to monitor the status of their compliance programs and therefore the status of their risk mitigation strategies.

Internal Information Security Management System

An information security management system (ISMS) is a systematic approach to information security consisting of processes, technology, and people designed to help protect and manage an organization's information. The ISO 27001 standard directly addresses the need for and approaches to implementing an ISMS, starting with an explanation of what the ISMS is and how it should align with other organizational processes:

> The information security management system preserves the confidentiality, integrity, and availability of information by applying a risk management process and gives confidence to interested parties that risks are adequately managed.

> It is important that the information security management system is part of and integrated with the organization's processes and overall management structure and that information security is considered in the design of processes, information systems, and controls. It is expected that an information security management system implementation will be scaled in accordance with the needs of the organization.

> This International Standard can be used by internal and external parties to assess the organization's ability to meet the organization's own information security requirements.
>
> Source: ISO/IEC 27001:2013
>
> Information technology — Security techniques — Information security management systems — Requirements

An ISMS is a powerful risk management tool and is most often implemented at medium or large organizations where there is a formal need to quantify risk, develop and execute strategies to mitigate it, and provide formal reporting on the status of these risk mitigation efforts. It gives both internal and external stakeholders additional confidence in the security measures in place at the company.

Though the function of an ISMS can vary from industry to industry, there are a number of benefits to implementation that hold true across all industries.

- **Security of data in multiple forms:** An ISMS can help protect data in all forms, whether the organization relies on hard-copy, on-premises, or cloud-based information systems.

- **Cyberattacks:** Having an ISMS can make an organization more resilient to cyberattacks, because the risk of these attacks is known and formal processes exist to mitigate them. As the threat landscape evolves, the ISMS's continuous improvement efforts and ongoing risk management activities help the organization to respond effectively.

- **Central information security management:** An ISMS will put in place centralized frameworks for managing information, reducing shadow systems, and easing the burden of data protection. Organizations with multiple units or dispersed authority can benefit from a centralized source of information security risk management by sharing best practices and resources.

- **Formal risk management:** Having a codified set of processes and procedures in place can reduce operational risks in a number of areas, including information security, business continuity, and adapting to evolving security threats. Although an ISMS does not explicitly address operational issues like financial risk, it can help address operational risks like system interruptions. Most organizations rely heavily on technology systems, and a security risk management framework that addresses availability also addresses operational risks.

As with any major organizational element, an ISMS requires buy-in from company leadership to be effective. For CSPs an ISMS can provide a single organizational function for addressing risks that customers will ask about, such as the security of the data they put into the cloud and availability of systems hosted in the CSP's environments. For cloud customers, their own internal ISMS is the implementation point for all the security controls discussed throughout this book, including risk management activities associated with migrating to and using cloud computing.

Internal Information Security Controls System

As a companion to an ISMS, a system of information security controls provides guidance for mitigating the risks identified as part of the ISMS's risk management processes. Often known as control frameworks, these are considered best practices guidance that can give the organization a starting point when addressing their identified risks. As with all shared resources, some modifications may be required.

Scoping controls refers to identifying which controls in the framework apply to the organization and which do not. There may be controls that deal with business processes, system types, or even technologies that are not in use in an organization. *Tailoring* is a process of taking the applicable controls and matching them to the organization's specific circumstances, such as removing any guidance for Windows systems if an organization is exclusively Linux based. To use a clothing analogy, scoping refers to excluding the sections of a store that sell clothes designed for other age groups—adults are unlikely to find anything wearable in the children's department! Once an appropriate outfit is selected, tailoring can ensure that it fits your individual body type, resulting in the best fit.

There are a number of control frameworks to choose from and various reasons to choose one or another. Organizations implementing an ISO 27001 ISMS will find the ISO 27002 controls very easy to use, since they are designed to fit together. Other control frameworks include NIST Special Publication 800-53, the NIST Cybersecurity Framework (CSF), the Secure Controls Framework, and the CSA CCM.

In addition to providing a set of standardized control activities, these frameworks may also provide guidance and processes for the tailoring and implementation of activities needed to meet the objectives. For instance, the NIST CSF organizes controls based on their intended risk mitigation functions.

- Identify
- Protect
- Detect
- Respond
- Recover

For example, Identify controls are useful for identifying threats and risks, while Protect controls are designed to proactively mitigate identify risks. Once controls are in place, the Detect category includes controls related to detecting whether a security incident has occurred, while Respond and Recover focus on mitigating the impact and returning to normal operations. More information on the NIST CSF can be found at `nist.gov/cyberframework/online-learning/five-functions`.

Policies

Policies are a key part of any data security strategy. Policies provide users and organizations with a way to understand requirements and provide the organization to enforce these requirements in a systematic way. Employees and management are made aware of their roles and responsibilities via policies, which is a way for organizations to govern activities occurring during the course of operations. Policies are an important piece of standardizing practices in an organization.

From a cloud computing perspective, policies can be an important tool to govern migration to and use of cloud resources. While cloud computing offers significant benefits like cost savings, it can also introduce unexpected or unwanted risk. Policies communicate expectations such as acceptable use of cloud services, helping to ensure that the organization balances the benefits realized via cloud computing without taking on unacceptable risks.

Policies are a formal and high-level document that should be approved by the organization's management. They support strategic goals and initiatives and generally do not contain highly specific details like system configurations or step-by-step procedures. Without formal management approval and proper education for relevant stakeholders, policies will be ineffective, so it is important for security practitioners to devote adequate attention to them.

Organizational Policies

Companies use policies to outline rules and guidelines, which are usually complemented by other documentation such as procedures, job aids, etc. Policies make employees aware of the organization's views and values on specific issues and what actions will occur if they are not followed. As an example, organizations typically define policies related to proper use of company resources like expense reimbursements and travel. These specify how and when employees can seek reimbursement and what rules they must follow when booking travel to ensure that the company complies with relevant accounting and fiduciary laws.

Policies are a proactive risk mitigation tool designed to reduce the likelihood of risks, such as the following:

- Financial losses
- Loss of data
- Reputational damage
- Statutory and regulatory compliance issues
- Abuse or misuse of computing systems and resources

Functional Policies

A functional policy is a set of standardized definitions for employees that describe how they are to make use of systems or data. Functional policies typically guide specific activities crucial to the organization, such as appropriate handling of data, vulnerability management, and so on.

One common policy at many organizations is a data classification policy, which communicates what types of data the organization handles and what protections must be in place. Other policies, such as cloud computing and acceptable use policies, can provide guidance for appropriate handling of data on employee workstations and cloud services based on the data's classification level. This might include requirements for applying encryption or even specify specific classification levels where data is not to be processed in the cloud at all.

Functional policies generally codify requirements identified in the ISMS and often align with the families of controls in security frameworks. The following, while not an exhaustive list, identifies several common policies that organizations might find useful:

- **Data classification:** Identifies types of data and how each should be handled

- **Network services:** How issues such as remote access and network security are handled

- **Vulnerability scanning:** Routines and limitations on internal scanning and penetration testing

- **Patch management:** How equipment is patched and on what schedule

- **Acceptable use:** What is and is not acceptable to do on company hardware and networks

- **Email use:** What is and is not acceptable to do on company email accounts

- **Passwords and access management:** Password complexity, expiration, reuse, requirements for MFA, and requirements for use of access management tools such as a password manager

- **Incident response:** How incidents are handled, and requirements for defining an incident response plan

Cloud Computing Policies

The ease of deploying cloud resources has led to a significant problem known as *shadow IT*, which is any IT service or information system that exists without formal knowledge of the organization. In an organization that uses SharePoint for filesharing and collaboration, a single team signing up for and using Dropbox to share files is an example of shadow IT. The controls in place for data security in SharePoint are unlikely to be applied to Dropbox, since the service was not formally approved and secured by the organization's IT department. Shadow IT can also create financial risks, as the organization's IT spending becomes harder to measure when multiple teams are involved.

Cloud services should not be exempt from organizational policy application. These policies will define the requirements that users must adhere to in order to make use of the services and may dictate specific cloud services that are approved for various uses. Because of the ease of provisioning cloud services, many organizations have specific policies in place that discourage or prohibit the use of cloud services by individuals outside of central IT oversight.

Since cloud computing is outside the direct control of the organization, policies may be written to guide the selection and use of cloud environments, rather than being used to govern the day-to-day activities of internal employees. When evaluating policies and how they should be applied to the cloud, security practitioners should address major areas of risk such as the following:

- **Password policies:** If an organization has password policies around length, complexity, expiration, or MFA, it is important to ensure that these same requirements are met by a cloud service provider.

- **Remote access:** Cloud services are inherently remote accessible, so organizations that previously prohibited or limited remote work will need to create remote access policies that apply to a large group of users (possibly even the whole organization). Secure remote network access can be cumbersome, requiring tools such as a VPN, while cloud computing often uses standard technologies like browser encryption to provide security. Ensuring that the correct tools are deployed and expectations are set for their use is a key element of a remote access policy.

- **Encryption:** Policies about encryption strength and when encryption is required should identify where and how these apply to cloud services. Key escrow can be an important aspect of policy to focus on, as well as minimum acceptable encryption algorithms and key lengths.

- **Data backup and failover:** Policies on data retention and backup must be enforced on cloud providers. Cloud services that offer built-in high availability and data replication features can make this process much easier, but selecting or architecting these solutions appropriately should be guided by the policy requirements.

- **Third-party access:** What third parties might have access to data stored with the CSP? Can this access be logged and audited? The answers to these questions could introduce risks, so the policy provisions on third-party access should be used as requirements when choosing a CSP.

- **Separation of duties:** Cloud services, especially SaaS, can introduce new user management models that could impact the organization's access controls, including separation of duties and minimum necessary access.

- **Incident response:** Incidents in the cloud are more complicated to investigate due to other parties who must be included, such as the CSP and any other tenants who might be affected by an incident. Policies and response plans should be updated to include these other stakeholders, coordination required, and any testing modifications that must be made due to a changed environment.

In some instances, a cloud service provider cannot meet a company's requirements when it comes to adhering to a specific policy. If this happens, it is important to consider the risks of using the provider, and any deviations from policy should be carefully documented. All policy exceptions should be treated as risks, which require compensating controls to mitigate. If the threat landscape changes significantly, these risks may increase above the organization's tolerance, which will necessitate action such as finding a new CSP or moving back to on-premises hosting.

Identification and Involvement of Relevant Stakeholders

One key challenge in the audit process is the inclusion of any relevant stakeholders. This includes the organization's management who will likely be paying for the audit, security practitioners who will be responsible for facilitating the audit, and employees who will be called upon to provide evidence to auditors in the form of documentation, artifacts, or sitting for interviews.

Cloud computing environments can include more stakeholders than on-premises systems, because there can be multiple CSPs involved. For instance, a SaaS application may introduce both the SaaS vendor as well as their infrastructure provider, where an on-premises environment would involve only the organization's internal IT department. When it comes to performing audits, certain challenges can arise from these complicated supply chains,

It is important to both identify and involve all relevant stakeholders. If this is not done, any audit performed risks missing important details and information the auditors need to uncover potential weaknesses. This applies even without additional vendors or stakeholders—auditors will need access to relevant personnel such as system administrators and management inside the organization. When auditing a cloud system, stakeholders from the CSP may need to be informed or involved.

To identify relevant stakeholders, some key challenges that cloud security practitioners face include the following:

- Defining the enterprise architecture currently used to deliver services, including all service providers.

- Identifying any contractual obligations or requirements that impact audits, such as a limitation on the right to audit or resources provided by the CSP that can be used by customers when performing an audit. Most CSPs publish their own audit reports that detail controls under their purview, such as physical and environmental. Cloud customers may carve these requirements out of their audit scope and instead rely on the findings of the CSP's auditors.

Specialized Compliance Requirements for Highly Regulated Industries

Responsibility for compliance to any relevant regulations ultimately rests with the cloud consumer, and organizations that migrate to the cloud do not absolve themselves of risks associated with their information systems. Some industries have cloud-specific regulatory or compliance guidance, and some industries have extensive regulatory frameworks due to the sensitivity of the data handled by that industry. This significantly impacts the work of security practitioners, who may find their entire job description dictated by the compliance requirements.

Many CSPs have compliance-focused cloud service offerings, which meet the requirements of specific regulatory or legal frameworks. An organization's cloud computing strategy should be designed with regulatory compliance in mind, including mandating the use of compliant cloud service offerings. The cloud customer is unlikely to perform their own audit of a CSP and instead will rely on the CSP's published audit reports to gain assurance that the CSP's services implement adequate protections to meet the regulatory requirements.

Highly regulated industries typically involve highly sensitive data, such as health or financial information, or provide services that make them critical infrastructure, such as power and other utility providers. Organizations in these industries need to be aware of the regulations governing their operations and ensure that their strategy for using cloud computing enables them to be compliant. Examples of these regulatory frameworks include the following:

- **North American Electric Reliability Corporation Critical Infrastructure Protection (NERC/CIP):** In the United States and Canada, organizations involved with power generation and distribution must regulate their operations according to the CIP standards. This includes the use of any cloud computing resources, which must meet requirements like maintaining adequate security protections to prevent disruption of power generation and delivery.

- **HIPAA and the Health Information Technology for Economic and Clinical Health (HITECH) Act:** Both HIPAA and HITECH deal with PHI and implement specific requirements for security and privacy protections, as well as breach notification requirements. While cloud computing is not specifically addressed, these laws do identify required controls that must be in place for any system handling PHI. Cloud customers should verify their chosen CSP's ability to meet these requirements before processing any PHI in the cloud.

- **PCI:** PCI DSS specifies protections for payment card transaction data. Similar to HIPAA, it does not specifically address the use of cloud computing, but any CSP chosen must be able to meet the PCI DSS standards for data security and privacy. Reviewing the CSP's audit reports to gain assurance is a key task for a security practitioner.

Since public CSPs do not generally allow individual customers to perform audits, organizations in highly regulated industries may seek out a different cloud deployment model. If enough organizations need cloud computing, creating a community cloud might be a feasible option. Since the user community shares the same regulatory requirements, the community cloud can be specifically designed to meet those needs. This simplifies the task of compliance, and any audits performed on the cloud will be specific to the industry-specific regulations, which will make security activities easier for all customers of that community cloud.

Impact of Distributed Information Technology Model

Cloud computing enables distributed IT service delivery, with systems that can automatically replicate data and provide services from data centers around the globe. Auditing such a complex environment requires significant modifications from traditional computing models, where it was possible to point to a specific data center and specific server rack where data or systems were hosted.

One obvious impact of this distributed model is the additional geographic locations auditors must consider when performing an audit. An important term in audits is sampling, which is the act of picking a subset of the system's physical infrastructure to inspect. For example, when performing a configuration audit on a system with 100 web servers, an auditor might pull configuration information for 20 of them to perform checks. The time needed to audit all 100 is prohibitive, so reviewing 20 percent is adequate to determine if the organization's configuration management policy is being followed.

Now expand this problem from 100 servers in a few data centers in one country: auditors now face hundreds of data centers in many different countries. Further complicating the issue is virtualization, which means the virtual servers that are part of a specific system could exist on any one of thousands of hardware clusters around the world—and their location can change almost instantly. This is an obvious benefit for system availability but makes the process of sampling much more difficult.

CSPs have found ways to collect evidence that provides auditors with sufficient assurance that they have collected a representative sample. This can include continuous monitoring strategies that capture information on a frequent enough basis to supply the auditor with sufficient, competent evidence. However, the cost of audits with geographically distributed systems will be greater, as the auditors may have to perform physical site inspections that require travel.

Legal jurisdiction issues can also complicate the process of conducting audits. While the process of auditing is not necessarily illegal, issues associated with auditors traveling and gaining access to facilities can add complexity to the audit process. For example, gaining access and approval to do business in some countries requires visas and work permits, which must be approved before an audit can take place. As with other aspects of cloud security, practitioners should coordinate with appropriate legal resources to determine any needs related to international auditing.

Understand Implications of Cloud to Enterprise Risk Management

If you compare how IT services were provisioned two decades ago to how they are done today, you would see a completely different landscape. In the dot-com era, provisioning systems took experts days or weeks to build out hardware, operating systems, and applications, and that assumed a facility was available—if not, building out a data center could take months. Companies spent millions of dollars on physical infrastructure in the form of data centers, wide area networks, and physical server hardware. Today, anyone can provision a multitier web application in a few minutes or sign up for a SaaS application in mere seconds.

This shift in how IT services is provisioned has significantly altered enterprise risk management practices. In the past, the thought of "accidentally" provisioning a server simply did not exist, much less the scenario of spinning up infrastructure in another country or legal jurisdiction. Today that scenario is not only possible but also highly likely in many organizations, which opens them up to new risks. These require new management and mitigation strategies, approaches, and tools.

It is vital for both cloud customers and CSPs to understand not only how enterprise risk management has changed, but how it continues to evolve as more organizations adopt cloud computing and novel cloud services emerge. New strategies can be employed for risk mitigation, and new ways of assessing, evaluating, and communicating about risk are needed.

Assess Provider's Risk Management Programs

Prior to establishing a relationship with a cloud provider, a cloud customer needs to analyze the risks associated with adopting that provider's services. The goal of this is the same as performing risk assessments for on-premises infrastructure, but the method of gaining assurance is different. Rather than performing a direct audit, the customer must rely on their supply chain risk management (SCRM) processes. Similar to shifting IT control away from the customer to the CSP, SCRM requires new approaches.

First and foremost in SCRM is evaluating whether a supplier has a risk management program in place, and if so whether the risks identified by that program are being adequately mitigated. Unlike traditional risk management activities, where the organization can directly review their own processes and procedures, SCRM may require an indirect approach. The major CSPs do not permit direct customer audits or assessments, so cloud customers must review audit reports furnished by the CSP to gain the information needed.

SOC 2, ISO 27001, FedRAMP, and CSA STAR have all been discussed in previous sections of this chapter. CSPs will engage a qualified third-party auditor to perform an audit and issue a report using one or more of these frameworks, and possibly others, depending on the markets the CSP is trying to win business in. Some customers are required to choose CSPs that are compliant with a particular framework, such as U.S. government agencies that must use FedRAMP-accredited CSPs. Nonregulated organizations may be able to choose a CSP that provides an audit report that offers adequate assurance, such as picking a CSA STAR Level 1 CSP. Although the Level 1 self-assessment provides only low assurance, the lower cost associated with a less-audited environment may be appropriate for lower-sensitivity data.

When reviewing an audit report, there are several key elements of the report to focus on. These include any scoping information or description of the audit target. Some compliance frameworks allow audits to be very narrowly scoped, such as SOC 2. If the CSP's SOC 2 audit did not cover a specific service a customer wants to use, then the audit finding does not provide any value. Also important to review are any findings, weaknesses, or deficiencies identified in the report, as these represent inadequate or nonfunctional risk mitigations. If the risk applies to a service the customer is not using, the finding can be ignored, but if it does impact a service in use, then that risk is inherited by the customer. This may drive changes, such as enhanced customer-side controls, tracking the CSP's mitigation and resolution efforts, or even migrating to another CSP altogether.

There are resources that can help organizations build out or enhance their SCRM program. NIST has a resource library that includes working groups, publications, and other resources, available here: csrc.nist.gov/Projects/cyber-supply-chain-risk-management. ISO 27000:2022 specifies a security management system for security and resilience, with a particular focus on supply chain management. It extends concepts found in the ISO 31000:2018 standard, which focuses on enterprise risk management. Both standards provide guidance for identifying and assessing a supplier's security controls, policies and procedures, and the effectiveness of their security risk mitigations.

Two other important aspects to consider when evaluating a CSP's risk management program include the company's risk profile and risk appetite. *Risk profile* describes the risk present in the organization based on all the identified risks and any associated mitigations in place. For example, technology startups typically have much higher risk than established financial services firms. This is due to several factors, including the age of the company and maturity of their risk management programs, as well as the varying amount of regulation each industry faces.

Risk appetite describes the amount of risk an organization is willing to accept without mitigating—once again a startup is likely to accept more risk than a bank simply due to the resources required to mitigate those risks. A cash-strapped startup cannot staff up a risk department, so it must accept more operational and technology risk. Both of these factors should be considered by any cloud customers when evaluating a provider's risk management program. These details may be provided in audit reports as part of the provider's description of their ISMS, or in other documentation like security whitepapers.

Differences between Data Owner/Controller vs. Data Custodian/Processor

An important distinction in data is the difference between the data owner (data controller) and the data custodian (data processor). While these nuanced definitions may seem unneeded, they do have implications for managing risks associated with privacy data. It is helpful to start with some definitions:

- A data subject is the individual or entity that is the subject of the personal data.
- A data controller is the person (or company) that determines the purposes for which, and the way in which, personal data is processed. This entity owns the data and, importantly, risks associated with any breaches of the data.
- The data processor is anyone who processes personal data on behalf of the data controller. This entity is a custodian of data, who is charged with implementing protections at the direction of the data controller.

For example, let's say BikeCo sells bicycles and allows users to provide personal data online to fulfill orders. They use a CSP, called CloudWheelz, to host their website and customer database, as well as an online payment processor, Circle, to handle payment card transactions. In this case, any customer is the data subject, and BikeCo is the data controller. Both CloudWheelz and Circle are data processors that act on behalf of the data owner. In the event that either CloudWheelz or Circle suffers a data breach, BikeCo is still legally liable for the data. If they have not taken adequate steps to ensure that their data processors implemented adequate protections, regulatory agencies are likely to assess significant penalties.

The distinctions are important for regulatory and legal reasons. Data processors are responsible for the safe and private custody, transport, and storage of data according to business agreements. Data owners are legally responsible (and liable) for the safety and privacy of the data under most international laws. When data controllers use processors, they must ensure that security requirements follow the data. This is often achieved via contract clauses that specify data protection and handling requirements, breach notification timelines, and possibly risk transfer such as the requirement for the processor to carry insurance that helps defray costs associated with a security incident.

Regulatory Transparency Requirements

A cloud security professional should be aware of the transparency requirements imposed on data controllers by various regulations and laws around the world. Many of these were written before cloud computing was as pervasive as it is today, so it is also important to stay informed about changes, as well as new regulations that come into force and impact the organization. Many legal firms will provide this kind of guidance as a service, and in-house legal counsel can also be a useful resource to identify regulatory requirements and any changes needed to come into compliance.

The following is a short and noncomprehensive list of several important regulatory frameworks that require transparency related to data security and privacy. Security practitioners in organizations regulated by these frameworks must be aware of the frameworks and work to implement the required controls. As a data owner or processor, cloud security professionals must be aware of all relevant regulatory requirements.

Breach Notification

Most recent privacy laws include mandatory breach notification. If an organization suffers a data breach, it is obligated to provide notification of that breach. There are some variations among the laws, mainly around issues of timing of the notification and who must be notified. Some regulations require notification within the specified time period of a suspected breach, while others are less strict and require only notification for a confirmed breach. Similarly, some regulations require notification only to the affected data subjects, while others require notification to a regulatory official such as a governmental data privacy official.

Regulations that require breach notification include, but are not limited to, GDPR, HIPAA (as amended by the HITECH Act), GLBA, and PIPEDA. In addition to these, numerous regional, state, and provincial regulations require data breach notification. Cloud security professionals should identify all relevant regulatory frameworks their organization is subject to, and build processes to ensure that obligations are met for notifying affected data subjects.

Incident response plans and procedures should include relevant information about the time period for reporting, as well as the required contacts in the event of a data breach. They should also include guidance on when it is necessary to contact specific data privacy officials. For example, a data breach that affects only U.S. citizens does not need to be reported to any data protection officials in the EU, since the GDPR does not apply to those data subjects.

Sarbanes-Oxley Act

If a company is publicly traded in the United States, they are subject to transparency requirements under the Sarbanes-Oxley Act (SOX) of 2002. Specifically, as data owners, these companies should consider the following:

- **Section 802:** It is a crime to destroy, change, or hide documents to prevent their use in official legal processes.
- **Section 804:** Companies must keep audit-related records for a minimum of five years.

SOX compliance is often an issue with both data breaches and ransomware incidents at publicly traded companies. The loss of data related to compliance due to external actors does not protect a company from legal obligations.

GDPR and Transparency

For companies doing business in the European Union or with citizens of the EU, transparency requirements under the GDPR are laid out in Article 12 (see `gdpr-info.eu/art-12-gdpr`). The exact language states that a data controller (data owner) "must be able to demonstrate that personal data are processed in a manner transparent to the data subject." The obligations for transparency begin at the data collection stage and apply "throughout the lifecycle of processing."

The GDPR stipulates that communication to data subjects must be "concise, transparent, intelligible and easily accessible, and use clear and plain language." Achieving this task may not be the responsibility of a security practitioner, but security should be present when requirements are developed for user interfaces and language presented to users. Legal counsel may also be involved to ensure that the requirements under GDPR are met by any system or application designs.

Meeting the requirement for transparency also requires processes for providing data subjects with access to their data. This process may be owned by customer-facing resources such as a support team, with input required from legal and security to ensure that the procedures meet the GDPR requirements.

In simple terms, this means that plain language must be used to explain why data is being collected and what it is being used for. Similar language is included in other privacy regulations, so building a robust process for providing transparent information is a requirement for many security teams.

Risk Treatment

Risk treatment is the practice of modifying risk, usually to lower it, which can be achieved in a number of ways. Risk treatment begins with identifying and assessing risks, typically by measuring the likelihood and impact of their occurrence. Not all risks can be treated equally, so risk management usually prioritizes those risks that are higher impact and likelihood first. These risk assessment procedures should be documented as part of the organization's ISMS.

Once risks are identified, risk treatments should be selected to reduce the likelihood or impact (or both). Treatments that reduce likelihood are proactive, and sometimes known as *safeguards*, while risks that reduce the impact after a risk has occurred are reactive and known as *countermeasures*. These are collectively referred to as *controls*, which should be using a cost-benefit analysis to achieve acceptable risk mitigation at an adequate price.

There are four main approaches to treat risk, and many organizations will use more than one treatment option for the same risk. The options are as follows:

- **Avoid:** The organization can avoid risk altogether by not engaging in a particular activity, such as not doing business with EU citizens to avoid GDPR compliance fines. However, this also means losing out on new customers, so it is not unusual for this treatment option to go unused.

- **Transfer:** The organization can transfer risk to another organization, which is typically an insurance company. An organization's insurance policy pays out in the event of a cyber incident, which helps to offset the financial impact. Insurance carriers are in the business of managing risk, and it is unlikely a carrier will offer insurance if the organization cannot show they have adequate risk mitigations in place. Therefore, risk transfer is often used in conjunction with risk mitigation.

- **Mitigate:** The organization implements controls to reduce the likelihood and impact of the identified risks. It is common for multiple controls to be layered in a risk mitigation, such as proactive access controls to prevent unauthorized system access, and data encryption to prevent an attacker from reading any data they do gain access to. This reduces the impact of a breach.

- **Accept:** All risks are accepted by organizations, and risks that are not mitigated or transferred are accepted as is. Mitigated risks should be evaluated to determine if the *residual risk*, that is, the risk that remains after the control is implemented, falls below the organization's risk tolerance. If the residual risk remains too high, other mitigations or risk transfer should be implemented.

It is important to remember that risks are never entirely eliminated. Mitigations and transfer reduce the risks, and cloud security practitioners should keep this in mind as they perform tasks like evaluating CSPs and selecting security controls for implementation.

Risk Frameworks

Similar to security control frameworks, there are several risk management frameworks available for security practitioners to use as guides when designing a risk management program. Many of these are published by the same bodies that publish the control frameworks, and they are complementary. Organizations designing an ISO 27001 ISMS can easily utilize the relevant ISO standard for designing a security risk management program. These standards are known as risk management frameworks (RMFs).

It is important to note that risk management is not only a security activity. Other departments typically pursue risk management as well, which means the security team might be required to work in a collaborative way when conducting risk assessment and management. Some organizations may find a single risk management function to be useful, so executives have a single view of risk and associated metrics. Other organizations may allow different departments to conduct risk management differently, especially if there are conflicting regulations that govern the activities.

In the cloud computing arena, a cloud security professional should be familiar with the ISO 31000:2018 guidance standard, the European Network and Information Security Agency (ENISA)'s cloud computing risk assessment tool, and NIST standards such as 800-146, "Cloud Computing Synopsis and Recommendation," and 800-37, "Risk Management Framework for Information Systems and Organizations: A System Lifecycle Approach for Security and Privacy."

ISO 31000

ISO 31000 contains several standards related to building and running a risk management program. ISO 31000:2018, "Risk management — Guidelines," provides the foundation of an organization's RFM, while IEC 31010:2019, "Risk management — Risk assessment techniques," provides guidance on conducting a risk assessment. The related ISO GUIDE 73:2009, "Risk management — Vocabulary," provides a standard set of terminology used through the other documents and is useful for defining elements of the risk management program.

This ISO standard provides generic recommendations for the design, implementation, and review of risk management processes within an organization. The 2018 update provides more strategic guidance and redefines risk from the concept of a "probability of loss" to a more holistic view of risk as the "effect of uncertainty of objectives," recasting risk as either a negative or positive effect. ISO 31000 recommends the following steps in planning for risk:

- Avoiding the risk by deciding not to start or continue with the activity that gives rise to the risk

- Accepting or increasing the risk to pursue an opportunity

- Removing the risk source

- Changing the likelihood

- Changing the consequences

- Sharing the risk with another party or parties (including contracts and risk financing)

- Retaining the risk by informed decision

ISO 31000 is a detailed framework but is not designed to be used in certification (there is no such thing as "ISO 31000 certified"). Adopting this framework will require extensive management conformity to accountability standards as well as strategic policy implementation, communication, and review practices. Documents and supporting resources can be found here: `iso.org/iso-31000-risk-management.html`.

ENISA

As a rough equivalent to the U.S. NIST, ENISA produces useful resources related to information and cybersecurity aligned with EU government objectives and programs. The "Cloud Computing Risk Assessment" is one of these documents and provides details of cloud-specific risks that organizations should be aware of and plan for when designing cloud computing systems.

This guide identifies various categories of risks and recommendations for organizations to consider when evaluating cloud computing. These include research recommendations to advance the field of cloud computing, legal risks, and security risks. Examples of the security risks identified include the following:

- **Loss of governance:** Gaps in the security defenses caused by differences in the understanding of responsibility between the client and the CSP.

- **Isolation failure:** The potential failures caused by lack of separation in storage, memory, and other hardware between cloud clients.

- **Compliance risk:** The CSP provides a new challenge to achieving certification.

- **Management interface compromise:** Management interfaces for cloud environments provide an additional attack vector.

- **Data protection:** How CSPs handle data in a lawful way.

- **Insecure data deletion:** Secure deletion of the cloud is complicated by its distributed nature.

- **Malicious insiders:** Addition of a CSP adds high-risk-access individuals who can comprise cloud architectures and data.

The full document can be accessed here: `enisa.europa.eu/publications/ cloud-computing-risk-assessment`.

NIST

Although a U.S. government agency, NIST publishes well-regarded information security standards that are free to download and may be used by any organization. NIST Special Publication (SP) 800-146, "Cloud Computing Synopsis and Recommendations," provides definitions of various cloud computing terms. These include the service and deployment models like SaaS and public cloud, which were discussed in Chapter 1. Although not a dedicated risk management standard, the various risks and benefits associated with different deployment and service models are discussed. These can be an important input to any discussion of cloud computing risk, and the document may be found here: `csrc.nist.gov/publications/ detail/sp/800-146/final`.

NIST also publishes an RMF, documented in NIST Special Publication 800-37. This document specifies the RMF to be used by U.S. government federal agencies and is often applied to organizations providing goods and services to these agencies. Although it shares some terminology with the ISO 31000 standard, the NIST RMF is specifically designed to address security and privacy risks. The RMF is flexible and can be applied at multiple levels of an organization, including the system level, an organizational unit level, or across the entire organization. The full publication and supporting documents are located at `csrc.nist .gov/publications/detail/sp/800-37/rev-2/final`.

Metrics for Risk Management

There are some key cybersecurity metrics that companies can track to present measurable data to company stakeholders. Each organization should evaluate its strategy, risks, and management requirements for data when designing a metrics program. Some metrics that are commonly tracked include the following:

- **Patching levels:** How many devices are fully patched and up-to-date? This is a useful proxy for risk, as unpatched devices often contain exploitable vulnerabilities.

- **Time to deploy patches:** How may devices receive required patches in the defined time-frames? This is a useful measure of how effective a patch management program is at reducing the risk of known vulnerabilities.

- **Intrusion attempts:** How many times have unknown actors tried to breach cloud systems? Increased intrusion attempts can be an indicator of increased risk likelihood.

- **Mean time to detect (MTTD), mean time to contain (MTTC), and mean time to resolve (MTTR):** How long does it take for security teams to become aware of a potential security incident, contain the damage, and resolve the incident? Inadequate tools or resources for reactive risk mitigation can increase the impact of risks occurring.

Metrics provide vital information for decision makers in the organization. Metrics that are within expected parameters indicate risk mitigations that are operating effectively and keeping risk at an acceptable level. Metrics that deviate from expected parameters, such as MTTD increasing, can indicate that existing risk mitigations are no longer effective and should be reviewed.

Assessment of Risk Environment

The cloud has become a critical operating component for many organizations, so it is crucial to identify and understand the risks posed by a CSP. Cloud providers are subject to risks similar to other service providers, but since they provide a critical service to many organizations, the impact of these risks is increased. It is important to consider a number of questions when considering a cloud service, vendor, or infrastructure provider.

- Is the provider subject to takeover or acquisition?
- How financially stable is the provider?
- In what legal jurisdiction(s) are the provider's offices located?
- Are there outstanding lawsuits against the provider?
- What pricing protections are in place for services contracted?
- How will a provider satisfy any regulatory or legal compliance requirements?
- What does failover, backup, and recovery look like for the provider?

It can be a daunting challenge for any cloud customer to perform due diligence on their provider. However, since the customer organization still holds legal accountability, it is a vital step in selecting and using a vendor. Designing a SCRM program to assess CSP or vendor risks is a due diligence practice, and actually performing the assessment is an example of due care. As a data controller, any organization that uses cloud services without adequately reviewing and mitigating the risks is likely to be found negligent should a breach occur.

There are frameworks for evaluating vendor and infrastructure risks, which provide guidance on designing and executing the required processes. Some of these are general technology risk management frameworks, while others are specifically designed for cloud computing.

ISO 15408-1:2009: The Common Criteria

The Common Criteria for Information Technology Security Evaluation is an international standard for information security certification. The evaluation process is designed to establish a level of confidence in a product or platform's security features through a quality assurance process.

Common Criteria (CC) evaluation is done through testing laboratories where the product or platform is evaluated against a standard set of criteria. This includes the Target of Evaluation (ToE) and Protection Profiles (PP), which describe the system evaluated and specific security services the product offers. The result is an Evaluation Assurance Level (EAL), which defines how robust the security capabilities are in the evaluated product.

Most CSPs do not have common criteria evaluations over their entire environments, but many cloud-based products do. One common example relevant to security practitioners is security tools designed to be deployed in virtual environments like the cloud. Defining a desired EAL level can be used when evaluating security products, as it allows the organization to select products that have been independently verified against a standardized set of criteria.

A product that has undergone CC evaluation cannot be considered totally secure. The ToE specifies the configuration of the product, and failure to configure a system to the same specification as the ToE can result in a less-secure state. Similarly, newly discovered vulnerabilities could lead to loss of security in a system even if it is properly configured. EALs are useful as a selection tool but are not an absolute guarantee of security.

An up-to-date list of certified products can be found at `commoncriteriaportal.org/products`.

CSA STAR

When evaluating the risks in a specific CSP or other cloud service, the CSA STAR can be a useful method for ascertaining risks. The CSA STAR contains evaluations of cloud services against the CSA's cloud-specific controls (the CCM), and organizations have the flexibility to select self-assessed or third-party-assessed cloud services. Organizations that are not regulated by other frameworks and that make extensive use of the cloud may find this a lightweight but useful risk management framework.

Since the registry of certified providers is publicly available, the STAR program makes it easy for a company to assess the relative risk of a provider and should certainly be consulted when assessing any new CSP.

EU Cybersecurity Certification Scheme on Cloud Services

ENISA has published a standard for certifying the cybersecurity practices present in cloud environments. The framework, known as EUCS, defines a set of evaluation criteria for various cloud service and deployment models, with the goal of producing security evaluation results that allow comparison of the security posture across different cloud providers. The standard is still under development as of 2022, but the draft scheme can be found here: `enisa.europa.eu/publications/eucs-cloud-service-scheme`.

The EUCs defines several elements needed to support certification, and many are similar to the Common Criteria. This includes assurance levels, necessary information for assurance reviews and tests, and a process for self-assessments. Newly discovered vulnerabilities are explicitly identified as an area of concern, and the scheme identifies a process for handling such vulnerabilities and updating any relevant certification documentation as needed. In addition, the scheme identifies conformance assessment body (CAB) criteria that detail the requirements an organization must meet to perform evaluations and issue certifications under EUCS.

Understand Outsourcing and Cloud Contract Design

Outsourcing refers to using a party outside the organization to perform services or deliver goods. Outsourcing can allow organizations to take advantage of higher-skilled resources that may be difficult or expensive to hire internally or take advantage of shared resources that benefit from an economy of scale. CSPs provide this type of outsourcing; by pooling and sharing resources, organizations gain access to a globally distributed network of data centers that would be prohibitively expensive for all but the largest multinational companies.

When entering into an outsourcing arrangement, organizations utilize a variety of legal agreements and must also perform oversight and monitoring functions to validate compliance with the agreed terms. Cloud security professionals are well served by understanding key contractual provisions that provide risk management options for the specific CSPs that are used by their organizations.

Business Requirements

Before executing a contract with a CSP, it is important for any business to fully understand their own business needs to select a CSP that can adequately meet those needs. The evolution of the cloud means that more and more IT functions can use cloud computing. Once an organization deems cloud computing fit for their needs, the process of codifying these needs and identifying CSPs that meet them can begin. In legal terms, a cloud customer and a CSP enter into a master service agreement (MSA), which is defined as any contract that two or more parties enter into as a service agreement.

Many organizations will have standardized contract templates, and the task of creating and maintaining these is usually not assigned to the security team. Legal counsel is most often responsible for these contracts, but input from the security team is essential to ensure that security requirements make it into these templates. Common areas of security that should be addressed in contracts include any compliance requirements the customer is passing along to the CSP, as well as important processes and parameters the CSP must meet, such as the duty to inform the customer of a breach within a specific time period after detection.

Another important legal document that may be required is a statement of work (SOW). SOWs are usually created after an MSA has been executed and govern a specific unit of work. For example, the agreement to use a CSP's services at specific prices would be documented in the MSA. A SOW could be issued under this MSA detailing requirements, expectations, and deliverables for a major project, such as paying the CSP to assist with a migration from on-premises to cloud hosting.

The greater specificity of a SOW allows for more granular security requirements that are specific to that unit of work, such as the use of physically secured transport and secure handling of hard drives that the CSP takes and migrates data into their systems. If this activity is performed only during the initial migration, these requirements do not make sense in the overall MSA since this physical data transfer is not part of the ongoing services the CSP provides.

The final legal document where business requirements can be captured is the service level agreement (SLA), which specifies levels of service the CSP is obligated to provide. SLAs measure common aspects of service delivery like uptime and throughput and are often tied to system requirements the organization needs in order to function properly.

The SLA is a legally binding agreement, and if the CSP fails to provide the specified levels of service, the customer usually has recourse options defined. These may include refunds or credits for the service and possibly the ability to terminate the contract without penalties. While this is a dramatic option, if a CSP is unable to meet the organization's required service levels, then the organization should be free to seek out another provider. Contracts often contain penalties for early termination without cause, so monitoring the service levels and properly documenting any shortcomings is essential, as this often enables the customer to terminate the contract with cause and avoid the termination fee.

Key SLA Requirements

Service level agreements can be a key factor in avoiding potential issues once a contract is in place. Service metrics, such as uptime or quality of service, can be included in this section of a contract. An uptime of 99 percent may seem adequate, but that level of allowed downtime would be equal to 87.6 hours a year. For a nonessential system, this may be acceptable, but a mission-critical system that must be available 24/7 cannot tolerate that much downtime!

SLAs should be written to ensure that the organization's service level requirements (SLRs) are met, and SLAs are best suited for defining recurring, discrete, measurable items the parties agree upon. This is in contrast to nonrecurring items that are better suited to a contract, such as agreed prices for specific services. Examples of these requirements, and common elements documented in SLAs, include the following:

- Uptime guarantees
- SLA violation penalties
- SLA violation penalty exclusions and limitations
- Suspension of service clauses
- Provider liability
- Data protection and management
- Disaster recovery and recovery point objectives
- Security and privacy notifications and timeframes

Vendor Management

As discussed previously, the process of managing risk is complicated when parts of the organization's IT infrastructure exist outside the organization's direct control. The practices of SCRM and vendor management overlap significantly, though in many cases vendor management will include more activities related to operational risks.

Vendor management concerns existed for traditional, on-premises infrastructure, but the activities required for cloud computing necessitate different processes and approaches. Selecting a vendor for on-premises hardware might have been a once-and-done activity, since hardware would be expected to last for a defined period of time; at the end of its useful life, assessment of replacement vendors would be conducted.

Cloud computing requires more continuous management activities, since it involves outsourcing ongoing organizational processes and infrastructure to a service provider. This redefined relationship requires a great deal of trust and communication with vendors. Cloud professionals need strong project *and* people management skills to be successful when performing activities such as the following:

- **Assess vendors:** Security practitioners should participate in the initial selection process for a CSP, which involves assessing security risks present in CSP and related services. Once a CSP has been selected, ongoing assessments should be conducted at a specified frequency. For many customers, this process will entail reviewing security reports like a SOC 2 on an annual basis after the CSP has undergone their yearly audit.

- **Assess vendor lock-in risks:** This assessment will require knowledge of not only the CSP's offerings but the architecture and strategy the customer organization intends to use. Simply moving physical services into virtual cloud-based equivalents is unlikely to face lock-in risks, as all CSPs offer basic IaaS that can host a virtualized server. Using any unique CSP offerings, such as artificial intelligence/machine learning (AI/ML) platforms, can result in a system that is dependent on that specific CSP. If the CSP suffers a breach or discontinues the service, the customer organization has no effective means of mitigating that risk, short of completely rebuilding the system from the ground up using another CSP's offerings.

■ **Assess vendor viability:** This is often a process that is not conducted by the security team, as it deals with operational risk. Customers assume significant risk if a CSP is hosting mission-critical systems but is unable to continue their operations, which could be caused by issues like bankruptcy. Assessing the viability of vendors may involve reviews of public information like financial statements, the CSP's performance history and reputation, or even formal reports like a SOC 1, which identifies potential weaknesses that could impact the CSP's ability to continue operations.

■ **Explore escrow options:** Escrow is a legal term used when a trusted third party holds something on behalf of two or more other parties, such as a bank holding money on behalf of the individuals buying and selling a home. In IT services, escrow is often used as a way to hold sensitive material like source code or encryption keys. Exposure of the information to unauthorized parties could be damaging but may be necessary in extreme circumstances. For example, a CSP that performed custom software development may wish to protect the intellectual property of their source code, but if they go out of business, their customers are left with an unmaintainable system. In this scenario, an escrow provider could hold a copy of the source code and release it to customers in the event the provider is no longer in business.

Contract Management

The management of cloud contracts is a core business activity that is central to any ongoing relationship with a CSP. Organizations must employ adequate governance structures to monitor contract terms and performance and be aware of outages and any violations of stated agreements. A standards body known as the OMG Cloud Working Group publishes a useful guide to cloud service agreements, including defining and enforcing contracts, managing SLAs, and building programs to govern these service arrangements. The guide can be found here: omg.org/cloud/deliverables/Practical-Guide-to-Cloud-Service-Agreements.pdf.

Contract Clauses

There are a number of specific elements that should be considered when engaging a CSP or other cloud provider. A contract *clause* is a specific article of related information that specifies the agreement between the contracting parties. Examples of clauses include language related to the customer's obligation to pay and any security requirements the customer expects the service provider to meet, such as implementing industry-standard security.

Writing and reviewing contract clauses may be outside the scope of a security professional's job, but understanding the function of these clauses and important considerations that should be addressed in the contract is important. This necessitates collaboration between security practitioners and legal counsel, especially as contract negotiations often involve very advanced legal knowledge. Some common contract clauses that should be considered for any CSP or other data service provider include the following:

- **Right to audit:** The customer can request the right to audit the service provider to ensure compliance with the security requirements agreed in the contract. Many CSPs do not accept these clauses due to the burden it would create on them to facilitate these audits, so the clauses are often written to allow the CSP's standard audits (e.g., SOC 2, ISO 27001 certification) to be used in place of a customer-performed audit.

- **Metrics:** Not all contracts will specify metrics, but if there are specific indicators that the service provider must provide to the customer, they can be documented in a contract.

- **Definitions:** A contract is a legal agreement between multiple parties, and it is essential that all parties share a common understanding of the terms and expectations. Defining key terms like security, privacy, and compliance, as well as specifying key practices like breach notifications provided within 24 hours of detection, can avoid misunderstandings.

- **Termination:** Termination refers to ending the contractual agreement. This clause will typically define conditions under which either party may terminate the contract and require notice that must be given, and it may specify consequences if the contract is terminated early. Failure to provide the services agreed on or failure to pay is often defined in this clause, providing both the CSP and the customer a way out of the contract without penalties.

- **Litigation:** This is an area where legal counsel must be consulted, as agreeing to terms for litigation can severely restrict the organization's ability to pursue damages if something goes wrong. For example, some providers require the use of arbitration instead of a court trial, which has different rules and may offer fewer options for the customer to recover damages.

- **Assurance:** Defining assurance requirements sets expectations for both the provider and customer. Many contracts specify that a provider must furnish a SOC 2 or equivalent to the customer on an annual basis, since the customer needs that document to gain assurance that the provider's risk management is adequate.

- **Compliance:** Any customer compliance requirements that flow to the provider must be documented and agreed upon in the contract. Data controllers that use cloud providers as data processors must ensure that adequate security safeguards are available for that data, and documenting the requirements in a contract is an example of exercising due care.

- **Access to cloud/data:** Clauses dealing with customer access can be used to avoid risks associated with vendor lock-in. For example, it could be catastrophic if a customer informs the provider that a contract will not be renewed and the provider deletes all that customer's data. Contract clauses guaranteeing right to access the customer's data provide protection against this risk and may specify legal recourse if access is not available.

Cyber Risk Insurance

Cyber risk insurance is designed to help an organization reduce the financial impact of risk by transferring it to an insurance carrier. In the event of a security incident, the insurance carrier can help offset associated costs, such as digital forensics and investigation, data recovery, system restoration, and even covering legal or regulatory fines associated with the incident. As discussed previously, cyber insurance carriers are in the business of risk management, so they are unlikely to offer coverage to an organization that is lacking in security controls designed to mitigate some of the risk.

Cyber insurance requires organizations to pay a premium for the insurance plan, and most plans have a limit of coverage that caps how much the insurance carrier pays. There may also be sublimits, which cap the amount that will be paid for specific types of incidents such as ransomware or phishing. It is important to understand what type of coverage is best suited to your organization's unique operating circumstances, and an insurance broker can be a useful resource when investigating insurance options. Factors to discuss with a broker include the amount of coverage needed, different types of coverage such as business interruption or cyber extortion, and security controls that the insurance carrier requires such as MFA. The broker can help to ensure that the insurance coverage is appropriate to an organization's unique circumstances and may be able to save money by eliminating unnecessary elements of the policy.

Cyber risk insurance usually covers costs associated with the following:

- **Investigation:** Costs associated with the forensic investigation to determine the extent of an incident. This often includes costs for third-party investigators.

- **Direct business losses:** Direct monetary losses associated with downtime or data recovery, overtime for employees, and, oftentimes, reputational damages to the organization.

- **Recovery costs:** These may include costs associated with replacing hardware or provisioning temporary cloud environments during contingency operations. They may also include services like forensic data recovery or negotiations with attackers to assist in recovery.

- **Legal notifications:** Costs are associated with required privacy and breach notifications required by relevant laws.

- **Lawsuits:** Policies can be written to cover losses and payouts due to class action or other lawsuits against a company after a cyber incident.

- **Extortion:** The insurance to pay out ransomware demands is growing in popularity. This may include direct payments to ensure data privacy or accessibility by the company.

- **Food and related expenses:** Incident often require employees to work extended hours or travel to contingency sites. Costs associated with the incident response, including catering and lodging, may be covered, even though they are not usually thought of as IT costs!

Supply Chain Management

Supply chain attacks are increasing in frequency and severity and have been on this track for some time. Back in 2015 the retail company Target was attacked using a vendor with weak security controls. In 2020, governments and major companies around the world were impacted by an attack against a popular SolarWinds network monitoring tool that was shipped to customers with compromised code. The popular open-source library npm has come under repeated attack, since so many open-source software (OSS) packages it hosts are incorporated into other software tools used by organizations all over the world.

Managing risk in the supply chain focuses on both operational risks, to ensure that suppliers are capable of providing the needed services, and security risks. This includes ensuring that suppliers have adequate risk management programs in place to address the risks that they face. Without these controls, risks that impact your organization's suppliers can easily turn into risks that impact your organization. If a major CSP does not enforce environmental controls and server equipment begins to fail, this translates to loss of availability for all of the CSP's customers.

The supply chain should always be considered in any business continuity or disaster recovery planning. The same concepts of understanding dependencies, identifying single points of failure, and prioritizing services for restoration are important to apply to the entire supply chain. Proactive measures including contract language and assurance processes can be used to quantify the risks associated with using suppliers like CSPs, as well as the effectiveness of these suppliers' risk management programs.

ISO 27036

The ISO 27000 family of standards has been discussed in many areas of this reference guide, and there is a specific standard dedicated to supply chain cybersecurity risk management. ISO 27036:2021 provides a set of practices and guidance for managing cybersecurity risks in supplier relationships. This standard is particularly useful for organizations that use ISO 27001 for building an ISMS or ISO 31000 for risk management, as it builds on concepts found in those standards.

ISO 27036 comprises four parts, including the following:

- ISO/IEC 27036-1:2021, "Cybersecurity — Supplier relationships — Part 1: Overview and concepts," which provides an overview and foundation for a supply chain management capability.

- ISO/IEC 27036-2:2014, "Information technology — Security techniques — Information security for supplier relationships — Part 2: Requirements," which provides a set of best practices and techniques for designing and implementing the supply chain management function.

- ISO/IEC 27036-3:2013, "Information technology — Security techniques — Information security for supplier relationships — Part 3: Guidelines for information and communication technology supply chain security," which is of particular concern for security practitioners, as it lays out practices and techniques specific to managing security risks in the supply chain.

- ISO/IEC 27036-4:2016, "Information technology — Security techniques — Information security for supplier relationships — Part 4: Guidelines for security of cloud services," which is the most relevant to cloud security practitioners. This standard deals with practices and requirements for managing supply chain security risk specific to cloud computing and CSP.

ISO 27036, like other ISO standards, is not a free resource. Additional resources worth review include the NISTIR 8276, "Key Practices in Cyber Supply Chain Risk Management: Observations from Industry"; NIST SP 800-161," Cybersecurity Supply Chain Risk Management Practices for Systems and Organizations"; and the 2015 ENISA publication "Supply Chain Integrity: An overview of the ICT supply chain risks and challenges, and vision for the way forward."

Summary

A cloud security professional must be constantly aware of the legal and compliance issues inherent in migrating and maintaining systems in the cloud. Understanding the legal requirements, privacy issues, audit challenges, and how these relate to risk and contracts with cloud providers is a must for any company taking advantage of cloud services. A cloud security professional must also be well versed in the frameworks provided by professional organizations such as ENISA, NIST, ISO, and the CSA. All information security activities are tied back to business risks, since security should always be aligned to the needs of the organization. Understanding, assessing, and mitigating these risks is critical to any business strategy, and requires collaboration between the security professional and other teams. Cloud security professionals should understand the role that IT plays in this larger picture and have the communication and people skills to involve the appropriate business, legal, and risk decision makers across the organization.

Index

E

S